*Sugawara no Michizane
and the
Early Heian Court*

Sugawara no Michizane
Courtesy of the Freer Gallery of Art
Smithsonian Institution, Washington, D.C. (Acc. no 1938.8)

Sugawara no Michizane and the Early Heian Court

Robert Borgen

University of Hawaii Press
Honolulu

To my parents
Evelyn and Herbert Borgen

First published by the Council on East Asian Studies,
Harvard University, 1986

Paperback edition
© *1994 University of Hawaii Press*

94 95 96 97 98 99   5 4 3 2 1

Library of Congress Cataloging-in-Publication Data

Borgen, Robert, 1945–
  Sugawara no Michizane and the early Heian court / Robert Borgen. –
Pbk. ed.
     p. cm.
  Includes bibliographical references and index.
  ISBN 0-8248-1590-4
  1. Sugawara, Michizane, 845–903. 2. Statesmen—Japan—
Biography.   I. Title.
[DS856.72.S9B67   1994]
952'.01'092—dc20
[B]   93–36993
                                                              CIP

Contents

Acknowledgments

A full chapter would be required to fully acknowledge all the teachers, colleagues, and friends whose help and encouragement over the years have made this book possible. The following is but a brief review of some of those individuals.

My study of Michizane began as a doctoral dissertation at the University of Michigan. There, I was privileged to study with many distinguished scholars. Special thanks go to Professors Robert H. Brower and William B. Hauser. Professor Brower introduced me to the complexities—and the beauties—of classical Japanese literature, and found time in his busy schedule to supervise the writing of my dissertation. Professor Hauser taught me both the substance of early Japanese history and the methods of a historian. In addition, Professors Charles O. Hucker, Noriko Kamachi, and Shuen-fu Lin read the dissertation version of my study and offered many helpful suggestions.

During the academic year 1980–1981, I was able to conduct further research on Michizane at the Historiographic Institute (Shiryō Hensanjo) of Tokyo University. Many scholars there assisted me in my research. I would especially like to thank Professor Yamanaka Yutaka, who has been a patient and helpful *sensei* since I was a graduate student. Professors Kanai Madoka, Tsuchida Naoshige, and Ishii Masatoshi were always willing to take the time to answer questions and made the arrangements necessary to facilitate my study. I also benefited from discussions with many other of the Japanese scholars whose works appear in my footnotes. Shinto priests at Tenjin shrines throughout Japan guided me through their institutions and provided me with helpful literature. In particular, I want to thank the Reverend Nishitakatsuji Nobusada of the Dazaifu Temmangū and the staff of its research institute. They made my brief stay in Dazaifu both pleasant and profitable. The staff of the Kagawa Prefecture Board of Education kindly provided me a thorough guided tour of sites associated with Michizane's stay in Sanuki. This research in Japan was made possible by generous support from the Japan Foundation and the Social Science Research Council.

Others who have offered valuable advice and encouragement include Professors Gisaburo Kiyose, Hsiang-po Lee, Jeffrey P. Mass, William H. McCullough, Hiroshi Miyaji, Edwin O. Reischauer, Edward G. Seidensticker, and Burton Watson.

The Edwin O. Reischauer Institute of Japanese Studies at Harvard University has also been very generous in its support. It has provided me with office space and library privileges, first during the summer of 1982 when I was revising this manuscript with the support of a summer research grant from the University of Hawaii at Manoa's Japan Endowment Fund, and again during 1985. Although principally engaged in a new project, I am fortunate to be just down the hall from the editor of this manuscript as it is readied for publication. That editor, Mary Ann Flood, of Harvard's Council on East Asian Studies, has offered many useful suggestions, as has Florence Trefethen.

Of the many individuals who have helped me with this project, my wife, Sophia Lee, is the one who deserves the most special thanks. Time and again, she willingly put aside her own graduate studies to read and discuss with me versions of my manuscript. I only hope that this book is worthy of the time and effort that she, and the others noted above, put into helping me produce it.

Explanatory Notes

The following conventions are employed throughout this book:

Names:
Following Japanese usage for historical figures, individuals are usually referred to by their given names after they are first mentioned in the text; cross references to their surnames appear in the index. Correct readings for some names are problematic. This is particularly true of women's given names. The readings I had adopted for most women's names are those suggested by Tsunoda Bun'ei in his various writings cited in the bibliography. Although many of these native Japanese readings are little more than educated guesses, they seem preferable to the Sino-Japanese readings for women's names that many scholars use today but certainly were not used in the Heian period. The Sino-Japanese readings appear in parentheses after the first reference to each woman's name, except in cases where a native reading is generally used (e.g., Kusuko) or relatively unambiguous (e.g., Nobukiko).

Ages:
Ages are given in the traditional East Asian manner that counted the number of calendar years in which an individual had lived. A child was considered to be one year old at birth and became two on New Year's Day. Because actual birthdays were not recorded, ages cannot be accurately converted to their equivalents in the Western system of reckoning, although an approximate

figure can be derived by subtracting one year from the ages appearing in the text.

Dates:

All pre-Meiji days and months are given according to the traditional lunar calendar. Years, however, are converted into their approximate equivalent in the Western calendar. Since the lunar new year usually occurred in February, most events described as taking place in the twelfth month of a given year in the Western calendar actually took place in January of the following year.

Offices and Titles:

In general, the translation of Heian bureaucratic terminology is based on Jean and Robert Karl Reischauer, *Early Japanese History*. Some modifications follow the usage found in more recent publications, notably the McCulloughs' translations of *Ōkagami* and *Eiga Monogatari*. I have distinguished the offices of *sesshō* (regent) and *kampaku* (chancellor) in keeping with Morita Tei, who stresses that these were not simply alternate titles for the same set of privileges. *Daijō daijin* has been translated as "grand minister."

Translations:

Most of the translations appearing in this book are my own. In translating the poetry, my principal goal has been to convey the basic sense of the original, although I hope I have managed to preserve at least some of the linguistic qualities that make the originals poetry rather than prose. A few translations are taken from other sources. Most notably, I have used Burton Watson's translations for four of Michizane's works, since I do not believe I could improve on his efforts. For the reader's convenience, notes clarifying allusions or textual problems within translations are indicated by letters rather than numbers and appear at the end of the translation rather than among the footnotes in the back of the book.

Illustrations:

The picture on the cover and frontispiece is a late fifteenth-century painting by Sesshin. It shows "Tenjin Visiting China" (Totō Tenjin), a popular theme among medieval artists. The poem in its upper-right corner is:

Kokoro dani	If only your heart
Makoto no michi ni	Follows the true way,
Kanainaba	Even though you fail to pray,
Inorazu tote mo	This god will protect you.
Kami ya mamoran	

The illustrations to the text come from three woodblock editions of accounts of Michizane's life: *Dazaifu Temmangū kojitsu*, by Kaibara Ekken (1685 edition, artist unknown, abbreviated as *Dazaifu Temmangū*); *Ehon Sugawara jikki*, text and illustrations by Kose Hidenobu (1842 edition of this work that was originally published in 1810, abbreviated as *Sugawara jikki*); and *Temmangū goden kiryaku*, by Hirata Atsutane (1820 edition with illustrations by Kuwagata Keisai, abbreviated as *Temmangū goden*). Obviously, none of these pictures is "historically accurate," but they vividly show how Michizane had come to be viewed in traditional Japan. The selection of events to be illustrated reflects the tastes of Edo-period artists who preferred to show the more colorful—and often legendary— aspects of Michizane's life. The Sesshin painting is reproduced courtesy of the Freer Gallery of Art, Smithsonian Institution, Washington, D.C. (Acc. no. 1983.8). I would like to thank the Harvard-Yenching Library for permission to reproduce the illustrations from its copy of *Daizaifu Temmangū*, and the Reverend Nishitakatsuji of Dazaifu Temmangū for those from *Sugawara jikki*. Those from *Temmangū goden* were taken from a modern reprint.

Preface
to the Paperback Edition:
A Scholarly Update

This is essentially the same book as the original edition. In order
to minimize production costs, I have resisted the temptation to
correct anything but the most obvious omissions and typographi-
cal errors. Moreover, since completing the book I have been
working on other projects, and so I am not in a position to substantially update the contents. Nonetheless, I would like to use
this introduction to modify a few details and introduce new
Japanese research on Michizane and Tenjin worship (parenthetical
page references all indicate relevant sections of my book).

If forced to pin down a scholarly trend, I would submit that,
since I completed my original research, the major new development has been a growth of interest in Japan's literature in Chinese,
including Michizane's works. In recent years, two of the major
Japanese journals of literary scholarship have published special
numbers, one focusing on "The World of Heian Court Literature in Chinese"[1] and the other on "Poetic Thought, Poetic
Criticism: Sugawara no Michizane and Ki no Tsurayuki."[2]

---

[1] *Kokubungaku: kaishaku to kanshō* 55.10 (Oct. 1990).
[2] *Kokubungaku: kaishaku to kyōzai no kenkyū* 37.12 (Oct. 1992).

Each includes a review of scholarship concerning Michizane by a leading specialist. The first, by Fujiwara Katsumi (whose first studies of Michizane's poetry were appearing as I was completing my research), is the most comprehensive; the second, by Kimbara Tadashi (whose surname appeared as "Kimpara" in earlier publications, including my own), acknowledges Fujiwara's essay and builds on it. These two surveys and the various other articles that appear in the same special numbers of the journals offer a comprehensive overview of the current state of relevant Japanese scholarship, and most of it is literary. In contrast, the standard guides to historical research reveal many items that might help us understand Michizane's age, but nothing focusing on the man himself. Readers unfamiliar with Michizane and the Heian period may want to read at least the introduction to my book before proceeding with the rest of this preface so they will have some sense of what it is updating.

Literary studies treat both Michizane's literary thought and practice. For some years Japanese scholars have been interested in early Heian theories of literature, which are introduced in my book (pp. 17–20 and 39–48 in particular). Attempts by some, however, at explaining Heian academic factionalism in terms of ideological disputes between poets *(shijin)* and scholars *(ju)* seemed misguided, since Michizane clearly identified himself as both, in keeping with Confucian teachings (pp. 84–85). The surveys of literary scholarship reveal that Michizane's self-identity as a poet and attitude toward other scholars remain central issues among Japanese specialists, whose research has added increasing sophistication to the discussion. Reading some of their arguments and reviewing what Michizane himself had to say have led me to believe that perhaps I was too hasty in dismissing the question.

To start with Michizane's own writings, Kawaguchi and Wakabayashi's concordance of his poetry confirms that, in his usage, intellectuals fell into two categories and he included himself in only one of them. The character *ju* that I translated as "scholar" or sometimes "Confucian scholar"—scholars were by definition Confucian—appears a total of seventeen times in Michizane's poetry (for example, pp. 123, 133, 139, 157, 172, 299). The character is used in various compounds but refers to Michizane himself in all but three instances. In these exceptions, it appears in compounds—*kōju* or *tsūju*—both meaning something like "erudite scholar." A partial explanation of this distinction would be that "erudite scholar" is an honorific usage necessarily reserved for those other than oneself. Emperor Uda politely referred to Michizane as an erudite scholar (p. 214), whereas Michizane occasionally described himself as a "worthless (literally, 'rotten') scholar" *(fuju)*. When Michizane wrote of "erudite scholars," however, he seemed to be using the term ironically rather than honorifically, and so at one point I translated *kōju* as "lofty Confucian scholar" (pp. 84–85) to convey something of the tone that I believe he intended. For example, in a poem mourning the death of a man he praised as a true poet, he uses that term disdainfully to describe other intellectuals who were not.[3]

The concordance reveals that Michizane used the word "poet" nine times, "poetic friend" *(shiyū)* three, and "poetic minister" *(shishin)* twice (the only two examples I translated are on pp. 178, 181). He uses these terms to refer sometimes to himself, sometimes to others, and sometimes to poets in general. Never does he use them ironically. Poets, unlike scholars, are always viewed positively, and he specifically notes that the poet whose death he mourned was neither a close friend nor a student of his. Still, according to Michizane, after his death, only two or three men at court could be regarded as true poets. Thus apparently factionalism was not Michizane's only criterion in classifying scholars. All, including himself, fell under the broad rubric of *ju,* but only a few, again including himself, were worthy of the name poet. Since at least one whom he praised as a poet did not belong to his own clique, perhaps we should acknowledge that the reverse could also be true: those whom he disparaged may not have been simply members of rival factions.

Fujiwara Katsumi has written a series of articles on this issue that hint at the substantive differences between the two groups of scholars and substantially illuminate what being a poet meant to Michizane.[4] He takes the Akō Incident (pp. 169–181) as a key to understanding the intellectual climate of Michizane's day. Scholars had been summoned to determine whether the elegant

---

[3] *KBKK,* item 502.

[4] The material that follows is based largely on his most recent piece, "Michizane: shi to shisō," *Kokubungaku kaishaku to kyōzai no kenkyū* 37.12 (Oct. 1992): 46–52. His previous research is summarized in the two survey articles noted above that also note other publications on this topic.

sinified title *"akō,"* used in the document appointing a new
chancellor, referred to a post that was merely honorary and hence
was meant as a discreet means of removing him from power.
Fujiwara notes that the professors of classics indeed looked
only to the orthodox Confucian classics for precedents whereas
scholars associated with the court university's literature program,
including Michizane, referred to later historical works as well.
Since history was regarded as a branch of literature, this hints at
real differences in the intellectual approaches of the two groups.

Fujiwara further observes that Michizane never referred to
literature as a force in the ordering of the state, the slogan of
his grandfather's day that had been borrowed from a Chinese
source (p. 43). Instead, Michizane alluded to another familiar
Chinese justification of poetry that originated in the Great
Preface to the *Book of Songs,* which states "Poetry is where one's
intention goes: that which is in the heart becomes poetry when
expressed in words." Although this is a view of poetry that
has been classified as "expressive," the same source goes on to
explain that people's feelings will mirror the quality of their
rulers and one of the functions of poetry is to allow inferiors
to subtly remonstrate their superiors. Hence, it merges with the
concept of "literature as a force for ordering the state" in also
upholding the familiar Confucian pragmatic theory of literature.[5]

According to Fujiwara, this view of poetry that combines
expressive and pragmatic elements lay at the core of Michizane's
poetic practice. It justified his composing poems extolling the
beauties of nature and, at the same time, encouraged him to seek
a moral basis for such poetry. More concretely, it gave Michizane
the moral courage to risk incurring the chancellor's displeasure
by protesting his behavior in the Akō Incident as detrimental
to literature, for Michizane regarded literature as a high calling
based on the expression of "intentions," including political

---

[5] James J. Y. Liu, *Chinese Theories of Literature,* pp. 69–70, 11–13. In ancient
China, the words for "poetry" and "intention" may have been in fact the same (see
Chow Tse-Tsung, "The Early History of the Word Shih [poetry]," *Wen-lin: Studies in
Chinese Humanities,* ed. Chow Tse-tsung [Madison: University of Wisconsin Press,
1968] pp. 151–209). Both the Chinese original and an English translation of the passage
from *The Book of Songs* to which Michizane alludes can be found in *The She King,* trans.
James Legge, in *The Chinese Classics,* vol. 4 (originally published in 1871 and reprinted
many times), pp. 34–36.

views. This attitude also led him to disparage the less courageous scholarly sycophants to whom he applied the two terms for "erudite scholar" noted above. Although we still lack a clear picture of what those who opposed Michizane's ideas actually believed, Fujiwara and others who have been working on this question have contributed much to our understanding of Michizane's own literary attitude.

Research on Michizane's poetic practice tends to seek distinctive elements in his work and show how it differed from his Chinese models. For example, a Chinese scholar has noted that his use of certain adverbs deviates from normal Chinese grammar. Thus Michizane seems to have been thinking of the Japanese verb suffix that indicates the passive voice when he used the adverbial character that serves a similar function in Chinese. Similarly, another specialist has discovered in Michizane's poetry the earliest known example of using the now-standard character to write the Japanese word *"niou,"* meaning "to be fragrant," or "to be colorful." According to this authority, in Chinese the character meant "resonance" or "to arrange." Standard dictionaries, however, indicate that the character Michizane used is in fact a Japanese original derived from the character that means "resonance." Could Michizane have invented it? Another scholar has investigated Michizane's descriptions of chrysanthemums, showing how he adopted Chinese metaphors and conventions. Still others have pointed out that he employed legal jargon from the *ritsuryō* codes, particularly in poems he wrote while serving as a provincial governor. As governor, apparently he became so involved in practical administrative problems that their technical vocabulary crept into his poetry, another deviation from Chinese literary models. Also, the question of Michizane's authorship of *Shinsen Man'yōshū* is still being debated among scholars. Regardless of who wrote it, it is a fascinating work that deserves more attention as a guide to understanding the relation between poetry in Chinese and in Japanese.

Continuing along these lines but in bolder strokes, the contemporary poet Ōoka Makoto has written a book on Michizane that puts his work in the context of a perceived fundamental pattern in Japanese culture: borrowing elements of foreign cultures and attempting to further refine them. He treats Michizane as an example, a "modernist" who confronted problems similar to those facing contemporary Japan.[6] Fujiwara too finds something very Japanese in Michizane's work. His analysis of Michizane's concept of poetry closes with the observation that it resembles the view of Japanese poetry presented in the introduction to the *Kokinshū* shortly after Michizane's death. Fujiwara concludes his review of scholarship on a similar note by suggesting, as others have before, that even if the motto "Japanese spirit, Chinese learning" may have been attributed to Michizane falsely (p. 4), it does accurately reflect his attitude. This is a somewhat different emphasis from the perspective I brought to Michizane. I chose to study him in part as an attempt to put a positive light on elements of Chinese culture in the early Japanese court, and so I portrayed a Michizane who wears his Chinese garb comfortably. Perhaps the Japanese views of Michizane may reflect an inclination to turn to exemplars from the past when seeking to confirm contemporary self-identity.

One expression of Michizane's assimilation of Chinese culture was his ability to compose poems in Chinese extemporaneously. I would like to correct an error that appears in my discussion of such poems. I state that he did not take time to "add punctuation" (pp. 97–98, 143, 236). This is a mistranslation. The character I rendered as "punctuation" does mean that (as a noun), but (as a verb) it can also mean "to make small corrections," and the phrase Michizane used is a standard one meaning simply "to revise a manuscript." When Michizane tells us he composed a poem without revision, we learn that even his extemporaneous poems are quite good, but we can not judge whether or not he was able to read them directly in Chinese without rearranging them into Japanese word order, as I had suggested. I still believe this to be a strong possibility, but I have lost one piece of supporting evidence.

Although I have focused on Japanese contributions to our understanding of Michizane's writings, I would also like to call attention to two studies in English. Helen McCullough's *Brocade by Night: 'Kokin wakashū' and the Court Style in Japanese Classical Poetry,* which came out after my book had gone to press, discusses Michizane's poetry, *Shinsen Man'yōshū,* early Japanese literary

---

[6] *Shijin Sugawara no Michizane: utsushi no bigaku* (Tokyo: Iwanami Shoten, 1989).

theories, and other topics related to my own study.[7] David Pollack's provocative *The Fracture of Meaning: Japan's Synthesis of China from the Eighth through the Eighteenth Centuries* incorporates and expands on his article mentioned in my bibliography.[8]

Moving from literary to historical issues, I would like to update my discussion of *kentōshi*, Japan's missions to T'ang China. Charlotte von Verschuer has published a meticulously detailed study that provides a wealth of information on the conduct of these missions. Among other important contributions to our understanding of these missions in general, she notes that they typically departed Japan when the weather was most favorable.[9] This contradicts the traditional view, adopted uncritically in my book (p. 34), that the early Japanese were unaware of the regular monsoon winds and sailed at the worst possible time, an interpretation that apparently originated with Mori Katsumi and was repeated by Edwin Reischauer.[10] The most detailed critique of Mori is presented by Ueda Takeshi.[11] He concludes that most of the missions left Kyushu between late July and late August (by the Western calendar), just after the rainy season when favorable winds were likely to be blowing. This was the best possible time of the year, as long as typhoons could be avoided. Although typhoons were unpredictable and did occasionally wreak havoc, this does not mean that Japanese sailors were ignorant of normal weather patterns.

My treatment of the abandonment of the *kentōshi* (pp. 240–250) also needs modification. In a tour de force of textual scholarship, Ishii Masatoshi has written an article that clears up one mystery principally by analyzing the usage of a single commonplace character.[12] Scholars have long been puzzled by the apparent speed of the Heian court in accepting Michizane's proposal that his mission to China be canceled. Ishii calls into question the reliability of the only source, *Nihon kiryaku*, that places this

[7] Stanford: Stanford University Press, 1985.

[8] Princeton: Princeton University Press, 1986.

[9] *Les Relations Officielles du Japon avec la Chine au VIIIe et IX siècles* (Geneva: Librairie Droz, 1985), p. 56.

[10] See, respectively, *Kentōshi*, pp. 55–60 and *Ennin's Travels*, pp. 60–61.

[11] "Kentōshi, Shiragishi, Bokkaishi no rekishi kikōgakuteki kenkyū: kodai kaijō kōtsū to kisetsufū to no kankei," *Hōsei tsūshin* (Aug. 1974): 16–28.

[12] "Iwayuru kentōshi haishi ni tsuite: *Nihon kiryaku* teishi kiji no kentō," *Chūō Daigaku bungakubu kiyō shigakka* 35 (Feb. 1992): 1–21.

decision just sixteen days after Michizane's proposal (p. 243). Ishii shows that it commonly confused two characters, similar in appearance, one meaning "this" and the other meaning "a certain." When the compiler introduced an event but knew only its month, not its exact date, he included it in the entry for the last day of the month and introduced it with the phrase "on a certain day," presumably of that month. The problem is that he, or a later copyist, often substituted the graphically similar character, changing the phrase to "on this day" and giving the entry a false appearance of precision. Furthermore, Ishii notes that the wording in this brief entry employs language also found in Michizane's proposal.

Ishii concludes that the court never made a formal decision to cancel Michizane's mission to China. Rather, as a result of Michizane's proposal, dispatch of the mission was first put off, and, without any formal decision, interest in it waned and eventually vanished. The compiler of *Nihon kiryaku* knew that the mission was never sent, but he had neither a record of the decision nor a precise date. Accordingly he improvised, placing a vague entry at the end of the month in which Michizane made his proposal. In a footnote, Ishii also dismisses as a later fabrication the source I quote stating that an edict canceling the mission was issued the year after Michizane's proposal. Its author, Ishii asserts, further garbled an already unreliable account in *Fusō ryakki* describing the arrival that year of envoys from the Manchurian kingdom of Parhae (pp. 250–252) and managed to confuse their appearance in Japan with the cancellation of Michizane's mission.

If Ishii is right, and I suspect he is, some modification of my argument is in order, although his conclusions are in keeping with the general outline of my treatment of the problem. My suggestion that, as late as 927, the Japanese had not precluded the possibility of sending further embassies to China seems more reasonable if we assume that the court never even formally canceled Michizane's embassy, much less decided to cut its diplomatic ties with China altogether. On the other hand, further doubts must be added to my suggestion, tentative from the start, that the source with a later date for the abandonment of Michizane's mission may be the more reliable one. Ishii seems to have solved the mystery of the all-too-prompt official response to Michizane's proposal, but I believe that otherwise my discussion of the circumstances surrounding Michizane's appointment and the failure to dispatch his mission to China remains valid, even if we now must suspect that no decision was formally made.

Finally, Tenjin, Michizane's deified spirit, has also received considerable scholarly attention in the form of at least six substantial books and numerous articles. Together, they offer fresh insights into many aspects of Tenjin worship. Most of the items, however, are rather narrow in focus, and a comprehensive overview of the subject is still needed. Perhaps a brief survey of some key publications will help explain why scholars still focus on details.

Three of the books are in fact collections of articles. Makabe Toshinobu's *Tenjin shinkō no kisoteki kenkyū* brings together his previously published articles—many already cited in my bibliography—updates them, adds a couple of new essays, and rounds out the collection with good editions of two early accounts of Michizane's life.[13] As careful readers of my footnotes will notice, Makabe is the leading authority on early biographies of Michizane and sources for the Tenjin legend, and his research on these texts clarifies how Tenjin worship evolved. Previously published essays by various scholars have been collected by Murayama Shūichi in *Tenjin shinkō*.[14] These articles, the oldest dating back to 1914, are central to our understanding of Tenjin worship, and again many appear in my bibliography. Murayama contributes a critical review of scholarship on Tenjin worship that reveals something of the subject's complexity, discussing fascinating topics that I omitted from my book. For example, the fear of angry ghosts that led to Michizane's deification had ties not only to popular Buddhism (p. 310) but also to other cults that may have originated in China and involved animal sacrifices. The third collection of articles, *Temman Tenjin: goryō kara gakumon no kami e,* edited by Ueda Masaaki, consists of new articles written by distinguished authorities for general readers.[15] Most of the authors treat material they have presented elsewhere in more technical articles. Others, however, cover

---

[13] Kondō Shuppansha, 1984.
[14] Yūzankaku, 1983.
[15] Chikuma Shobō, 1988.

less familiar topics. One that I found particularly intriguing introduces various daily records that were kept at Kitano Shrine in Kyoto from 1449 to 1688 and briefly describes their contents. In addition to the spread of Tenjin worship, we read about *shōen*, shoguns, and peasant uprisings: topics familiar to readers of most books about medieval Japanese history that are lacking in my own study, even when the concluding chapter does venture into the period. A fourth book is Stanca Scholz's *Aspekte des Mittelalterlichen Synkrestismus im Bild des Tenman Tenjin im Nō*, which discusses noh plays, some familiar, others obscure, based on the Tenjin legend.[16] It includes, for example, a translation into German of a noh play, *Kinzanji*, not even available in a modern Japanese edition, that is based on the legend of Michizane's posthumous journey to China (p. 327).

The two remaining books are collections of documents. One, *Dazaifu*, edited by Nakano Hatayoshi, appears in the series *Shintō taikei*.[17] Whereas the previously published volume in that series on Kitano shrine included many familiar texts that are key to the history of Tenjin worship, the documents in this volume are more diverse. They are divided into five groups: histories of the Dazaifu shrine, descriptions of shrine rituals, records of its construction, documents concerning its economic foundations, and genealogical accounts of its head priests. A second valuable collection of documents is *Tenjin densetsu no subete to sono shinkō*, compiled by Yamanaka Kōsaku.[18] It includes 966 variations of 118 basic stories concerning Tenjin, plus the first modern edition of a detailed recounting of the Tenjin legend dating from the Edo period. Some of the stories such as the plum tree that flew to Kyushu are familiar (pp. 290–295). Others are not: "Once upon a time, Tenjin was chased by a white dog and fled into a field where he slipped on a taro plant, poked his eye on a sesame leaf, and fell into a well. Afterwards, it is said, they did not keep white dogs, raise taro and sesame, or dig wells there."

As this summary, incomplete though it is, demonstrates, Tenjin worship is a diffuse phenomenon. Its history is all-too-

---

[16] Stuttgart: Franz Steiner Verlag, 1991.
[17] *Jinja hen*, vol. 48 (Shintō Taikei Hensankai, 1991).
[18] Dazaifu: Dazaifu Temmangū Bunka Kenkyūjo, 1992.

well documented and can be approached from many directions. This very complexity of the subject discourages scholars from attempting to write a comprehensive survey.

The items mentioned so far point to a need to expand rather than correct my treatment of Tenjin worship. A series of articles by Takei Akio, however, suggests that my treatment of the Dōken legend (pp. 315–319) may need revision.[19] Two early versions of the story survive, and Makabe believes that at least the longer text was probably written not long after the events presumably took place in 941 but acknowledges that the dating is problematic. Takei on the other hand argues that the longer version, which shows more influence of esoteric Buddhism and includes the story of Dōken's visit to hell, may date from as late as 1100. If he is right, parts of the story are products of the growing popularity of Tenjin worship rather than contributions to it. Finally, at the risk of seeming immodest, I would like to mention an article I have written, "Sugawara Denju: Life, Religion, and Drama," that analyzes the biographical, legendary, and theatrical elements that went into the making of the ever-popular play *The Sugawara Secrets of Calligraphy.*[20]

I hope this preface, in addition to updating and correcting my own book, will suggest new areas for future research. Also, I would like to thank my colleague Professor Marian Ury for sharing with me her list of details needing correction and Patricia Crosby of the University of Hawaii Press for facilitating the publication of this paperback edition of my book.

---

[19] "Nichizōden tenkai no issokumen: toku ni Shingon mikkyō to no kanren ni tsuite," "Nichizō meikai henrekitan oboegaki," and "Eikyūjibon 'Dōken shōnin meidoki' ni kansuru ni san no mondai," all appearing in *Kodai bunka* 28.3 (March 1976), pp. 57–69; 29.6 (June 1977), pp. 42–49; and 39.1 (Jan. 1987), pp. 24–37, respectively.

[20] In *Literary Relations East and West,* ed. Jean Toyama and Nobuko Ochner (Honolulu: University of Hawaii Press, 1990), pp. 166–173.

Introduction
Michizane:
The Man and the Legend

Throughout Japan at the beginning of every year, youthful worshipers throng to certain Shinto shrines. They give the impression that Japan's largely secular youth is experiencing a religious revival. Such, however, is not necessarily the case. The season for entrance examinations is approaching, and students are praying for acceptance at the schools of their choice. They purchase such items as charms to ensure academic success or wooden plaques on which they write their specific requests. The charms are taken home, but the plaques are left at the shrines and hung on a special rack where they may be read by all. Some are piteous: "I want to get into Waseda University. This will be the fifth time I have tried." Others seem out of place at a Shinto shrine: "I want to get into the Department of Christian Studies at Heian Women's College." Less confident students may enumerate as many as twenty schools in declining order of academic prestige, while those who want to study abroad will write a list of, for example, American business schools. But most are straightforward requests for acceptance at schools ranging from the better elementary schools to the best medical schools.

This type of "worship" thrives at shrines commonly known as "Temmangū." They are dedicated to a deity whose full name is Temman Daijizai Tenjin (Heaven-Filling Great Self-Sufficient Heavenly Deity), but who is known affectionately to all Japanese as "Tenjin-sama." Only shrines to Inari, the god of the harvest, and Hachiman, the god of war, are more numerous. Most Tenjin shrines are small and unknown outside their local communities, but several are nationally renowned, the most famous being those at Kitano in Kyoto and Dazaifu in Kyushu. Tenjin is so revered a deity that even in Hawaii, at one of the few remaining Shinto shrines, members of the local Japanese-American community recently dedicated a new altar to him.

The nature of divinity in Shinto belief is not clearly defined, and "gods" (kami) are of many types. Tenjin belongs to the special category of gods who were originally mortals, for he is the deification of a historical personage, Sugawara no Michizane (845–903). Although not regarded with the same affection as Tenjin-sama, the man Michizane, too, is a familiar figure. In centuries past, legends concerning his life and deification were popular. Since the founding of Japan's modern education system in 1872, historical accounts of his activities have appeared regularly in primary school textbooks.

Michizane was a poet, scholar, teacher, diplomat, provincial governor, and minister of state. As a poet, he excelled at kanshi (poetry in Chinese) and his best works are far more expressive and individualistic than the imitations of Chinese models produced by most of his contemporaries. The two histories of Japan that he helped compile remain valuable sources for modern scholars. Teaching both at a family-run preparatory school and at the court university, he trained so many students for official careers that rivals came to fear they constituted a dangerous clique. In an age when Japan's official contacts with the Asian mainland were sporadic, he helped receive three missions from the then-flourishing Manchurian kingdom of Parhae. Ironically, however, it was at his instigation that Japan finally abandoned its own missions to T'ang China. Although distinctly a man of the court, Michizane served four years as a conscientious, but not necessarily very effective, provincial governor. Upon his return to the capital, he was promoted to a position of considerable power, but his success aroused the jealousy of rivals who slandered him and had him exiled to Kyushu. There he died. Despite his many varied achievements, his political career ended in failure.

Some years later, when a series of disasters befell the capital, people thought them to be the revenge of Michizane's angry ghost. As a result, he was posthumously pardoned and promoted, and eventually he came to be revered as a deity. Images of Michizane as Tenjin are diverse. They have reflected both differing concerns of worshipers and changing times. At first, the courtiers who had helped to drive Michizane into exile feared Tenjin's vengeful wrath. On the other hand, opponents of the court, both noble and common, looked upon him more sympathetically as a fellow victim of oppression at the hands of entrenched political interests. Bookish men regarded Tenjin as a patron saint because of Michizane's literary accomplishments, and Murasaki Shikibu too alluded to him in *The Tale of Genji* when she described her hero's exile. Through the centuries following Michizane's death, legends—some quite fantastic—evolved. As the god Tenjin, he was thought capable of performing miraculous deeds. For example, Zen monks believed that he posthumously went to China to seek enlightenment under a Chinese master of their sect. As a result, "Tenjin Visiting China" (Totō Tenjin) became a conventional theme among Japanese painters, even though Michizane had declined to make the journey when he was named ambassador to the T'ang (*kentō taishi*). During the Edo period, Tenjin worship flourished and calligraphy came to head the list of Michizane's reputed talents. Schools, both those for samurai and those for commoners, conducted rites to honor him, and he became the subject of the still-popular play, *The Sugawara Secrets of Calligraphy* (*Sugawara denju tenarai kagami*).[1]

The Edo period also witnessed the growth of critical scholarship. Men trained in the secular Confucian tradition began to distinguish more clearly the facts of Michizane's life from the legends of Tenjin, although even these more skeptical men continued to honor Michizane. Veneration of Michizane, as opposed to worship of Tenjin, reached a peak in the years between the Meiji Restoration and the end of World War II. In 1902, Tenjin shrines grandly celebrated the one-thousandth anniversary of his death. This event inspired the publication of biographies by

many leading figures of the day, including the politician Ōkuma
Shigenobu (1838–1922), the writer Takayama Chogyū (1871–
1902), and the Tokyo Imperial University professor of philosophy Inoue Tetsujirō (1855–1944). Inoue's biography, revised in
1936, remained for many years the standard treatment of Michizane's life. In it, Japan's pioneer specialist in Western philosophy lavished overblown praise on Michizane and compared him
favorably to Confucius, Socrates, Buddha, and Jesus.[2]

The appeal of Michizane in those years was based on stories
of his supposedly unwavering loyalty to the emperor, even after
he had been driven into exile, and also on the motto attributed
to him: "Japanese spirit, Chinese learning" (Wakon Kansai). Although the phrase first appeared in a source that even in the Edo
period was recognized as a late forgery, still, many scholars felt
that it accurately reflected Michizane's views. It was taken to
mean that Michizane had advocated borrowing the more advanced knowledge and techniques of a foreign country, in this
case China, but using them in the context of Japan's native traditional values. This basic concept was widely supported in the
Meiji period, when the original slogan was modified to "Japanese
spirit, Western learning" (Wakon Yōsai). Thus, more on the
basis of legendary words and deeds than on his real accomplishments, Michizane became a hero to conservative Meiji intellectuals. Whereas in Hawaii immigrants from rural Kyushu set up
an altar to the god Tenjin, in Boston, under the influence of
more sophisticated Japanese—perhaps indirectly via Ernest
Fenollosa—Michizane joined the ranks of the world's great literary men, artists, scientists, statesmen, and soldiers whose names
appear on the facade of the public library, completed in 1895.[3]
The only other Japanese so honored was the scholar Rai San'yō
(1780–1832). China was also allotted just two representatives,
Confucius and Mencius. The remaining names—over 500 of
them—were of great men, virtually all from the Western world.
As in Inoue's biography, here too Michizane's name appears in
truly exalted company.

If Tenjin worship led to fantastic legends about Michizane,
the "Michizane worship" of Meiji scholars produced a picture
that may have been less supernatural, but was still questionable.
Inoue's views of Michizane were, in their own nationalistic way,
as fanciful as those of the medieval monks who wrote of his

journey to China. After World War II, Michizane quickly fell from favor as stories of his loyalty to the emperor lost their appeal. The play, *Sugawara Secrets of Calligraphy*, was banned by occupation authorities for being too "feudalistic," and his picture was removed from the five-yen note where it had first appeared in 1888. But gradually, as Japanese began to reexamine their ancient past more objectively, critical studies of Michizane appeared, written by leading specialists in Japanese literature and history. They examined Michizane and his poetry without the distortions of either medieval Tenjin worship or prewar nationalism.[4] Thanks largely to the research by these scholars, today it is possible to view the man Michizane with considerable accuracy, despite his having died more than a thousand years ago and been elevated to a god. Exaggerated comparisons with Confucius et al. are not needed to justify the study of Michizane. His actual contributions may be of a lesser order, but they are indeed significant. This study will try to present a balanced picture of Michizane and his position in Japanese history. It will focus on his career as a scholar, poet, and court official, with passing attention to Tenjin-sama's legendary deeds.

Michizane is of interest not only for his individual achievements but also for the many ways he symbolized his age. The second half of the ninth century was a transitional period in Japan's institutional and cultural history. Through the mid-sixth century, Japan had remained a primitive land, largely isolated from the centers of East Asian civilization. Then, a series of important changes began, traditionally said to have been triggered by the introduction of Buddhism from Korea in 552. Many elements of continental civilization were enthusiastically welcomed into Japan, first via Korea and later directly from China. Among them were Buddhist thought, art, and architecture, originally from India but brought to Japan largely in their Chinese guise. Also imported was the Chinese writing system and with it the Confucian classics and Chinese poetry. In addition, the Japanese learned about Chinese concepts of imperial rule and centralized bureaucratic government. During the seventh century, these and other aspects of Chinese civilization increasingly influenced the formation of Japan's own traditional culture.

The first decades of the eighth century witnessed the completion of three important projects that firmly established the court's commitment to government and culture in the Chinese manner. In 701, following a few preliminary attempts, the Japanese promulgated their first comprehensive criminal and administrative codes, the Taihō ritsuryō. These codes largely followed Chinese political theory and, with only modest revision, remained the basis for civil administration, in practice, for at least two centuries, and, in theory, through the Meiji Restoration. Then, in 710, a new capital was built at Nara, its symmetrical plan in accordance with Chinese ideals for an administrative center. It provided a proper physical setting in which to run a Chinese-style government, as did its successor, the Heian capital established in 794. The third project, completed in 720, was the compilation of Nihon shoki (Chronicles of Japan), Japan's first national history that accurately followed Chinese historiographic models and was written in proper Chinese. An earlier history, the Kojiki (Records of ancient matters), completed in 712, had focused more on ancient legends and employed a hybrid language that mixed elements of Chinese and Japanese. The more polished Nihon shoki authenticated the legitimacy of the imperial family and the recently sinified court government.

These projects were made possible by Japan's continuing contact with the more advanced nations of continental Asia. In 600, the Japanese court dispatched its first formal diplomatic mission to China, and these embassies continued on a more or less regular basis for more than two centuries. They became the principal channel for study and trade in China and also served to further confirm Japan's new status as a civilized member of the East Asian community of nations.

Through the eighth and ninth centuries, the Japanese court attempted to preserve its sinified appearance. The depth and pervasiveness of Chinese influence, however, is difficult to gauge precisely. In practice, elements of Chinese and native culture existed side by side, as is illustrated by the example of the two anthologies of poetry that survive from the eighth century. The first, the Kaifūsō (Fond recollections of poetry, compiled in 751) consists of poems written in Chinese. The second, the Man'yōshū (Collection for ten thousand generations, compiled c. 759), contains what some Japanese consider the most pristinely pure of their native poetry. Similarly, the law codes that include sections copied verbatim from their Chinese models also present distinctively Japanese features such as the Department of Shrines (Jingikan). The Japanese never abandoned their native traditions, but, for a period of roughly two centuries, the court did attempt to govern in the Chinese mode (modified to suit native custom), and court culture (at least officially encouraged higher culture) was distinctly sinified.

Starting in the mid-ninth century, however, the Japanese court gradually began to abandon its commitment to functioning in the Chinese manner. This change can be seen in many spheres of activity. Politically, a single lineage from the Northern House (Hokke) of the Fujiwara family came to dominate high court offices, and lesser posts as well eventually became hereditary preserves. Thus the Confucian ideal of a bureaucratically organized meritocracy was abandoned. Land, which was supposed to be controlled by the government and distributed to peasants, increasingly came to be accumulated into large privately managed estates (*shōen*). Revenues from these estates flowed into the hands of powerful court families and temples rather than into government coffers. Japan's interest in diplomacy waned. Foreign contacts became if anything more frequent, but took the form of private trade dominated by Chinese merchants. Only rarely did Japanese venture abroad seeking the cultural glories of China. Literature in Japanese, which had virtually disappeared from sight after the *Man'yōshū*, once again began to flourish, and, when the imperially sponsored *Kokinshū* (Collection of ancient and modern times) was compiled in 905, the native poetic tradition was given the official recognition that earlier had been accorded only to literature in Chinese. During the middle and late Heian periods, roughly the years 900 to 1185, a more purely Japanese culture came to the fore. The *ritsuryō* codes were not revoked and interest in Chinese culture never died, but they did lose their preeminent position.

Michizane's life corresponds closely to the half-century when these important cultural changes were occurring. He was born six years after the return of Japan's last official mission to T'ang China, and he died just two years before the completion of the *Kokinshū*. He had connections with both of these major cultural watersheds: his uncle had served on the last mission to China, and two of his poems appeared in the *Kokinshū*. He himself gave impetus to the changing cultural patterns when he declined to make the journey to China. Although Michizane in this way contributed to the growth of the new culture, on the whole he belonged to the older, more Chinese order. In many ways Michizane's career resembled that of a Chinese scholar-official. After an education in the Confucian classics and Chinese literature, Michizane entered Japan's court bureaucracy by means of a civil service examination similar to those given in China. He served in many offices at court and in the provinces. He produced a substantial body of writings in Chinese. Even his final exile was a variation of the familiar Chinese theme of the literatus who lost out in court struggles with men less learned but more influential. Unlike the case of his Chinese counterparts, however, Michizane's political downfall represented more than the end of an individual career. It also helped mark the end of an age in which Chinese culture had dominated the court. Thus, Michizane's life throws light on important changes in Japanese history.

Politically, the early Heian period witnessed a shift in power from emperors to members of the Fujiwara family who served first as ministers (*daijin*) and later as regents (*sesshō*). The Heian period began with Emperor Kammu (737–806, r. 781–806) firmly in control of the court government. Many of his policies, including his move of the capital, were intended to strengthen imperial power, which in the Nara period had been compromised by the influence of Buddhist monks and institutions. To achieve his goal, he attempted to revive the *ritsuryō* system and promoted able men from less influential court families. Similar policies were adopted by his son Saga (786–842, r. 809–823) and, decades later, by his great-great-grandson Uda (867–931, r. 887–897). Between the reigns of Saga and Uda, however, control of the court fell into the hands of two ministers from the Fujiwara family, first Yoshifusa (804–874) and then his adopted son Mototsune (836–891).

The Fujiwara were an ancient noble family that historically had been active supporters of the *ritsuryō* system. Yoshifusa's ancestors had assisted in the creation of Japan's sinified state and later had held high office during the Nara period. In the Heian period, however, most Fujiwara leaders followed a policy of modifying the codes to suit changing conditions and to strengthen their own position. Thus, the conflict between the emperors and the Fujiwara involved broader institutional issues. The emperors favored a return to the *ritsuryō* system and its bureaucratic government, code law, and taxes on individuals. In contrast, the Fujiwara generally sought to emphasize aristocratic elements in the government, acknowledge a new customary law, and use land as the basis for taxation.[5]

Japan's emperors turned to the *ritsuryō* system for support because the codes placed them at the top of a national administrative hierarchy, even though historically their political power had been limited. Originally, the forebears of the imperial family had constituted one of the many noble clans (*uji*) that had dominated Japan. By the sixth century, the head of the imperial family had come to be recognized as the national sovereign. Rival clans, however, were not eliminated; instead they were incorporated into the new bureaucratic framework and given positions commensurate with their earlier status. Contrary to the view of many Japanese historians who characterize the system as "despotic," in fact, the codes provided for a balance of power between the emperor and the principal administrative body, the Council of State (Daijōkan, see chart 1). Its highest officers, known collectively as "senior nobles" (*kugyō*), were in practice usually descendants of other powerful ancient clans. Together, they served as a deliberative body that had a strong voice in determining policy. Because of the codes' Chinese basis, they proclaimed the supremacy of the emperor, but Japanese political considerations did not allow them to grant the emperor absolute power. A comparison of Japan's codes with their T'ang models reveals that Japan's emperor was less able to act independently than was his Chinese counterpart, whereas the Council of State had greater authority than any corresponding T'ang body.

How the Council of State served to limit the free exercise of imperial power can be illustrated by examining the procedures for issuing edicts, the official expressions of the emperor's will. The codes provided for two types of edicts. The more formal type required the assent of all senior nobles. That would have been a strong restraint on the emperor, although in practice such edicts were issued principally for matters of ritual importance such as the changing of era names. But even the less formal type of edict that was used more commonly could not

CHART 1

The Ninth-Century Central Government and Michizane's Career at Court

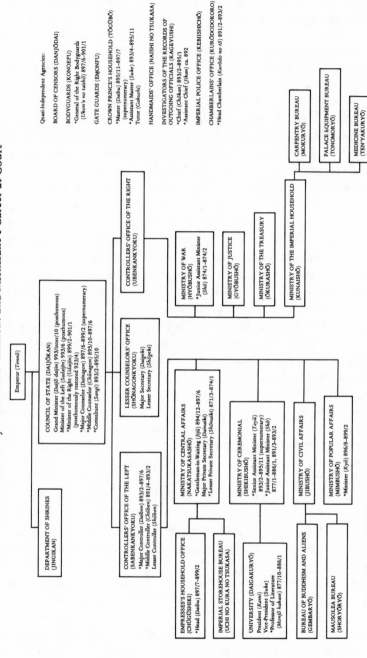

Quasi-Independent Agencies:

BOARD OF CENSORS (DANJŌDAI)

BODYGUARDS (KONOEFU)
*General of the Right Bodyguards
(Ukon'e no taishō) 897/6–901/1

GATE GUARDS (EMONFU)

CROWN PRINCE'S HOUSEHOLD (TŌGŪBŌ)
*Master (Daibu) 895/11–897/7
(supernumerary)
*Assistant Master (Suke) 893/4–895/11
Tutor (Gakushi)

HANDMAIDS' OFFICE (NAISHI NO TSUKASA)

INVESTIGATORS OF THE RECORDS OF
OUTGOING OFFICIALS (KAGEYUSHI)
*Chief (Chōkan) 893/2–895/1
*Assistant Chief (Jikan) ca. 892

IMPERIAL POLICE OFFICE (KEBIISHICHŌ)

CHAMBERLAINS' OFFICE (KURŌDODOKORO)
*Head Chamberlain (Kurōdo no tō) 891/2–893/2

EMPEROR (Tennō)

COUNCIL OF STATE (DAIJŌKAN)
Grand Minister (Daijō daijin) 993/inter/10 (posthumous)
Minister of the Left (Sadaijin) 993/6 (posthumous)
*Minister of the Right (Udaijin) 899/2–901/1
(posthumously restored 923/4)
*Major Counselor (Dainagon) 897/6–899/2 (supernumerary)
*Middle Counselor (Chūnagon) 895/10–897/6
*Consultant (Sangi) 893/2–895/10

DEPARTMENT OF SHRINES
(JINGIKAN)

CONTROLLERS' OFFICE OF THE RIGHT
(UBENKANKYOKU)

LESSER COUNSELORS' OFFICE
(SHŌNAGONKYOKU)
Major Secretary (Daigeki)
Lesser Secretary (Shōgeki)

MINISTRY OF WAR
(HYŌBUSHŌ)
*Junior Assistant Minister
(Shō) 874/1–874/2

MINISTRY OF JUSTICE
(GYŌBUSHŌ)

MINISTRY OF THE TREASURY
(ŌKURASHŌ)

MINISTRY OF THE IMPERIAL HOUSEHOLD
(KUNAISHŌ)

CARPENTRY BUREAU
(MOKURYŌ)

PALACE EQUIPMENT BUREAU
(TONOMORYŌ)

MEDICINE BUREAU
(TEN'YAKURYŌ)

CONTROLLERS' OFFICE OF THE LEFT
(SABENKANKYOKU)
*Major Controller (Daiben) 893/2–897/6
*Middle Controller (Chūben) 891/4–893/2
Lesser Controller (Shōben)

MINISTRY OF CENTRAL AFFAIRS
(NAKATSUKASASHŌ)
*Gentleman-in-Waiting (Jijū) 894/12–897/6
Major Private Secretary (Dainaiki)
*Lesser Private Secretary (Shōnaiki) 871/3–874/1

MINISTRY OF CEREMONIAL
(SHIKIBUSHŌ)
*Senior Assistant Minister (Tayū)
893/2–895/11 (supernumerary)
*Junior Assistant Minister (Shō)
877/1–886/1, 891/3–893/2

EMPRESSES'S HOUSEHOLD OFFICE
(CHŪGŪSHIKI)
*Head (Daibu) 897/7–899/2

IMPERIAL STOREHOUSE BUREAU
(UCHI NO KURA NO TSUKASA)

UNIVERSITY (DAIGAKURYŌ)
President (Kami)
Vice-President (Suke)
*Professor of Literature
(Monjō hakase) 877/10–886/1

MINISTRY OF CIVIL AFFAIRS
(JIBUSHŌ)

BUREAU OF BUDDHISM AND ALIENS
(GEMBARYŌ)

MAUSOLEA BUREAU
(SHORYŌRYŌ)

MINISTRY OF POPULAR AFFAIRS
(MIMBUSHŌ)
*Minister (Kyō) 896/8–899/2

Note: This chart shows all the major institutions of court government plus lesser agencies mentioned in the
text. Names of these government institutions are written in all capitals. Also included are titles of officials
discussed in the text; Michizane's offices are indicated by an asterisk and followed by the dates he held them.

be issued without the assistance of at least one senior noble who held the office of middle counselor (*chūnagon*) or above. An emperor thus could not exercise his authority without some cooperation from the Council of State.

Although the codes did not guarantee absolute imperial authority, Heian emperors turned to them, nonetheless, because they did provide a framework within which an ambitious ruler might be able to restrict the independent power of the dominant aristocratic family, the Fujiwara. The same procedures that could limit an emperor's ability to act independently could also be manipulated to the advantage of a politically able and ambitious emperor, who could effectively control the council through an alliance with just a single official holding one of the posts of middle counselor or above. Men in that position were potentially very powerful. Not only could they assist in proclaiming imperial edicts, but they could also approve routine directives on their own without reference to higher authority, either the emperor or the Council of State. Moreover, all such officials had similar powers, despite the differences in their formal status. Therefore, one way for emperors to exert their authority was to promote reliable allies to the office of middle counselor. In practice, these allies usually were either able men from lesser court families who could be trusted to be loyal to their imperial patrons or descendants of emperors who had been removed from the imperial family with the grant of surnames such as Minamoto (or "Genji," the Sino-Japanese reading for "Minamoto clan") and Taira (or "Heike," the Sino-Japanese reading for "Taira family").

Because all of the higher senior nobles had similar powers, no one minister could easily dominate the government by gaining appointment to the highest regular office. The minister of the left (*sadaijin*) may have been the highest ranking regular member of the Council of State, but his function in the government was much the same as that of a middle counselor. This situation allowed an emperor to tip the balance of power in his own favor with a few key appointments. Another consequence was that an ambitious court aristocrat could not easily control the government from a regular appointment to the Council of State. Accordingly, Fujiwara leaders sought ever grander posts, first within the *ritsuryō* system and later outside the system in

the form of new offices that allowed them to dominate both
the emperor and the Council of State.[6]

Toward the end of his career Michizane was promoted to
high office by Emperor Uda. He became the most conspicuous
example of a man placed in the Council of State to aid in the
exercise of imperial power. For most of his years in government
service, however, Michizane held regular posts in the extensive
bureaucracy both at court and in the provinces. This bureaucracy functioned under the general supervision of the Council
of State. At court, it consisted of eight ministries (shō), plus a
wide range of lesser offices, each with specialized functions.
Most of the lesser offices were subordinate to an appropriate
ministry, although a few were independent.

The men who staffed these governmental organs were divided
into two broad categories: officials (kanjin) and menials (zōnin).
The officials, in turn, were of two types, administrative and
specialist. Most governmental organs, including ministries, provinces, and lesser offices, had four levels of administrative officials (shitōkan), some of which might be further subdivided
into junior and senior grades. In addition, many offices had specialists (honkan) assigned to them. For example, the court
university (daigakuryō) was, in fact, a regular government
bureau (ryō) under the Ministry of Ceremonial (Shikibushō).
As such, it had the usual four classes of administrative officials, with the two lower level posts each having junior and senior
grades. The men assigned to these offices held the same ranks
as corresponding officials in other bureaus. The university also
included specialists—professors (hakase)—and some of them
had relatively high ranks. Beneath all these officials were a
large number of anonymous menials. They were mostly men
without court rank, although some men with the lowest ranks
might be grouped together with them.[7]

In the ninth century, two systems were used to indicate a
man's status. The newer and more important was court rank
(kurai), but an older system of noble titles (kabane) also survived, a vestige of the age before the introduction of bureaucratic government. These titles were awarded to families and
were strictly hereditary. For example, Michizane's ancestors
had held the title of muraji until 684 when the system of titles
was reformed and they were granted the more noble title of

sukune. Eventually, in his grandfather's generation, the family was awarded the title of *ason,* the highest one available to those not descended from the imperial family. Every Sugawara held this title, and hence Michizane's full name appears as Sugawara no Ason Michizane. Originally, the use of a title had been a sign of membership in a noble clan, and the specific title had designated the status of that clan. Japan's ruling class continued to use these titles until the Meiji Restoration, but already in the eighth century they had basically lost their original function and remained only as general indications of a family's noble status.

The *ritsuryō* codes created a system of ranks that largely superseded the ancient titles. From the most noble minister down to the most obscure clerk, a man's status at court was determined by his rank. All officials were assigned ranks ranging from the first down to the eighth. At the bottom beneath the eighth rank was an initial rank (*soi*). The initial rank granted few privileges, and men who held it were not always distinguished from menials without rank. The highest three ranks were divided into junior and senior levels, and all the remaining ranks were further subdivided into upper and lower grades. Thus, the system consisted of a total of thirty ranks ranging from the "senior first" down to the "junior initial lower." According to the codes, a man was first to be granted a specific rank and then assigned an office appropriate to that rank, although provisions were made for men to be given offices higher or lower than prescribed for their rank and such appointments were common.

Ranks and titles differed in two fundamental ways: ranks were awarded to individuals, titles to families; and ranks were periodically raised in recognition of achievement, titles normally were fixed. Thus, rank was the more precise measure of an individual's position and was highly prized. Aristocratic (*ki*) status, for example, came to be defined in terms of rank. Those with the third rank or above were considered true aristocrats. Typically, at any given time during the ninth century, they numbered only about seven or eight men, the most senior of the nobles on the Council of State. Officials with the fourth and fifth ranks, perhaps a little over a hundred individuals, were considered lesser aristocrats (*tsūki*), and filled important regular bureacratic posts. Positions for non-aristocratic minor officials with ranks down to the eighth numbered about four hundred. At the very bottom of the governmental hierarchy were perhaps 6,000 menials with no rank at all or perhaps only the initial rank.

High rank conferred many privileges: eligibility for important offices, the guarantee of rank to one's heirs, and potentially enormous income. According to the codes, an official of the sixth rank was entitled to an annual salary equivalent to twenty-two *koku* of rice. A promotion of only one grade to the junior fifth rank, and hence low aristocratic status, raised that figure more than tenfold to 255 *koku*. With the third rank and true aristocratic status, it became 6,957 *koku*. At the junior first rank, the highest actually awarded in the ninth century, the prescribed salary was 22,406 *koku*. The Heian *koku* was roughly equal to two bushels, approximately 40 percent the size of the more familiar *koku* used in the Edo period. Still, the prescribed income of a high official was comparable to that of a minor daimyo in later centuries, and the daimyo probably would have had far greater expenses. Whether Heian aristocrats actually collected all of their generous salaries is difficult to determine; however, evidence suggests that when government finances were straitened (as they often were) the highest officials were paid first, in full. Men of lower rank were given only a portion of their due.[8] If indeed that was the practice, court ministers may well have collected their enormous salaries.

For purposes of awarding rank and, hence, also for admission to government service, the codes divided men into three categories. Sons of aristocrats—also grandsons of the high aristocrats—were automatically awarded a specified rank on the basis of hereditary privilege (*on'i*) at age twenty-one after serving brief apprenticeships as attendants (*toneri*). These ranks ranged from the already aristocratic junior fifth awarded to the heir of a first rank official down to the eighth for sons of fifth rank officials. Aristocratic youths were also assured admission to the university, and, if they passed a civil service examination, they could obtain a slightly higher rank. Sons of minor officials were allowed to become attendants, although of a less prestigious type. After six years, if their performance was judged satisfactory, they too would be awarded rank, but at a much lower level than the hereditary rank for sons of aristocrats. Alternatively, sons of minor officials could apply for admission to the university (for them, admission was not assured) and gain rank through the examinations. Here too they were at a disadvantage, for the ranks awarded to successful examinees were lower than most hereditary ranks. For example, the son of a minor official might only earn the senior initial rank through service as an attendant or the senior eighth rank for passing the examination. Finally, for men whose fathers had no rank, entry into government service as a menial was possible, but to obtain rank was exceedingly difficult.

Men in government service were thus divided into three distinct tiers: aristocrats, lower officials, and menials. The gaps between each group were enormous. Hereditary ranks could be far higher than those achieved through the examinations or service as an attendant. Moreover, promotions to the fifth rank and above were determined by the Council of State, and so a well-connected young aristocrat with relatives on the council might receive special favor and be promoted rapidly. In contrast, an able but less noble man could spend years in the same low rank from which promotions were granted through slow routine bureaucratic procedures. Political considerations were minimal; instead, long years of diligent service were required. These practices ensured that the various levels of officialdom would tend to reproduce themselves from within fixed groups of families. Sons of high officials could be expeditiously raised to high rank. Sons of minor officials would advance so slowly they would never attain the fifth rank and aristocratic status. A limited number of aristocratic families, descendants of the most powerful ancient clans, produced most of the senior nobles of the Nara period. During the Heian period, the number of such families gradually shrank.[9]

Despite the dominance of hereditary privilege, advancement through study at the university and success in the civil service examinations was possible and allowed a small number of intellectually able men to attain ranks far beyond those of their fathers. Usually, these men were either sons of minor officials not entitled to hereditary privilege, or sons of lesser aristocrats eligible only for very low hereditary rank. Academic success was one of the few ways they could significantly improve their position at court. A handful of scholars from obscure families attained aristocratic status, and some were even promoted to the Council of State. But sons of these men rarely maintained their fathers' positions, for academic ability was not inherited automatically like rank, and even high-ranking scholars did not have the political influence to win special promotions for their sons. Michizane's lineage, however, was a rare example of a family that was able to achieve and then preserve aristocratic status on the basis of its scholarly abilities. For the Sugawara, the university and the examinations were of paramount importance.

The fortunes of the university were closely tied to those of the imperial family, since one way for emperors to strengthen their own position was to favor men with scholarly rather than aristocratic backgrounds. This policy could be justified in terms of the Confucian ideals that lay behind the *ritsuryō* system, and it also allowed emperors to promote men more dependent on imperial favor than were established aristocratic politicians. The situation resembled that in China. T'ang society too was aristocratic, and the examination system remained relatively unimportant until later when, in the Sung dynasty, powerful rulers found they could control the aristocratic families by promoting successful examination candidates.[10] Japanese emperors attempted to follow a similar strategy, but with markedly less success. Japan's emperors failed in part because their position institutionally was weaker than that of Chinese sovereigns, whereas the status of the hereditary aristocracy was more secure. Moreover, a single lineage of the Fujiwara came to dominate first the highest offices at court and subsequently, by intermarriage, the imperial family itself. No single aristocratic family in China attained a comparable position. A final problem was that Japan's examination system remained fundamentally alien. Questions were based on Chinese thought and history; the answers written in ornate Chinese prose. Little effort was made to assimilate the system either in form or in content, and it became increasingly anachronistic in the middle centuries of the Heian period when interest in native traditions revived and flourished.

Michizane's family background and career illustrate many of the processes outlined above. In the Nara period, his ancestors had served as minor bureaucrats who were customarily barred from regular promotion to the fifth rank. They were typical members of lower officialdom. Michizane's rise to the highest offices was made possible in part by the success of his immediate forebears, who were able to attain aristocratic status by virtue of their literary and scholarly achievements during the reigns of emperors who valued their talents. Michizane's own career began with his experiences as a student and then as an examination candidate. Between 871 and 886, the first period of his service at court, he held various posts of moderate importance, culminating in nine years as a professor of literature. During these years, Michizane's life was that of a typical court scholar-official. This period came to an end when he was named to a four-year term as governor (*kami*) of Sanuki province, the modern Kagawa prefecture in Shikoku. Although details of his administration are scanty, in his poetry Michizane portrays himself as a hard-working governor and offers rare glimpses of ninth-century provincial life.

While Michizane was serving in Sanuki, important political changes were occurring in the capital. Through the early years of Michizane's career, the court government had been under the sway of the Fujiwara. However, in 887 Uda became emperor and tried to rule without Fujiwara interference as his predecessors had done at the beginning of the Heian period. When Michizane returned to the capital in 890, he fit perfectly into Uda's plans, for he was a man of learning and experience, but lacked close ties to established political powers. During the following decade, through Uda's patronage, Michizane rose to become the most influential minister at court. His activities in this period reveal the workings of the government at its highest level. In 901, however, his years in high office came to an abrupt end when he was accused of attempting to manipulate the imperial succession. Even his patron, the now-retired Emperor Uda, could not prevent his exile to Kyushu.

Just as Michizane's official career illustrates the workings of ninth-century court government, so his writings shed light on literature and scholarship of the period. In early Japan, literature (*monjō*) was a broadly inclusive term. Following Chinese concepts, the Japanese grouped together under the rubric of literature many forms of writing that demanded an elevated style.[11] Literary anthologies included poetry, prose essays, examination papers, and even official documents. Although the university briefly had maintained a separate program in history (*kiden*), by Michizane's day it had been subsumed into the literature course. This lack of distinctions was not restricted to the conceptual level. In practice too, the same men who were summoned to present poems at court functions were also called upon to draft government documents or edit official histories and legal compendia. Since the making of compilations was the usual scholarly enterprise, the realms of scholarship and literature also overlapped. One distinction, however, was important: that between writing in Chinese and in Japanese. In the ninth century, most serious writing was in Chinese, either prose (*kambun*) or poetry (*kanshi*). Writing in Japanese was generally limited to poetry (*waka*).

In the early Heian period, literature in Chinese flourished under imperial sponsorship. This was not simply because the emperors were great admirers of literature, although some of them indeed were. Rather, it was the cultural side of their policy of reviving the *ritsuryō* system. By summoning their ministers to compose poems in Chinese, they were reaffirming their status as proper Confucian sovereigns. By ordering the compilation of court histories, they demonstrated the legitimacy of their reigns. By encouraging proficiency in Chinese composition, they were able to conduct the diplomatic exchanges that enhanced national prestige. Confucian theory provided ample justification for court sponsorship of literature, and emperors turned to these theories for support at a symbolic level just as they looked to the codes as a source of institutional strength.

Because of its highly ritualistic and symbolic function, most of early Japan's literature in Chinese that survives is public and formal. *Kanshi* were written at court ceremonies on prescribed themes; they expressed conventional sentiments in elegant language. Poets strove to demonstrate their knowledge of Chinese literary lore rather than their own individual genius. Michizane's *kanshi* are noteworthy because among them are conspicuous exceptions to these generalizations. To be sure, most of his poems are formal and remarkable only for the great erudition they display. In addition, however, Michizane also left a large body of less formal poetry that is more expressive of his personal thoughts, feelings, and observations. Whereas most men composed *kanshi* principally to satisfy the demands of court ritual and to demonstrate their learning, Michizane wrote also in response to inner needs. Moreover, his command of Chinese was adequate to the challenge of creating works of real literary interest. With reason, Michizane came to identify himself as a poet and in occasional moments of frustration set himself apart from the larger group of court literary men.

To a Japanese poet, the use of Chinese as a literary language had advantages and disadvantages. The most obvious drawback was that it required the mastery of a foreign language and literary tradition. This problem was rendered more difficult, because in Michizane's time the Japanese felt obliged to follow contemporary Chinese rules of prosody requiring both rhyme and, for certain forms, meter based on the arrangement of tones. These features were totally alien to Japan's native language and literature. Despite such difficulties, *kanshi* did allow certain freedoms not found in *waka*. Although the *Man'yōshū* had included long poems, the mid-ninth century *waka* revival focused on the thirty-one-syllable short poem. In addition, poetic decorum had come to limit the vocabulary and range of themes acceptable for *waka*. By writing in Chinese, Michizane was able to express himself on subjects not allowed in *waka* and to develop his thoughts at considerable length.

Michizane's *kanshi* also benefited from the influence of the great T'ang poet Po Chü-i (772–856). Early Heian *kanshi* had been patterned on the more mannered styles of the Six Dynasties and early T'ang. Po Chü-i's poetry, however, included works that were more informal and colloquial. By 838, if not earlier, the poetry of Po Chü-i was known in Japan, and it soon became very popular. Its influence on Michizane's *kanshi* is apparent. Most obviously, Michizane alluded to poems by the Chinese master and borrowed their form or diction. More significantly, Po Chü-i's example legitimized the use of less formal language. One scholar has even suggested that Michizane's occasional deviations from correct Chinese usage may not have been errors but rather attempts at introducing more colloquially Japanese expressions into his *kanshi,* as suggested by Po Chü-i's use of colloquial Chinese.[12]

The best of Michizane's works, including some of his prose, have universal appeal. The problems that troubled him—and his troubles were conveyed more vividly than his pleasures—seem familiar even to readers living in a completely different culture more than a thousand years after his death. We can all sympathize with a man who sadly tells of seeing a deceased son in his dreams. Perhaps because East Asia's traditional respect for old age is so familiar, we are pleasantly surprised to discover Michizane worrying about his first gray hairs. Present-day teachers may find some small comfort in Michizane's complaints that his students spilled ink on their texts and carved on their desks. Michizane's eventual deification in no way altered the essential humanity of his poetry.

Michizane also participated in the ninth-century revival of native poetry, and a few of his *waka* are today familiar to all Japanese. On the whole, however, his *waka* are less noteworthy than his *kanshi*. Most of his *waka* are skillful but unremarkable examples of the highly "reasoned" poetry that was fashionable in his day. One difficulty in judging his talents as a *waka* poet is that his poems in Japanese are not as well preserved as his works in Chinese. Whereas Michizane himself compiled the latter into two chronologically arranged anthologies with a few explanatory notes, he does not seem to have valued his *waka* so highly. After his death, some appeared in imperial anthologies, notably in a sequence of twelve poems in the *Shinkokinshū* (New collection of ancient and modern times, compiled in 1205). Later enthusiasts extracted his *waka* from various sources and made collections of them, but often they mixed poems of dubious authenticity with genuine works. Today, scholars estimate that forty to fifty of the *waka* attributed to Michizane are authentic.[13] They show him to be a capable, if not outstanding, *waka* poet, but they are less distinctive and less revealing of his personality than are his *kanshi*.

Michizane's writings offer a perspective on the Heian court different from the more familiar image conveyed by later masterpieces of Japanese prose. *The Tale of Genji* and *The Pillow Book* focus their attention on a narrow segment of society dominated by a subtle concern for beauty, refinement, and romance. They are perhaps the supreme expressions of what Donald Keene has termed "the feminine sensibility in the Heian era."[14] In contrast, Michizane's *kanshi* reveal to us something of the age's "masculine sensibility." Although Michizane also wrote of the court's elegant pastimes that so interested the women writers, romance was not one of his literary concerns. This does not mean that in his private life he was more ascetic or strait-laced than others at court. His reported twenty-three children suggest quite the opposite. His writing, however, was grounded in a Chinese literary tradition that did not take romance as a central concern.

Michizane's writings depicted a man's world of official busi-ness. He portrays himself as a busy official, a conscientious gov-ernor, and a maligned teacher. Even if these self-portraits are idealized, they do show us aspects of Heian life neglected in the writings of women, who would have known little about such matters. Through his academic training, Michizane became familiar with the major systems of East Asian thought. Inspired by Confucian principles—and Po Chü-i's poetry—he sympa-thetically described the suffering of the poor. In moments of leisure or frustration, he comforted himself by writing in a Taoist vein, replete with allusions to *Lao-tzu* and *Chuang-tzu*. And he expressed his faith in Buddhism, a religion that did not have a strong influence on Chinese poetry but dominated the spiritual life of the Japanese court. Although Michizane may not have been a philosopher, he did find literary inspiration in the major East Asian intellectual traditions. Heian literature in Japanese, too, was deeply tinged by the influence of Buddhist ideas, but Confucian and Taoist thought found expression prin-cipally in the literature in Chinese. Neglect of that literature can lead to a distorted view of the age.

Because Michizane lived over one thousand years ago, it is hardly surprising that gaps exist in our knowledge of him. For example, we know little about his childhood and virtually noth-ing about the women in his life. Traditional biographies focused on the events of his public career, supplemented by platitudes about his righteousness and spiced with a few miracles. Not long after Michizane's death, private peccadillos of high-ranking courtiers were being noted with relish in diaries, historical ro-mances, and collections of anecdotes. Documents from Michi-zane's day, however, maintained more of a dignified Confucian tone and did not record intimate or less seemly details of his private life. If these were the only sources available, a detailed study of Michizane's life would be impossible. Fortunately, in addition to the dry chronicles of his official career, his writings survive and reveal to us something of his inner life and sensitive personality.

This book will focus principally on the achievements of a remarkable individual, Sugawara no Michizane, but the man cannot be removed from his historical context. Crucial to an understanding of Michizane are his family background and the structure of the court university, since the academic success of his immediate ancestors paved the way for his unprecedented rise to the highest ranks of court society. Therefore, these two topics must be treated more fully before addressing Michizane himself.

1 · A Family of Scholars

Family background was an essential consideration in determining a man's position at court, and, by the middle of the Heian period, the Sugawara were well established as a family whose members had the status of lesser aristocrats: they typically rose to the fourth or fifth ranks, but rarely higher. No Sugawara after Michizane attained high office; instead, his descendants served in a wide range of offices appropriate to men of their rank. In particular, many held posts at the university, where they came to be one of only three families from which professors of literature were commonly chosen. The Sugawara maintained this status until the late Edo period, long after court ranks and offices had become largely meaningless. They were not the most noble of court families, but the Sugawara were sufficiently important to warrant a full genealogy in surviving texts of the great record of the court aristocratic lineages, *Sompi bummyaku* (Noble and base lineages, originally compiled in the late fourteenth century). Such complete treatment is given to just six families other than branches of the Fujiwara or descendants of the imperial house.[1]

At the time of Michizane's birth in 845, however, the Sugawara were not yet securely established as a family of noble scholars. They were, in fact, a rather new family. Only sixty-four years earlier, a branch of the ancient Haji family had requested a new surname, Sugawara, and established itself as an

23

independent family. Michizane's father and grandfather were indeed scholars who achieved aristocratic status, but their immediate ancestors in the Haji family had been legally restricted to low court rank. Moreover, in the ninth century the Sugawara were merely one among many families from which the court university drew its professors, and Michizane's lineage was the only one in the Sugawara family that held posts there. Other Sugawara lineages sought careers elsewhere, and one became known for its medical expertise.[2] In order to understand Michizane's own career, one must consider his family's status at court and how it was achieved. A review of lives of his immediate ancestors will also throw light on the political, cultural, and literary milieu into which he was born.

THE ORIGIN OF THE SUGAWARA

The Sugawara family was created in 781 when fifteen members of the Haji family under the leadership of Haji no Furuhito, Michizane's great-grandfather, presented the new Emperor Kammu a petition outlining the family's history and requesting a new surname:

> The ancestor of the Haji family was the god Amenohohi, whose descendant in the fourteenth generation was named Nomi no Sukune. In ancient times, when Emperor Suinin reigned from the Tamaki Palace at Makimuku, customs were still primitive and funeral rites were not properly conducted. When a person died, his retainers were buried alive along with him. Thus, after Empress Hibasuhime passed away, her coffin was placed in a courtyard and the emperor asked the assembled ministers, "How should the empress's funeral rites be conducted?" The ministers replied, "The precedent of Prince Yamatohiko [whose retainers were buried alive with him] should be followed." However, our distant ancestor, Nomi no Sukune, offered this suggestion, "In my humble opinion, the practice of burying retainers alive is absolutely contrary to the principles of benevolent government and is not the way of developing the nation and benefiting the people." Then, on his own, leading over three hundred potters, he took clay and made images of various things, which he presented to the emperor. When the emperor saw the images, he was very pleased and used them in place of the live retainers. "These objects are to be known as *haniwa*," he proclaimed.
> The virtue of this former emperor and the heritage of our ancestor have benefited later generations both of our own family and of all

people. But our ancestors served with equal frequency on both fortunate and unfortunate occasions, taking charge both of sad funeral rites and also of joyful festivities. Thus we served the court and such was the normal course of events. Now, however, the custom is different and we only take charge of funerals. This was not the intention of our ancestor. Therefore we request that our surname be changed from Haji to Sugawara, the name of the place where we dwell.[3]

The request was granted and so the Sugawara family was created from one branch of the Haji family. Later, other branches adopted the surnames Ōe and Akishino. The history of the Haji family as presented in Furuhito's petition is a mixture of myth, legend, and fact. Although the claim to divine origin may be mythical, it points to the family's beginnings in Izumo, for the Haji's ancestral deity was the same as that of the Izumo Magistrate (Izumo no Kuninomiyatsuko) family. Around the fifth century, members of the Haji family migrated to the Yamato region. The apocryphal story of Nomi no Sukune's inventing *haniwa* reflects the fact that the Haji came to take charge of pottery making for the Yamato court, which was then consolidating its control over Japan. The name Haji (literally, "master potter") points to this tradition. Because burial objects were among the wares it produced, the family also came to be responsible for imperial funerals. This development occurred sometime in the early seventh century.

The Haji did not maintain their position as hereditary undertakers very long. As the Japanese court gradually reorganized itself into a more bureaucratic form of government based on Chinese principles, the earlier tradition of hereditary occupations was modified. According to the new *ritsuryō* codes, although an individual's entry into officialdom was determined largely by his father's rank, subsequent promotions and assignments to bureaucratic posts were supposed to be based on merit. In theory, most court offices were no longer hereditary preserves, but old usages lingered both in law and in practice. For example, the codes explicitly specified that members of the Haji family were to supervise funerals of the highest ranking aristocrats and princes. Moreover, custom dictated that the family should also provide directors of the Mausolea Office (Shoryōshi). Thus, in the Nara period, while the Haji family retained vestiges of its hereditary occupation, members of the family also were

1. *Making the first* haniwa *under Nomi no Sukune's supervision*
Source: Sugawara jikki.

able to become regular officials in the new court bureaucracy and serve according to their individual abilities.

In fact, contrary to Furuhito's assertion, funerals were not the Haji family's main concern during the Nara period. Increasingly, the Haji branched out to serve in a wide range of official posts and to perform a variety of duties. Members of the family developed a number of special interests that helped to lay the foundation for the activities of their more famous Sugawara descendants. First, the Haji were often involved in Japan's relations with continental Asia. Second, perhaps as an outgrowth of their contacts with men from more advanced Asian cultures, the Haji acquired a tradition of literacy and scholarship. One Haji, after studying in China, helped to compile the Taihō Codes. Others contributed poems to the Man'yōshū, the first anthology of Japanese poetry. Many were employed as sutra copyists, a profession reflecting not only literacy but also an interest in Buddhism. In the Nara period, the Haji were not principally a family of scholars, but the beginnings of a tradition of learning were apparent.

Despite these activities, the fortunes of the Haji family did decline during the Nara period, although not because of involvement in funerals, as Furuhito claimed. The problem lay in the system of ranks. In 728 the court made a small but significant modification when it created a new rank, the "outer" (ge) junior fifth lower. Once given this rank, a man was normally unable to receive further promotion. Members of certain families were automatically given this outer rank when they became eligible for promotion to the fifth rank, and, as a result, they could rise no higher and were barred from regular aristocratic status. One of the newly stigmatized families was the Haji. They were indeed a numerous and important court family, but they definitely were not aristocratic. Furuhito's branch of the family desired to change its surname, less because of unpleasant associations lingering from its former occupation than because of the restriction to outer rank.

During the Nara period, many other families also abandoned names associated with lost hereditary occupations, but changing the family name was not merely a matter of following fashion. Rather, the name change was the last in a series of rewards granted Furuhito by Kammu immediately following his accession in the fourth month of 781. At the time, Furuhito held the outer junior fifth rank lower with no recorded office. The next month, he was named lieutenant governor (*suke*) of Tōtōmi, an absentee appointment with a salary but no duties attached. On the first day of the sixth month, an imperial proclamation stated, among other things, that incompetent officials should be punished and good officials promoted. In response to the proclamation, on the sixteenth day of the month, Furuhito was singled out for transfer from outer to inner rank, and a Fujiwara accused of bad administration was demoted. Only nine days later, Furuhito presented his petition that the name of his family be changed from Haji to Sugawara. With their new name of Sugawara, members of the family were no longer doomed to being appointed to outer ranks; they were eligible for entry into the ranks of the aristocracy.

Furuhito was able to change his name because he had close ties to the new emperor. One obvious tie was through Kammu's grandmother, who was a Haji. This family connection, however, was not the most important one: the emperor's grandmother came from a different branch of the Haji family that did not change its name until nine years later. More significantly, Furuhito was a learned man and had once taught Kammu, who at the time was merely a prince not in line for the imperial succession. As a prince, Kammu went on to serve as president (*kami*) of the university, a post normally held by scholars, not by members of the imperial family, and after he became emperor he continued to show great respect for learning. Accordingly, he promoted his former tutor and thereby helped one branch of the Haji family escape from the restrictions attached to its name.

Furuhito's contribution to the future of his family was enormous. By changing its name, he made promotion to high rank possible for his descendants. Moreover, it was he who truly initiated the scholarly tradition that was developed so successfully by Michizane's lineage. Details of Furuhito's life are scanty, but, by the time of his death, around the year 785, he had not risen above the modest rank and office he had held four years earlier when he had petitioned to have his family's name changed. Some years afterwards, it was said that "he was renowned in his day for his correct Confucian behavior, which surpassed that of others, but his family was not wealthy and his children suffered from the cold."[4] This description probably was not empty rhetoric. Following Furuhito's death, his four sons were given special grants of food and clothing to support their studies in recognition of their father's services as an imperial tutor.[5] To be an imperial tutor, Furuhito must have been a man of considerable Confucian learning and of high moral character, yet the special support his sons required to continue their studies after his death would suggest that indeed the family was not wealthy. In short, Furuhito was, as stated, a proper but not prosperous Confucian gentleman.

SUGAWARA NO KIYOKIMI (770–842)

Of Furuhito's sons, the youngest, Kiyokimi, proved the most outstanding. Kiyokimi was born in 770, the year after Empress Shōtoku (r. 765–770) died and her corrupt priestly adviser—and perhaps lover—Dōkyō (d. 772) was driven from the court. In his early years, Kiyokimi lived through a series of political crises that eventually led to the transfer of Japan's capital, first from Nara to Nagaoka in 784 and then to Heian, the modern Kyoto, in 794. Although various high ministers and even imperial princes were exiled or occasionally even murdered during these years, Kiyokimi successfully avoided the intrigues and scandals and gradually rose to a position of prestige, if not power. Today, unlike his grandson Michizane, Kiyokimi is virtually unknown except among specialists, but he, too, was a remarkable figure. He followed in his father Furuhito's scholarly footsteps to become the first Sugawara scholar-aristocrat. Michizane looked back to him, not Furuhito, when he wrote of his family's academic tradition. Kiyokimi had a noteworthy career and is deserving of attention in his own right, not simply as Michizane's grandfather.[6]

A studious youth, Kiyokimi was selected in 784 at the age of fifteen to be a companion of the eleven-year-old Prince Ate (774–824). This was not only an honor but turned out to be a stroke of good fortune as well because the next year Crown Prince Sawara (d. 785) was implicated in the assassination of a powerful minister who had been supervising the move to Nagaoka. After Sawara was sent into exile and died—or was murdered—en route, Ate became the new crown prince and later reigned as the Emperor Heizei (r. 806–809). It was a month after Ate became crown prince that Furuhito's sons were given the grants to support their studies. Although that was ostensibly in recognition of Furuhito's services to the emperor, his son's relationship to the new crown prince may have also influenced the decision.

In 789, when he was twenty years old, Kiyokimi passed the entrance examination and became a student of literature (*monjōshō*) at the university in the capital, then located at Nagaoka. The next year he received the distinguished title of *ason*. This was a reward in recognition of the emperor's grandmother, a Haji, who had just been given the highest court rank earlier the same month. Unlike the name change that had applied only to one branch of the family, this new title was granted to all descendants of the old Haji family.[7] At the university, Kiyokimi proved to be an able scholar and eventually was promoted to graduate student (*tokugōshō*). His new status entitled him to financial assistance in the form of the salary from a nominal provincial post, junior secretary (*shōjō*) of Mino province. After studying at the university for nine years, the maximum period allowed, he took the civil service examination in the third month of 798. By this time, the court had settled in the new Heian capital. The examinations consisted of two essay questions; one of Kiyokimi's was on ancient Chinese history, the other on philosophy. Unfortunately, the questions survive only in a truncated form and their precise meaning is not clear. One month later, it was announced that he had failed the examination, but in the fifth month the matter was reconsidered and he was at last given a passing grade.

Civil service examinations were very difficult, and Kiyokimi's experience of having a failing grade revised to a passing one was not unique. Having finally passed the examination, Kiyokimi was awarded the junior sixth rank lower and appointed to a minor administrative post at the university, one suitable to a young man of scholarly ability. Curiously, despite his own difficulties on the examination, this office placed him in the position of being an examiner, and two sets of his examination questions survive. The questions on the first dealt with "The Beginning and End of Heaven and Earth" and "Worship at the

Shrine of the Imperial Ancestors." Those on the second set concerned "Harmonizing the Five Elements" and "With Peaceful
Government the People Prosper."[8] Both the questions and
the answers, which are also preserved, show the Confucian
orientation of the examination system.

At this point, Kiyokimi seemed on his way to a successful,
if perhaps unremarkable, career as a court scholar and bureaucrat. His fortunes changed in 801 when he was named to serve
on the last but one of Japan's official missions to the court of
T'ang China.[9] This appointment meant great danger, but potentially even greater honor: danger, because many, perhaps a
majority, of the Japanese sent to the Asian mainland were lost
at sea or for other reasons never returned; honor, because
during these early years of the Heian period, Japanese adula-
tion of T'ang culture reached a peak, and great prestige was
accorded to those who had actually visited China. Kiyokimi's
selection for the mission was appropriate, both because of his
knowledge of Chinese acquired at the university and because
of the Haji family's long involvement with diplomacy and foreign
culture, a family tradition that was not totally forgotten.
Diplomacy remained an area of Sugawara activity, and one of
Kiyokimi's sons and later his grandson Michizane would be similarly appointed to visit China. But the most important consideration from Kiyokimi's point of view was that his experiences in
China provided a cachet of legitimacy to his new position as a
court scholar specializing in Chinese literature.

Preparations for the mission to China formally began in the
tenth month of 801 when its principal officers were appointed.
Fujiwara no Kadonomaro (755–818), from one of the less influential Fujiwara lineages, was named ambassador (*taishi*), and
Ishikawa no Michimasu (d. 805), vice-ambassador (*fukushi*).
Ranking just below them were four administrative officers
(*hangan*), one for each of the mission's four ships. Among the
administrative officers was Kiyokimi. Others who joined the
embassy included the student Tachibana no Hayanari (d. 842),
who later became a famous calligrapher, and the monk Saichō
(767–822, posthumously known as Dengyō Daishi), who would
go on to establish the Japanese Tendai sect after his return from
China. Saichō sailed on the same ship as Kiyokimi, and so began
a long association of the Sugawara family with the Tendai sect,

one that continued through Michizane's lifetime and lasted for centuries after his death as that sect came to control Kitano Shrine, the principal center of Tenjin worship in Kyoto.

After the mission's officers had been appointed, it was not mentioned again in the chronicles until the early months of 803, when a series of audiences, banquets, and gifts for the emissaries were noted. The grandest ceremony was held on the twenty-ninth day of the third month:

> There was a farewell banquet for Ambassador Kadonomaro and Vice-Ambassador Ishikawa no Michimasu. Chinese custom was followed throughout. At the height of the festivities, the emperor summoned Ambassador Kadonomaro to his dais, offered him a cup of wine and recited a poem:
>
> | | |
> |---|---|
> | *Kono sake wa* | This cup of wine |
> | *Ō ni wa arazu* | Is not large, |
> | *Tairaka ni* | But it is wine |
> | *Kaerikimase to* | In prayer for |
> | *Iwaitaru sake* | Your safe return. |
>
> Kadonomaro's tears fell like rain and there was not one among the assembled nobles who did not weep. The emperor granted to Kadonomaro three quilts, one complete outfit of clothing, and 200 ounces of gold; and to Michimasu, one outfit of clothing and 150 ounces of gold.[10]

Emperor Kammu's poem is noteworthy, not for its literary merit but because it is one of the very few surviving *waka* from the early decades of the Heian period. Why Kammu chose to recite it at an otherwise highly sinified court ceremony is something of a mystery. Possibly such Japanese elements at court rites were not uncommon, but were simply omitted from most official records. Alternatively, perhaps the emperor was not skilled at composing *kanshi,* despite his interest in the university.

The mission departed from Naniwa, the modern Osaka, the following month, but a storm struck on the Inland Sea. One ship went down with most of its men, and two ships, including the ambassador's, were blown back to port. Kiyokimi's ship, however, weathered the storm and proceeded to Kyushu, where its party waited a year while the other ships were repaired. At this point, the monk Kūkai (774–835, posthumously known as Kōbō Daishi) took advantage of the delay and belatedly joined the mission. Like Saichō, Kūkai subsequently achieved great renown as the founder of a sect, in his case Shingon. All four ships finally gathered in Kyushu and in the seventh month of 804 set sail for China. Although this had become the customary time for the departure of embassies to China, it was also the typhoon season and a period when the monsoon winds were not favorable. Predictably, no sooner had the ships begun their voyage than their troubles resumed. Again a storm struck and two of the ships were blown back to Kyushu. Despite many hardships, however, the principal members of the mission, including the ambassador, Kiyokimi, Saichō, and Kūkai, successfully made the crossing to China.

The ambassador's ship unfortunately was blown far to the south, but Kiyokimi's landed at a more convenient port. From it, he and his party began their long westward journey to the T'ang capital of Ch'ang-an. On their way, they were caught in a snowstorm. Kiyokimi wrote, in Chinese:

> Encountering Snow on a Winter Day
> at Shang-yuan Inn, Pien Province
> Clouds and mist have not yet departed from the old year,
> But plums and willows unexpectedly encounter the spring.
> Alas, the jewel dust
> Comes and soaks the traveler's handkerchief.[11]

This poem displays a cleverness resembling that of the Japanese poetry in the *Kokinshū* and shows how techniques and conventions characteristic of it were adopted from Chinese poetic practice. For example, it incorporates the standard literary conceit of confusing late snow for early plum and willow blossoms; it also puns upon the Chinese word for "dust" (*hsieh*), which was then pronounced similarly to the word for "snow" (*hsueh*). Customarily, a traveler always longed for home, and therefore it was actually tears, not snow, that soaked his handkerchief. In 1660, a Japanese scholar claimed "this small quatrain is worth a hundred—even a thousand—poems," probably because it so closely conformed to what by then was firmly established Japanese poetic usage. But the most interesting feature of this generally conventional poem is that the word translated as "alas" (*pu-fen*) is a T'ang colloquial expression that Kiyokimi probably had learned since his arrival in China. Thus, in this poem, he was displaying a small item of newly acquired knowledge.

Significantly, it was a colloquial expression, which suggests that perhaps Kiyokimi was learning to converse in Chinese. He was quick to incorporate newly acquired expressions into his Chinese poetic vocabulary. Although this is but a small example, it shows Kiyokimi's enthusiasm for learning and utilizing elements of Chinese culture that he would not have known from the books he had read in Japan.

In the eleventh month, Kiyokimi's party arrived in Ch'ang-an. However, his compatriots from the other ship, including the ambassador, were delayed because they did not have proper documents with them. The Chinese expected foreign envoys to bring tribute and obsequious oaths of fealty, but the Japanese found these practices offensive and had come to dispatch their embassies with gifts but not documents. Kiyokimi had avoided difficulties because his ship had landed at a port where officials were familiar with this Japanese custom, but in the southern province to which the ambassador had been blown, the local governor questioned the diplomatic status of the Japanese envoys. Their ship was moored in a swamp and they were allowed to land only after Kūkai had drafted an elegant appeal for official recognition. In the twelfth month, all the Japanese at last gathered in the Chinese capital, where they were granted an imperial audience. Kiyokimi, in particular, is said to have made a good impression on the emperor. They greeted the new year in Ch'ang-an, but the emperor soon fell ill and died on the twenty-third day of the first month. The Japanese joined in the mourning rites. Soon after the new emperor was enthroned, they departed on their uneventful homeward journey. Just about a year after the envoys had left Japan, they landed safely in Kyushu.

The mission had been a trying one and many lives had been lost. Moreover, upon their return, the envoys reported that conditions in China were unstable. The T'ang dynasty would survive for another century, but signs of decay were already apparent to the Japanese observers. Although they had suffered many adversities in the course of performing their duties, they were well rewarded for their efforts as representatives of the Japanese nation. Promotions were granted to all the members of the mission, including a posthumous reward for the vice-ambassador, who had died in China, and a promotion for a shrine at which prayers had been offered for the mission's safe return. The ambassador

Kadonomaro was promoted three grades and shortly afterwards named middle counselor. Kiyokimi, too, was not overlooked. In the seventh month of 805, he was promoted one grade to the junior fifth rank lower, and the following month was appointed vice-president (*suke*) of the university, a respectable position appropriate to a man of his scholarly achievements.[12] His status was not yet imposing, but at the age of thirty-six, he had equaled his father's highest rank. Success in the civil service examinations and a completed mission to China provided the basis for a brighter future than would otherwise have been expected of an individual from a minor court family.

After serving as vice-president of the university for less than six months, however, Kiyokimi was sent off to be a provincial lieutenant governor. Heian courtiers viewed provincial appointments with distinctly mixed feelings. On the one hand, they did not welcome the prolonged separation from their homes and polite society in the capital, but, on the other hand, they did relish the lucrative salaries of provincial offices. As a result, the practice of "absentee appointments" (*yōnin*) developed. These were nominal provincial posts with no duty other than that of collecting the salary. Kiyokimi's father Furuhito had held such an office in Tōtōmi and Kiyokimi himself had held one as a graduate student. In later years he would be given the absentee governorships of Awa, Shinano, Settsu, and Tamba. He could not have served in any of these provinces for he held concurrent posts in the capital.

If meritorious officials were given absentee appointments as a form of financial reward, officials accused of crimes were dispatched to isolated provincial posts as a form of punishment. Such would be Michizane's fate almost a century later. And, in 824 when Kiyokimi was already an influential man at court, he, too, was sent to the provinces with an undesired assignment, supernumerary (*gon*) governor of Harima. Although Kiyokimi was not charged with a crime, courtiers objected that this was tantamount to exile. By then, Kiyokimi had become a respected senior court official, and his absence was generally lamented. Hence, at the recommendation of the high court nobles, the emperor soon recalled him to the capital.[13]

Kiyokimi's first tour of duty in the provinces was more typical. From 806 until 812 he served in Owari, the province in which the modern city of Nagoya is located. During those years he was neither absentee nor exile. Although he was nominally lieutenant governor, in fact, he was the chief administrative official. While he was posted in Owari, at least four men held the title of governor, and a fifth was appointed supernumerary lieutenant governor. Because records are not complete for almost half of the years Kiyokimi served in Owari, possibly even more court nobles—their names now lost—were also given nominal offices in that province. None of these men, however, left the capital, where they all concurrently held other regular appointments. Moreover, Kiyokimi's court rank was that of a governor, four grades too high for his actual office as lieutenant governor. This suggests that, although in name only a lieutenant governor, he was, in fact, expected to do the work of the governor for whose office he was fully qualified. Such arrangements were common in the Heian period.[14]

As de facto governor, Kiyokimi was given the opportunity to put into practice the Confucian theories of government that he had learned at the university, and apparently he did so successfully. His obituary claims that "without using punishments, he governed in the manner of Liu K'uan," a Later Han dynasty official who is said to have whipped offenders painlessly with reeds to shame them into good behavior. A brief item mentioned in the court chronicles offers fragmentary evidence in support of this praise. During Kiyokimi's tour of duty, eight *chō* (approximately twenty acres) of land that a certain Prince Sami had developed in Owari were reclaimed into the public domain because this private holding had "disturbed the people."[15] Some may question who benefited more from bringing land back into government control: the peasants who farmed it or the officials who taxed them. But, according to the principles of the *ritsuryō* system, Kiyokimi's act would have been taken as a sign of good and benevolent administration. Moreover, although famines, epidemics, unpaid taxes, and other difficulties were reported in many provinces, no such problems were recorded as occurring in Owari during Kiyokimi's term there. Judged by the standards of his day, Kiyokimi was a good governor.

Kiyokimi was fortunate in the timing of his provincial service, for while he was in Owari the Heian court was wracked

by a series of political crises. Soon after Kiyokimi's departure
from the capital, the great Emperor Kammu died and was succeeded by his son, Kiyokimi's former companion, who became
Emperor Heizei. Heizei's reign began auspiciously with a series
of reforms in local administration, but scandal ensued. First, a
prince was accused of plotting against the emperor and was
driven to suicide. Many of his followers were also sent into
exile, and as a result the Southern House (Nanke) of the Fujiwara family was seriously weakened.

Even more scandalous was Heizei's resumption of an old
love affair with Fujiwara no Kusuko (d. 810), the mother of
one of his own concubines. To make matters worse, Kusuko's
brother tried to take political advantage of her intimacy with
the emperor. Finally, in 809 after only three years as sovereign,
Heizei abdicated on account of illness. He was succeeded by
his younger brother, who became Emperor Saga. Heizei subsequently recovered his health, however, and found retirement not to his liking. When, in turn, Saga fell ill in 810,
Heizei seized the opportunity to regain his power and proclaimed that the capital was to be returned to its former site at
Nara, where he had taken up residence with Kusuko. Fighting
eventually broke out between the emperor and the former
emperor. Heizei was captured, but the blame was placed on
his advisers, most of whom were members of Kusuko's Ceremonial House (Shikike) of the Fujiwara, and they were duly
sent into exile. Kusuko herself committed suicide and earned
the dubious distinction of having the disturbance named after
her, "The Kusuko Incident" (Kusuko no hen). Off in the
provinces, Kiyokimi was spared involvement in these disagreeable
events.

Although Saga's reign got off to an uncertain start, the intrigues that had followed Kammu's death proved beneficial
to the imperial house, because they seriously weakened the
Fujiwara. The two branches of the family that had suffered
most never did recover their power. As a result, Saga was able
to rule with relative freedom from interference by the Fujiwara, even though ministers from the Northern House of the
family were to become all powerful only a few decades later.
Saga himself abdicated in 823, but until his death in 842 he
continued to exercise considerable influence during the reigns

of his half-brother, Emperor Junna (786–840, r. 823–833) and his son, Emperor Nimmyō (810–850, r. 833–850).

Saga followed the example of his father Kammu and attempted to put into practice the ideal of imperial rule through the *ritsuryō* system. Saga's approach, however, differed from Kammu's. Kammu had vigorously pursued policies aimed at restricting the power of the great monasteries and noble families, encouraging able but less well-born men to enter government service, enforcing land-distribution laws, overseeing the activities of provincial officials, and reducing the corvée and military service burdens of the peasantry. He also sent large armies to subdue rebellious non-Japanese tribes in northern Honshu. All this was in addition to the construction of two new capitals, Nagaoka and Heian. Although many of his policies were successful, they resulted in a major drain on the government treasury. Saga's reforms were neither so bold nor so expensive. He created two important new government agencies, the Chamberlain's Office (Kurodōdokoro) and the Imperial Police Office (Kebiishichō). The former was particularly significant, because it facilitated the exercise of imperial power by allowing the emperor to by-pass some of the complicated procedures required for issuing edicts. The latter functioned as a metropolitan police force for the capital city. Saga also sponsored the compilation of important legal commentaries that clarified the meaning of the *ritsuryō* codes.[16]

Saga's greatest enthusiasm, however, was reserved for cultural reforms that served to strengthen Confucian values. He took particular interest in Chinese literature—he was an able *kanshi* poet himself—and court ritual. Poetry and ritual may hardly seem significant elements of political reform, but, according to the Confucian ideals that Saga was trying to revive, they had an intimate relation to government. According to the *Analects* (*Lun-yü*), Confucius repeatedly stressed the importance of literature, especially poetry, and ritual in the cultivation of the "true gentlemen" (*chün-tzu*), whom he considered to be the bulwark of the ideal state.[17]

When the ancient Japanese court set about to become civilized in the manner of the continent, it discovered that in Chinese "to become civilized" (*wen-hua*) meant, among other things, "to become literate." The Japanese quickly learned from their continental teachers an attitude of respect for the power and beauty of the written word, particularly if the word happened to be written in Chinese, for, in East Asia, China was the principal source of learning. Therefore, even before they built the capital at Nara, the Japanese established a university to teach the Confucian classics as an essential element in their evolving sinified state. A civil service examination system based on these classics soon followed. In keeping with Chinese standards, the Japanese judged examination essays on the basis of two criteria: reasoning and elegance. The highest grades were given to those papers that achieved the Confucian ideal of "art and substance harmoniously blended."[18] Literacy in any form, however, was essential to the functioning of Japan's bureaucracy, and so even students whose classical scholarship was not up to par for the examinations could be recommended for government service, provided they were skilled in the art of Chinese composition. Thus, in early Japan as in early China, the ability to read and write became a highly valued technical skill that was all the more esteemed when embellished with a touch of artistry.

Respect for aesthetic values has been a persistent trait in Japanese society, and the Japanese did not neglect China's less pragmatic theories of literature. For example, Japan's earliest anthologies of *kanshi* contain allusions to the Chinese concept of poetry as an expression of personal feelings. But even as an expression of personal feelings, poetry could be interpreted as having political significance. If poetry contained its writer's private sentiments, then it should be collected and studied in the same way that during the Former Han dynasty folk songs had been collected in order to judge popular sentiments. Indeed, the introduction to one imperial *kanshi* anthology refers specifically to the Chinese idea of collecting poetry as a means of gauging popular opinion.[19] To be sure, the works in early Japanese imperial anthologies were all written by members of the court elite and thus were a far cry from the Chinese model of collecting folk songs. Japanese compilers may have reasoned that the opinions and feelings of educated officials were most worthy of attention. More likely, the Japanese court simply was following another Chinese practice: applying pragmatic justifications to poetry that was admired for other reasons—for its value as a symbol of high cultural achievement or for its beauty alone.

Some societies that came under Chinese influence virtually abandoned their native languages as a means of literary expression. This was not the case in Japan. The Japanese learned to use Chinese characters to record their native language and in a remarkably short time were writing polished verse in Japanese. However, the compilation of the *Man'yōshū* around 759 was followed by roughly a century in which literature in Chinese was preeminent. This period is often referred to as "the dark age of native literature" for nearly all the extant writings from it are in classical Chinese.[20] As noted, the *waka* composed by Kammu before the departure of the mission to China is one of the few exceptions. It suggests that *waka* were still composed, but most were deemed unworthy of preservation. Despite the highly sophisticated literature in Japanese that had developed during the Nara period, the early ninth century was a time when literature in Chinese enjoyed overwhelming prestige.

When Kiyokimi returned from his provincial post in 812, the political situation at court had settled down after the chaos that had ensued upon Kammu's death, and Saga had embarked on his program of cultural reforms. Thus Kiyokimi's return, like his departure, came at a most opportune time when his expertise in Chinese literature and culture were in particular demand, and he went on to become a leading participant in Saga's attempts to sinify court literature and ritual. Saga proved his commitment to Japan's literature in Chinese by sponsoring three anthologies devoted exclusively to it, the first of Japan's imperially sponsored literary collections. Today they are the best remembered literary monuments of early Heian Japan's infatuation with Chinese culture. The importance of Kiyokimi's contributions is demonstrated by his service on the editorial committees for all three. These imperial anthologies, however, were not Japan's earliest collections of *kanshi*. That distinction belongs to the *Kaifūsō*, compiled in 751 and consisting of 116 poems, all written in the simplest of Chinese verse forms. In form, the poetry of the *Kaifūsō* resembled that of the Six Dynasties; rhyme was employed, but the rules developed during the T'ang dynasty for tone patterns were ignored. These earliest examples of Japanese efforts at writing poetry in Chinese were more impressive as cultural achievements than as works of literature.

Technical standards, if nothing else, had risen considerably by 814 when Saga ordered the compilation of the *Ryōunshū* (Cloud-borne collection), the first imperial *kanshi* anthology. Most of the *Ryōunshū*'s ninety poems followed the elaborate T'ang rules for tone patterns and thus were in the contemporary Chinese style. Twenty-three poets were represented, including emperors Heizei, Saga, and Junna, then still crown prince. Only four years later, Saga ordered a second anthology, the *Bunka shūreishū* (Collection of literary masterpieces). The 148 poems in this collection were stylistically similar to those in its predecessor, but their arrangement was significantly different. Whereas poems in the *Ryōunshū* were ordered according to the rank of their authors—emperors first, low-ranking courtiers last—those in the *Bunka shūreishū* were classified by theme under headings adopted from the *Wen-hsuan* (Selections of refined literature), a much admired Chinese anthology. In later collections of poetry in Japanese, this thematic arrangement of poems was to become an art in itself. The classifications used in *waka* anthologies included some that had first appeared in the *Bunka shūreishū*, including travel, parting, and grief, although the most popular categories for *waka,* the seasons and love, were not used for the *kanshi*. Another interesting feature of this second *kanshi* anthology is that it included works by women. This would have been surprising in later years of the Heian period when Chinese poetry had come to be regarded as a masculine art.

The *Keikokushū* (Collection for ordering the state), Japan's third and last imperial anthology of literature in Chinese, was compiled in 827. By then, Saga had already abdicated, but he remained a power in court political and literary life, and he probably was responsible for this collection too. The *Keikokushū* was the most ambitious of the three anthologies, both in its size and in its range of materials. It had twenty chapters, compared to only three in the *Bunka shūreishū,* and for the first time, prose as well as poetry was included. Unfortunately, only six of its chapters survive: chapter one, containing seventeen poetic essays (*fu*), a Chinese genre that combined elements of prose and poetry; chapters ten, eleven, thirteen, and fourteen, containing a total of ninety-seven poems similar to those in the earlier anthologies; and chapter twenty, consisting of questions and answers from civil service examinations. Thus, the *Keiko-*

kushū was closely patterned after the *Wen-hsuan,* which was even longer but included a similar assortment of genres. If the contents of the *Wen-hsuan* are a reliable guide, the missing chapters of the *Keikokushū* probably contained a wide variety of official documents in addition to the examinations.[21]

Kiyokimi was one of only two men who served on the editorial committees for all three anthologies, and his own work was fairly well represented in them. Included were fifteen poems, two poetic essays, and two sets of examination questions. Other than a few scattered fragments, these are the only extant examples of Kiyokimi's writings, although they are but a small fraction of his total output. When Michizane compiled his grandfather's works, they filled six chapters.[22] Because so little of his writing survives, generalization about his individual merits as a poet is impossible; however, the items from the imperial anthologies do provide excellent examples of early Heian court taste in *kanshi.* They are typical of the works selected for official recognition in the anthologies, even if we have no way of knowing whether or not they are representative of his writing in general.

Kiyokimi's works illustrate how literature was supposed to serve a pragmatic function. That was the standard Confucian theory to explain the importance of literature and also the official rationale for the Japanese court's sponsorship of poetry collections. The introduction to the first anthology began by quoting a famous Chinese work of literary criticism that stated "literature is a vital force in the ordering of the state."[23] This same line provided the title for the final anthology, *Collection for Ordering the State.* But, as noted, the Japanese also recognized China's less practical theories of literature. The same source that provided the pragmatic title for the last anthology had gone on to espouse a more expressive, aesthetically oriented theory of literature, one the Japanese also acknowledged. In his writings, Kiyokimi demonstrated how the Japanese combined their expressed concern for the pragmatic value of literature with a love for the beauty of Chinese poetry.

In his most interesting extant work, Kiyokimi argued that even a very minor art could prove useful as well as pleasing:

Poetic Essay on Whistling [*Hsiao*], with Introduction

As a child I enjoyed music, and as an adult I appreciate it all the more. Although it should be only a passing diversion, I cannot take my mind off it even for a moment. My life is a mixture of likes and dislikes, successes and failures, but unfortunately I am completely unable to play any stringed instrument or produce a single note on the flute. Resting at a pavilion by the pond, when the sun sets and all grows cool, I gradually tire of reciting poetry. Then I begin to whistle. The great and small are contained in my mouth. The long and short obey my wishes. It has no formal melody, nothing to transcribe; no lyrics, nothing to memorize. In short, whistling is the best means to learn the beauty of sound. Therefore, I take brush in hand and write this poetic essay to convey something of my thoughts.

Whistling, the glorious consonance of the eight sounds,
Produces the five notes, their variations and harmony.[a]
It summons the gods of heaven and earth to gather
And arouses the dark mysteries of yin and yang.
Tune its marvelous melody to the pitch pipes,
Run the subtle resonance through the many-piped flute.
It is like the ringing of the bells of metal or stone,
Or the beating of the drums of war.
To make an instrument, one must
Traverse the many peaks, pass through the pine gardens,
Cross the dangerous valleys and enter the bamboo grove.
The musicians K'uei and Hsiang were devoted to contrivance.
The craftsmen Pan and Ch'ui planned carefully.[b]
To polish bright, straighten and renew,
To engrave decoration, design and construct,
All this is the result of human endeavor
And borrowing objects to produce sound.
But the tone made by whistling
Rises and falls on one's lips.
Reflecting on bamboo, one imitates the bamboo flute.
Thinking of the silk string, one sounds like the zither.
The song of the oriole in a spring forest is expressed.
The cry of the gibbon on a peak at dawn is made clear.
One breath can be divided into the notes *chueh* and *yü*.[c]
The resonances grasp the cold depths.
They flow to the melodic play of mountains and rivers,
Follow the tunes of songs from Wu and Yueh.[d]
Thus, its melody is not of the ordinary
And never fails to be mysterious.
The time to enjoy it is not fixed,
But when inspired, one delights in it.
It is not a thing of dawn like the cry of a roosting cock,

Nor is it like the evening call of a marsh crane.
It avoids the regulated intervals of the dragon voice,
And shuns entering the shrine of the phoenix wings.
For example, the peak of Su-men
Heard the din of drum and flute,[e]
And the summit of Mount Yin
Was startled by the thundering in its forests and valleys.[f]
Such deeds of former sages
Are recorded in ancient verses.
In addition, when the Chin general was at the frontier fort,
The barbarian bandits were moved by the beauty of the rising
moon,[g]
Or when Chao Ping came to the river,
The boatman saw the mystery of summoning the wind.[h]
Thus, whistling is not merely a means of whiling away leisure hours,
But also has awesome powers for averting danger.
Although not an esoteric instrument to arouse the gods,
It is a delicate art, the virtues of which ought to be extolled.[24]

Notes:

a. The eight sounds are those produced by (1) metal bells, (2) stone chimes, (3) zithers, (4) bamboo flutes, (5) gourd flutes, (6) ceramic flutes, (7) leather drums, and (8) wooden drums. The five notes are those of the ancient Chinese pentatonic scale.
b. K'uei was a musician in the court of the legendary emperor Shun. Shih Hsiang is said to have taught zither to Confucius. Pan and Ch'ui were both legendary craftsmen; the former came to be worshiped as a god of craftsmanship.
c. The names of the third and fifth notes in the ancient Chinese pentatonic scale.
d. Two Chinese states of the Eastern Chou period (770–403 B.C.).
e. Juan Chi, one of the Seven Sages of the Bamboo Grove (c. A.D. 300), once visited a Taoist hermit on Mount Su-men. When the hermit would not answer his questions, Juan Chi began to whistle, and the hermit responded in kind. The hills resounded as if there were several drums and flutes.
f. Juan Chi went to visit another hermit on Mount Yin. Again the hermit would not speak. This time Juan Chi and the hermit whistled together, and the mysterious sound is said to have shaken the forests and valleys.
g. One moonlit evening when his city was besieged by barbarians, Liu Yueh-shih climbed a tower and whistled. The barbarians heard him, were deeply touched, and lifted the siege.
h. When a boatman refused to take him across a river, Chao Ping whistled to summon the wind, which disordered the current so that he could walk across.

Kiyokimi began his poetic essay with a personal introduction describing his lack of conventional music talent, just as many years later, Michizane would also complain that the rigors of preparing for his examinations forced him to abandon his music lessons. The personal tone of the introduction was unusual for a work included in an imperial anthology; however, the essay itself closely followed Chinese convention, both in form and content. Elegant descriptive language, generously enriched with learned allusion, was characteristic of the Chinese poetic essay, and in this piece Kiyokimi took the opportunity to display his superior knowledge of Chinese lore. Although the subject, whistling, may seem eccentric, it was derived from Chinese precedents. An essay on whistling also appeared in the *Wen-hsuan,* and Kiyokimi borrowed phrases from it and from other Chinese essays on music. Whistling was esteemed as a Taoist exercise for communication with nature through music. It was considered particularly effective because, as Kiyokimi noted, no manmade instruments were required.[25] In Kiyokimi's last few lines, however, he parted from his Chinese models. First, he alluded to Chinese anecdotes illustrating the idea that beauty can calm even the rude barbarian soul. Then he concluded by asserting that the art of whistling also can have its practical applications. Kiyokimi thus brought his poetic essay into line with the pragmatic view of literature that prevailed in the early decades of the Heian period.

Unlike "Whistling," most of the poetry in the imperial anthologies was expressly written for such formal occasions as court rituals, imperial outings to scenic spots, or receptions for foreign guests. Formal public poetry of this type was more a group activity than a private pastime. At court functions, the assembled nobles composed verse on assigned themes or poems "harmonizing" (*wa*) with those written by the emperor. Harmonizing meant that the emperor would offer a poem of his own, and the assembled courtiers would then present matching poems, using the same theme, verse form, and concluding alternate lines with identical characters as rhymes. Such exchanges were valued as an expression of accord between emperor and subject, or at least emperor and minister. For example, *Bunka shūreishū* contains a group of five poems based on the familiar Chinese story of Wang Chao-chün, a princess who was sent off to become the bride of a barbarian chieftain as part of a peace agreement during the Former Han dynasty. The following poems are, first, Saga's original and, second, Kiyokimi's response written in harmony with it:

Wang Chao-chün
by Emperor Saga

Still young she left the Han Palace
And grief-stricken entered the barbarian land.
To the end of the earth—a thousand, ten-thousand leagues—
She journeyed, never to return.
Desert sand destroyed her delicate hair.
Wind and frost ravaged her jewel-like face.
Only the moon of Ch'ang-an remained,
Its glow seeing her off over the vast mountain ranges.

In Harmony with "Wang Chao-chün"
by Sugawara no Kiyokimi

Why no other plan to quell the barbarians?
Her gentle body was used to pacify one border.
Her tears followed the endless fortifications and finally ceased.
Her grief reached to the far heavens, eternal.
In a distant province, the moon reflected in a wayfarer's mirror.
And in barbarian lands, the ice froze her traveling dress.
How could she bear to live in a rude cloth tent,
And abandon forever her fine silken chamber?[26]

These poems are typical of the works appearing in the imperial anthologies of literature in Chinese. Their subject matter is Chinese and wholly conventional. Not only the original story, but also the vast deserts and barbarian tents described could have been known to most Japanese courtiers only through books. Kiyokimi suggested a political message in his poem— that better planning might have prevented the need to sacrifice the princess in the interest of peace. However, one suspects that both he and Saga were less concerned with such issues than with the pathos of a beautiful princess doomed to spend her remaining days in the rude tent of a desert tribesman. Poems like these appeared in imperial anthologies because of their symbolic value. They demonstrated that the Japanese emperor could summon his ministers for an edifying exchange of verse in Chinese, thereby proving that the Japanese had more in common with Wang Chao-chün and the civilized Chinese than with the uncouth barbarians to whom she had been sent. The essay on whistling and the poems on Wang Chao-chün contain purely aesthetic and expressive elements, but they appeared in imperially sponsored anthologies because they also were regarded as literature that helped "order the state."

Kiyokimi's contributions to early Heian sinification were not limited to literature. In 818, he assisted in the reform of court ritual and dress standards, and later he helped rename the gates to the palace compound. Originally, these gates had been named after twelve families closely tied to the imperial house; however, the Chinese characters used in writing these names were selected for their phonetic, not semantic, values. With Kiyokimi's guidance, new and more auspicious names were selected that in most cases sounded very much like the old names. For example, the Ōtomo Gate, named for the ancient and noble Ōtomo family, became the Ōten Gate (Ōtemmon), literally, the "In Accord with Heaven Gate." Another of Kiyokimi's contributions to improving court manners was his book *Newly Established Wine Etiquette (Shintei shushiki)*. Unfortunately, only fragments survive, but they reveal that the work dealt with such matters as how wine cups were to be exchanged between guest and host, and "punishments" for improprieties at imperial banquets: "Those who are late five times shall be made to drink three cups as punishment." *Newly Established Wine Etiquette* was sufficiently important that it was included in an early Heian list of "Necessary References for Civil Servants," under the heading of "Political Science" (*seiri*),[27] for wine drinking was considered an essential element in court ritual.

In addition to serving as an arbiter of court taste, Kiyokimi also pursued a successful career as an official. His steady rise through the court bureaucracy was interrupted only once when, as noted, he was briefly and inexplicably sent to the provinces in 824. Most of the posts he held were appropriate to a man of his scholarly background. In 812, after completing his first provincial tour of duty as a lieutenant governor, Kiyokimi was appointed president of the university. Although he served as president for only one year, his career at the university was a long one, for in 819 he was named professor of literature and he remained in that post until his death twenty-three years later. As professor of literature, he lectured to Emperor Saga on the *Wen-hsuan* and later to Emperor Nimmyō on the *History of the Later Han Dynasty (Hou-Han-shu)*. Kiyokimi also held offices

in the Ministry of Ceremonial on the Board of Censors (Danjōdai), again offices customarily assigned to men of learning.[28]

In the best Confucian tradition, Kiyokimi was not simply a
scholar with no knowledge or ability in practical affairs. In addition to serving on a mission to China, he was given a variety of
administrative offices at court, including director of the Palace
Equipment Bureau (*tonomo no kami*), lesser controller (*shōben*), middle controller (*chūben*), and mayor of the right capital district (*ukyō no daibu*). The following story illustrates the
respect with which he was treated:

> Kiyokimi was then [c. 821–822] appointed middle controller of the
> left. However, that office was not to his liking, and he sought a trans-
> fer to the post of mayor of the right division of the capital. Emperor
> Saga discreetly asked the court rank appropriate to that office. Kiyo-
> kimi replied that it was the senior fifth. On that day, the office was
> changed to the junior fourth [the rank that Kiyokimi held].[29]

Kiyokimi's request for the transfer was also granted. In addition
to these administrative duties, Kiyokimi also helped with the
compilation of *Ryō no gige* (An explication of the civil codes),
the first official commentary on the *Yōrō Ryō*, the revised version of the Taihō Civil Code then in effect.[30]

Ultimately, in 839, Kiyokimi was promoted two grades to
the junior third rank, thus placing him among the highest ranking court nobles. He was treated as an honorary consultant
(*hisangi*). This meant that although his new rank entitled him
to the office, he was not formally named a consultant (*sangi*).
Probably Kiyokimi was not given a regular appointment for two
reasons. The Sugawara were a new family whose ancestors had
been minor functionaries. For Kiyokimi, promotion to the third
rank alone was exceptional. A regular position as a consultant
on the Council of State would have been unthinkable. Moreover,
Kiyokimi was already seventy years old, and the infirmities of
age had begun to set in. His official obituary would state that
his face retained its youthful appearance because he took special medicines, but walking had become exceedingly painful for
him. Therefore, out of respect for learning, but not, we are told,
at his own request, the emperor granted him special permission
to ride an oxcart into the palace as far as the pear tree in the

Great South Garden. Nonetheless, Kiyokimi gradually ceased
coming to court and finally, in 842, he died at the age of
seventy-three.

Kiyokimi had been successful both as a scholar and as an official. Moreover, his achievements, like those of his father Furuhito, had important consequences for later generations of the
Sugawara. Furuhito, by changing his surname, had freed his
family from the traditional restrictions that had been placed
on their promotion to high rank. Kiyokimi, in recognition of
his literary and sinological abilities, had been rewarded with
aristocratic status. Equal status could not be guaranteed to his
descendants, but by virtue of his junior third rank, his sons and
grandsons were assured court rank on the basis of hereditary
privilege. The Sugawara had not become a major power at court,
but they were now far removed from their ancient position as
supervisors of court funerals.

SUGAWARA NO KOREYOSHI (812–880)

Like his father, Kiyokimi had four sons, and again it was only
the youngest—theoretically the least favored—who proved himself able to follow in his father's footsteps. Of the two eldest
sons, virtually nothing is known. The third son, Yoshinushi
(803–852), was given all the benefits normally due the son of an
influential court scholar, but he lacked either the ability or the
inclination to take full advantage of his position. Although he
passed the university's entrance examination to become a student of literature at the age of twenty-three in 825, he never
took the civil service examination. Ten years later, he was appointed to serve as an administrative officer on an official embassy to China. Despite numerous difficulties, the mission was
completed and he returned to Japan in 839, after having visited
Ch'ang-an as his father had done thirty-four years earlier. This
would turn out to be Japan's last official mission to T'ang China.

Yoshinushi was rewarded with a promotion to the junior
fifth rank lower. He was then thirty-seven years old and potentially at the threshold of a career parallel to that of his father.
But when he died fourteen years later, he still held the same
rank and he had served only in minor offices. His obituary eulo-
gizes him, stating "as a youth he was brilliant, his appearance

handsome and his speech eloquent."[31] Possibly he never lived up to his youthful potential. The obituary appeared in a history that his more successful younger brother helped compile, and so a more likely explanation is that the younger brother was expressing proper Confucian respect for an elder brother who was not remarkably able. Kiyokimi's influence may have helped in gaining admission to the university and an appointment on a mission to China, but he could not guarantee a noteworthy career at court.

The scholarly traditions of the Sugawara family were maintained by Kiyokimi's youngest son, Koreyoshi, who was regarded as an academic child prodigy. In 822, the sinophile Emperor Saga summoned him to the palace, where the eleven-year-old Koreyoshi impressed the courtiers with his ability to read texts and compose poems, all in Chinese. At the age of twenty, Koreyoshi entered the university as a student of literature, and four years later he became a graduate student. In the seventh month of 839, he took the civil service examination, and after four months it was announced that he had passed. Earlier that year, his father had been promoted to the junior third rank, and so on the basis of hereditary privilege, Koreyoshi was entitled to the junior sixth rank lower. For his success on the examination, he was awarded a rank three grades higher, the senior sixth upper. Thus he entered government service auspiciously, just one grade below the aristocratic fifth rank.[32]

Koreyoshi went on to a long and distinguished career as a court scholar. Unfortunately, surviving records provide little more than a list of the offices he held, with hardly any details on what he did in those offices. Still, this list holds some interest as an illustration of the type of career a court scholar could expect in the middle decades of the ninth century. Unlike his father, who displayed some skill as a practical administrator, Koreyoshi served almost exclusively in offices that called upon his scholarly abilities. His first appointments were to minor administrative offices in the university. Then, in 842, he was named major private secretary (*dainaiki*) in the Ministry of Central Affairs (Nakatsukasashō), an important post that involved the sensitive task of drafting documents for the emperor and high officials. These documents had to be written in elegant

Chinese, and hence the office was only given to men possessing the necessary literary skills. Two years later, he was promoted to the junior fifth rank lower, which placed him among the lesser aristocrats.[33] His superior ability is indicated by his achievement of this rank at the age of thirty-three, whereas his older brother did not receive it until age thirty-seven.

Koreyoshi's most noteworthy accomplishments were as an educator. In 846, he became a professor of literature, and he remained in that post for twenty-one years. During that time, he concurrently held a variety of additional offices. Among them were a total of eleven absentee provincial appointments, granted at different times, that provided him with supplementary income. Other positions were at court and some involved actual duties. In 847, he was named tutor to the crown prince (tōgū no gakushi). When the prince he tutored later became Emperor Montoku (827–858, r. 850–858), he rewarded his former teacher with an exceptional promotion of two grades to the senior fifth rank lower. Among the other offices Koreyoshi held concurrently with his professorship were president of the university, mayor of the left capital district (sakyō no daibu), senior assistant president of the Board of Censors (danjō daihitsu) and minister of justice (gyōbu kyō), a post he held twice. A few of these offices may have been largely ceremonial. For example, his appointments as minister of justice do not reflect a special interest in legal matters. Typically, the actual responsibilities of a ministry were principally in the hands of its second- or third-ranking officials. Koreyoshi's appointments in the Ministry of Justice were essentially honorary, inspired by the fact that the great Chinese poet Po Chü-i, whose works had recently become popular in Japan, had also been a minister of justice.[34]

After finally leaving his post as professor of literature, Koreyoshi was named senior assistant minister (tayū) of ceremonial, and then in 872 he became a consultant, the lowest-ranking position on the Council of State. Because he was not further promoted to middle counselor, he never exercised political power, but he did participate in discussions of government policy at the highest level. Unlike his father, he was not merely an honorary consultant. He was the first Sugawara to be a regular member of the Council of State. Subsequently, he was given one more important post, chief investigator of the records of outgoing officials (*kageyushi no chōkan*). This placed him in charge of an office responsible for monitoring the honesty and effectiveness of provincial administrators, but again it was probably his immediate subordinates who principally were responsible for directing the office. By the time of his death at the age of sixty-nine in 880, he had reached the junior third rank.[35] Koreyoshi's official career had been one of steady advance. In his later years, he ranked among the highest court nobles and held a position surpassing that of his father.

The most remarkable fact about Koreyoshi's career is that he seems never to have fallen into disfavor. As will be discussed in the next chapter, most nobles who relied on their scholarly abilities to gain positions in the court bureaucracy found their status to be relatively insecure. Koreyoshi succeeded probably because of his lack of involvement in political matters. According to his obituary, "He showed little natural disposition for practical affairs and was forgetful of his appearance, but he appreciated the beauties of nature and enjoyed reciting poetry. He had a deep reverence for Buddhism, loved all mankind, was filial to the utmost, and did not approve of killing."[36] Although details of Koreyoshi's accomplishments are scanty beyond the outline of his offices, still, what little information that does survive tends to confirm the characterization in his obituary.

His recorded activities—as distinguished from the list of offices he held—reveal an interest in scholarship, literature, religion, and ritual, but not in administration or politics. For example, he served as a judge when literary men were summoned to court to compose poems. When Emperor Montoku lay suffering from his final illness, Koreyoshi drafted the document calling for a pardon of all criminals, except those guilty of unpardonable crimes. Subsequently, he helped select the site for Montoku's tomb, and then at that tomb he announced the accession of Montoku's successor Seiwa (850–880, r. 858–876). He joined in offering an opinion on calendar reform that was good enough to be accepted in the place of the proposals made by professional calendar specialists. When repairs on the Great Buddha at Nara were completed after its head had fallen off in an earthquake, he composed the special prayer for the dedication ceremonies. He drafted part of an inscription that was copied by one of the court's most skilled calligraphers and cast into a bell for the monastery Jingoji in the hills northwest of the capital. The bell is still there today, offically designated a National Treasure. He reported a palace fire to the Kamo Shrine and assisted when a new imperial virgin was named to that shrine.[37] None of these duties was overtly political.

A curious problem that required Koreyoshi's special expertise occurred in 844, two years after Emperor Saga's death. The powerful major counselor (*dainagon*) Fujiwara no Yoshifusa summoned Koreyoshi to court along with Haruzumi no Yoshitada (797–870), a man of modest provincial origins who had risen to become an important court scholar known for his interest in the occult. Yoshifusa explained:

> The testament of the late Emperor Saga stated, "In this world, every strange occurrence is said to be a message from ancestral ghosts. This does not seem reasonable." Recently, there has been a strange occurrence. We ordered the officials to conduct a divination ritual, and a message from ancestral ghosts was made clear. If we believe it, then we will be in conflict with the late emperor's last testament, but, if we ignore it, we may risk bringing a curse on this generation. We are completely bewildered and do not know which course to follow. After a last testament has been made, can it be altered? Please consider the matter and give us your opinion.

This shows that Saga's Confucianism went beyond his love for Chinese poetry. He also accepted the Chinese sage's admonition to keep a safe distance from ghosts and spirits. Generally, in the Heian court, ghosts were taken quite seriously. Caught between a desire to respect an emperor's last wishes and popular belief in the supernatural, court leaders finally sought the professional opinions of the most learned scholars. After consulting various Chinese classical sources, Koreyoshi and Yoshitada presented the following opinion:

> In ancient times, after Wang Chi had died, he was summoned and appeared as a ghost. King Wen asked him about conditions in the underworld and was duly informed.[a] Therefore, one cannot deny the possibility of reports from ancestors. However, the way of ghosts is different from the way of living creatures. Their thoughts and emotions are not the same. For example, consider the case of the wealthy Mister Liang of the northern Ch'i dynasty [550–589]. His last words were that his faithful servant should accompany him,

even in death. Following these instructions, his family killed the servant; however, the servant came back to life and reported that immediately after death he had been taken to an official building where he saw his late master. The master said, "I had thought that the dead would need servants, and therefore I summoned you in my last words. But we no longer have any ties and I shall ask the officials to release you. Tell my family to pray for my salvation.[b] Also, according to the *Tso Commentary* (*Tso-chuan*) to the *Spring and Autumn Annals* (*Ch'un-ch'iu*), Wei Wu-tsu had a favorite concubine who was childless. When Wu-tzu grew ill, he ordered his son K'o to arrange for her remarriage after his death. However, as his condition worsened, he changed his mind and ordered his son to bury her alive with him. The son decided to follow the order given when his father was still in full control of his faculties. Years later, because of this good deed, he was rewarded by the old grass weaver.[c]

Moreover, the *Classic of Documents* (*Shu-ching*) states that when one has doubts, he should confer with his ministers and consult divination.[d] *Po-hu t'ung* (The comprehensive discussion in White Tiger Hall) too asserts that "for determining good or ill in the universe and filling its men with industry, nothing is better than divination."[e] Finally, Liu Liang's *Pien ho-t'ung lun* (Essay explaining harmony) states, "In some cases, by violating a king's last order one achieves the Way and following it one loses the Way. The superior man approaches such problems with an open mind. This is indeed righteousness."[f] From these examples, it is clear that the results of divination ought not to be doubted, and a man should critically judge his ruler's orders before following them. Orders can be changed, and one need not feel uneasy about having done so.[38]

Notes:

a. These were the son and grandson of the founder of the Chou royal family. They ruled before the Chou defeated the Shang at the end of the second millennium B.C.

b. The original Chinese version of this story can be found in *T'ai-p'ing kuang-chi* (Vast record of the T'ai-p'ing era [976-984]), a Sung anthology of early short stories compiled circa 976-984 by Li Fang and others. Koreyoshi and Yoshitada accurately summarize the Chinese story, although the original is more vivid in describing the master's tortures in hell: "The servant heard the magistrate [of hell] ask a guard, 'How much oil did you squeeze from him [the master] yesterday?' 'Eight measures,' the guard replied. 'Well, try once more and see if you cannot squeeze out another six measures.'"

c. Before an important battle, the son, Wei K'o, saw an old man making rope of grass. The powerful leader of the enemy troops later tripped over this rope and was captured. In a dream, Wei K'o learned that the old man was the father—or the ghost of the father—of the woman whose remarriage he had arranged. The father had returned to reward Wei K'o for having made the correct decision.

d. The original text reads, "If you have doubts about any great matter, consult with your own heart, consult with your nobles, consult with the
   masses of people, consult with divination."
e. *Po-hu t'ung* is a collection of opinions on the classics compiled in A.D. 79
   by the historian Pan Ku. Koreyoshi and Yoshitada's preceding abbreviated
   quotation from the *Classic of Documents* is also taken directly from this
   source.
f. The *Essay Explaining Harmony* itself is no longer extant; however, the
   passage quoted here can be found in Liu Liang's biography in the *History
   of the Later Han*, which is probably where Koreyoshi and Yoshitada also
   found it.

This opinion reveals the extent of Heian belief in the supernatural—a belief that would lead to Michizane's eventual deification—and it also demonstrates how Chinese precedents were
used to determine government policies. More importantly, it
suggests that a subtle change had taken place within Heian
scholarly and literary circles. During the first decades of the
period, Japan's emperors had attempted to rule directly in accordance with the law codes adopted a century earlier. In keeping with the spirit of these codes, Confucian scholarship—and
scholars—had been officially encouraged as essential to a properly
run government. But following Saga's death, political power
gradually fell into the hands of the Fujiwara. The most powerful of early Heian Fujiwara leaders was the same Yoshifusa who
had requested the opinion on ghosts. In 858 when his grandson
was enthroned as Emperor Seiwa at the age of nine, Yoshifusa
became the first regent who was not a member of the imperial
family. His personal power became virtually absolute.

Later Fujiwara leadership has been characterized as "the rule
of taste," but Yoshifusa was a ruthless politican who used whatever means available to dispose of his opposition.[39] Under Buddhist influence, the Heian court had indeed all but done away
with capital punishment. On occasion, however, men suspected
of plotting against the Fujiwara died suspiciously early deaths.
Skillfully manipulating two "incidents," Yoshifusa drove his
rivals from the court and consolidated his ties to the imperial
family. First, shortly after Saga's death in 842, Yoshifusa succeeded in having his cousin, the future Emperor Montoku,
named crown prince and having two important non-Fujiwara
courtiers banished from court. One was the calligrapher Tachibana no Hayanari who had accompanied Kiyokimi to China.

He died, possibly of unnatural causes, before reaching his place of exile in Izu. The second incident occurred in 866 when Tomo no Yoshio (809–868), a descendant of the formerly powerful Ōtomo family, was accused of having set fire to a gate of the imperial palace. He and seven others, including an influential member of the Ki family, were sent into exile. To oppose Yoshifusa was to place oneself in a very dangerous position, and Koreyoshi was lucky not to have had his name besmirched in the second of these incidents, for it involved men who were associated with him, as will be discussed below.

Although Yoshifusa and other early Fujiwara leaders continued to operate within the framework of the *ritsuryō* system, Yoshifusa in particular had little interest in the system's Confucian basis. While he dominated the court, literature was no longer stressed as being a "vital force in the ordering of the state," and imperial sponsorship of literary anthologies ceased. Men of culture and learning but not of aristocratic status found their chances for official preferment more limited than had been the case in Saga's day. Therefore, many turned to the reclusive teachings of Taoism and Buddhism, or took an interest in the occult.[40] During the early decades of the ninth century, Kiyokimi was consulted on questions of court dress and renaming the palace gates, issues that reflected a Confucian interest in ritual and the rectification of names. During the middle decades of the century, however, his son Koreyoshi was consulted on divination and ghosts. These were not completely alien to the Confucian tradition, but they represent a more peripheral aspect of it.

Koreyoshi's otherworldly leanings, which his obituary noted, were encouraged by the political realities of his day: scholars were not being as well rewarded as they had been earlier. Koreyoshi's interests are clearly reflected in his two surviving poems:

> Visiting a Mountain Recluse and Failing to Meet Him
> The moon wanes: in this hut dwells only a crane.
> Spring closes: one oriole is perched within the gate.
> The mushrooms are gathered; no more need for fences.
> When the cinnabar cauldron goes out, he suddenly vanished.[41]

> Untitled
> Eastern sky, cold, clear, without a wisp of haze.
> The golden sun illumines the vast dawn heaven.
> From my window I spot a goose flying in from afar

And above the clouds, cranes exchange their cries.
The fog lifts; distant trees emerge frail as ferns;
The river at the far border is fine as a hair.
In a deep pool, how can the waters be roiled?
The mirror needs no wiping to make it clean.[42]

The first poem is filled with Taoist elements. A crane is the usual companion of an immortal. The mushrooms would be auspicious ones cultivated by hermits, and the cinnabar cauldron would be used to compound rare potions. Presumably the subject of Koreyoshi's poem has produced a magic elixir and drifted off into the realm of immortality, a conventional theme of Chinese Taoist poetry.

The second poem is somewhat more interesting. It begins by portraying a vast landscape of the sort common to Chinese poetry, but rare in Japanese. The final couplet describes a calm pool in which one would hardly expect to see waves, and implies that the surface of the pool is like a mirror that does not need to be cleaned. This is an allusion to a famous Zen story. The fifth Chinese patriarch of the sect had announced that whoever wrote the best verse would become his successor. His leading disciple thereupon wrote:

The body is the Bodhi tree,
The mind is like a clear mirror.
At all times we must strive to polish it,
And must not let the dust collect.

But the patriarch was not satisfied with this poem. Then a menial who had been working at the temple offered a verse:

The mind is the Bodhi tree,
The body is the mirror stand.
The mirror is originally clean and pure,
Where can it be stained by dust?

The patriarch immediately recognized the menial as his successor.[43] The point of the second poem is that striving to achieve knowledge and insight—"polishing the mirror"—ultimately is unnecessary because the source of enlightenment, a person's buddha-nature, is already present within each individual.

In Koreyoshi's metaphor, naturally waves do not form in the

deep pool just as naturally one need not seek religious insight from external sources. Because the poem is intended to convey a Zen message, its descriptive passages take on additional meaning, beyond the beauty of the scene they describe. In the morning, the haze disappears and the sun rises of their own accord, not through human endeavor. The trees and river in the distance seem small and delicate because our senses do not necessarily perceive truth accurately. Therefore, even the landscape described by Koreyoshi is symbolic of Zen teachings.

These poems point to often overlooked aspects of early Heian court culture: the popularity of Taoism and the introduction of Zen. Superstitions based on religious Taoism have been frequently noted, but the influence of philosophical Taoism has received little attention. Probably the reason is that, after Ōtomo no Tabito's *Man'yōshū* poems in praise of wine, Taoist ideas appeared principally in Japan's literature in Chinese, whereas modern views of Heian culture are based largely on its literature in Japanese. However, as Michizane's many poems on Taoist themes will demonstrate, Koreyoshi's poem is by no means an isolated example. Like their Chinese counterparts, Heian literati wrote on Confucian themes while serving in official capacities, but often turned to Taoism in moments of leisure. The influence of Zen on Japanese culture is familiar, but it is generally associated with the Kamakura and Muromachi periods. The history of Zen in Japan, however, goes back much further. Even in the Nara period, the Japanese had known of "*zen*" in its basic sense of "meditation," and, as a distinct sect, it was first introduced in the early ninth century when Emperor Saga invited a Chinese Zen monk to Japan. By Koreyoshi's day, the text to which he had alluded had long been known to the Japanese.[44] The court's early interest in Zen, however, proved short-lived. Perhaps the paradoxical nature of its teachings and the austere rigors of Zen meditation did not appeal to early Heian aristocrats who preferred the lavish ceremonies, richly artistic displays, and promises of salvation offered by other sects. Koreyoshi's poem is one of few surviving literary artifacts of the Zen sect in the early Heian court.

In the years following Saga's death, the interests of Japanese scholars shifted subtly but discernibly from the socially oriented teachings of Confucius to the more abstract concepts and reclusive ideals of Buddhism and Taoism. This shift, however, was neither complete nor sudden. On the one hand, it was Saga who had invited the first Zen monk to Japan; on the other hand, even during the years when Yoshifusa dominated the court, the university continued to teach the Confucian classics. Similar contradictions can be found in specific works. The conclusion of Kiyokimi's poetic essay on whistling may stress a pragmatic view of the art, but most of his essay follows China's Taoist whistlers in describing its more mystical qualities. Even though Koreyoshi's two extant poems concern esoteric subjects, they are but two out of his complete works, which came to ten chapters when Michizane compiled them.[45] No doubt many of his lost poems expressed more conventional Confucian themes. Thus, the change in intellectual climate was not total. In general, however, Saga did encourage poetry as a state function, a policy based on Confucian ideas of government. In contrast, under Yoshifusa's domination, the government's concern for poetry waned, and court scholars became increasingly interested in the esoteric mysteries of Taoism and Buddhism.

Koreyoshi's Taoist and Buddhist inclinations may have helped him avoid political entanglements, but they did not turn him into a recluse, for he took an active interest in his duties as a professor of literature. He proposed a regulation to make it easier for successful students to enter the government bureaucracy. The regulation was adopted, and many of his former students became important court scholars and officials.[46] Of more lasting significance were the four works he compiled, apparently for use by his students. Unfortunately, except for a few fragments, none of these works is extant, but enough information does survive to give some idea of their contents and to demonstrate that they were respected and used throughout the Heian period. They are excellent examples of the principal Heian scholarly endeavor, the making of compendia.

The most important of Koreyoshi's works was *Tōgū setsuin* (A phonetically arranged dictionary of rhymes).[47] This lexicon in twenty chapters was compiled from thirteen Chinese rhyming dictionaries. It gave the definitions and pronunciations of Chinese characters arranged according to their tones and rhymes, a classification particularly useful to students of T'ang-style regulated verse, which had strict rules concerning both tone patterns and rhyme. For each character, Koreyoshi carefully cited the various definitions and pronunciations given in his Chinese sources. As a result, his dictionary was far lengthier than any of its models. Its importance is revealed by the frequency with which it was quoted in various other early Japanese dictionaries and commentaries. In 1144, a court scholar noted that, when his students were uncertain of a character's pronunciation, he had them consult Koreyoshi's *Tōgū setsuin*. Still later, in 1276, a manuscript of the work, copied by Michizane—who is said to have assisted in its compilation—was listed among the treasures of the Fujiwara family.[48] Koreyoshi's dictionary became a basic reference work for Heian students of Chinese poetry.

Koreyoshi's three other compendia were of literature in Chinese. Two of these probably consisted of poems written by Japanese poets. *Shūin risshi* (Regulated verse gathered by rhyme), in ten chapters, presumably contained poems arranged according to their rhymes for easy reference by students. *Gimbō kanritsu* (Poems by courtiers) also had ten chapters and was more than simply a textbook. In 1008, we are told that it was read at an all-night literary gathering in the mansion of the great statesman Fujiwara no Michinaga (966–1027). Koreyoshi's final anthology, *Kaishō bunrui jū* (Classified literary works of the Hui-ch'ang era), a mammoth work in seventy chapters, was probably a collection of works written during the Hui-ch'ang ("Kaishō" in Japanese pronunciation) era (841–847) of the T'ang dynasty. This was an anthology of very recent Chinese literature. No doubt the poetry of Po Chü-i figured prominently, for the great Chinese poet had died during the sixth year of the Hui-ch'ang era and was already known in Japan and admired by Koreyoshi.[49] In addition to these literary anthologies, Koreyoshi also assisted in the compilation of two official collections of legal statutes and served on the editorial committee for the *Montoku jitsuroku* (Veritable records of Emperor Montoku), the fifth of Japan's official Chinese-style histories, for which his son Michizane drafted the introduction. Koreyoshi's contributions to these works, however, was probably rather limited.[50]

Although the official careers of early Heian courtiers such as Kiyokimi and Koreyoshi were recorded in detail, virtually no information survives about their private lives. This is in marked contrast to conditions in later years of the Heian period when "marriage politics" became a more firmly established element in court life. During the tenth century, family ties and the strategic marriages that created them developed into a routine means of ensuring power at court. At the same time, new literary forms appeared. They were written in Japanese prose, often by court women. Some were fictional, but others were autobiographical or historical and carefully described the romances of influential government leaders. Men also kept diaries in Chinese that recorded details of their private lives. As a result, women became more visible, either as pawns in the marital designs of Fujiwara politicians or as heroines in the new Japanese-language literature. Making use of these sources, modern scholars can trace with surprising detail the marriages and love affairs of important Fujiwara leaders from the tenth century onwards.

The situation in the ninth century was different. Although strategic marriages were already important, there was not yet a permanent position of regent or chancellor held by a maternal relative of the emperor. Moreover, most surviving sources are more impersonal than those from only a few decades later. The surname of a man's mother might be noted, or more rarely that of his principal wife, but the Confucian histories of the period certainly did not describe a man's passing amorous liaisons. Judging from mid-ninth-century love poems in Japanese by Ono no Komachi and Ariwara no Narihira—and from their legendary love affairs—early Heian society seems to have been no more puritanical than that described in *The Tale of Genji*. An extant fragment from Emperor Uda's diary, cited in a later chapter, is surprisingly frank. Thus, the difference between the first century and the later centuries of the Heian period does not lie in their social customs. Rather, women became increasingly conspicuous in court politics and hence appeared more frequently in the histories. Also, more varied sources of information survive to present modern scholars with a better rounded view of life at court.

The names of Kiyokimi's mother and wife, or wives, are lost. In the case of Koreyoshi, one of his wives—Michizane's mother—is identified as a member of the Tomo family, although neither her given name nor her parentage is recorded.[51] If Koreyoshi had married well, she may have been a close relative of Tomo no Yoshio. Unlike the Sugawara, the Tomo were a family who claimed ancient noble lineage. In the Nara period and earlier, their ancestors, the Ōtomo family, had produced important political leaders and eminent poets, but by the Heian period their fortunes had declined. Yoshio, an able and ambitious man, strove to improve his position at court, and in 848, three years after Michizane's birth, he was placed on the Council of State as a consultant. Gradually he rose to the office of major counselor, but in 866 he was accused of setting fire to a palace gate, as noted earlier. Ironically, the gate was the one that had originally been named after his own ancestors the Ōtomo until Kiyokimi had helped sinify it to Ōtemmon. Whether or not Yoshio was guilty, a question that today cannot be answered, Yoshifusa took advantage of the incident to have Yoshio exiled, along with seven other officials from the Tomo and Ki families. Among them was Ki no Natsui (active c. 858–866) an experienced administrator and scholar who is thought to have had academic ties to the Sugawara.[52]

The Sugawara themselves did not suffer directly from the incident, but it caused them great distress. At the time, Koreyoshi was minister of justice, and so he was obliged to serve as one of Yoshio's judges, even though his wife was also a member of the Tomo family. This was Koreyoshi's only official duty that clearly did have political implications, and the outcome of the trial indicates that he followed the safe course of agreeing with Yoshifusa, regardless of his wife's family ties with Yoshio. To make matters worse, another of the accused men, Natsui, also was associated with Koreyoshi and a member of the court's literary community. As a result, some men openly began to question the Chinese concept of literature as a bulwark of the state. Instead, they suggested that "poets are useless." At the time, Michizane was already a twenty-two-year-old student of literature. He expressed his dismay in a poem:

> Autumn Night
> Dispersed are the elder statesmen,
> Knife-like is the fierce night wind.
> I feel autumn's profound grief.
> Alas, for me times are bad.[53]

The poem employed a form of word play in which elements of the first characters in lines one and three become the first characters in lines two and four. This display of verbal erudition does not obscure Michizane's clear expression of his sentiments. The Ōtemmon incident had besmirched the name of his mother's family and had even raised doubts about the value of literature. Fortunately, because Koreyoshi always had avoided political entanglements and on this occasion did not challenge Yoshifusa, the Sugawara were spared. However, the Tomo family was disgraced and never did recover its position at court. This may have contributed to our lack of data about Michizane's mother.

Traditionally, Michizane is said to have been born at Koreyoshi's residence, the Sugawara Mansion (Sugawara In). Its site is just west of the present imperial palace in Kyoto, although it was to the east of the original Heian palace. According to a legend first recorded in 1070:

> The Sugawara Mansion was the home of the late Sugawara Consultant Koreyoshi. Once, when he was still alive, a small child of about five or six years appeared in its south garden. His face and figure were out of the ordinary. "Whose son are you and whence did you come?" he asked. The small child replied, "I have no fixed home and neither do I have a father or mother. I would like you to be my father." Knowing the child was not an ordinary person, Koreyoshi reared him with great care, and every day the boy's genius became more apparent. He is known as the Sugawara Posthumous Grand Minister (Kan Zōdaishōkoku).[54]

As the centuries passed and Michizane's renown as the god Tenjin spread, the story of his birth was gradually improved upon. A rather late version stated:

> Koreyoshi had reached the age of forty but had no sons. . . . For twenty-one days he prayed together with his wife. Shortly after they had gone to sleep, a loud voice called to her. With a start she awoke and saw above her head a long purple cloud from which a beautiful child descended on a plum branch, holding a shining jewel in his hand. Saying, "Take this from the gods you have worshiped," he threw it towards her. Although surprised, she reached out to catch it, but suddenly it entered her womb. She immediately awoke from her dream and recounted it to Koreyoshi, who was very pleased that their prayers had been answered. From this day his wife became

pregnant. . . . In the twelfth year of Jōwa [845], a child was born, his first cry a loud one. He was Michizane.[55]

Unfortunately, colorful legends aside, little is certain about Michizane's birth and childhood. In addition to the Sugawara Mansion, two other sites are also said to have been Michizane's home. They are located about a mile south of the Sugawara Mansion and are adjacent to one another. Michizane himself noted that his father gave him the use of the study in one of them, the Red Plum Hall (Kōbaiden). That study was part of the Sugawara family school, which had been founded by Kiyokimi. One possible explanation is that Michizane took up residence in his grandfather's former home, which the Sugawara had continued to use as a school even after Koreyoshi had established his own household in the Sugawara Mansion. When Michizane became an influential minister, he may have further acquired the third property just south of the Red Plum Hall.[56] Today, all three sites associated with Michizane are marked by Tenjin shrines. But, wherever Koreyoshi's mansion or Michizane's later residence may have been, Michizane was probably born elsewhere, for Heian custom dictated that wives remain in their original family homes or return to them for the birth of their children.

Contrary to the second legendary account, at the time of Michizane's birth, Koreyoshi was only thirty-four and Michizane was, in fact, his third son. None of the older sons, however, seems to have survived beyond his youth. In 865, Michizane composed a prayer on the occasion of a memorial rite to one brother, a former student of literature, who had died a year earlier. Subsequently, Michizane would refer to himself as an only son.[57] However, he probably did have sisters, even though family records did not bother to mention them. Sugawara women served in the palace under Emperors Saga and Montoku, and another was a concubine to Kōkō (830–887, r. 884–887) before he became emperor. The presence of such women in the palace was not necessarily significant politically. According to one estimate, the total number of court ladies was usually over a thousand, and any of them might have become an object of the emperor's fancy. Only the most well born and well connected, however, could produce a candidate for the imperial succession. None of the Sugawara court ladies held so exalted a position. Although the ties between them and Michizane are not recorded, one—Kōkō's former concubine—may have been his sister.[58] Years later when Michizane rose to high office, he strengthened his position by means of marital ties to the imperial family, but earlier Sugawara ladies who served at court were merely a few among the multitude of women selected for their fine appearance or special talents rather than their political connections.

When Michizane was a small child, he fell seriously ill. Naturally, his mother was very distressed. She prayed to the bodhisattva Kannon, vowing that, if Michizane regained his health, she would dedicate an image of the goddess. Her son recovered, but by the time of her death in 872, she had not yet fulfilled her vow. Therefore, when she lay suffering from her final illness, she asked Michizane to take as much as he could afford from his salary and save it until he had accumulated enough to carry out her vow. Michizane dutifully cut down on his private expenses so that he might fulfill his mother's last wish. Eventually, he mentioned his plan to his father. Koreyoshi, being a devout Buddhist, was very pleased and vowed himself to build a temple to enshrine the image. Michizane composed a hymn to be cast onto the temple's bell. The hymn was inscribed in a single row of characters around the circumference of the bell; it could be read in either direction.[59] Whichever way it was read, it expressed appropriate religious sentiments.

Koreyoshi did not live to see the completion of this last pious project. In the second month of 880, he fell ill. Michizane tended his ailing father, but the medicines he provided were ineffective; Koreyoshi died on the last day of the eighth month. His last words were, "I will not live until the period of repentance in the tenth month. Although I die today, pray for my salvation when that month comes."[60] The Sugawara family had a tradition, probably dating back to Kiyokimi's day, that in the tenth month they held a service of repentance, dedicated to the goddess Kisshōten. In the tenth month of the year following Koreyoshi's death, Michizane sponsored a special service at the new Kisshōin, the Sugawara family temple enshrining Kisshōten that Koreyoshi had ordered built.[61] For the service, Michizane composed a prayer for the salvation of his late parents and installed an image of Kannon in keeping with the vow his mother had made many years earlier. The family temple was located just south of the capital and is still in existence. Today, however, Kisshōin is a shrine dedicated to Michizane.

2 · Student Years

When Michizane celebrated his coming of age, his mother wrote the following poem:

Hisakata no	Strong enough to break
Tsuki no katsura mo	The cassia tree
Oru bakari	On the far off moon
Ie no kaze o mo	May you vigorously maintain
Fukaseteshigana	Our family tradition.[1]

Breaking a branch of the cassia said to grow on the moon was a conventional metaphor, taken from Chinese literature, for success in the civil service examinations. Thus, the poem expressed his mother's hope that Michizane would study diligently and one day pass the examinations. Both his father and grandfather had passed them, and she wanted him to continue what had become a family tradition. Success in the examinations would be vital to Michizane's chances for a distinguished career at court. His relatives who had not passed the examinations, his uncle Yoshinushi for example, also had failed to achieve high position.

Western scholars have tended to belittle the importance of early Japan's civil service examinations and the schools that prepared men to take them. The schools, it is argued, were only open to men whose fathers' ranks automatically entitled them to enter the bureaucracy on the basis of hereditary privilege. One standard textbook goes so far as to state that "the Chinese practice of recruitment on the basis of examinations was never adopted."[2] Certainly, Japan's government was not to be dominated by men selected by examinations until modern times. Throughout most of Japan's history, lineage and personal ties were more highly valued than ability as measured by an examination. However, this does not mean that the education and examination systems of Nara and early Heian Japan were mere ornaments on a fashionably Chinese façade. During most of the eighth and ninth centuries, they functioned and were taken quite seriously. Men regularly studied at the court university in preparation for bureaucratic careers. Most entered government service directly after a few years' formal training and joined the obscure ranks of minor officials. Particularly able individuals who managed to pass the difficult examinations might have more noteworthy careers, and an exceptional few rose to positions of considerable influence. The training offered at the university could be essential to sons of minor officials or provincial magnates if they desired careers at court. For those men, who were not entitled to hereditary privilege, Japan's university and civil service examinations were vitally important institutions.

The example of the Sugawara family clearly illustrates both how able men could use the examinations to improve their status, and how the system eventually broke down. To the Sugawara family in the ninth century, success on the examinations was as important as strategic marriages of fecund daughters were to the Fujiwara leaders in the tenth century. In that later century, the Fujiwara were establishing themselves as, in effect, hereditary imperial fathers-in-law and grandfathers, and, at the same time, the position of the Sugawara as court scholars also became hereditary in all but name as members of the family from one generation to the next continued to pass the examinations and hold posts in the university. In Michizane's day, however, the situation was different. The status of the Sugawara family was not yet so clearly established, and the examination system still functioned largely in accordance with the regulations of the Taihō Codes. The examinations were difficult, and Michizane's youth was spent in studying for them. After passing them, he devoted much of his adult life to preparing others to take them. Michizane's personal attitudes were molded by years of schooling in the Confucian classics, and his career was determined in part by his success on the examinations. These institutions have already been mentioned in the context of his father's and grandfather's careers, but because they are so essential to Michizane's own experiences as a scholar and official, a detailed review of them is necessary as a preface to discussing Michizane's youth.

THE ORIGINS OF THE UNIVERSITY

The *ritsuryō* codes provided for instruction in a wide range of specialized fields, including yin-yang studies, astronomy, medicine, acupuncture, and water-clock technology; but these were technical subjects, the mastery of which never led to high office.[3] Of far greater prestige was the training provided at the court university in the Confucian classics, which already had long been studied in Japan. Japan's earliest teachers of the Confucian classics were Koreans from Paekche, the first of whom was said to have been the groom accompanying two horses sent as tribute to Emperor Ōjin (c. 270–310) from the king of Paekche. The story may be apocryphal, but the fact of Korean influence on early Japanese education is beyond doubt. When Japan's first university was established, probably as part of the Ōmi Codes (Ōmi ryō) promulgated around 670, its first president was a Korean. Details of this early institution are few, but the names of five professors from the seventh century survive, all with Korean surnames.[4] The services of such men were officially recognized when two groups of low-ranking scribes said to have been descended from Japan's earliest Korean teachers were specifically given the privilege of admission to the university. Korean influence continued through the Nara period, when of the twenty-two professors whose names survive, nine were of Korean origin, as were seven of the thirteen men known to have taken the civil service examinations.

In 701, the Taihō Codes were issued with detailed provisions expanding the education system and establishing Japan's first civil service examinations. Schools principally teaching the Confucian classics were to operate on two levels: a central university in the capital and a college in each province. The university also had a program in mathematics, as well as professors of calligraphy and phonetics, and medical doctors were affiliated with the colleges. These, however, were distinctly secondary concerns. Whereas the university was to have four hundred students of classics, the number in mathematics was to be only thirty. Moreover, the court rank of the mathematics professor was five grades lower than that of the classics professor. Mathematics had been made a part of the university curriculum because it was an important administrative skill necessary for the efficient management of the complex land distribution and tax systems. Although the Japanese gave a higher rank to their professors of mathematics than did the Chinese, they, too, accepted the Confucian view that classics was the more important subject. [5]

Most students, both at the university and at the colleges, were to study specified Confucian texts and their commentaries. Students were first taught to read a text in Chinese by the professor of phonetics, who was usually a Chinese immigrant. [6] Having mastered the reading of the text, the students then attended lectures on its meaning given by the professors of classics. Every ten days, students were to be examined and then given a day off—in contrast to regular officeholders who had one day off in every six. The codes demanded punishment for students who did poorly on the examination. According to the commentaries, this was to take the form of whipping, from which even sons of high-ranking courtiers could not escape by paying a fine. [7] At the end of the year, students sat for final examinations. Those who failed three years consecutively were expelled, as were those who after nine years still were not ready for the civil service examinations. The best students, on the other hand, were recommended for those examinations. The only forms of recreation allowed students were koto playing and archery practice.

The question of who made up the university's student body is a subject of some controversy. According to the original code, four categories of students were to be admitted: (1) sons and grandsons of officials of the fifth rank or above; (2) sons of scribes descended from the Korean scholars who had first brought Confucian learning to Japan; (3) sons of officials of the eighth rank or above upon special application; and (4) students from the provincial colleges—mostly sons of local district officials—whose admission was contingent on passing a special examination. Thus, entry into the university was primarily determined by the rank of one's father. Only sons of aristocrats or members of a special group of scribes were automatically accepted. Sons of lower-ranking courtiers or district officials from the provinces either had to make a special petition or pass an examination if they wished to attend. However, most sons and grandsons of aristocrats whose entry into the university was assured were also guaranteed court rank on the basis of hereditary privilege, regardless of whether or not they passed a civil service examination. Therefore, some scholars maintain that the university was strictly aristocratic, intended to give a modicum of learning to sons of the nobility, but not to train men of talent who could then be brought into the government through the examinations.

The intentions of the men who drafted Japan's codes for the education and examination systems are difficult to ascertain. Obviously, the regulations for the university, like the rest of the *ritsuryō* system, assumed the legitimacy of aristocratic privilege. For the university, however, the exceptions to the rule, the provisions for admitting lower-ranking courtiers, proved more significant than the general principle that admission was primarily open to sons of the highest nobles. In practice, the youths whose status was guaranteed by their noble birth did not flock to the university, despite periodic orders requiring them to attend and inducements for them to take the examinations.[8] The university's curriculum was rigorously academic and not merely that of a finishing school for young gentlemen. Accordingly, ample room remained to permit the admission of young men not so well born. In 730, specific provision was made for the admission of commoners. Precise information on who actually attended the university is scarce, but of the few students whose names survive, most came from relatively minor or even totally obscure families.[9] The very lack of data suggests that most men who attended the university were not sons of aristocrats but of minor officials. Like their fathers, they went on to modest careers and, hence, were not honored with biographies that would have noted their university studies.

In addition to the university, the codes provided for the establishment of one college in every province, each with a single professor responsible for teaching the classics to a group of students numbering between twenty and fifty, depending on the size of the province. As noted, the students were primarily sons of the locally recruited district officials who, in turn, were descendants of the virtually independent local magnates of an earlier age. The *ritsuryō* system had given such men secure but very minor positions in local governments, and few of them played significant roles on a national level. Those who did were often men who had first earned reputations for their scholarship. The best known examples are Kibi no Makibi (695–775) and Haruzumi no Yoshitada. Makibi, the son of a minor official from Bitchū province, studied for nineteen years in China, and, after serving in posts at the university, he eventually rose to the office of minister of the right with the junior second rank. Yoshitada, the man who had joined Koreyoshi in offering the opinion on ghosts, was from Ise province. He studied at the university, passed the civil service examinations, and attained the office of consultant with the junior third rank. These examples show that the training in the Confucian classics might have proved valuable to sons of provincial families.[10]

The problem with the colleges was that they rarely functioned as intended and could not be maintained in all provinces. The chief difficulty was in finding teachers. Each college professor was supposed to have been selected from among learned men in the province, but few men with suitable training in the classics were to be found outside the capital. In 723, the number of colleges had to be reduced to only thirteen, although in 779 the court again decreed that colleges were to be established in all fifty-eight provinces. Eventually teachers were sent from the capital, but this proved no real solution to the problem. The men sent were apt to be the less-able university students who had little prospect of passing the civil service examinations. On the whole, the provincial colleges were not particularly successful. The one exception was at Dazaifu, the government headquarters in Kyushu; the college there did develop into a lasting institution with a variety of courses paralleling those at the university in the capital.[11]

Closely related to these educational institutions was the examination system created in the Taihō Codes. Successful students were to be directly recommended for the examinations, which covered generally the same texts as were taught at the university. Although the university clearly was intended to prepare men for the examinations, the two institutions functioned separately. Most university students did not take the examinations, and specific provision was made for talented men in the lowest rungs of government service to be recommended for the examinations so that they could improve their status through them even without study at the university. Moreover, the examinations included some subjects not taught at the university, a situation that led to various changes in the university's curriculum.

Candidates took one of four civil service examinations: *shūsai* ("flourishing talent"), *myōgyō* (classics), *shinshi* ("presented scholar"—the Chinese *chin-shih*), and *myōbō* (law), in descending order of the rank awarded to those who passed. The prestigious *shūsai* examination consisted of two essay questions requiring students to "summarize great matters." One early commentary proposed a sample question: "Why do horses smell the ground after they defecate; why do dogs lift their legs when they urinate?" Then as now, legal commentaries were not known for their levity, but that question surely was suggested in jest. Extant examples show that actual questions dealt with problems of morality, philosophy, classical Chinese history, or other issues generally within the Confucian intellectual tradition, although elements of other Chinese philosophical systems also appeared.[12] The questions were abstruse and could not have been answered without training in Chinese classics such as that which was provided at the university.

On the classics and law examinations, candidates were asked meanings of ten passages from either specified Confucian classics or Japanese law codes respectively. These examinations apparently were oral. The *shinshi* examination consisted of two essay questions on "the essential business of governing the nation" and a test of the candidates' memorization of two Chinese texts—*Wen-hsuan* and *Erh-ya,* the former being the then popular literary anthology and the latter an early lexicographic work. Neither was among the texts taught at the university. Candidates were shown passages from these works with a few characters blocked out and were expected to supply the missing characters from memory. These three examinations were all difficult, but offered only small reward in the form of rather low court ranks to successful candidates. As a result, they were rarely taken. Learned men who sought to pass one of the examinations usually chose the most demanding but also the best rewarded and most esteemed *shūsai* examination.[13]

Both the education and examination systems of the Taihō Codes were based on Chinese models, but neither was a direct copy of its T'ang-dynasty original. Japan radically simplified China's elaborate education system. For example, the T'ang Ministry of Rites (Li-pu) included a Directorate of Education (Kuo-tzu chien) that was responsible for six public institutions of higher learning in the capital. Three schools taught the Confucian classics, each to students of different social classes. The remaining schools taught law, calligraphy, and mathematics respectively. Together, these schools had approximately thirty teachers and 2,000 students.[14] This was obviously far too elaborate for Japan's needs or capacities, and consequently these various schools were scaled down to only one university with nine teachers and 430 students. Whereas the Chinese provided a wide range of government-sponsored local schools outside the capital, the Japanese reduced this to one college for each province, and even this provided more than the nation could support. Japan's four civil service examinations all had Chinese counterparts, but the Chinese also had an examination in calligraphy that the Japanese never adopted. Moreover, the Japanese examinations were all much shorter than their T'ang models. For example, Japan's *shūsai* examination required two essays; its Chinese equivalent required five.

If the organizational outlines of Japan's education and examination systems did not closely follow T'ang precedents, the actual substance of these systems did. Even the wording was almost identical in certain sections of the Chinese and Japanese codes, such as those prescribing details of the biannual Confucian memorial rites, the lists of officially approved texts and commentaries, and the tests that were given every ten days. Although the curriculum at the Japanese university was generally identical to that of its Chinese counterparts, there were small but significant differences. For example, *Lao-tzu* was a required text in T'ang China, reflecting the fact that the T'ang emperors considered themselves descendants of its author, but it was not even taught in Japan. Also, Japan's professors of phonetics had no Chinese model, since there was no need to teach Chinese pronunciation in China.

The factors influencing Japanese modifications of T'ang institutions have been divided into five categories, all of which can be illustrated by changes the Japanese made in adopting the T'ang education and examination systems. First was the influence of Korean versions of Chinese institutions. Korean precedents can be found for the idea of one rather than six central universities, the exclusion of law from the university, the use of certain mathematics texts, and the inclusion of the *Wen-hsuan* in the examinations. This Korean influence is hardly surprising in light of the major Korean role of bringing Chinese learning to Japan. A second factor was the influence of traditional institutions and entrenched interests. This explains why descendants of the first Korean teachers in Japan and provincial magnates of an earlier age were singled out for the special privilege of admission to the university, despite their relatively low status. Third was the Japanese love for classical aspects of Chinese culture. Thus the Japanese based the name of their university on that of a Han rather than a T'ang institution. Fourth was native Japanese innovations, such as the creation of professors of phonetics and a provision that students who did not do well in their classical studies but were skilled in writing could be specially recommended for appointment. The final factor was the desire to emulate the success of the T'ang and eliminate what were felt to be weaknesses in the system. This explains why *Lao-tzu,* with its anarchistic sentiment, was eliminated from the Japanese university curriculum.[15]

The Japanese were following their usual practice of modifying what they adopted from foreign lands. In this case, contrary to the usual view, they did not simply take an egalitarian system and make it into an aristocratic one. A comparison of the original Chinese and Japanese codes reveals that the principal changes made by the Japanese involved simplification and innovation to make the new institutions more suitable to Japanese conditions and needs.

In a few respects, the Japanese system was actually more egalitarian than its T'ang model. Japan's university from the start admitted children of both high- and low-ranking nobles and eventually came to admit commoners as well, whereas T'ang China's six schools in the capital were strictly segregated by rank. In 820, the Japanese declared that their own university should follow the precedent of one of China's aristocratic schools and restrict admission to sons of officials holding the third rank or higher. Seven years later, however, a Japanese professor responded by objecting that the new policy interfered with scholarship. "The university," he noted, "is a place that reveres talent and cultivates virtue." He went on to point out that some of China's greatest scholars were from poor families, and that "great talent is not limited to the aristocracy; aristocrats do not necessarily have great talent." The rule he was protesting had never been strictly enforced, and, as a result of his objections, it was abandoned.[16] Some Japanese courtiers had attempted to use Chinese example as an excuse for making the Japanese university more restrictive, but their move did not succeed.

Modestly egalitarian features were not limited to admission policies. In Japan, but not in China, a regulation specifically stated that at rituals within the university, the students were to be arranged according to their age, not their fathers' rank. Because Japan's civil service examinations were shorter, they were in a sense easier than those in China. During the T'ang, hereditary rank for the well born, who did not need to take the examinations, extended to the great-grandchildren of the highest nobles, but in Japan it did not extend beyond grandchildren. Like Nara and Heian Japan, the T'ang—particularly the early T'ang, which was Japan's model—was very much an aristocratic age, and the examination system was still a relatively new innovation.

The Japanese did not eliminate, but in fact may have even added, egalitarian elements to their method of official education and recruitment. Still, it cannot be denied that on the whole the T'ang system did allow more room for entry into government service based on individual merit than did the Japanese modification of that system. In China, the government provided many opportunities for the education of nonaristocrats, albeit at segregated institutions, whereas in Japan a commoner's chances of getting a formal education at publicly run schools were slim indeed. Although shorter, Japan's examinations had to be taken in a difficult foreign language, classical Chinese. The principal advantage given Japanese aristocrats, however, did not lay in the education or examination systems, but rather in the rules governing hereditary privilege. In Japan, hereditary ranks were considerably higher than those in China, but for successful examination candidates, the situation was reversed, the Chinese being far more generously rewarded. Moreover, in Japan all sons of high nobles could receive hereditary rank, but in China only eldest sons were granted this privilege.[17]

The most important difference between the Japanese and the Chinese systems lay not in their laws or even in the spirit of their laws, but rather in their historical evolution. In Japan, court offices gradually tended to become hereditary and the examinations, which had always functioned on a limited scale, eventually degenerated into empty rituals. In contrast, China's examinations became the usual path to official position. In the early T'ang, successful examinees may have constituted a relatively small percentage of officialdom, but by the following Sung dynasty they dominated the bureaucracy. Knowing the ultimate fate of the two systems, modern scholars can easily dismiss ancient Japan's attempt at official recruitment by examination as a half-hearted attempt at copying a more vigorous institution. In the early years of the eighth century when the copy was being made, however, the Chinese system might have appeared less vital and the Japanese copy less eviscerated than they seem today.

In creating a bureaucratic government based on Chinese models, the Japanese emphasized aristocratic elements in these models, but not to the exclusion of more egalitarian strains. The Japanese university certainly was intended, in part, to "educate the sons of the court aristocracy whose positions were already assured," as the textbook quoted earlier states.[18] But it also provided such training to sons of low-ranking court nobles and provincial magnates for whom official positions at court were not at all assured. If such men excelled at their studies, they could take examinations that permitted them to enter the court bureaucracy with sufficiently high rank that they might on occasion rise to positions of considerable influence. Theoretically, even commoners could have worked their way up the educational ladder to obtain positions at court, although no examples are known today. In practice, most university students were from minor court families. They did not take the examinations, but entered the court bureaucracy directly with low rank and served in a wide variety of posts, particularly those requiring a high degree of literacy. Presumably, the men who framed the Japanese codes intended to provide such opportunities to intellectually able men who were at least moderately well born, and in this limited way, the institutions they created did serve a useful and important function. Moreover, the experience of the Sugawara demonstrates that in exceptional cases the university and examinations could also be a path to high office for men from minor court families.

DEVELOPMENT: THE POPULARITY OF LITERATURE

The university went through many changes in the almost two centuries between its founding around 670 and Michizane's entrance in 862. The codes of 701 give us our first clear picture of how the university was supposed to operate in theory. The decades immediately after the issuance of the codes witnessed a number of reforms, among them the addition of Chinese literature to the curriculum. This attention to the university suggests that the Japanese were seriously trying to improve the institution and make it better suit their own needs and interests. From the mid-Nara period, however, concern for the university and its Confucian curriculum waned as the court came increasingly under the influence of Buddhism, symbolized by the dedication of the Great Buddha in 749 and the political rise of the monk Dōkyō in the 760s.[19]

After Dōkyō was driven from the court in 770, efforts were made to revive the more Confucian style of government that had been proclaimed in the ritsuryō codes, of which the university was a part. Following the establishment of the Heian capital in 794, the university began to flourish. The number of university students had been rather small in the Nara period, but in the ninth century, the enrollment approached the 430 students specified in the original codes.[20] Competition for admission to the more popular courses of study became so intense that entrance examinations were established and private academies appeared to prepare young men for them. New regulations facilitated the entry of successful examination candidates into the bureaucracy. Various forms of economic support were created to maintain the university and provide extra income for teachers and support for students. One clear indication of the respect newly accorded professors was that after 791 their salaries were supplemented with the income from special "office-paddies" (*shikibunden*), untaxed lands that they were given the right to exploit. This was a perquisite otherwise attached only to the highest offices. [21]

Perhaps the most significant development within the university was the introduction of literary studies. Originally, in keeping with Chinese precedents, the university's curriculum had emphasized the Confucian classics. In 728 and 730, new regulations established the office of professor of literature, with a rank equal to that of an assistant professor of classics, and stated that there were to be twenty students specializing in literature selected from among intelligent commoners—sons of men without rank—regardless of age. In addition, ten able and industrious university students, two of them from the literature program, were to be selected as graduate students and given stipends. [22]

Graduate students had Chinese precedents; formal professors and students of literature did not. [23] A number of theories have been proposed to explain why the Japanese created this course of study. Possibly it was to prepare students for the civil service examinations, which, in fact, required skill in Chinese composition as well as familiarity with the Confucian classics. Knowledge of one literary anthology, the *Wen-hsuan* was required for the *shinshi* examination. Alternatively, the Japanese may have recognized that good birth, the official criterion for admission to the university, was no guarantee of literary talent, and this program, open to men on the basis of ability rather than birth, was intended to train poets who could compose Chinese verse, which was then becoming an important element in court ritual. Whatever the reason for its creation, the eventual popularity of the literature course reflected the Japanese court's taste for the artistic over the philosophical. [24] The Japanese did seriously study the Confucian classics, but they found Chinese poetry more to their liking.

During the Nara period, the literature program gradually increased in prestige. Although the professor of literature was originally supposed to rank with the assistant professor of classics, in 722 one professor of literature was given the additional office of president of the university, and eight years later, still holding those offices, he was promoted to the junior fourth rank lower, thus far surpassing in rank the full professor of classics, who normally held only the senior sixth rank lower. Finally, in 821, the professor of literature's rank was officially raised to the junior fifth.[25] Students too, by the mid-Nara period, came increasingly from the same low- to middle-ranking court families that had from the start provided most of the university's students, in spite of the original rule that literature students were to be selected from among commoners.

In the early ninth century, even princes were studying literature, which by then had become the most respected course at the university. Although the number of students may have been increased in 834, the total probably did not exceed forty, far fewer than the four hundred allowed in classics. As a result, competition to become a student of literature grew increasingly stiff, and some students entered the classics program as preparation for the entrance examination to the now more exclusive literature course. Eventually, a special category of preparatory students of literature (*gimonjōshō*) was created. It, also, required an examination, and those who passed were then trained for the more difficult examination to become a regular student of literature.[26] In Michizane's day, literature was the most selective and highly regarded program at the university. Men who only studied classics had little chance of significant careers at court.[27]

The precise content of the literature course is unclear, beyond the fact that the literature in question was Chinese, not Japanese. Emphasis probably was placed on the *Wen-hsuan* and *Erh-ya,* the two texts covered in the *shinshi* examination. In addition, history became part of the literature program. Beginning in 757, the court records occasionally mentioned professors and students of history who specialized in China's "Three Histories" (*San-shih*): the *Records of the Historian* (*Shih-chi*), *History of the Former Han Dynasty* (*Han-shu*), and *History of the Later Han Dynasty.* Finally, in 808, the position of professor of history was officially established, only to be abolished in 834 and replaced by an additional professor of literature. At that time, the openings for students of history similarly may

have been allotted to students of literature. History lost its independent status as an academic discipline within the university
and became part of the literature curriculum, but professors of
literature regularly lectured on the Three Histories and occasionally were even referred to as professors of history.[28] Thus, in
the early Heian period, the university's literature program included both Chinese literature and history.

The usual path for young men seeking to enter government
service by means of the examination system was to begin their
education in private academies. The more able of them then
took the examination to become students of literature. Others
readied themselves for that examination through further study
either as students of classics or as preparatory students of literature. A sign of the respect accorded students of literature was
that they came to be known as *shinshi,* a term that originally
had referred to those who had passed the civil service examination by that name. The best students of literature were then
recommended to become graduate students, who in turn were
known as *shūsai* after the examination for which they were
preparing. Finally, if the graduate students passed the civil service examination, they would enter the court bureaucracy, although with somewhat more honor than rank. Only later, as
in the *Tale of Genji,* were professors regarded as slightly pom-
pous and old-fashioned objects of aristocratic derision.

Sugawara involvement in the university began during the
reign of Emperor Kammu who sought to strengthen the institution. Throughout the ninth century, the family maintained its
association with the university as the institution continued to
enjoy high student enrollment and generous financial support.
Michizane was fortunate to live in an age that respected his
scholarly and literary skills. However, he did have to face certain
difficulties—first as a student, later as a teacher and official—
caused by problems within the education and examination systems as they functioned in the ninth century. One was the
fierce competition for admission to the literature course. The
total number of students of literature is unclear, but a group of
ten poems Michizane wrote in 884 to congratulate men who
had just passed the entrance examination suggests that they
may have been admitted ten at a time. The poems mention the
ages of three of the new students: forty-nine, forty-two, and

thirty-eight respectively. A fourth, probably also in his forties, had finally passed on his thirteenth try.[29] The remaining six successful candidates presumably were more youthful. Still, interest in Chinese literature and the prestige of the university were such that men no longer young sought to become students of literature. Most of them came from relatively minor court families such as the Tajihi, Wake, or Ono. In that year, of the seventeen men listed as senior nobles, seven were Fujiwara and six Minamoto, yet no member of either family was among those accepted into the literature course.[30] To influential aristocrats, the struggle to gain admission was not worth the effort. To men from less powerful court families, it was.

A second problem lay in the difficulty of the civil service examinations and the limited rewards they offered. Only an exceptional few were able to pass the examinations, receive rank, and enter the bureaucracy. Although the selection process may have been stringent, the ranks bestowed on successful examinees were not as generous as those automatically awarded to sons of high aristocrats. Significantly, none of the ten students whom Michizane congratulated in 884 can be positively identified. Despite their academic efforts, they were not able to achieve sufficient eminence that their names became easily recognizable. A few of the most outstanding scholars were rewarded with suitable positions at court, but most served obscurely in minor posts. Learning was encouraged more actively than it was rewarded, and competition for desirable positions at court was comparable to that for admission to the literature course. However, there were no examinations to select candidates for office on the basis of ability.

This competition, first for admission to the university's preferred programs, and then for suitable appointments, produced undesirable results. In the bureaucracy, men with private connections to those in power were at an advantage, and, even within the scholarly community, personal ties became increasingly important as a means of assuring career success. The outcome of this situation was the growth of academic cliques and bitter rivalries. Occasionally, scholars stooped to slandering one another in attempts to gain the favor of influential courtiers. The resulting feuds sometimes appeared ideological—as one faction protested the activities of the "lofty Confucian scholars," another group complained that "poets are useless." The real conflicts, however, were based more on personal loyalties than intellectual convictions. For example, in moments of literary exuberance Michizane proclaimed himself "at heart a poet," but he never abandoned the traditional ideal of combining literature and scholarship, for he also referred to himself as a Confucian. Nonetheless, he did participate in the quarreling, and just as his rise to high office was in part a result of his academic success, so his eventual downfall would begin with accusations made by a resentful former examination candidate whom he once had failed.[31]

A further problem was that the position of scholars at court was in some ways ambiguous. Scholars appointed to university professorships had duties resembling those of present-day professors. They taught students, gave lectures on appropriate occasions, composed literary and scholarly works, and sometimes were called upon to offer learned opinions on public issues. Their official status, however, was quite different from that of their modern counterparts. The university was not an independent institution but an ordinary government bureau. A professor, although a specialist, was also a regular member of the bureaucracy. Any official with the necessary rank and academic credentials could be named a professor, and, conversely, any professor could be routinely transferred to another post at court or in the provinces. No professor was guaranteed tenure at the university.

Michizane, for one, had a strong sense of vocation as a scholar and poet. But as a bureaucrat holding the junior fifth rank, he was subject to appointment to a wide variety of posts ranging from professor of literature to director of the Carpentry Bureau (*moku no kami*) or governor of a province, all offices held by men of that rank. Michizane's Confucian training stressed that men of learning such as himself had a duty to serve the state. Accordingly, he greeted the news of his eventual transfer from professor to provincial governor with conflicting emotions. On the one hand, he strongly felt it his duty to serve his emperor to the best of his abilities. On the other, he bitterly lamented leaving an office that he considered far more appropriate to his particular talents and station in life. Michizane's feelings were shared by other scholars who would have liked to be professors, but, as regular members of the court bureaucracy, found themselves appointed to less desirable posts.[32] At the same time, again because they were regular bureaucrats, scholars could also hope for an exceptional promotion to high office. Michizane's was the most conspicuous but not the only example. Both his father and grandfather had achieved high rank after building reputations based on their learning. As a court scholar, Michizane was devoted to his vocation, but as an official he had to accept the bureaucratic post to which he was assigned, a post that could be inappropriately obscure or unexpectedly exalted.

Finally, the ninth century witnessed not only the flourishing of the university but also the beginnings of the Fujiwara domination of the court, a development that contributed to the problems noted above. Early Fujiwara leaders worked within the framework of the *ritsuryō* system, but some of their policies would eventually help to undermine it.[33] Thus, during the middle decades of the century when the Fujiwara dominated the court, they continued to support the university and treat scholars with respect. The already uncertain official position of men whose status depended largely on their intellectual abilities, however, was rendered all the more precarious by the conflicting principles of the *ritsuryō* bureaucracy and of the Fujiwara hegemony. The former, in theory, followed the concept of appointments based on merit; the latter, in practice, awarded office largely on the basis of birth. Thus, scholars might be given suitable appointments in recognition of their abilities, but if they got into quarrels with the Fujiwara, the outcome was predictable. Similarly, those without Fujiwara patronage were apt to find themselves among the first sent off to undesirable provincial posts in order to create vacancies at court for friends and relatives of those in power. Michizane's many farewell poems to colleagues departing for service in the provinces demonstrate that this was a common experience. A particularly famous example was the appointment in 930 of the senior court poet Ki no Tsurayuki (868?–946) to the office of governor of Tosa, the most isolated region of Shikoku.[34]

During the ninth century, scholarship was encouraged and men of learning were respected, but the positions of such men at court were rarely secure. In part, institutional considerations such as the difficulties both in admission to the university's literature course and of the civil service examinations generated the personal rivalries and insecurities of scholars. In addition, scholars had to compete for office not only with each other but also with members of the Fujiwara family and imperial descendants whose hereditary positions and personal ties guaranteed that the competition would not be an equal one. On occasion, able men could be promoted to high offices on the basis of merit in accordance with the Confucian principles underlying the *ritsuryō* system. More commonly, however, such men were accorded considerable respect but only modest rank and office.

Eventually, in the tenth century, the university began to decline. Earlier, for a lucky few, success at the university had been rewarded at court in accordance with the principles of the *ritsuryō* system. As Fujiwara domination of the court became complete, however, personal ties and family background became the paramount criteria for success. A university education was no longer as useful as it had been. In part, that was because the university continued to teach Chinese subjects despite increasing interest in Japan's native culture, especially its literature. Thus, not only was university training less useful for an official career, it was not even as fashionable as it had been. Worse, the quality of the university deteriorated. The most talented men were no longer attracted to it, and, in addition, professorships came to be assigned more on the basis of family than of talent.

In the ninth century, it was a remarkable achievement for three generations from the Sugawara family to serve as professors of literature, but from the tenth century onward, the Sugawara became one of only three families from which professors of literature normally were appointed. The same pattern appeared in the university's other programs. By the late Heian period, a Sugawara professor of literature is said to have "passed the office on to his son," as if it were a private possession rather than a public office. Not only the official positions but even learning itself became, in effect, family property as each of the families that supplied university professors developed its own esoteric methods for reading Chinese texts.[35] Such secretive practices helped protect a family's status but were detrimental to the intellectual vitality of the university. In 1177, the university burned down and was not rebuilt, although the Fujiwara family school, which was destroyed in the same conflagration, was reconstructed. Still, the university as an institution, apparently one without its own buildings, managed to survive until the mid-fourteenth century, and as late as the first decades of the nineteenth century, members of the Sugawara family, some still in their teens, continued to be given the empty title of professor of literature.[36]

The civil service examinations, too, gradually lost their importance. They had always functioned on a small scale, administered individually only when a suitable candidate appeared who was prepared to take one of them. In the first two hundred years of their operation, only sixty-five men are said to have passed the most difficult of them, and other examinations appear to have been administered even less frequently.[37] Like the university, the examination system began to seriously decay during the tenth century, when, for example, Emperor Murakami (r. 946–967) parodied the examinations by having a student write an essay on *sangaku,* a popular form of entertainment consisting of music, dance, acrobatics, and juggling. In the Muromachi period, a Sugawara descendant treated this obvious farce as a real examination. By his day, examiners were providing candidates not only with questions but also with draft answers that only needed to be copied over.[38] The system had totally degenerated. The limited scale and eventual demise of early Japan's civil service examination system have served to discredit it in the eyes of modern historians. Comparisons with later developments in China make Japan's system look all the worse. But to men in Michizane's position, on the fringes of aristocratic society, even the limited functions of early Japan's university and examinations were vitally important.

THE STUDENT MICHIZANE

Michizane's family was one of scholars and had high hopes he would continue its traditions, hopes that were expressed in his mother's poem. Because of his family's scholarly heritage, Michizane as a child had educational advantages that were not shared by many of his contemporaries. In fact, as early as his grandfather's time, a Sugawara residence had been used as a private school preparing young men for admission to the university.³⁹ Michizane probably began studying Chinese there when he was still quite young. Years later, he proudly noted that his eldest son had begun to read at the age of four, and another son at six had already memorized a long work, "Poems on the Capital" (Ti-ching p'ien) by the T'ang poet Lo Pin-wang.⁴⁰ Michizane's own education would have begun similarly around the age of five with the memorization of such works.

When he was eleven, Michizane composed his first poem in Chinese:

> Viewing the Plum Blossoms on a Moonlit Night
> The moon glitters like pure snow.
> The plum blossoms resemble twinkling stars.
> How charming! The golden orb crosses the heavens
> And the jewel petals perfume the garden.⁴¹

The poem correctly follows the rules for versification in the then-current T'ang style. Most of its phrases were adopted from familiar Chinese models; however, the juxtaposition of the plum blossoms and the moon is said to have been an original idea by the precocious Michizane.

Although the most impressive feature of the poem is its author's youth, its enthusiastic description of the plum blossoms' beauty inspired one of the most popular legends about Michizane: that he had a special love for the plum. Before being sent off into exile many years later, he wrote what was to become his best known poem—one in Japanese addressed to the plum blossoms, but this time in a more melancholy mood. From these two poems, the legend grew. Centuries later, painters would customarily portray him with a spray of plum blossoms.

Michizane's admiration for the plum cannot be denied, but the degree of his admiration is open to question. Although over the years he did compose many poems on the plum, he composed more on the chrysanthemum and many on other trees, plants, and flowers, among them the willow, bamboo, cherry, and pine. A count of the natural images in the titles of Michizane's poems reveals only twelve poems on the plum versus twenty-two on the chrysanthemum. Images more popular in Japanese poetry lag far behind, with just five poems on the cherry blossoms and four on the autumn leaves. A concordance of Michizane's *kanshi* reveals a similar pattern.⁴² These figures

2. Eleven-year-old Michizane composing his first poem
Source: Dazaifu Temmangū.

do not necessarily represent Michizane's own poetic tastes, for many of his *kanshi* were written at imperial command on set themes. They do, however, cast doubt on the legend of his special affinity for the plum blossom. If anything, the chrysanthemum would seem to have been his favorite poetic subject. Michizane did choose to write more often of the plum and chrysanthemum rather than the cherry blossoms and autumn leaves usually favored by poets who wrote in Japanese. This preference reflects his training in Chinese literary traditions, in which poets wrote more often of those flowers than of cherry. Michizane's choice of imagery was less the product of personal taste than of literary convention.

A poem written at the age of fourteen was the second one Michizane chose many years later to preserve in his anthology. It reveals the youth's increased facility at expressing himself in Chinese. In the poem, Michizane lamented that, although another year was about to pass, he had made little progress in his studies. Thus, he was already using the medium of Chinese poetry to express his own personal concerns, not simply conventional Chinese themes: far more likely that at fourteen Michizane was worried about his schoolwork than that at eleven he had developed a lifelong attachment to the plum. Also, the *Wakan rōeishū* (Japanese and Chinese poems for chanting), an early eleventh-century anthology of couplets in Chinese and *waka* on related themes, deemed a couplet from this youthful poem worthy of inclusion:

Ice envelopes the water's surface; the sound of waves is not heard.
Snow dots the forest top; the trees seem as if in bloom.[43]

The appearance of a couplet in an important anthology from so youthful an author suggests that he was making rapid progress in the study of Chinese composition, despite the anxiety expressed in the poem.

Michizane wrote these poems while he was studying at the Sugawara family school, where he was under the tutelage not of his father but of one of his father's students, Shimada no Tadaomi (828–891). Tadaomi was to become an important figure in Michizane's life. He was not only Michizane's first teacher, but also would become his father-in-law and lifelong friend. Tadaomi's career provides an interesting contrast with that of Michizane. Tadaomi had passed the university entrance examination and became a student of literature under Michizane's father Koreyoshi. His literary ability was widely recognized, and Koreyoshi thought well enough of him to select him to be Michizane's tutor. At the time, however, he was already twenty-eight and still only a student, not a graduate student. Apparently he never took the civil service examination, but, like most university students, entered the bureaucracy directly with low rank.

At the age of thirty-two, when he was specially summoned to compose poems in response to those by an ambassador from the Manchurian kingdom of Parhae, he was merely the junior secretary of Echizen province with the junior seventh rank lower. Seven years later, he was named lesser secretary (*shōgeki*), a post of modest rank but one appropriate to a man of his literary ability for it involved the drafting and revising of official documents. In 869 at the age of forty-two, he was promoted to the junior fifth rank lower, but just over a month after his promotion, he was again sent off to the provinces, this time as supernumerary lieutenant governor of Inaba. Most of his remaining years were spent either serving in provincial posts or living in the capital with no official position. The only exceptions were two years as junior assistant minister of war (*hyōbu no shō*) and the final year of his life as director of the Medicine Bureau (*ten'yaku no kami*). In 883, he was once again specially summoned to help receive an embassy from Parhae, this time along with Michizane. By then, his former student, seventeen years his junior, held the same rank he did and had been serving as professor of literature for nearly six years. At the time of Tadaomi's death in 891, he still held the junior fifth rank, although he had been advanced to its upper grade in 879 at the age of fifty-two.[44] Michizane had attained that rank when he was thirty-five, and his future rival, Fujiwara no Tokihira (871–909), would already hold the junior fourth rank while still in his teens.

Clearly, Tadaomi's career was not so impressive as that of Kiyokimi, Koreyoshi, or Michizane. One reason was that, by the mid-ninth century, the Sugawara were well established as court scholars, whereas Tadaomi's ancestors were virtually unknown. Offices may not yet have become strictly hereditary, but well-placed and high-ranking parents were definitely assets. Nonetheless, a few individuals from families just as obscure as the Shimada did rise to high office both before and after Tadaomi. One key difference was that they passed the civil service examinations, which Tadaomi did not even take. Certainly Tadaomi was a learned man and a capable poet, but apparently he was not quite good enough to be recommended for the civil service examinations. Other evidence also suggests that Tadaomi was not of the same intellectual caliber as Michizane. Michizane's first poem was composed at the age of eleven; Tadaomi's was at the age of sixteen. More importantly, his writing does not display the mastery of Chinese that Michizane would eventually achieve.[45]

Tadaomi spent many years in minor provincial offices, and later in life abandoned hope of an outstanding official career, taking instead to writing poetry on reclusive themes. His education had not brought him the rewards he might have liked. Only the most able—and lucky—literary men had their abilities rewarded with suitable office; most university students went on to careers like Tadaomi's. The young and sensitive Michizane's concern that his studies were not proceeding smoothly shows his realization that if he did not do well, he would not be able to maintain his family's reputation.

As the time approached for Michizane to take his university entrance examination, Koreyoshi personally began to supervise his studies. Every day, Koreyoshi had him compose a poem on an assigned theme with a specified form and rhyme. Of the many poems Michizane wrote at this time, he selected the four most noteworthy examples for inclusion in his collected works. All dealt with conventional Chinese themes and were written in very learned and allusive language. Despite his worries, Michizane displayed remarkable erudition, the result of years of diligent study. His ability is even more impressive when one remembers that he had not been a healthy child. The following is the least recondite of the poems he wrote for his father when he was preparing for the examination. It shows Michizane at the age of perhaps seventeen writing in a thoroughly Chinese manner:

Cultivating the Mulberry
(In sixty characters, with the rhyme taken from the title)
　　Inside the palace gates they observe their rites,
　　Except in spring when they cultivate mulberry.
　　Awaiting that season, they can not miss the time.
　　With pure hearts, carefully they cull the leaves.
　　A sickle is caught as the moon is caught on a branch.
　　Pollen falls; the leaves seem coated in frost.
　　Their hands move; their bracelets chime.
　　They look down and find their baskets full.
　　Like peach or plum blossoms rustling in a breeze
　　Their gauzy silks move in the warm air.
　　Please nurture the hungry silkworms,
　　And offer their silk at the ancestral shrine.[46]

In 862, on the fourteenth day of the fourth month, Michizane took his entrance examination, which was given at the Ministry of Ceremonial. He was required to compose "six eulogies (*san*) for contemporary auspicious events." The "eulogy," written in four-character rhyming lines, was a Chinese literary form commonly used in examinations during the T'ang dynasty. Michizane's eulogies praised various natural phenomena that were taken as auspicious signs in accordance with the Chinese concept that the natural world reflected the political order. The first extolled the wonder of a purple cloud that had appeared over Mino province:

　　Deep its purple hue,
　　The merit-seeking cloud.
　　It dots the sky a moment
　　In respect for imperial virtue.[47]

The other eulogies similarly praised such things as a white dove, a white sparrow, and a white swallow. After the far more elaborate and challenging poems his father had assigned him, this examination would not seem to have been very difficult. A little over a month after he took it, he was officially accepted as a student of literature at the university. He was eighteen at the time, and later, traditional histories would claim he was the youngest man admitted to the literature course. At least two other contemporaries, however, gained admission at the same age, so Michizane's youth was not unique. Still, he had skipped the stage of provisional student and was as young as anyone who had been matriculated in the university. Most men entered the literature program in their twenties, and, as noted, a few were much older.[48] Michizane's student years had begun on an auspicious note.

As a student at the government university, Michizane found himself on the fringes of officialdom and was soon invited to participate in a ceremony at the palace on the ninth day of the ninth month. There he joined with other literary men in composing a poem on a theme ostensibly selected by the thirteen-year-old Emperor Seiwa: "The Wild Geese Visit." This was the first of many occasions throughout his career when he would be summoned to offer formal poems as part of palace rituals. Many of the rituals, including the celebration of the ninth day of the ninth month, had been borrowed from Chinese custom, and by making them occasions for the composition of Chinese poetry at court, the Japanese were symbolically reaffirming their commitment to the Confucian principles underlying the *ritsuryō* system. Following Saga's death in 842, the court's interest in literary gatherings waned; and they continued in a merely perfunctory manner. But, just as Michizane entered the university, the regent Yoshifusa showed a brief interest in reviving them.[49] Students of literature, despite their low official status, were frequently called upon to compose *kanshi* at such rituals. This was a singular honor, for otherwise only men of high rank participated. Thus, even though he did not yet hold rank as other students did, Michizane now had formal standing at court.[50]

His new status also allowed Michizane to take part in the university's biannual Memorial Rites to Confucius (Sekiten), in which he was also to continue to participate throughout the rest of his career. This was one of the most purely Chinese of court rituals, which even involved animal sacrifices. It retained its austere Confucian tone far more faithfully than other court ceremonies, which had a tendency to emphasize aesthetic pleasures more than moral rectitude. The memorial rites were followed by a lecture on a specified classical text and composition of poems on that text. The first time Michizane attended, the lecture was on the *Li-chi* (Book of rites), and afterwards he wrote

The rites are over; once again the *Rites*.
Majestic ceremonies have been twice performed.
These edifices here since ancient times,
Their colors glisten, the feeling is fresh.
As the lamb on bended knees reveres his mother,
As the geese in flight follow their elder brothers,
So to Confucius, lofty and virtuous,
We raise our eyes and strive to raise ourselves. [51]

Unfortunately, details of Michizane's life as a student are scattered and not always clear. Customarily, university students received free room and board at special dormitories, some run by the government, others by private families. One of the government dormitories for students of literature was said to have been founded by Michizane's grandfather, Kiyokimi. When he became a professor himself, Michizane wrote a poem encouraging a student—apparently not a very diligent one—to live in that dormitory and devote more time to his studies. [52] Probably, at some point during his student days, Michizane too resided there himself, although he did not mention this fact in his writings.

The precise content of Michizane's studies also is not easily discerned. As noted, the curriculum for the literature course was not explicitly prescribed, and Michizane never mentioned either studying or later teaching any distinctly literary works. His many learned allusions to Chinese literature, however, prove that he indeed studied the subject. Michizane did refer to lectures on Chinese history and classics. The former had been incorporated into the literature curriculum, and the latter was to some degree a required subject for any educated man. One of Michizane's teachers was his own father, then professor of literature. In 864, Koreyoshi completed a seven-year series of lectures on the *History of the Later Han Dynasty,* and afterwards a group of his students, including Michizane, gathered for a commemorative banquet. Each celebrated the event with a poem on a figure from the work they had just finished studying. Michizane was assigned Huang Hsien, a famed scholar who, unable to find employment at court, retired and devoted himself to occult practices. Every line but the first of Michizane's eight-line poem managed to include a phrase borrowed from the biography of

Huang Hsien in the *History of the Later Han Dynasty*. Michizane also wrote an introductory essay briefly surveying China's history and historiography through the Later Han, and praising Koreyoshi's lectures. Later, as a graduate student, Michizane would compose a poem at a similar banquet, this time observing the completion of a reading of the *Analects*.[53]

Significantly, whereas Koreyoshi had "lectured" on the *History of the Later Han*, the *Analects* was merely "read." The use of these terms, "lecture" (*kō*) and "read" (*toku*), seems to refer to the teaching method specified in the Taihō Codes, which stated that students first were to be taught how to "read" a text by a professor of phonetics and then to be "lectured" on its contents by a professor of classics.[54] The *Analects* was read by a certain Wang Tu, whose name indicates he was not a Japanese but rather an immigrant—or descendant of one—and therefore qualified to teach authentic Chinese pronunciation. That he had not adopted a Japanese name suggests that he was a recent arrival to Japan. Even if his family had come some generations earlier, he may still have spoken Chinese, for immigrant communities near the capital seem to have continued using their ancestral language.[55] Probably he taught the correct Chinese reading for the *Analects,* and a native Japanese professor then lectured on its meaning as Koreyoshi had lectured on the *History of the Later Han*.

If these conjectures are correct, two conclusions can be drawn. First, in the mid-ninth century, the university was still using the same basic teaching method that had been officially authorized over a century and a half earlier, and thus the Japanese were remarkably faithful to the letter of the ancient codes well into the early Heian period. Second, Michizane had the opportunity to study Chinese as Chinese, not simply as a form of writing to be converted into Japanese before being understood. Already in Michizane's day, Chinese texts customarily were read by transposing them into Japanese; however, Michizane apparently learned both to read and to write directly in Chinese, a skill that contributed to his growing ability as a poet in the language. Michizane would later note that a number of his poems were composed hurriedly with no time to "add punctuation." This punctuation was presumably an aid to reading the poems in Japanese, and Michizane had no need of such aids. At the same time, Michizane's making special note of the omission of punctuation suggests that its use was customary.[56]

These two points regarding the university's teaching methods and Michizane's knowledge of Chinese could be made with more assurance if we had better information about Wang Tu's identity, but unfortunately data are scanty. We know neither his nationality (he might have been Korean) nor his status at court (he is never referred to as a professor of phonetics). Whoever he was, whatever his official position, he must have been a close friend of Michizane's, for otherwise Michizane could hardly have offered him a poetic caricature such as:

> Seeing Wang Tu Play *Go* and Presented to Him
> A life or death struggle over the Way!
> Instead of talking with your moves, you talk with your mouths:
> After time and again shamelessly taunting each other,
> In a fury, you shout, "Chi-hsin's my relative!"[57]

In a note, Michizane explained that Wang Chi-hsin of the T'ang was well known for his *Classic of Go* (*Wu-ching*).

Almost twenty years later, when he was passing through Kaya, a post station on the Yodo River south of the capital, Michizane lamented:

> When I Reached the Post Station at Kaya,
> I Was Moved to Tears
> Last year my old friend, His Excellency Wang,
> in the post house tower gripped my hand, wept when we parted.
> Arriving, I inquire of the official in charge;
> "Some time ago," he answers, "—that little grave there."[58]

Kaya was both the site of a detached palace famed for its beauty, and a major port. Wang Tu might have spent his last years there serving as an interpreter. One would like to imagine that shortly before his death, he had been pleasantly surprised by the visit of a former student from the capital. Unfortunately, there is no way of confirming that the impatient *go* player who had taught the young Michizane was indeed the same individual who was buried at Kaya many years later after one last meeting.

Michizane's studies proceeded smoothly, and on the seventh day of the first month, 867, at the age of twenty-three, he was named a graduate student of literature.[59] Graduate students were selected on the basis of their ability as judged by their professors rather than by an examination. For example, years later as a professor, Michizane would recommend one of his best students:

> Student of Literature, Junior Eighth Rank Lower, Ki no Haseo
> Report: This student's desire to emulate Yen Hui [Confucius's most able disciple] never ceases. His health too is admirable. Truly he deserves to be selected as a graduate student and appointed according to the usual procedures.
> The eighth year of Gangyō [884], eleventh month, twentieth day.
> Junior Fifth Rank Upper, Junior Assistant Minister of Ceremonial and Professor of Literature, Sugawara no Michizane[60]

Michizane himself was named a graduate student only a month before his father stepped down from his long tenure as professor of literature. At the time, there was no other professor of literature, and thus Michizane must have been selected as a graduate student in one of his father's last acts as professor.[61] Although he would prove himself worthy of his father's recommendation, in this instance, suspicions of favoritism cannot be easily dismissed.

Almost two months after becoming a graduate student, Michizane was awarded the senior sixth rank lower and an absentee appointment as supernumerary junior secretary of Shimotsuke. These were typical rank and office for a ninth-century Japanese graduate student. His rank was awarded on the basis of hereditary privilege that accrued from his grandfather's high position, and the income from the nominal provincial office was intended as a form of stipend.[62]

Originally, graduate students had been able university students who were awarded special financial support, but by Michizane's day, they had come to be regarded more specifically as promising young men who were preparing for the civil service examinations. Because the examinations were difficult, as a graduate student Michizane again found his time taken up by study, as had been the case when he was preparing himself for admission to the university. Later he would recall:

> In my youth I was a graduate student
> And the days passed by too quickly.

I ceased exchanging pleasantries with friends;
I had no more time for intimacy with my wife and children. [63]

To facilitate his studies, his father Koreyoshi gave him a room in the family mansion that was already in use as a classroom for private students or perhaps as a library. "This room is famous as a place of learning. Make it your home as long as you are a scholar," Michizane afterwards remembered his father as saying. [64] Following his father's counsel, Michizane moved in with his books and furnishings.

Details of Michizane's graduate studies are no clearer than those of his earlier education; however, a deceptively commonplace poem reveals his growing erudition:

Rejoicing over the Rain
To spread its name, it moistens a thousand leagues.
Proclaiming beneficence, it comes forth from the heavens.
Plentiful rain, such a blessing!
Black clouds forming magnificent peaks!
They foretell abundant crops
And presage happiness in the villages.
Auspicious times result from virtuous administration;
Ample rain encourages agriculture.
A timely shower fills even the smallest space.
All encompassing, it flows everywhere.
Long lasting, it means a bountiful harvest.
Empty skies are not desired.
Eventually we should hear the copper phoenix.[a]
Who needs to worship the clay dragon?[b]
The old farmer has returned home
To relax, blessed with prosperous times. [65]

Notes:
a. A copper phoenix atop a palace in the T'ang capital was said to cry out on the occasion of a good harvest.
b. A clay dragon was worshiped to bring rain.

The poem seems conventional enough, but a note to it explained that each line employed the name of a good minister from the Han dynasty. For example, the character in the first line translated as "to spread" is also the given name of Chu Po, an important official from the last years of the Former Han. Also, the poem had a specified length and rhyme. Although the exact circumstances of its composition were not stated, perhaps it was an exercise in composition that a professor had assigned.

Michizane's student days were not without distractions, despite his claims of having had no leisure and demonstrations of academic effort such as the above poem. Occasionally his friends would gather to relax and enjoy the quiet delights of wine and poetry:

> Spending the Day Reciting Poetry in my Study
> Why waste such a splendid day
> When good friends have come to visit!
> In this fine new room,
> Let us recall the sages of old in their bamboo grove.
> A few cups will intoxicate us
> And quietly we can exchange friendly verses.
> Time, easily lost, is impossible to regain.
> Alas, I see night is about to fall.

In 866, about the time this poem was written, complaints against drunken, disorderly officials had resulted in a prohibition against drinking, complete with stern punishments for those who disobeyed. But there were exceptions. Wine was allowed for ritual and medicinal purposes, and among small groups of friends—provided permission was obtained in advance. Michizane had made the new law an excuse for gathering a few of his like-minded friends, among them his former tutor Tadaomi, for an evening of wine and poetry. Later in life, Michizane would lament that wine brought him no pleasure, but in his youth it had the desired effect that Chinese poets had often sought.[67]

In addition to enjoying the pleasures of wine and poetry, Michizane cultivated a taste for arts other than literature. On occasion he was privileged to enjoy visits to the imperial park, the Shinsen'en, where the famous painter Kose no Kanaoka (active late ninth century) served as superintendent. Michizane so delighted in the park—and in Kanaoka's skill as a painter—that he wrote:

> To Mister Kose, Requesting a Painting
> Generously you let me visit the forbidden imperial precincts,
> But I fear the scene will not last long.

No one yet has been able to carry away mountains and streams,
So I beg you paint me a likeness of their elegance.[68]

All of Kanaoka's works are now lost, but a group of poems
Michizane composed almost two decades later to accompany
five of them gives us some idea of what his paintings must have
been like, for example:

Thanking a Taoist for the Wine of Longevity
Gazing at the cup, I wonder for how many springs will it preserve me
And hope that I too may live to have your frosted beard and side
  locks.
Rather than debate immortality with the sorcerers,
The sage Ma Ku[a] needs only to thank the inhabitants of Drunken
  Village.[69]

Note:
a. Ma Ku was a Later Han woman immortal.

This and the other poems Michizane wrote indicate that Kanaoka's paintings were very Chinese, at least in subject matter,
and thus through Michizane's writings we can obtain a precious
glimpse of art now lost.

According to tradition, Michizane was more than a connois-
seur of the arts; he was a master of many, including painting
and sculpture. In particular his genius as a calligrapher became
legendary. Unfortunately, no reliable evidence survives to show
that he excelled at any art other than poetry. To be sure, as an
educated man he must have possessed some skill with the brush,
but when his contemporaries listed the great calligraphers of the
day, his name was not among them. During the later Heian
period when genuine examples of his handwriting were extant,
they were prized less for their aesthetic merit than because
Michizane already had been deified. Today, experts agree that
none of the samples of calligraphy long attributed to him is
authentic.[70] Michizane's fame as a calligrapher was largely the
product of the Edo period. And whatever his ability at other
arts, music definitely was not Michizane's forte, as he noted
when a graduate student:

I Cease Practicing the Koto
I believed in the koto and brush as aids to the scholar
And even now my seven-stringed koto rests under my window.

In vain I concentrate; uselessly I study the score.
My technique is clumsy, I ask my teacher for help.
My "Deep Valley" sounds nothing like an autumnal stream.
My "Cold Crow" lacks the plaint of a bird's night cry.
All the musicians say I am wasting my time.
Much better our family's traditional art—the writing of poems! [71]

Eventually, in 870, on the twenty-third day of the third month, Michizane took his civil service examination at the age of twenty-six. Michizane had been among the youngest of university entrants, and he was also one of the youngest examination candidates. His father and grandfather did not take their examinations until they were twenty-eight and twenty-nine years old respectively. Michizane's student, Ki no Haseo (845–912), whose recommendation was quoted above, did not pass his until he was thirty-nine. Michizane had been a graduate student four years, and only one individual in the ninth century is known to have passed his examination after fewer years of graduate study. That was Haruzumi no Yoshitada, who may not have been a student many years but was already thirty-four when he took the examination. [72]

Michizane's examiner was the lesser private secretary (*shōnaiki*), Miyako no Yoshika (834–879), another representative early Heian scholar and official. Yoshika's family background was hardly eminent, although his uncle had served as professor of literature from 821 to 829 and was the man who had insisted that university admission not be restricted to the aristocracy. Perhaps this uncle had been able to help in Yoshika's early training and career. Yoshika passed his civil service examination and spent most of his relatively short career as a private secretary, a post requiring considerable literary skill because it involved drafting documents for the emperor. [73] In 875, he became professor of literature and helped compile the *Montoku jitsuroku* with Koreyoshi. It was not uncommon for private secretaries to administer civil service examinations, and Yoshika was well qualified to do so. In fact, he gave four civil service examinations along with a number of university entrance examinations. [74]

A famous story relates that Michizane visited Yoshika's mansion shortly before taking his examination. A group of Yoshika's students were practicing archery, and Yoshika invited Michizane to demonstrate his skill. All thought that Michizane, a bookish young man, would be a poor shot, but to their surprise

3. *Requesting a painting from Kose no Kanaoka*
Source: Sugawara jikki.

his two arrows were both right on target. Yoshika was impressed and said, "This is a portent that you will hit the mark on your examination."[75] Most modern scholars are inclined to agree with those who did not expect Michizane to be a good archer. This story does appear in a generally reliable biography of Michizane written only about fifty years after his death. However, even that earliest biography does contain a few questionable anecdotes, and that of Michizane's prowess as an archer is one example. The story probably originated among literary men who borrowed words from one of Michizane's later poems, translated in chapter seven (p. 299), and from them invented Yoshika's clever remark referring to the examination in vocabulary suggestive of archery. In medieval times when the military enjoyed greater prestige, admirers of Michizane amplified the story in an attempt to demonstrate that he excelled in the martial arts as well as the literary ones.[76] The anecdote became a part of the Michizane legend along with the stories of his great love for the plum blossoms and skill as a calligrapher. Those legends, however, could well have been exaggerations of fact. This one surely was pure fiction.

Another story concerning Michizane's examination appears in the *Gōdanshō* (Selections from Ōe's talks), an early twelfth-century collection of anecdotes related by the scholar Ōe no Masafusa (1041–1111). According to Masafusa, when Michizane was taking his examination, he could not bear being confined in the examination room and stepped out to stretch his legs by the gate. There he happened to meet Tachibana no Hiromi (837–890), one of Koreyoshi's former students who until recently had been serving as professor of literature. They spoke and Michizane confessed that he did not understand one point on the examination. Hiromi then mounted his horse and rode off to consult the Saga Hermit. The story ends with its teller admitting uncertainty about the hermit's identity. Although the story may not be totally implausible, it, too, is generally dismissed by modern scholars. Many stories in the *Gōdanshō* are more entertaining than factual, and the appearance of a mysterious recluse in this one does not add to its narrator's credibility.[77]

Contrary to legend, the circumstances of Michizane's examination were neither remarkable nor suspicious. For his first essay, Yoshika asked him to "Elucidate Surnames," a problem in Chinese history. The question began, "Bestowing surnames and dividing them into categories is a method of leading the common people," and proceeded to point out that in ancient China surnames and offices were created to bring order to society, but as generations passed people increased in number and confusion ensued. It then gave a series of obscure and perplexing examples of what, in fact, were peoples' names for Michizane to identify. Michizane's answer first explained the evolution of Chinese surnames. Originally the government had maintained an office to regulate them and thereby preserve the moral order of society. Under the Ch'in (221–206 B.C.), however, this order broke down. Subsequent dynasties attempted to revive the regulation of surnames but to little avail as surnames lost their significance. Michizane then defined the term "surname" and noted that most surnames were taken from such things as offices, occupations, and place names. Finally, he identified the various individuals to whom Yoshika had alluded.

In his second essay, Michizane was to "Analyze Earthquakes." Yoshika asked why the normally still earth moved, how the Chinese explained this phenomenon, and how the Buddhists in India explained it. The issues were not scientific but philosophical. Michizane first presented the Confucian view that earthquakes occurred when the emperor's virtue was inadequate and the government was in disorder. He clarified the allusions in the questions and added a Taoist interpretation of earthquakes. Then he discussed Buddhism, first asserting that both Lao-Tzu and Confucius had acknowledged the Buddha's teachings. For a Buddhist analysis of earthquakes, he referred to the *Nembutsu sammai kyō* (Contemplating the Buddha's name sutra) and the *Daichi doron* (Great wisdom śastra). Modestly, he concluded his examination essays:

> I, Michizane, gaze in awe towards the Yangtze and Han rivers, but am ashamed of my inability to span the broad ocean. I wish to master the art of clear expression but get lost on the path amidst the clouds. How can I deal with the dark mysteries or discuss what is beyond my sight and hearing? I have not the leisure to visit the land of the Duke of Chou and Confucius, or let my spirit wander with Chuang-tzu or the Buddha. Unable to solve all the difficulties, I cannot avoid error. [78]

4. Examinee Michizane's skill at archery
Source: Sugawara jikki.

A humble disclaimer was the conventional conclusion to examination papers, but at least in Michizane's case, a modern reader might think it unnecessary. The range of knowledge Michizane displayed was awesome, covering China's history, its philosophical traditions, both Confucian and Taoist, and even Buddhism. Although the university was generally considered a center of Confucian orthodoxy, the examination covered the various major intellectual traditions that the Japanese had assimilated from the Asian continent. Moreover, both the examination questions and the answers were written in a most learned and recondite style of classical Chinese. Even with the aid of the best modern reference works, they all but defy full comprehension. One can well imagine that Michizane just might have felt the need of aid from a hermit sage. His performance on the examination certainly seems very impressive.

Yoshika, however, was not particularly impressed. When he completed his grading almost two months after Michizane had taken the examination, he noted that some of the obscure names in the first essay were not quite properly identified, and in the second essay the Buddhist sources were not cited with sufficient precision. Moreover, he pointed out a few characters that he believed had been incorrectly used. The objections seem minor, but Yoshika concluded:

> Although there are many errors and grammatical solecisms, still, the prose style is noteworthy. The prose and reasoning are barely passable according to the terms of the codes, and thus I pass the candidate with a grade of "D." [79]

The *ritsuryō* codes had specified four passing grades to be determined on the basis of both prose style and reasoning. If style and reasoning were superior, an "A" was awarded; if one was superior and the other was average, a "B"; if both were average, a "C"; and, as Yoshika observed, if both were barely passable, the lowest passing grade of "D" was given. Michizane would later propose clarification of this grading system. It is interesting to note that the standards for grading gave equal weight to the candidate's literary style and his reasoning. In fact, style was perhaps of greater importance because a candidate whose logic was deficient but style excellent could be specially recommended for appointment.[80] This was not simply a case of rampant aestheticism. Certain official documents were customarily drafted in an elevated style of classical Chinese, and such documents were often included in literary anthologies, in keeping with Chinese precedent. The Chinese-style bureaucracy required men skilled in the art of composing in the Chinese language, and therefore Yoshika was not damning Michizane with faint praise when he took special note of Michizane's superior prose style.

Michizane's poor grade was not a reflection of his ability but of contemporary grading practices. Yoshika awarded the same grade to all the candidates he examined. One, Fujiwara no Sukeyo (d. 897), a student of Koreyoshi's, was only passed with the usual grade of "D" after Yoshika had been forced to reconsider.[81] Moreover, Yoshika was not a uniquely strict grader. Michizane's grandfather had similarly passed only after an initial failing grade was revised, and his father too had received a "D." In fact, apparently everyone who passed the examinations in the ninth century was given a "D," and thus Michizane had no need to feel ashamed of his poor performance. Rather, he should have been satisfied that he had passed. The examinations were not yet an empty ritual and not all failing candidates had their grades revised.[82]

Nonetheless, when he received a congratulatory poem from his Chinese teacher Wang Tu, he replied:

In good times, passing the examination makes one's name.
Treading in my father's footsteps, I will not break with tradition.
Fortunately, I do not return home a failure to become a frustrated old man.
Unexpectedly, I am ranked among the clouds in the blue sky.
Your congratulatory note deeply touches me,
But I wipe my eyes when with dismay I look at the criticism of my essays.
Do not say I have succeeded and shall receive noble office.
I must apologize to my father for breaking off only a worm-eaten branch of the cassia.[83]

The last line is a reference to the same cassia tree on the moon to which his mother had alluded when he celebrated his coming of age more than ten years earlier. Michizane concluded with a note explaining that his last line referred to the sharp criticism his examination essays had received. Under the circumstances, etiquette surely demanded a certain amount of demurral, but Michizane's concern over Yoshika's criticism may have been more than mere polite modesty. Michizane would always be very sensitive to criticism, which he usually regarded as unjustified.

Regardless of his grade, passing the examination was a vitally important achievement for the youthful Michizane. Time after time he mentioned the fact that both his father and grandfather had been scholars; clearly he felt obliged to maintain this tradition, all the more so because his brothers had died and there was no one else to do so. In addition, he must have known that men with scholarly backgrounds who did not pass the examinations had little chance of noteworthy careers at court, his uncle Yoshinushi or his teacher and friend Tadaomi being all too familiar examples. Success may not have guaranteed that he would rise to high office as his father and grandfather had done, but it did make him eligible for the more honorable posts to which a literary man could aspire, including those at the university, which already were being regarded as part of the family tradition.

3 · Bureaucrat and Educator

As a student at the court university, Michizane had found himself on the fringes of officialdom. Only after he had passed his civil service examination in 870 was he ready to take on a regular post in the government. The court bureaucracy, however, moved slowly and he did not receive his first appointment until the following year. So began the first stage in Michizane's official career. It lasted until he was named a provincial governor in 886. The period might be further subdivided into two phases. Before 877, Michizane's career roughly paralleled that of many officials with scholarly backgrounds who did not hold academic posts: his offices were not distinguished. He did hold one that called upon his literary abilities, but he also served in other routine administrative positions. Then, in 877, he was named to two posts, one within the university, the other closely related to it. He thereby obtained two of the choicer plums the court had to offer a scholar. Although throughout this stage in his career Michizane's offices were of only moderate importance compared to those he would later hold, after 877 he gradually consolidated a position as the most influential scholar at court.

Today, surviving sources do not allow one to paint a detailed picture of the public life and official responsibilities of a ninth-century Japanese bureaucrat. Court records and early biographies tell us what posts Michizane held, but we know little about his regular duties. In a few of his poems and other writings,

113

however, Michizane does offer glimpses of himself at work. He shows us a man conscientious in performing his duties and concerned about his professional advancement. Also, when special problems arose at court, he occasionally was called upon to present statements expressing his views, and some of these documents are preserved in court chronicles. Thus, we do have some knowledge of Michizane's official activities.

Michizane's poetry offers a slightly clearer view of his private life and individual temperament, of his likes and dislikes. Some of what we find is attractive: visits to a suburban villa, for example. Some is deeply touching, such as his sad memories of a son who passed away in childhood. In other places he reveals himself to be less saintly, but at the same time more human, than legend would have one believe. From this period we begin to recognize something of Michizane's distinctive personality.

YOUNG BUREAUCRAT

On the eleventh day of the ninth month, 870, six months after Michizane had taken his examination, his name first appears in Japan's official chronicles:

> The graduate student of literature, senior sixth rank lower, Sugawara no Michizane, was promoted one grade because he passed the civil service examination with a "D." According to regulation, he ought to have been advanced three grades; however, because his original rank was the senior sixth lower, he was only promoted one grade.[1]

The regulation mentioned had been issued in 802 and was one of a series of revisions in the system of awarding rank.[2] It was aimed at encouraging study by favoring successful examinees.

The original codes had prescribed four passing grades but had specified that rank was to be awarded only to those with the two highest grades. The regulation of 802 noted that in China those with lower passing grades were awarded rank too and stipulated that the same practice should also be followed in Japan. The rank for those who received a "D" was to be the senior initial lower, the third lowest rank in the system. The regulation further stated that a successful candidate who already held rank and passed with a "D" would be promoted three grades. That was, in fact, how Koreyoshi and others were treated. Michizane, however, had already attained a relatively high rank through hereditary privilege and promotions. Had he been further advanced the full three grades, he would have received the junior fifth rank lower, and hence aristocratic status. By special edict, sons of the most powerful Fujiwara leaders occasionally attained the fifth rank while still in their teens, but custom did not allow successful examination candidates to be awarded so high a rank, and thus Michizane did not receive the full reward he had earned through the examination.[3]

Michizane had to serve for three years as a minor official before he was finally granted the junior fifth rank lower at the age of thirty. If he had formally joined the ranks of the aristocracy later than did some members of the Fujiwara family, still he was younger than most of his scholarly colleagues, who were generally in their forties when they were promoted to the fifth rank.[4] Michizane's relatively rapid advance in rank reflects the new status of the Sugawara family. Because he came from a family of influential scholars, Michizane enjoyed the advantages of a superior education and relatively high hereditary rank. However, even the most influential scholars were not so powerful as scions of Fujiwara ministers, and so, compared to them, Michizane found that his promotions came slowly.

In terms of his initial appointment, too, Michizane's official career began unspectacularly. After he had passed his examination and been promoted one grade, he was not immediately assigned a new office; he still held only the nominal provincial post he had been granted as a graduate student. Nonetheless, in 870 Michizane expressed new optimism in a poem he sent to Tadaomi, his former tutor who was then serving as lieutenant governor of Inaba:

> Thoughts on the Occasion of the Winter Solstice
> Who would be ashamed of the simple shoes and stockings, the
>   customary ritual offerings?
> Thousands of households celebrate that now the days will grow
>   longer.
> But no sign of mild weather has yet appeared;
> We still lament the long nights when we awaken from cold dreams.
> Since the spring, I have been called "the former graduate student."
> With the coming of the new year, I hope to be known as "the
>   previous provincial secretary."

Today's ceremony is not yet that for the new year.
I look forward to hearing from you again before then.

Michizane concluded with a note explaining that his term
as supernumerary provincial secretary would be over at the end
of the year. He went on:

The duties of a Confucian scholar are to conduct the rites and study
the classics. Because I have done both, I write the above couplets. [5]

Michizane's optimism proved justified. When new appointments were announced in the first month of 871, the year after
he took his examination, he was named assistant director of the
Bureau of Buddhism and Aliens (*gemba no suke*). This was an
office of the Ministry of Civil Affairs (Jibushō) responsible for
keeping registers of monasteries, monks, and nuns, as well as receiving foreign envoys. [6] Michizane would, in fact, later help
greet three missions from the Manchurian kingdom of Parhae;
however, he did not long serve in the bureau charged with greeting such foreign guests. Just one month after that initial appointment, he was named lesser private secretary, the same post still
held by his examiner, Yoshika. At the age of twenty-seven,
Michizane not only held the same office as Yoshika but also
equaled him in rank, even though Yoshika was eleven years his
senior.

Private secretaries worked in the Ministry of Central Affairs,
where their principal duty was the drafting of imperial documents. Because it was in charge of matters pertaining to the imperial household, Central Affairs was considered the most exalted
of ministries. Its superior status was indicated by the fact that
its officials held higher rank than comparable officials in other
ministries, and, if Michizane and Yoshika's cases are typical,
their actual ranks may even have been higher than those prescribed in the codes. The post of lesser private secretary was
supposed to be held by an official of the senior seventh rank
upper. When Michizane and Yoshika held that office, their
ranks were four grades higher. [7] Michizane remained in this honorable if not outstanding post for three years, from 871 to 874.

Regular promotions were announced in the early days of
each new year, and, in the first month of 874, both Michizane

and his father were among those rewarded. Koreyoshi was advanced to the senior fourth rank; Michizane received his key promotion to the fifth rank. As a result, Michizane was eligible for higher office when a list of appointments was issued eight days later, and indeed he was named junior assistant minister of war. Junior assistant ministers were more important than their title might suggest. In theory, they were the third-ranking official in a ministry. In most ministries, however, the actual ministers were aristocrats of the most noble birth, often members of the imperial family. Such men received honor and income, but probably did not take an active part in running their ministries. The assistant ministers, on the other hand, were usually men of more modest birth who were selected for their practical abilities and who were actually in charge. In practice, therefore, the junior assistant minister was the second-ranking official. Moreover, although a post in the Ministry of War may appear to have been a sinecure because Heian Japan showed little enthusiasm for armed combat, still, noble courtiers delighted in decorating their names with the military titles bestowed as honors by that ministry.[8] Battle may not have appealed to peace-loving aristocrats, but official titles certainly did. As junior assistant minister of war, Michizane's military responsibilities would not have been onerous, but he could have found himself in the politically delicate position of helping to determine who would be awarded military titles.

Michizane did not remain long in the Ministry of War, however, for just one month after being appointed to it, he was transferred to the Ministry of Popular Affairs (Mimbushō), again as junior assistant minister. He remained in his new post for three years. In one sense, this may have been a demotion, for in his new assignment he was no longer the de facto second-ranking official. Popular Affairs was the exception to the rule that ministries were headed by men selected principally for their nobility. Central Affairs may have been the most honored ministry because of its close ties to the imperial family, but Popular Affairs was economically the most important because it controlled the budget, taxes, transportation, and the census. Such essential matters were not entrusted to a noble figurehead. The minister of popular affairs often was the only minister who was actually an experienced bureaucrat, and usually he also held a concurrent position on the Council of State. For example, at the time of Michizane's appointment, the minister of popular affairs was Minabuchi no Toshina (807–877), a scholarly friend of Koreyoshi's who was also a middle counselor. The next year he was replaced by Fujiwara no Fuyuo (808–887), a veteran official with the concurrent post of consultant.[9]

As junior assistant minister of popular affairs, Michizane became, in fact as well as in theory, the third-ranking official, but he was now the third-ranking official in a ministry that had heavy responsibilities, not one that primarily distributed honorary titles. It was the second post that Michizane held for an extended period of time. Unlike his earlier office of private secretary, this was not one that required special literary skills, but it was a key position in a vital ministry.

After passing his examination, Michizane thus spent the six years from 871 until 877 learning the art of practical administration through service in posts that gave him valuable experience. Both of his appointments to relatively responsible positions came after serving very briefly in two distinctly less significant ones; the reason, however, for this pattern is not certain. The court may have decided to move him to offices in which his talents could be put to better use. Alternatively, to take a more cynical view, because Michizane could be a haughty and difficult young man, perhaps he was transferred to place him among individuals with whom he was on better terms. Another possibility is that his father, still active in court affairs, may have been able to arrange Michizane's assignment to the more desirable posts. However he managed to get the better posts, Michizane as a young official showed the same concern for his career advancement that he had expressed earlier as a student. It can be seen, for example, in the poem he sent to a certain "Major Secretary (Daigeki) Shimada," perhaps Tadaomi's brother Yoshiomi:

> Thoughts on Having been Appointed Junior Assistant
> Minister of Popular Affairs
> I hear the Ministry of Popular Affairs is a busy post,
> But how should an official decide whether his duties will be light or
>   heavy?
> For three years I served as private secretary,
> Then I was favored by more than a month in the Ministry of War.

> Handling documents now for the first time, I am ashamed of my
>   ignorance of government.
> For the present I must abandon the pleasures of literature.
> Your duties require your presence at high official discussions.
> Please do not fail to report on evaluations and promotions.[10]

Michizane concluded the poem with a note observing that Shimada's office required his presence when the Council of State
met to discuss the performance of officials, and Michizane was
anxious to learn how he himself was being evaluated.

In his poem, Michizane also noted that he had no time for
literature, and that seems to have been no empty claim of over-
work, for Michizane left relatively few poems from his years as
a minor bureaucrat. In one he portrayed himself as an energetic
official rushing to work at the crack of dawn:

> Morning Duty
> By candlelight, I don my official robes for morning duty.
> On the road, I ceaselessly whip my weary horse.
> Where can the beating of the morning drum be heard?
> Here, between the Ministries of Ceremonial and Central Affairs.[11]

The Ministry of Popular Affairs, where Michizane was then
assigned, was located between the ministries mentioned in the
poem, and Michizane was there at work early enough to hear
the morning drum, which was sounded at approximately 7:30.
His new responsibilities inspired Michizane to turn from literature to a scholarly project more closely related to his current
situation. Perhaps because he found that his academic training
offered inadequate preparation for his official duties, he began
to study precedents for recent events at court. He planned to
classify them into sixty categories and compile them into a
work that he tentatively entitled *The Essentials of Government*
(*Chiyō shakuen*). It was intended to be a reference for examination candidates and officials.[12] Although the project was never
completed and only a draft introduction survives, Michizane's
attempt at such an endeavor shows that he took his official
duties seriously. His Confucian training—and his personal ambitions—did not allow him to neglect government service, even
when he might have preferred to be writing poetry.

Michizane may not have had time to compose many poems

or finish his compilation of official precedents, but he drafted many documents, among them imperial edicts, petitions, and Buddhist prayers. Such documents make up the majority of prose works in Michizane's literary anthology, and almost all of them were written on behalf of others. As a private secretary, his duties included drafting edicts for the emperor, and during his years in that office he composed his first one. He would continue to draft them throughout his career at court.[13] In practice, literary men, regardless of their office, were regularly summoned to draft edicts, which were written in an elevated style requiring considerable knowledge of Chinese. This was an important duty and even minor errors could have serious consequences: Michizane's friend Hiromi—the man said to have helped him on his examination—precipitated a political crisis by his injudicious choice of a term in an edict he drafted, as will be discussed in the next chapter.

In addition to drafting edicts, Michizane also composed many petitions, often for the highest ranking officials. For example, he wrote three petitions for the grand minister (*daijō daijin*) and regent Fujiwara no Yoshifusa declining certain privileges. He wrote another for Yoshifusa's heir Mototsune declining the office of minister of the right (*udaijin*). These petitions were conventional formalities, and despite Michizane's eloquence, they were duly rejected. Michizane's popularity as a writer is indicated by the fact that twice he not only composed petitions to the emperor, but also the imperial replies. Such documents are interesting less because of their contents than because of the circumstances of their composition. The aristocrats who called upon Michizane to draft petitions and prayers lacked sufficient training in Chinese composition to do so themselves. Less clear is the reason why Michizane once drafted a petition for an assistant professor of classics.[14]

If Michizane received anything in exchange for his services as a drafter of petitions and prayers, the fact is not recorded. This does not altogether rule out the possibility that he was paid, for he virtually never discussed finances anywhere in his writings. Probably, however, he was not paid. Rather, as a court scholar, he was expected to perform such favors for high-ranking nobles whose Chinese may not have been the best but who were in a position to aid a scholar in his official career. As a professor,

Michizane would continue to draft many documents, but later when he himself became a high official he virtually ceased to do so except for members of the imperial family. By then he had more pressing duties; however, at the start of his career, composing documents was one of his major responsibilities.

Michizane's activities during his early years as a bureaucrat were not limited to his regular official duties and the drafting of documents. After Emperor Seiwa's grandmother died in 871, it was revealed that she had requested the court not to observe full mourning for her. The emperor, however, had doubts about the propriety of this, and at her funeral rites a few days later he asked court scholars to present their opinions on how the mourning ought to be observed. Together with his former examiner Yoshika, Michizane recommended, on the basis of Japanese regulations and Chinese precedents, that "truly, although grief is felt within, there is no need to wear mourning without." Five other opinions were offered, and after some discussion the court concluded that, although the emperor ought to mourn in his heart for five months, he need wear mourning dress only for three days. Eight years later, after Michizane had become a professor, a similar problem arose when a consort of Emperor Junna died after also requesting that mourning not be observed. This time, Michizane argued that her relationship with the current emperor, Yōzei (868–949, r. 877–884) was sufficiently distant that he need not mourn, although the late consort's immediate family ought to. Some objected, but her last wishes were respected as Michizane had advised.[15]

Michizane's experiences as a diplomat also began during this stage in his career. In 872 he was assigned to escort a mission that had arrived from Parhae. This would have been the beginning of his long involvement with Japan's foreign relations, another family tradition, but his mother died only eight days after he was appointed and he himself was now obliged to go into mourning. Based on Confucian models, the law stated that officials were to retire from office for a year upon the death of a parent, but the Japanese did not observe filial mourning as strictly as did the Chinese, and customarily, men were recalled to office before the year had passed. In Michizane's case, he was summoned after five month's retirement to draft an edict replying to the message from the king of Parhae.[16] In Michizane's day, diplomatic exchanges with Parhae were Japan's principal means of official contact with continental Asia and thus were highly valued. The edict sent to Parhae's king was of such importance that the court's need for Michizane's skills outweighed his personal obligation to mourn for his mother. Later, in 883 as a professor and again in 895 as a consultant, Michizane would be more directly involved in receiving embassies from Parhae.

In 876, Japan was plagued by drought, and one of Michizane's last duties as junior assistant minister of popular affairs was to pray for rain at Kehi Shrine in the town of Tsuruga, a port on the Japan Sea. Tsuruga was only about fifty miles from the capital, but the route was mountainous and the roads primitive. This arduous journey, which took more than five days, was Michizane's first extended trip away from the capital. The impression it made on him inspired his first attempt at extended poetic narrative:

> Mountain Journey on an Autumn Day
> Ever onward, through the endless mountains;
> Ever nervous, I cannot relax.
> According to the calendar, autumn nears its close;
> Since leaving home, the morning of the fifth day.
> From which valley stream do the white clouds drift upwards?
> To how many crags do crimson trees cling?
> The arrival of each chill wind
> Brings more travel anxieties.
> We spread out mats, eat our cold meal,
> And ready the vehicles at dawn by candlelight.
> Winding and steep, our road is carved into the mountains.
> High swaying bridges cross the gorges.
> In the valleys is the danger of falling rocks;
> On the peaks we almost caress the sky.
> Although physically we remain unchanged,
> We seem to have crossed into another world.
> Our weary horses cry out at wild cascades,
> And old retainers suffer on precipitous paths.
> On our way we pass a monk holding his staff.
> We meet a woodcutter and exchange greeting.
> Looking down we see a village;
> With hands raised in greeting we proceed through a bustling town.
> Houses are arranged like a thousand *go* stones,
> And a broad lake spreads out before us.
> The vines and creepers form a hermit's new robe,
> But the coin-like elm buds have disappeared.

To quench our thirst we dip into the flowing brook.
To warm ourselves we burn the fallen leaves.
The smoke-like mist saddens our hearts,
And the chilling vapors penetrate to the marrow.
I seek not the secrets of longevity
Nor do I look for the fees of new students:
To worship the gods, I press on to the shrine
And with my offerings hope to ward off disaster.
The sun's rays quickly wane
And colors fade near the end of the year.
The wind will surely blow till dawn
As the moon shines on us through the night.
I ask how much farther we have to travel
And suddenly realize our destination is still far off.[17]

Michizane may have exaggerated the danger and excitement of his journey for the sake of literary effect, but still it must have seemed a perilous trek to the young scholar from the capital. Whether or not all his vivid details were literally accurate, the sense of adventure and purpose expressed were sincerely felt. Having arrived in Tsuruga and completed his mission, Michizane had a chance to relax there. In his last poem as junior assistant minister of popular affairs, he saw the town in a new light:

Moon over the Sea
This autumn night, an ocean breeze lodges amidst reed flowers.
How can I be melancholy before this vista?
Words and laughter issue from my heart and mingle with the
    sounding waves.
I recite poems and use my finger to write them in the sand.
I slowly stroll; the low grasses are covered in the rising tide.
I sit a while; into the night sky the moon's rays sink.
If I were free to wander and could select my favorite spot,
The province of Echizen would acquire a solitary Confucian scholar.[18]

Today, an ancient plum tree survives on the grounds of Kehi Shrine. A sign by it states that Michizane brought it from his garden in the capital, and local legend elaborates by claiming that Michizane had come in 894 to pray for a safe voyage after having been named ambassador to China.[19] Michizane did visit the shrine and he was named ambassador, but the events occurred almost two decades apart. As is often the case with elements of the Tenjin legend, the story is a blend of truth and

124 · *Bureaucrat and Educator*

fabrication. In this case, however, the people of Tsuruga had little need to improve upon the facts, for, despite the arduous journey, Michizane had enjoyed his visit to their town.

EDUCATOR

On the fifteenth day of the first month, 877, Michizane was named junior assistant minister of ceremonial. Although this was not a promotion—he was still a junior assistant minister— Michizane's new post must have pleased him. The functions of the Ministry of Popular Affairs were indeed important, but a man of Michizane's background would have felt more in place at the Ministry of Ceremonial, for its responsibilities included supervising both the university and the civil service examinations, in addition to regulating court rituals and civilian bureaucratic appointments. Whereas in Popular Affairs, Michizane had been required to concern himself with unfamiliar problems of financial administration, in his new post at Ceremonial, he would look after precisely the educational and intellectual matters he knew best. His appointment came only twelve days after the accession of the young Emperor Yōzei, and in the ninth month of that year, he was assigned an important role in the Great Thanksgiving Festival (Daijōe) that commemorated the first harvest of the new reign.[20] For Michizane, this was another great honor.

In the same year, on the eighteenth day of the tenth month, Michizane received a still greater distinction. In addition to his office in the Ministry of Ceremonial, he was appointed professor of literature. Never before had three generations of the same family served as professors, and Michizane was justly proud of having successfully maintained his family tradition.[21] In 879, he continued a series of lectures on the *History of the Later Han* that had been begun by his predecessor, and after one of his lectures, he sent a poem to his students. Although he claimed it was written in jest, the pride expressed was very real:

Lonely, like Cheng I-en, I have no brothers.[a]
When I passed my examinations, I was too busy studying to admire
  my garden.
I was drawn to literature by family tradition.
My post in Ceremonial too is a reward for ancestral accomplishments.

Students, I warn you: Do not bring shame on your families!
Abandon your life to the struggle for an honorable position!
My son at age four is beginning to read
And perhaps will pass my offices on to future generations.

Note:
a. Cheng I-en was an only child whose name appears in the *History of the Later Han.*

After line four, Michizane inserted a note:

One cannot become professor of literature without talent nor be appointed junior assistant minister of ceremonial without ability. For three generations, starting with my grandfather, we have held these two offices without losing them and thus I express my thanks.[22]

Upon his appointment as a professor at the age of thirty-three, Michizane had achieved one of his great ambitions. A few years later, his young son was showing promise of being able to continue the remarkable academic success of the Sugawara family for yet another generation. When Michizane became professor, Koreyoshi was serving on the Council of State as a consultant and may have been able to aid in his son's professional advance. As long as Michizane stayed within the realm of scholarship, he would benefit from the reputation established by his father and grandfather, but his own qualifications for his new office cannot be denied. As a youth he had shown himself to be a precocious student and poet who had completed his formal higher education with uncommon speed. Moreover, already when he was a private secretary, he had lectured on the *History of the Former Han,*[23] perhaps to his father's students, and he had accumulated six years of practical experience in the court bureaucracy. Michizane had the necessary combination of academic skills and good connections.

A new phase in Michizane's official career thus began in 877 when he was appointed to the concurrent offices of junior assistant minister of ceremonial and professor of literature, posts he was to hold until 886 when he left the capital to serve as a provincial governor. In addition to his two offices at court, Michizane was rewarded in 883 with an absentee appointment as supernumerary governor of Kaga province, the modern Ishikawa prefecture to the north of Kyoto:

My family is known for its humble tradition of scholarship,
But my father's greatest joy was an appointment to this province.[a]
Because of its monthly tribute, we were able to eat our fill.
Although he is now departed, I still appreciate his goodness.
I too need not suffer on the northern road through the lingering
   snow,
But simply wait for autumn with its bountiful harvest.
How proud I am that at my waist I wear the symbols of three offices!
This spring, imperial beneficence is overflowing.[24]

Note:
a. During Michizane's childhood Koreyoshi had served as supernumerary governor of Kaga from 850 until approximately 854.

This poem is of interest because it is a rare instance of Michizane's mentioning a source of his income and also because it
clearly shows how one courtier viewed his absentee provincial
offices. His attitude may seem at best cynical to a modern reader, for today the custom of granting absentee appointments is
regarded as an abuse that contributed to the breakdown of provincial administration under the *ritsuryō* system. The pride
Michizane expressed, however, demonstrates that Heian courtiers considered their absentee appointments to be fully legitimate sources of extra income. On the basis of this poem,
Michizane might be accused of boasting, but at least in the eyes
of his contemporaries, he would not have been guilty of harbor-
ing a corrupt or dishonest view of his official responsibilities as
supernumerary governor.

During his years as professor, Michizane became the most influential scholar at court. He held key posts in the university
and the Ministry of Ceremonial. In addition, after the death of
his father in 880, he assumed control of the private school that
had been begun by his grandfather at the family mansion.
Under Michizane's leadership, it became an important institution that prepared many young men for admission to the
university.

The Sugawara were but one of various families that had
established private educational institutions during the ninth century. Most were created specifically for the relatives of their
founders. The best known example is the Fujiwara's Kangakuin
(Institute for the Encouragement of Learning), which served
two functions. In part it was a private dormitory for university

students from the Fujiwara family. In that respect it was similar to the university's Monjōin, the official dormitory for literature students said to have been founded by Michizane's grandfather. By Michizane's day, the Monjōin had come to be split into two divisions, one supervised by the Sugawara, the other by the Ōe family. All students of literature were expected to affiliate with one or the other division. Despite its ties with the Sugawara and Ōe families, however, the Monjōin remained essentially a public institution. In contrast, the Kangakuin was a strictly private preserve of the Fujiwara.

In addition to being a dormitory for university students, the Kangakuin also provided elementary education for Fujiwara children. Lectures for university students were also held there. It was well endowed with financial support, although not necessarily with academic talent. The Fujiwara family was sufficiently concerned with the education of its youth to create this institution, but the family's status was not dependent on its member's intellectual abilities. Although they already dominated much of the bureaucracy, few Fujiwara held official posts in the university during the ninth century, and those who did were from the politically less influential branches of the family. [25]

The Sugawara school was distinctly different from its Fujiwara counterpart. The contrast began with its informal name, Kanke Rōka, which meant, simply, "Sugawara Family Hallway." The name reflected yet another difference. Whereas the Kangakuin had its own elaborate buildings adjacent to the university, students of the Kanke Rōka met, as the school's name suggests, in a crowded hallway leading to Michizane's private study. Although it lacked the trappings of the Fujiwara institution, the Sugawara school was the most successful of private schools in preparing young men for admission to the university and careers at court. It accepted students from all families, and even those Fujiwara who had intellectual ambitions, chose it rather than their own family's Kangakuin. Under Michizane, the Kanke Rōka grew, and several hundred students were said to have studied there. Of them, Michizane boasted, nearly a hundred gained admission to the university. Four eventually became counselors, and another four passed their civil service examinations. Because of its students' success, the school acquired a nickname: "The Dragon Gate" (Ryūmon). [26] This was the name of a turbulent rapids on China's Yellow River. Any fish able to swim up it was thought to become a dragon. Consequently, "to pass the dragon gate" came to be a fixed metaphor for passing the equally challenging civil service examinations.

From its founding, the Kangakuin had been viewed as a threat to the university. Its older residents ought to have been living at a government, not a family, dormitory while they attended the university, which was where all of their lectures should have been held. The Kangakuin thus tended to duplicate some of the functions of public institutions. In addition, most of its younger students aspired only to obtaining a modicum of education, not to university admission. The Sugawara school, on the other hand, became a major support to the university, since it stressed preparation for the university and examinations. Unlike the Fujiwara school, it tended to promote, not subvert, the institutions of the *ritsuryō* system. The Kanke Rōka enjoyed its heyday under Michizane's tenure, but it survived long after his death. The last known reference to it dates from the early twelfth century, although by then its character surely had changed.[27]

Michizane's successful pupils at the Kanke Rōka who entered the university as students of literature probably continued their studies under him, for he was one of two professors of literature, and students did not normally change teachers. Not only did he become principally responsible for the education of many literature students, he and his family's associates came to dominate the university, especially its literature course. In 867 when Koreyoshi was promoted from his professorship to a higher office, the second position as professor of literature was already vacant, and so two new men were appointed. One was Koreyoshi's former student Hiromi. The other was Kose no Fumio (824–892), who was given the additional post of president of the university in 871. Fumio was a well-known scholar from a relatively minor court family. Although his own teacher had been a student of Koreyoshi's, he himself was not closely associated with the Sugawara. Hiromi served for two years, after which one professorship again was left unfilled until 875 when Michizane's examiner Yoshika was appointed to it.[28] Thus, after Hiromi's departure, the office was removed from the purview of the Sugawara and their associates until 877 when Michizane himself took over the professorship in literature that

Fumio had held. Fumio remained on as president, but from this point onward, Michizane's position within the university gradually strengthened.

When he was first appointed professor, Michizane once again found himself holding the same office as Yoshika, with whom he had also served as private secretary three years earlier. Both men were known for their literary abilities and thus nothing is remarkable in their having held similar specialized posts. They did not, however, become friends or develop the patron-client relationship that came to be common in China between a successful candidate and his examiner. In Heian Japan, a scholar's loyalty was to his teacher or academic clique, whereas his examiner was supposed to be from another faction within the scholarly community. Probably Michizane remained bitter over Yoshika's severe criticism of his examination essays. Michizane's earliest and partisan biographer would relate boastfully that in the first month of 879, Michizane was promoted to the junior fifth rank upper, and thereby surpassed the rank of his former examiner and current fellow professor Yoshika. [29]

Two months later, Yoshika died at the age of only forty-six and one of the professorships again became vacant. Michizane waited five years before submitting a petition:

> Requesting that the Vacant Post of Professor of Literature
> be Filled with a Person to Assist in the Various Duties
> It is my observation that of all the curricula at the university, classics is the greatest. Thus, the positions of professor of classics are never left vacant, and a total of five men are always employed [including the assistant professors and lecturers]. Also, there are always two professors in each of the other subjects—mathematics, law, calligraphy, and phonetics—even though the students are few.
> Literature is in fact no less vital a scholarly discipline than classics, but the number of professors is still the same as in calligraphy or mathematics. Not only is the number of professorships small, but one is now vacant. My native ability is limited and the duties of a professor are too great for one man. At present, among able scholars there is a suitable person whom I wish to have appointed to the vacancy so that together we can fulfill the responsibilities of professor of literature.
> Submitted with the utmost humility, on the twenty-fifth day of the second month in the eighth year of the Gangyō era [884]; by the Junior Fifth Rank Upper, Junior Assistant Minister of Ceremonial, Professor of Literature, and Supernumerary Governor of Kaga; your servant, Sugawara [30]

Michizane's "suitable person" turned out to be his old friend Hiromi, who was duly reappointed professor of literature three months later. Meanwhile, the office of president of the university recently had become vacant when Fumio was sent off to a provincial office. He was replaced by Fujiwara no Sukeyo, who not only was one of Koreyoshi's former students, but who also took a daughter of Michizane's as one of his wives.[31] Thus, in addition to Michizane, two of his father's former students held key positions at the university. As Michizane's petition pointed out, although the classics course had the largest number of teachers and students, the literature course that the Sugawara faction now dominated was by far the university's most prestigious program.

Michizane's most able students at the university could be recommended for the civil service examinations supervised by the Ministry of Ceremonial where the Sugawara faction also was dominant. On the same day that Michizane had been appointed junior assistant minister, Hiromi had replaced Koreyoshi as senior assistant minister. Four years later, that post went to Fujiwara no Harukage. Although Harukage was indeed the son of a high-ranking official, he was not closely related to the current Fujiwara regent Mototsune. He did, however, have ties to the Sugawara, for his mother was of that family and he himself had been a student of literature.[32] The assistant ministers were the most important officials at the Ministry of Ceremonial, for like other ministries it was headed by men whose titles were honorary and responsibilities minimal. After 812, the post of minister of ceremonial was monopolized by a succession of imperial princes. For example, during Michizane's years as junior assistant minister, the minister was Imperial Prince Tokiyasu, who would later reign as Emperor Kōkō.[33] He is thought to have been an able man, but still the actual affairs of his ministry probably were left in the hands of his subordinates. Thus, the Sugawara, along with their friends and relatives, were as influential at the Ministry of Ceremonial as they were at the university.

The Sugawara had a vested interest in the Ministry of Ceremonial, because it was responsible for the university and was also where both the university entrance examinations and civil service examinations were given. While serving there, Michizane had occasion to give four civil service examinations, one of them in 892 after he had been reappointed to the ministry following his term of office in the provinces.[34] Clearly, the potential for abuse was great. Michizane could have prepared a young man at the Kanke Rōka for the university entrance examination that he himself administered, taught the same man at the university, and finally recommended him for the civil service examination that again he might have administered.

Customary practice, however, served to restrain excessive favoritism. Unlike Yoshika, for example, Michizane never administered a university entrance examination. Probably Michizane was precluded from doing so because at Kanke Rōka he was training youths to take them. Such a practice would be in keeping with the one already noted that governed the selection of civil service examiners, who were chosen from outside the candidates' academic clique. This custom would become an inflexible rule around 940, but even in Michizane's day, when factions were not yet so clearly defined, the practice had already begun, at least informally.[35] For example, in Michizane's own case, it was because Koreyoshi was then senior assistant minister of ceremonial that Yoshika, a private secretary, was called upon to administer his examination. Favoritism was not unknown, and on occasion Michizane's judgments of students and fellow scholars were colored by questions of personal allegiance. Nonetheless, he always claimed to be fair in evaluating his students, and customary practice restricted his ability to favor them on examinations.

Michizane showed his concern for the fairness and effectiveness of the examination system in a group of three proposals written in 883. First, he pointed out that although the examinations still consisted of the two essays specified in the original codes, the length of the questions and answers had significantly increased since the Jōwa era (834–847). Michizane recommended a limit on the length of the examination and more emphasis on the candidate's reasoning rather than empty displays of erudition. Second, he noted that, despite a ban on private ownership or even study of certain books on astronomy, prophecy, and military strategy, examinations occasionally referred to those issues. He observed:

> If the examiner follows the custom of posing questions on forbidden subjects, he risks his career. If the candidate states that out of respect for the law he has not studied such matters, he will not pass the examination and will surely protest. . . . I suggest that the punishments for discussing banned topics be dropped and interference with the examinations cease.

Finally, Michizane objected to the grading standards. In particular, he felt that the distinction between a "B" and a "C" was unclear, both indicating an average paper. Michizane requested that the standards for those grades be specified more precisely. As noted, successful candidates all seem to have been given a grade of "D," and Michizane may have hoped that with clearer standards examiners would be encouraged to award higher grades.[36]

All of Michizane's proposals would have strengthened the examination system. If put into effect, they would have shortened the essays to a more reasonable length, eliminated the fear of punishment for discussing proscribed subjects, and clarified standards to make possible higher grades and thus higher rank upon passing. Michizane knew the importance of the examinations to his own family's success and hoped to assist other able men who sought to follow a similar path. At the same time, his proposals could have strengthened his own position by increasing both the number and rank of his own former students at court. In addition to possible personal benefits, bringing more men selected for their ability into the bureaucracy might have served to counterbalance the rising power of the Fujiwara, and perhaps this was the reason his proposals were not implemented. Michizane may have been the most influential individual within the court scholarly community, but his influence was not so great at the highest levels of government.

"PROFESSORIAL DIFFICULTIES"

Despite Michizane's prominent position as a scholar, he could not avoid:

Professorial Difficulties

We are not a family of generals.
As Confucian scholars we earn our living.
My revered grandfather held the third rank.
My compassionate father served as a high court noble.
Well they knew the power of learning
And wished to pass it on for their descendants' glory.
The day I was promoted to graduate student,
I determined to follow the ways of my ancestors.
The year I became a professor,
Happily, the lecture hall was rebuilt.
When everyone rushed to be first to congratulate me,
My father alone expressed concern.
Over what did he express concern?
"Alas that you are an only child," he said;
"The office of professor is not mean,
The salary of a professor is not small.
Once I too held this post
And lived in fear of people's criticism."
Having heard this kind admonition,
I proceeded uneasily as if treading on ice.
In the fourth year of Gangyō [880], the Council of State ordered
    that I begin my lectures.
But after teaching only three days,
Slanderous voices reached my ears.
When preparing recommendations for graduate study,
It was perfectly clear who did or did not deserve to advance.
But the first student to be failed for lack of ability
Denounced me and begged for an undeserved grade.
I have not failed as a teacher;
My recommendations were made fairly!
How true was my father's advice
When he warned me before all this occurred.[37]

As noted, feuds and rivalries were common in the faction-ridden academic community of the late ninth century. Because of his conspicuous position, Michizane could not avoid attracting criticism, just as his father had predicted. The more reclusive Koreyoshi too had been in a similar situation and had chosen

to shun dispute. Michizane, however, was not so tolerant or retiring an individual. As a student, he had grumbled about having
to put up with dull aristocratic snobs at the university.[38] As a
teacher, he would be sorely tried by the antics of his more un-
ruly pupils at the Kanke Rōka:

> A brush is an implement for writing, and a scraper a tool for
> scratching out mistakes. But some of that flock of crows who de-
> scend on me, apparently unaware of the proper use for such imple-
> ments, pick up the scraper and immediately start hacking at the
> desks, or fiddle with the brush until they've spattered and soiled my
> books. On top of this, in scholarship the most important thing is to
> gather data, and to gather data one has first of all to take notes. But
> since I am not a person of very proper or methodical nature, I often
> find I have to lay down my brush in the midst of my researches,
> and at such times I leave a lot of little slips of paper lying about with
> notes on them concerning the data I have collected. At such times
> people come wandering into my library without permission; though
> what they're thinking about I can't imagine, the clever ones, when
> they spy my notes, fold them up and stuff them into the breast of
> their robe, and the stupid ones pick them up, tear them in two, and
> throw them away! Occurrences like this distress me intensely, and
> in addition there are countless petty little annoyances I could men-
> tion. One more thing—there are times when one of my friends for
> some reason comes to see me on important business. But after he has
> entered my library, one of the idle intruders, not bothering to ascer-
> tain whether someone with important business has entered ahead
> of him, comes marching straight in with his wholly unimportant
> affairs—it's enough to make one despair! . . .
> I am particularly ashamed to think that I have been unable to
> establish the kind of unofficial academy that would attract real men
> of worth, but instead am reduced to laying down regulations to keep
> uninvited intruders out of my library. Such remarks are intended
> only for those who do not really understand me, though those who
> do understand me number only about three. I hope in spreading a
> small net to keep out swallows and sparrows I won't be driving any
> phoenixes away.[39]

Apparently some of Michizane's young charges did not take
their studies as seriously as he would have liked, and one can
sympathize with his distress. Michizane's own attitude, however,
tended to exacerbate the problem. He seems to have divided
people into two categories, worthless "swallows and sparrows"
on the one hand and precious "phoenixes" on the other. His

remark that only three men understood him suggests he placed most of his associates in the former category. Personally, he was not a forgiving man and did not make friends easily.

An anecdote from the *Gōdanshō* further reveals Michizane's sometimes intolerant nature and concern for factional loyalty:

> Miyoshi no Kiyoyuki [847–918] was Kose no Fumio's student. Fumio's recommendation for him stated, "Kiyoyuki's talent surpasses that of his contemporaries." Michizane sneered and changed the word "talent" to "ignorance." Hiromi said this was unfair, but Michizane got angry and replied, "As a student of my father's, you ought not to have sympathy for Kiyoyuki."[40]

Although, like other tales from the *Gōdanshō*, this can hardly be accepted as historical fact, still it does reflect Michizane's attitude towards Kiyoyuki. Michizane would later become Kiyoyuki's examiner. A comparison of how he treated two of his examinees, Kiyoyuki and Ki no Haseo, reveals the difference in his attitude toward those who were and those who were not personally associated with him.

The Miyoshi were another obscure court family, their history virtually unknown prior to Kiyoyuki. His father was a minor official who had served primarily in the provinces. Kiyoyuki shared neither Michizane's educational advantages nor his hereditary rank, and therefore his advance at court was conspicuously slower. He entered the university around 866 at the age of twenty, probably as a classics student, and only in 873 did he manage to become a student of literature. His teacher Fumio thought well of him, and the next year he was recommended for promotion to graduate student. Finally, in 881, at the age of thirty-five, Kiyoyuki took his civil service examination. Having studied under Fumio, Kiyoyuki had to be examined by a member of a different faction, and so, even though in mourning for his father, Michizane was specially summoned to administer the examination. His two questions were on Chinese poetics and astrology. Contrary to Michizane's reported opinion, Kiyoyuki was an able and learned man. He would later serve as both professor of literature and president of the university, and eventually he rose to a position on the Council of State as a consultant. Nonetheless, Michizane failed him on the examination. Two years later, the decision was reversed, and

Kiyoyuki was passed, with the usual grade of "D."[41] The reason for Michizane's negative attitude is not known, but certainly he treated Kiyoyuki with undeserved harshness.

Ki no Haseo, in contrast, became a lifelong friend of Michizane's. Unlike the families of most Heian scholars, the Ki had once been politically powerful during the Nara period, but by the ninth century their influence had declined. Nothing is known of Haseo's father beyond his name and his final office, one that normally was held by an official of only the senior sixth rank. If indeed that was his rank, Haseo would not have been entitled to hereditary rank. The identity of his first teacher is not certain, but Haseo would later lament that his abilities had gone unrecognized. He did not become a student of literature until 876 at the age of thirty-three. Three years later, a poem he composed at a palace banquet attracted the attention of Michizane. Although he was the same age as Haseo, Michizane was already a professor of literature and promptly recommended Haseo's promotion to graduate student.

In 833, at the age of thirty-nine, Haseo passed the civil service examination with essays on the use of rites to improve public morality and the mystical effects of personal virtue. Contrary to the usual practice, one of his own teachers, Michizane, served as examiner. Probably this was allowed because Haseo had studied with various teachers and was not clearly affiliated with a specific clique. Throughout his life, Haseo managed to avoid becoming embroiled in factional disputes. For example, many years later when Michizane and his followers were driven from power, Haseo was unaffected and continued to rise to high office, despite his friendship with Michizane. Kiyoyuki, however, was jealous of the favorable treatment Haseo had received in the examinations and came to despise him. Again quoting the *Gōdanshō*, when Haseo was named professor, Kiyoyuki is said to have asserted, "This marks the beginning of incompetent professors."[42] Like Kiyoyuki, Haseo was without doubt a capable man. He too served as professor of literature and president of the university, and ultimately would attain the position of middle counselor, a post above that which Kiyoyuki held on the Council of State.

Despite his claims of objectivity, as an examiner Michizane treated his friend Haseo more fairly than he did Kiyoyuki and, as a result, Kiyoyuki was to become Michizane's enemy. In grading Kiyoyuki's examination, Michizane was probably influenced by factional considerations. Scholarly cliques had existed from Koreyoshi's time and would later become increasingly rigid as court appointments became hereditary. In the tenth century, the Sugawara came to lead one of the two distinct factions within the university's literature program, and students from specified families automatically entered their faction. Koreyoshi had kept aloof of such factionalism and had warned Michizane that he needed to be careful as a professor to avoid criticism. Although Michizane may have considered his motives and actions beyond reproach, his concern for maintaining family tradition and for the welfare of his own students left him open to charges of favoritism. Attitudes such as his would eventually bring about abuses, including hereditary professorships and rigid academic factions determined by family.[43]

Because Michizane had become the most influential of court scholars, complaints from disgruntled students were only to be expected. Michizane's personal opinions and behavior made matters even worse. His account of the Kanke Rōka indicates that he had little tolerance for those whom he regarded as his intellectual inferiors. Furthermore, if the anecdote from the Gōdanshō is true, his attitude toward Kiyoyuki suggests a tendency to place members of rival cliques into the category of the academically second rate. In Michizane's defense, it should be noted that he did not always strictly observe factional distinctions. He remained a friend of Kiyoyuki's teacher Fumio, and he would occasionally enjoy visits to the Fujiwara and Wake family schools.[44] Still, had Michizane been like his father, a more compromising and less argumentative individual, his "professorial difficulties" might not have been so irritating.

Despite Michizane's willingness to criticize others, he reacted strongly when others found fault with him:

A Distressing Matter
(At the end of the summer in the sixth year of Gangyō [882], someone wrote an anonymous poem slandering Counselor Fujiwara no Fuyuo. The counselor judged the poem to be technically superior and suspected it had been written by Professor Sugawara. I felt totally humiliated. Could this be my fate?)

Must a gentleman fear suspicion?
When suspicion becomes real, it must be feared!
In our world, small men are many, gentlemen few,
And so troubles thrive in the realm.
One man comes to warn me: I do not believe.
A second comes to warn me: I still withdraw.
But should a third man come, I grow alarmed—
And the fear increases with the fourth and fifth warnings.
I have searched my soul and found no taint,
But those who know me not say I am naive.
Anonymous words have shattered my bones;
Perhaps I shall fall, a corpse by some roadside.
Daily matters, once so quiet, are now in chaos,
My life, once so tranquil, is now filled with danger.
Before Chiao-yuan Peak, the valley seems shallow,
And the mountains at Meng-men today appear level.
No one would call me a wild violent man.
This "master of literature," who could he be?
A four-horse chariot can not keep pace with a three-inch tongue.
I grieve not for wounds to my face, but wounds to my name.
Neither famous nor yet an elder,
I pray for good reputation and many long years.
But now I may die of grief, my name tarnished.
Gods of heaven and earth, bring my innocence to light!
O luminous deities, if your mysterious judgements are still unfailing,
How long must I endure this slander?
Awesome gods, if you still have power to punish in secret,
Bring calamity down on the man who has sinned.
Accept my pure heart as an offering,
Gods, may you answer my prayer.
These words may seem trivial, yet they are true,
While he who should suffer laughs secretly.
At home, no brothers to share my troubles,
But outside, my friends know my suffering.
Although because of a poem I am accused of wrong,
With what but a poem can I express my despair.[45]

Michizane has been described as "mild and bookish."[46] Certainly he was bookish, but the vengeance he demanded in this poem—and others—could hardly be considered mild. He has also been called "pathologically sensitive."[47] That may be a more accurate characterization. Indeed, Michizane reacted strongly to criticism, although the diagnosis of his sensitivity as pathological is a bit extreme. In this particular instance, Michizane's concern might have been justified, for he was accused of a serious matter: anonymously slandering a high-ranking and influential statesman who seven years earlier had been his superior in the Ministry of Popular Affairs. Michizane, however, responded almost as vigorously to less serious criticism. A year after the incident of the anonymous poem, Michizane helped to receive an embassy from Parhae and had occasion to write many poems in public. Again tongues began to wag, and Michizane responded with:

A Poem on Frustration

Last year, the world was amazed: how skillful my poem!
This year people grumble: how crude my poems!
Those at the Foreign Envoy's Quarters are not precious jewels,
Although the one before the Counselor's gate was a work of rare
    genius.
It is not that acknowledged poems are bad and anonymous works
    superior,
Nor that early works are excellent and later ones inferior.
If one man opens his mouth, ten thousand people spread the word.
When a wise man speaks, the fools all take delight.
Speeding over ten leagues, a hundred, even a thousand,
Even a dragon-like four-horse chariot cannot keep up with a tongue,
Flowing onward for six years, seven, even eight,
Man's life is like a river, it cannot be dammed up.
Man's life is like a river, his name can be fouled.
This name, what water can restore its purity?
Indeed, heaven can distinguish right from wrong.
Surely man ought to be able to do the same.
My enemies all said that only a scholar could write such a poem.
But last year's commotion has finally subsided.
Those who deride me made the anonymous poem mine,
So the objections this year cannot be true.[48]

Michizane sent copies of this poem to Haseo and Sugano no Korenori, another scholar who would later become professor of literature, but about whom little else is known. Michizane and Korenori proceeded to exchange a series of poems. Korenori responded to Michizane's poem with a pair of his own, which Michizane in turn answered. Korenori again responded, and Michizane concluded the exchange with a final pair of poems. In this exchange, starting with Korenori's first pair of poems, they followed the convention of concluding alternate lines of each poem with an identical sequence of rhyming characters.

The exchange between Michizane and Korenori thus became something of a tour de force as Korenori's original rhymes were maintained through all four pairs of poems.

Unfortunately, Korenori's poems are now lost, but Michizane's responses reveal something of their contents. Korenori was trying to comfort and reassure his friend, and at one point he had noted that the ambassador from Parhae had praised Michizane's poems, saying they resembled those of Po Chü-i, the Chinese poet Michizane most admired. Michizane modestly answered that this was mere flattery. He was not to be easily soothed, and his four poems responding to Korenori's essentially repeated the same complaints he had voiced in his original poem. Because he wrote in a poetic tradition that encouraged expressions of grief and even self-pity, perhaps he exaggerated his displeasure for literary effect.[49] That suspicion is reinforced by the fact that the exchange of poems had become something of a display of literary virtuosity. However, even if overstated for literary effect, his annoyance was real. For a man who was quite willing to criticize others, Michizane accepted criticism of himself with very little grace.

PROFESSORIAL PLEASURES AND PERSONAL MISFORTUNES

Despite Michizane's "professorial difficulties," his years as professor also had their pleasant moments. Shortly after complaining of his difficulties, he was honored with the privilege of welcoming a group of high court nobles who had come to visit the university. He wrote his former tutor Tadaomi:

> My Feelings after a Literary Banquet
> at the North Hall of the University
> Proudly the university greeted its honored guests.
> Humbly I welcomed the imperial consultants who stayed until sunset.
> The musicians, using their drums as pillows, sleep by the pond.
> Students, clutching their poems, crouch by the walls.
> How splendid once again to have heard stories from the past told by
> the elders!
> Naturally they will be recited to our descendants for many
> generations.
> High officials came to join us and for the first time we truly enjoyed
> the banquet.
> For the rest of our lives, we will be thankful for their great
> beneficence.[50]

Later, when a small wing was added to his study, he wrote a poem on its wall:

The walls of the new corridor, several yards square, are leafed with
    gold.
Bamboo flourishes like green mist above the white garden sand.
The small door to the north leads to my library.
The lattice window to the east serves as my moon-gazing pavilion.
I can barely see the feet of horses as they pass by on the road.
I can hear the voices of people close by as they approach the gate.
Naturally, I despise vulgar intruders when they laugh and chatter.
Instead, I long for visits from mountain priests who chant sutras
    through the night.
Still, I think I shall keep my window open throughout the year
Not shutting myself up for even a single day.
Although I could find fulfillment in simply cleaning this room,
Dirt accumulates, because my duties keep me busy from dawn to
    dusk.[51]

Writing poems on walls, it should be noted, was not an eccentricity. Michizane wrote a number of poems on walls, and so did his friends, perhaps inspired by Po Chü-i.[52] These two poems show Michizane delighting in different types of pleasures. In the first, he expressed his pride in his official position. As a professor he had the honor of receiving noble visitors to the university. In the second, his enjoyment came from a moment of solitude offering a respite from the demands of his official duties. Michizane's feelings were at times conflicting. As a conscientious Confucian official, he took his responsibilities seriously and was proud of his very respectable status in the court bureaucracy. At the same time, he was also a poet—and a somewhat temperamental one at that—who could delight in relaxing, freed from the cares of office. Some of his best poetry would be written when he was living in the provinces, his career ambitions frustrated, rather than when he was at court serving in the sort of offices he considered more appropriate to a man of his status and ability. These two poems were an early hint that Michizane the poet would not necessarily be happiest and most productive in the same situations that appealed to Michizane the official.

During his years as professor, Michizane the poet took particular pleasure in the company of one Taira no Masanori. Masanori was a great-grandson of Emperor Kammu. His father had been granted the surname Taira and had served twenty-four years as a high court noble. One of Masanori's brothers also rose to high office. Masanori, however, appears to have been a cultivated man who enjoyed his leisure more than he aspired to office. For most of his career he served in absentee provincial posts or honorary positions in the palace guards, and only late in his life was he finally given an office with real duties: director of the Carpentry Bureau. Although he may have lacked ambition, the fact that he was summoned with Michizane to help greet an embassy from Parhae suggests he was a man of learning, for that was a duty likely to require exchanges of Chinese poetry.

It was in 883 when they were both greeting the mission from Parhae that Michizane and Masanori became acquainted. Shortly afterwards, Michizane recorded his first visit to Masanori's country estate west of the capital, probably near the modern Katsura Detached Palace (Katsura Rikyū). Michizane commemorated the occasion with a sequence of four quatrains:

> Late Autumn at the Mountain Villa of General Taira
> Ten million human dwellings within this single world;
> If by chance one meets a true friend, he does not speak of parting.
> I gaze at the somber blue water nearby with its cold sound,
> Then face the lonely mountains in the evening light.
>
> The villa is beneath the mountain; the road covered with mist.
> I trust my horse to make his way through the fields, but flowers
>   distract him.
> General, do not accuse me of wasting my time.
> The professor has come for spiritual cultivation.
>
> Spiritual cultivation to excess is a vain affectation.
> I sincerely regret that we were so late in becoming acquainted.
> Clouds and mud! Do not calculate the difference in our stations.
> Wind and moon! I hope we may forever enjoy their beauties.
>
> Several rounds of *go* invite us to sit in tranquility.
> A few sips of wine make us forget our troubles.
> If the world wishes a model of genuine friendship,
> It needs only to look at our pleasure this autumn day. [53]

On another visit two years later, Michizane wrote a series of twenty poems, beginning with a note:

> On the twenty-sixth day of the ninth month, I accompanied the supernumerary governor of Awa, Taira no Masanori, to his small

villa west of the river. After drinking several cups of wine and while enjoying our elegant conversation, I asked a student who had come with us to select twenty topics for poems. The sun was setting over the western mountains and the time for our return was gradually approaching. Licking the tip of my brush, I wrote quickly, without adding punctuation, not paying attention to the proper tones, and generally ignoring the rules. People will surely laugh at these poems and conclude I have no talent.

The poems are all on conventional Chinese themes, for example:

> The Sounds of the Rapids
> Although by nature I avoid noise,
> I love the river's gentle sound.
> It rouses the hermit from his pillow.
> It resembles an ancient tune played on the koto.
> A solitary pine on the bank serves as shelter.
> The fallen leaves are like boats tied to the waves.
> This evening I have no work
> Other than the first book of *Chuang-tzu*.

> The Fishing Boat
> Along the twisting river bank, no other calling
> For the solitary old fisherman.
> His small boat drifts like a fallen leaf.
> His frail line shudders in the cool breeze.
> Do not ask about what he does at home.
> He simply hopes to spend his later years thus.
> Should I wish to copy his bamboo pole,
> I have a small thicket at my home. [54]

The relationship between Michizane and Masanori is an interesting one. As Michizane noted, the two men were in some ways very different. The Sugawara indeed had become an aristocratic family, but in terms of birth, Michizane could not compare with Masanori, a descendant of emperors. Michizane was an ambitious man, anxious to maintain his family's hard-earned reputation for scholarship. Masanori was content with his inherited status and was satisfied to be a wealthy patron of the literary arts. Michizane clearly enjoyed Masanori's company and the opportunity to visit his country estate. The poems he wrote there are virtually the only ones he composed outside the capital during his years as professor. All are elegantly Chinese in tone, yet they are different from the equally Chinese poems Michizane produced for various court rituals. At court, Michizane wrote on more serious subjects in learned language and often used Confucian themes. The poems he wrote with Masanori instead extolled the pleasures of the countryside in rather simple language and with Taoist sentiments.

These poems can also be compared with the ones he had written previously on his journey to Tsuruga. In both cases, because he was away from the court and its conventions, he was free to write in a rather uncomplicated informal style, without learned allusions and obscure vocabulary. Yet the tone of the poems is different. The earlier ones accurately reflect Michizane's experiences: his fear and wonder on the journey; his relief and pleasure at the destination. The later ones, although attractive, are conventional in their sentiment. Michizane met with Masanori to enjoy the approved recreations for leisured Chinese gentlemen, who customarily turned Taoist in their spare moments away from the cares of office. Accordingly, Michizane wrote on Taoist themes, with frequent references to *Chuang-tzu*. Elegant and pleasant to read, the poems were appropriate to the occasion but seem to lack conviction. Michizane simply was following a different set of less formal conventions than those he followed at court.

In addition to his work and his poetry, Michizane also took pleasure in his growing family. While still a graduate student, he had married his tutor Tadaomi's daughter Nobukiko, five years his junior. His oldest children apparently were daughters and we hear little of them until many years later. His first son, Takami (876–913), was born the year before Michizane was named professor, and, in a poem already quoted, Michizane proudly noted that the boy had begun to read at the age of four.[55] Another son who had also shown promise, however, died in childhood:

Dreaming of Amaro

Since Amaro died I cannot sleep at night;
if I do, I meet him in dreams and tears come coursing down.
Last summer he was over three feet tall;
this year he would have been seven years old.
He was diligent and wanted to know how to be a good son,
read his books, and recited by heart the "Poems on the Capital."
Medicine stayed the bitter pain, but only for ten days;
then the wind took his wandering soul off to the Nine Springs.
Since then, I hate the gods and buddhas;

better if they had never made heaven and earth!
I stare at my knees, often laugh in bitterness,
grieve for your little brother too, buried in an infant's grave.
. . .

How can I bear to hear your sisters call your name, searching;
to see your mother waste away her life in grief!
For a while I thought the ache in my bowels had mended;
now suddenly it comes boiling up again.
Your mulberry bow over the door, the mugwort arrows;
your stilts by the hedge top, the riding whip of vine;
in the garden the flower seeds we planted in fun;
on the wall, words you'd learned, your scribblings beside them—
each time I recall your voice, your laugh, you are here again;
then I hardly see you day or night and all becomes a daze.
A million missteps in this realm of Sumeru,
three thousand darknesses in this world of life—
O thou Bodhisattva of Mercy,
watch over my child, seat him on the great lotus! [56]

Amaro's death was a profound shock that would continue to haunt Michizane's dreams. This poem's vividly detailed imagery of children's toys and scribblings on the wall is highly effective. Its language may be classical Chinese, but its location is clearly Michizane's home. The feelings expressed are authentic, not literary clichés. Contrary to what he stated in one of his poems written at Masanori's villa, Michizane never gave serious thought to cutting a bamboo pole from his garden and becoming a fisherman. That was simply a Chinese literary convention that suited the moment. Michizane's grief over his son's death was real, and he expressed it in a style distinctly his own. This is a poem that in Michizane's day could not have been written in Japanese, since the long poem was no longer a commonly accepted form. It is an excellent example of how literature in Chinese allowed a Heian poet to expand the range of his expression.

Throughout his life, Michizane would continue to refer periodically to his children—he is said to have had twenty-three—with obvious pride, affection, and concern. [57] His devotion to his family went beyond a mere desire to maintain the Sugawara scholarly tradition. Curiously, Michizane hardly ever mentioned his wife, or more likely, wives. Considering the number of his children, certainly he must have had secondary wives; however, no record of them survives. Poetry in Japanese as a medium for amorous exchange had already been perfected by such poets as Ariwara no Narihira and Ono no Kamachi. Love poetry in Chinese, however, was not written; in part because Chinese precedents were few, in part because women commonly did not master Chinese, and thus love poetry in that language normally would not have played a part in courtship. Perhaps if more of Michizane's poetry in Japanese had survived, it would provide some insights into his relations with women. As it is, all we can say with certainty is that the number of his children suggests he could not have led a strictly monogamous life.

4 · Governor of Sanuki

Under the *ritsuryō* system, provincial governorships were of vital importance to the central government, for they were the means by which the court controlled and administered its territories. Virtually all of its revenues came from the provinces, and, as later events were to demonstrate, without control of the land, it could no longer function as an effective government. Despite the importance of provincial administration, however, the court sometimes treated the system in a cavalier manner. As noted, absentee appointments were commonly used as a means of augmenting the salaries of men in the capital, and a full complement of officials was not necessarily dispatched to govern each province. At the same time, the land itself within the provinces was being divided up into estates that were controlled by religious institutions and powerful court families. In later centuries of the Heian period, the abuses worsened as aristocratic families came to treat the governorships of certain provinces as, in effect, their private property. These practices, most of which had already begun in the Nara period, benefited the individuals who dominated the court but also led to the decline of the central administration.

Most of these problems that would gradually debilitate the *ritsuryō* system of provincial administration had already appeared in Michizane's day, but the system itself was still functioning, essentially in the manner its creators had intended. In

147

theory, provincial appointments were treated in much the same manner as posts at court. Any man holding the prescribed rank could be assigned to a term of duty in the provinces and upon completing it become eligible for a new appointment, either back in the capital or again in the provinces. In practice, however, provincial service often was scorned and assigned to officials from lesser families who eventually would form a distinct class of provincial administrators. An exception to this pattern was the occasional aristocrat who welcomed the opportunities for personal gain that accompanied a post in the hinterlands. Michizane's experience was typical and provides insights into how the system of provincial governorships functioned. In particular, the circumstances surrounding his appointment and his attitudes toward provincial service are recorded in some detail. Although information concerning his official activities is not as well preserved, still, his is the best-documented example of a ninth-century governorship.

We know about Michizane's years in Sanuki not from government records, few of which survive, but from his *kanshi*, for he truly came into his own as a poet during his term in the province. As a student and minor court official, Michizane had demonstrated his ability to use Chinese poetry as a means of personal expression, but most of his poems were primarily intended as displays of erudition or ornaments to court rituals. In Sanuki, however, almost all of his many poems were written as personal responses to the events and scenes that surrounded him. This was his first extended period away from the capital and much of what he saw was new to him. He became aware of the hardships suffered by the lower classes and was moved at least to poetry, if not to political action. Rustic life he found sometimes pleasing, sometimes depressing, but always a source of literary inspiration. The four years from 886 until 890, when Michizane was in Sanuki, constitute the second stage in his official career. Overall, this was not a happy time in his life, but it had important consequences for him. Michizane's experiences in Sanuki contributed to his development as a poet and gave him useful experience in provincial affairs. Moreover, his involvement in political events concurrently taking place at court led to his subsequent rise to high office.

AN UNEXPECTED APPOINTMENT

The first month of 886 witnessed two events that would significantly influence Michizane's subsequent career. The year began conventionally with the customary formalities on New Year's Day. The next day, Grand Minister Mototsune's eldest son, Tokihira, celebrated his coming of age. In itself this too was nothing unusual; however, the circumstances of the ceremony were remarkable. It was conducted at the imperial palace, where the emperor himself placed the cap of adulthood on Tokihira's head. Then, with a proclamation drafted by Michizane's friend Hiromi but copied in the emperor's own hand, Tokihira was granted the senior fifth rank lower. Afterwards, the grand minister held a banquet in his official chambers. Never before had a noble—even a Fujiwara—celebrated his coming of age so grandly, and Tokihira's senior fifth rank, awarded when he was only sixteen, was in marked contrast to the ranks awarded most young courtiers. Neither the emperor nor Hiromi was altogether pleased with Tokihira's special treatment, but they felt constrained to follow the wishes of Mototsune, who dominated the court.[1] Both the ceremony and the rank were clear indications of his power. With his head start, Tokihira would become Michizane's superior and rival within only ten years, despite the great gap in their ages and experience.

The following days were taken up with the usual activities of the first month. Promotions in rank were announced on the seventh day for men and on the eighth day for court ladies, who also were eligible for rank, although theirs were largely honorary without the perquisites that accompanied men's ranks. Various festivities were enjoyed, and then on the sixteenth day, new appointments were announced. Michizane's associate Sukeyo was awarded an office in the Controllers' Office of the Left (Sabenkankyoku), which supervised the four most important ministries, and he retained his post as president of the university. Michizane's friend Masanori was transferred from the post of supernumerary governor of Awa to supernumerary governor of Sanuki. And Michizane himself, to his dismay, was named governor of Sanuki. This was not an absentee appointment, and after nearly nine years as professor of literature,

Michizane was obliged to serve a four-year term as provincial
governor, for the court did not tolerate regular provincial appointees who failed to take up their duties. Only two weeks
after Michizane's appointment, there was a protest that ten governors, one of whom had been appointed two years earlier, had
not yet departed for their provinces. Four were subsequently
punished with demotions in rank. Weaknesses had long been
apparent in the system of provincial governorships established
in the *ritsuryō* codes, but the system definitely was still funtion-
ing in Michizane's day.[2]

The new year's festivities continued, but the newly appointed
Governor Michizane was no longer enjoying them. One annual
event was the palace banquet at which poems in Chinese were
composed on a theme selected by the emperor. Michizane had
become a regular participant in these banquets, and he was invited on the twenty-first day of the month. Provincial appointees
normally did not attend, but an exception was made for Michizane in recognition of his literary abilities. After a musical entertainment, the assembled poets were asked to compose on the
topic, "Hearing the Palace Dancing Girls Perform 'Willow Blossom Lament.'" Michizane's contribution went:

> Our palace dancers, do they not equal those of the
>   venerable T'ang?
> Their elegant makeup is the flower of our emperor's
>   favor.
> The music, played on the flute of the western nomads,
> Is filled with sentiment, but is hardly a lament!
> Together the dancers wave their green branches,
> Drunk with pleasure, they do not notice the silver hairpin fall,
> Although the delicate sounds linger in this humble servant's
>   ears,
> How sad he is that he must cross the sea alone for a distant
>   shore![3]

After Michizane and the other poets had offered their compositions, a wine cup was passed to each in order of his rank.
On Mototsune's turn, which should have come immediately
after the emperor's, Mototsune kept the cup, walked over to
Michizane, and stood before him. Mototsune then recited the

last line of a poem by Po Chü-i and asked Michizane to recite the whole poem. The poem was:

> On Night Duty with Yuan Chen,
>   in Answer to His Poem
> Together we commiserate over our lack of leisure.
> Night duties are all too frequent; days of prohibition many.
> On hearing the sound of the morning drum we shall part.
> To whom shall belong the scenery of the coming day?[4]

By stressing the last line, Mototsune was hoping to comfort Michizane. The prime minister took Po Chü-i's message to be that, although parting was truly sad, a sojourn in the provinces might at least offer a pleasant change of scenery. But the distraught Michizane was not so easily consoled with literary allusions. No sooner did he begin to recite the poem than his eyes filled with tears and his throat choked with sobs. Unable to continue, he hurried home to spend a sleepless night lamenting his imminent departure from his home in the capital.

Michizane's appointment raises two questions. First, was a provincial governorship actually as undesirable as Michizane obviously thought it was, and second, why was Michizane named to an office for which he was not prepared either by training or by temperament? Both questions are complex and cannot be answered with complete certainty.

Heian literature suggests that courtiers regarded the provinces— indeed anything provincial—with disdain. This attitude is also seen in fact that at the time of Michizane's appointment ten governors were tarrying in the capital rather than serving in their provinces. Aristocratic reluctance to leave the capital, however, is not the whole picture. If some governors preferred to stay home, others settled in the provinces to which they were assigned and refused to return to court. Such men were not necessarily from insignificant court families. In 842, Dazaifu protested the actions of a certain Prince Nakai. Although a member of the imperial family, Nakai held only the senior sixth rank upper and had been appointed lieutenant governor of Bungo, a province in Kyushu. There, he had illegally acquired extensive lands and great wealth. When his term of office expired, he chose to stay in Kyushu where, now known as "The Former Lieutenant

Governor," his powers increased. The government's response was to pardon him, but demand that he return home.[5] The outcome of this incident is unknown, but clearly Prince Nakai preferred to live as a scorned but wealthy provincial rather than an honored but impoverished courtier.

Nakai's riches may have been ill-gotten; however, legitimate wealth could also be gained through provincial service. The framers of the original codes had anticipated that remote provincial posts would prove unattractive to cultured men from the capital, and therefore they provided special material benefits so that officials serving in the provinces would be more amply rewarded than those with comparable ranks at court.[6] Michizane's salary was supplemented by an absentee governorship, and thus he did not feel the need to seek a lucrative post in the provinces. But his attitude was not necessarily shared by other less well-rewarded courtiers.

In a farewell poem, Michizane would remark, "I do not consider governorships part of my family tradition."[7] In fact, however, this was not altogether true. Michizane's grandfather had been praised for his able administration as lieutenant governor of Owari, and his uncle, too, had served as a lieutenant governor. Michizane's father indeed had never been sent to the provinces, but he was exceptional. Most courtiers whose status depended more on their literary abilities than their family ties found themselves assigned to the provinces at some point in their careers. Later in the Heian period, men who served in the provinces came to form a distinct class inferior to those who served in the capital, but such was not yet the case in the ninth century. While he was governor, Michizane would be rewarded with a promotion of one grade to the senior fifth rank lower, and his activities would bring him to the attention of the new Emperor Uda who later became his great patron. His chances for later official preferment may have even been enhanced by his broadened experience in practical administration.[8] At best, a governorship could provide opportunities for the legitimate—or illegitimate—accumulation of wealth. At worst, it was merely the sort of temporary setback that a Heian noble of Michizane's status had to expect occasionally. Although not as prestigious as a professorship, it was not the disaster that Michizane seems to have thought it to be.

Michizane's dismay at a provincial appointment should have been somewhat ameliorated by the fact that Sanuki was not an undesirable province. It corresponded to the modern Kagawa prefecture in Shikoku and was only of moderate distance from the capital, approximately a six-day journey away. Also, it was relatively advanced both economically and culturally. Most of its extensive arable land had been divided up according to the rules of Japan's land distribution system. In addition, a wide variety of handicrafts and industries flourished: among its many products were salt, fish, silk, paper, ironwork, medicinal herbs, and ceramics. Perhaps Sanuki's prosperity is best demonstrated by the fact that its tax burden was among the highest of all provinces. Sanuki was known not only for its material goods, but also for its men of learning. The most famous was the priest Kūkai, who had begun his studies at the Sanuki provincial college, and a number of his more eminent disciples were also from the province. In addition to priests, numerous legal scholars came from there. Of the ten renowned Heian legal experts listed in a medieval source, eight originally came from Sanuki. Perhaps this was related to the reputation for contentiousness that the people of Sanuki had acquired.[9]

The two most common explanations for Michizane's provincial appointment are either that the Fujiwara were already viewing him as a potential rival and wished him out of the way, or that enemies in the academic world plotted against him. These would later become two of the principal elements in his subsequent exile to Kyushu, but his appointment to Sanuki cannot be explained so simply. The most powerful Fujiwara at court, Mototsune, was a personal friend. He had tried to comfort Michizane at the palace banquet and later would hold a farewell gathering for him. This was not the way the Fujiwara customarily had treated rivals of whom they wished to dispose. Also, although Michizane was sent to Sanuki, many of his academic colleagues, notably Hiromi and Sukeyo, were receiving promotions. Hiromi had recently been named consultant, and Sukeyo was subsequently given Michizane's old post as assistant minister of ceremonial. Another of Michizane's friends, Sugano no Korenori, succeeded him as professor of literature. Moreover, Michizane was not the only scholar relegated to the provinces about this time, and the others represented different factions.[10]

Thus, there is no evidence that the Fujiwara were already viewing him as a threat in 886, nor does there appear to be any pattern of demotions only for members of his scholarly faction. Michizane was not sent to Sanuki simply because of Fujiwara jealousy or academic factional strife.

Michizane's appointment to Sanuki can best be explained in relation to the political situation under the then-reigning Emperor Kōkō. Like his Gilbertian namesake, Kōkō had unexpectedly risen from relative obscurity rather late in his life. His predecessor, Yōzei, had come to the throne in 876 as a ten-year-old boy under the regency of his maternal uncle Mototsune. Three years later, Mototsune was also given the title of grand minister. Gradually, Yōzei showed himself to be mentally disturbed. After he had reportedly murdered the son of his own wet nurse, Mototsune had no choice but to force his abdication. Mototsune could have easily placed another child nephew or grandson on the throne and continued as regent, but rather than again take a chance with an immature sovereign, he arranged to have his friend and cousin, Prince Tokiyasu, the minister of ceremonial, named Emperor Kōkō. At the time, Tokiyasu was fifty-five years old, and as a son of Emperor Nimmyō, he was far removed from the current line of succession. Traditionally, Mototsune was condemned for interfering with the imperial family, but more recently, he has been praised for acting in the best interests not of himself but of the court, for he replaced a criminally insane emperor with a mature, stable man, instead of another easily dominated but potentially unreliable child.[11]

An adult emperor, however, made Mototsune's official position at court ambiguous. Obviously he could no longer continue as regent with a grown man as emperor, but still he remained the most powerful individual at court, and the grateful Kōkō could not slight him. Mototsune retained the impressive title of grand minister, but the duties and privileges attached to that office were vague. The position of grand minister was not a regularly filled office but one to which individuals of special merit on occasion were appointed. According to the ritsuryō codes, the ministers of the left and right were actually responsible for managing the affairs of the government. In contrast, the grand minister, if appointed, was to be "a model individual, setting an example for all within the four seas. He shall regulate the nation, debate the Way, and harmonize the yin and yang." A commentary stated quite explicitly that the grand minister had no duties.[12] The title was intended to be largely honorary.

Three months after he became emperor, Kōkō ordered all the professors to present opinions on whether or not the grand minister had any duties and to which T'ang office it corresponded. In other words, he wanted Mototsune's position at court clarified. Obviously, the politically judicious conclusion to offer would have been that the office of grand minister was in fact a very powerful one. Of the five opinions presented, two completely ignored the commentary that stated the grand minister had no duties, and two mentioned it but stressed instead that the office was still a very important one. A variety of corresponding T'ang offices were proposed. One opinion—Michizane's—was distinctly different from the others. Michizane began forthrightly by quoting the commentary on the grand minister's lack of duties, and added, "How can there be further doubts about the intepretations of the time-honored authorities?" He then presented a list of Chinese offices beginning with ones from the Han dynasty and ending with the same T'ang offices mentioned by the other scholars, but he concluded that "the intent of our Japanese codes is quite different from that of the T'ang regulations." The status of Japan's grand minister, he reasoned, should not be determined on the basis of Chinese precedent. But in the end, he clouded his argument by admitting that although the grand minister had no regularly assigned duties, he did belong to the Council of State, the most powerful organ of government.[13] Although Michizane temporized somewhat, his views more closely reflected the spirit of the original codes than did those of the other scholars.

Michizane had been admirably outspoken, and Mototsune, to his credit, does not seem to have immediately objected. Nevertheless, Michizane had not endeared himself to the most powerful man at court. The outcome of this debate was that Kōkō issued an edict granting Mototsune special powers. Although the term "chancellor" (kampaku) was not used, the intended status was essentially the same and this is often considered the beginning of that office.[14] As chancellor, in fact if not in name, Mototsune remained friendly towards Michizane, but that friendship must have been tempered by the knowledge that Michizane was anything but an uncritically loyal supporter.

A second problem resulted from Kōkō's status as a mature emperor with experience in the government. Unlike his boy-emperor predecessors, Kōkō was as eager to reward his own friends and relatives as were the Fujiwara. A study of high court officialdom under Kōkō's reign reveals an increase in the number of men belonging to or descended from the imperial family, while the number of Fujiwara related to the regent's family was stable. A new element was thus brought into the upper echelons of the court government, but not at the expense of Fujiwara interests. Although the number of top officials rose from fifty-nine to sixty-three, still, the number of vacant positions proved insufficient.[15] Some officials had to be removed to make room for the newly appointed imperial relatives, and scholars such as Michizane became victims of these circumstances. The scholars who did well under Kōkō's reign were generally those with close ties either to the emperor or to Mototsune. For example, Hiromi had a variety of complicated marital ties to the imperial family, and his own family, the Tachibana, claimed an emperor as an ancestor, albeit many generations earlier. Sukeyo, in addition to belonging to the Sugawara academic faction, was a household official (*keishi*) of Mototsune.[16] Michizane, also, had ties with Kōkō. As noted earlier, a sister of his was probably one of Kōkō's concubines, and Michizane had earlier worked under Kōkō in the Ministry of Ceremonial. The Sugawara, however, were not nearly so aristocratic a family as the Tachibana, and Michizane's ties with Kōkō proved inadequate to warrant patronage. Michizane was appointed to Sanuki because he was politically expendable.

Contemporary gossip was suggesting that Michizane's new post, in fact, represented banishment from court, but such was not the case.[17] The emperor Kōkō and his minister Mototsune were anxious to promote their own associates. Somehow, vacancies had to be created at court and Michizane found himself among those with insufficient influence in the highest places to retain his posts in the capital. The source of his problem was the dual nature of his position as a court scholar and official. Although he had come to dominate academic circles, as a bureaucrat his status remained modest and insecure. Perhaps Mototsune and Kōkō hoped to temper Michizane's disappointment by assigning him to a reasonably prosperous and advanced province, but that was small comfort.

THE POET AS GOVERNOR

Before Michizane's departure, he was invited to farewell banquets, first at Sukeyo's mansion, then at Mototsune's, and finally at the university. The poem he wrote at Mototsune's banquet suggests he had resigned himself somewhat to leaving the capital:

> A Farewell Banquet at Mototsune's Eastern Pavilion
> Whether as governor or scholar, one should serve the
>   nation loyally.
> Our one emperor's beneficience supports hundreds of lives.
> When I leave this eastern pavilion, over what shall I
>   grieve?
> Only that I shall not see the flowers in the capital
>   next spring![18]

Michizane left the capital on the twenty-sixth day of the third month. The last day of that month marked the end of spring, and so during his journey westward to Sanuki, he wrote:

> While on My Way, I See Off the Spring
> Spring saw off the departing traveler; the traveler now
>   sees off the spring.
> Sad at heart is this man of forty-two years.
> I think of home and tears fill my eyes; my vacant study
>   grows old.
> On the road, sadness increases, but the wild grasses are
>   renewed.
> As time passes, the lingering color of the wild flowers
>   fades.
> The birds know my feelings and at night cry out ceaselessly.
> The breeze and sunshine today have returned home to
>   the east.
> If only they could carry one or two of my thoughts![19]

Details of early Heian provincial administrative procedures are not well documented, but in his poetry, Michizane provides us with rare glimpses of life in ninth-century Sanuki. The view he offers is subjective and in places distorted for literary effect. Certainly he does not give us a minute guide to governmental practice. Still, his poetry paints a colorful picture of the province, and to the extent that details can be corroborated, they are generally reliable.

Soon after his arrival in Sanuki, Michizane went on his first tour of inspection of the province. These tours were among the duties of governors prescribed in the codes:

> Each year, governors shall tour all the districts of their provinces in order to examine the customs, inquire about the elderly, make a record of prisoners, and offer justice to the falsely accused. They shall carefully investigate the fairness of legal judgments, look into the complaints of peasants, sympathetically teach the five constant virtues, and encourage agricultural prosperity. In the villages, if there are individuals who excell at scholarship, follow the way of righteousness, behave filially, perform exceptional deeds, or are notably loyal or pure, they shall be recommended to the court. Those who are not filial, ignore the rites, bring about disorder, or disobey the law shall be reformed. [20]

Michizane described his second tour of inspection in a long poem that reveals his concern for carrying out the duties assigned him in the codes:

Spring Tour

No one will despise me for wishing to see the face of the
    spring breeze,
And so, gazing in the four directions, I try to focus my
    vision on it.
My talents are limited; I must avoid damaging the brocade.
My thoughts are shallow; how can I unravel the tangled
    twine?[a]

. . .

Sitting atop a moss-covered rock, my spirit penetrates the
    earth.
Before the willow flowers, my feet tread on ice.
I excuse myself when persistent callers come to pay their
    respects,
And endure the clerks who see me off so obsequiously.
Surrounded by my writing implements, I idle away my leisure time,
And when poetry flows from my mouth, I am unable to stop it.
Every affair ought to be based on the principles of goodness
    and virtue.

All activities should be as prayers for the harvest of rice
and millet.
At a mysterious shrine, an aged shaman tells strange tales.
At an ancient temple, the venerable priest recites occult
parables.
When the rain falls, the provincial warehouse is repaired.
While fields are being burned clear, irrigation ditches are
marked.
Opening the prison door, I check that no one is unjustly
held.
Lightly raising my reed whip, I gently chastise habitual
wrongdoers.
I try to teach the youths and lower classes to respect their
elders and superiors.
I fear the poor and weak will suffer at the hands of the
rich and powerful.
The aged who cannot afford meat must be cared for and
comforted.
The orphans who would otherwise starve and sleep without
pillows must be aided.
Before the gate of a dilapidated hut, I inquire of its owner's
welfare.
By a field that two men ought to cultivate, I ask, "Why is
there only one?"
Children playing on their bamboo horses neglect to welcome
me outside their village,
But a recluse by the roadside lifts his humble staff in
greeting.
Although I have not been so fortunate to have white deer
come up to my carriage,
At least I do not hear myself referred to as a pale hawk.[b]
If I govern poorly, my good name will be ruined.
How can I earn a good rating and advance in the world?
Reining my horse, I set off for the office building at the crack
of dawn
I do not put on my cap to return to my residence until the
evening clouds gather.
On top of the post station are three drums.
In the window of the public office there is a single lamp.
When people have dispersed and all is quiet, I often grow
sad.
When night deepens and I sleep alone, with difficulty I control
my tears.
Since my arrival, half a year has passed; I have tried
to be honest and conscientious,

But how bitter to be surrounded by corruption like a swarm
of dirty black flies.[21]

Notes:
a. In other words, avoid damaging the brocade of well-ordered government
   and unravel the complexities of administration. The meaning of the following couplet is unclear and so it has been omitted.
b. White deer were said to tamely approach the carriage of a good official;
   cruel officials were said to behave like merciless pale hawks.

On his tours of inspection, Michizane was performing the
tasks required of him by the codes, but his attitude toward his
official duties was ambivalent. This and other poems show that,
in the best Confucian tradition, he intended to govern correctly and to the best of his abilities. In particular, he was concerned
about maintaining the high standards set by his two predecessors,
whom the local populace was said to have remembered with
affection.[22] Yet at the same time, as governor he had to deal
with local functionaries—some of them corrupt—whom he liken-
ed to "a swarm of dirty black flies."

As governor, Michizane bore ultimate responsibility for the
administration of Sanuki, but he was assisted by many other
officials. Local administration operated on two levels. On top
were the governor and his immediate subordinates who were
sent from the capital for terms of four to six years. The number
of these officials varied. Provinces were divided into four categories according to size, with the larger provinces assigned more
officials. Nominally, Sanuki was in the group that consisted of
the second-largest provinces. Thus, Michizane should have had
as assistants—and companions—eight officials from the capital.[23]
In fact, however, all officials appointed did not necessarily serve
in the province. While Michizane was governor, at least five
courtiers held absentee appointments in Sanuki, among them
both Michizane's friend Masanori and his future rival Tokihira.
Although most of these men held explicitly supernumerary
appointments, both the lieutenant governor and the supernumerary lieutenant governor of Sanuki remained at court while
Michizane served in the province.[24] Often, one high-ranking
official was considered adequate for each province, regardless of
whether he was nominally a governor or lieutenant governor.
For example, Michizane's grandfather had been the chief admin-

istrative officer of a province, even though he only held the title of lieutenant governor.

Although the full complement of officials may not have been present, Michizane did have the assistance of some men from the capital, at least one of whom was sufficiently well educated that he and Michizane could enjoy an occasional exchange of poems expressing their commitment to effective administration of the province:

> Answering Provincial Secretary Fujiwara's Poem
> "The Blossoms at the Office Building"
> The pink cherry bursts into a smile, like the famed
>   mountain pear.[a]
> The former Governor Abe left its fragrance for us.[b]
> But the boundless beauty of the spring garden is of no
>   practical use.
> Instead, we should hope to see an abundant harvest in the
>   autumn.[25]

Notes:
a. During the Chou dynasty, when Lord Chao was touring the provinces, he fell asleep under a mountain pear tree. The local people respected him so much that after he departed, they protected the tree.
b. Michizane noted, "This flowering tree was planted early in the Gangyō era [877-884] by Governor Abe." Abe no Okiyuki, one of the men Michizane hoped to emulate, had served as lieutenant governor from 878 to 882. In his case, the nominal governor seems to have remained at court, leaving him in charge.

Serving under these officials sent from the capital were the locally appointed district officials (*gunji*) responsible for most of the practical details of governing the province. They were selected from the descendants of men who in an earlier age had been independent local magnates. In Sanuki, this class of men was apparently rather well educated and able, for from it came Sanuki's famous priests and legal scholars. Michizane recognized the importance of these men, and a year after his appointment, he had the number of officials in each district doubled. On the other hand, at the end of his term in office, he noted that, although local difficulties were generally blamed on the governor, in fact the fault often rested with the district officials.[26] As a governor sent from the capital, he was very much dependent on their good will, and accordingly he would sometimes invite local dignitaries to his quarters to share a drink with him:

> On New Year's Day at My Temporary Residence
> I Invite Guests for a Drink with Me
> I invite guests from the village by the river for a cup of
> New Year's wine.
> But it arouses in the host a traveler's thoughts of home.
> Members of the household drink little, hastening instead
> to offer wine to others.
> The village elders pass the cup around many times with
> punishment drinks for latecomers.
> Last year, I sadly parted hands with my family,
> But today a smile shows on my face.
> They stumble onto their carriages, their drunkenness
> not feigned,
> And return home, leaving behind their oars and fishing
> poles.[27]

Michizane described his guests as if they were rustic fishermen. More likely these "village elders" were, if not actually district officials, at least men of similar background, for invitations to the governor's residence could only have gone to men of some status.

Michizane's most serious difficulty as a governor occurred in 888, his third year in Sanuki, when the province suffered a severe drought. Early in the summer, he wrote:

> A Quatrain Sent to Ōe no Koreo, Head Official
> of Utari District
> A drought is certainly the result of bad government.
> We can rely only on the Sutra of Supreme Wisdom.[a]
> When provincial and district officials mingled at the
> reading,
> You and I, both born in the year of the ox [845],
> already had hair tinged with frost.[28]

Note:
a. *Daihannya kyō* (*Mahāprajñāpāramitā Sutra*), which was commonly recited for relief from drought.

And later he began another poem with a long introduction:

On the seventh day of the fourth month in the second year of Ninna
[886], I first arrived in this province and looked about the provincial
capital. A little to the north was a lotus pond and just east of the
pond lived an aged man. He told me, "During the Gangyō era
[877-884], the lotuses here had leaves but no flowers. However,
since the beginning of the Ninna era [885-888], both leaves and
flowers have burst forth." Then, toward the end of summer, after
the season for the flowers had arrived, the old man's words were
proved correct. I addressed my fellow officials and had them compose poems in praise of the blooms. From among the countless
plants in the pond, I plucked enough to distribute to the twenty-eight
temples in Sanuki. Those who heard of this were filled with joy;
those who saw it were inspired with piety. Moreover, I made offerings
of fragrant oil to all the temples and proclaimed that this practice
should continue on to later generations. Last year, I repeated this
rite. I must do as I vowed, but this year, since spring, there has
been no rain and by summer, not even a cloud. Dust has appeared on
the bottom of the pond and the roots of the lotus have dried up.
Gods and men are no longer in accord. Human hearts and natural
phenomena are no longer in harmony. It is not that the Buddha's
power is inadequate, but rather that men lack faith. Accordingly, I
write this poem to express my grief:

Beyond my gate is a small pond abundant with lotuses.
Who planted the seeds?—who dug the pond?
Tender new leaves glisten with dew.
The clear stream flowing from the valley never
    grew stagnant.
Leaning on my staff, the view was always
    fresh.
Three times I rode there, beneath the full moon.
Finally I witnessed the new flowers gaily burst forth,
And at last I believed the white-haired old man's tale.
I was confused: had a red banner been planted at the edge
    of the pond?
My eyes were uncertain: did crimson candles shine forth
    from the mud?
I am told that the Pure Land in the West glitters like a
    jewel,
But here in a southern district, I was touched by these
    glorious flowers.
With my religious offerings, I judged the receptivity of
    the people,
And hoped my small deed would help them gain salvation.
My fellow officials, working by the pond, praised me as
    their leader.

Throughout the province, people rushed to make offerings
  before the Buddha.
All together, just twenty-eight temples,
But the flowers seemed enough to fill the three thousand worlds.
People gathered to pluck them, then departed on their
  separate ways.
Alone I meditated on the Pure Land and slept with hands
  clasped in prayer.
From of old, my loyalty has been fixed upon the august
  imperial palace.
Surely this will avail me now and good fortune will not
  desert me.
First I prayed that our nation's quarrels should forever
  cease.
Then I begged that my province should produce a bountiful
  harvest this year.
Having come here and made my vow,
I hoped my rite would be continued by later generations.
How could I have anticipated that this year no rain would
  fall?
Because of what wrong have the clouds over this province
  grown dry?
In spring, the wind blew around the mountains and clouds
  settled in the valleys,
But summer days have burned like fire and fields grow only
  smoke.
A greedy poison-dragon has begrudged sending the divine
  downpour.
An evil demon has altogether stopped the flow of the
  benevolent spring.
The shrine priests are exhausted from running about
  distributing offerings.
The monks in meditation weary of sitting and reciting
  sutras.
How sad if the sources of the Cheng and Pai rivers should
  run dry!
Now, talk of virtues of Kung and Huang is but an empty
  dream.[a]
Nearby, I see dust floating and fragrant flowers dying.
I know that everywhere the earth burns and young sprouts
  are scorched.
We have exhausted our accumulated good fortune and must
  seek the sweet tree of immortality.
We have sincerely performed all the rites and must wait
  for the harvest of the fields of blessedness.[b]
Please do not laugh at the impotence of the exalted rituals.
I am ashamed of my administration's many errors.

While in confusion I wonder how to control the reins, the
    exhausted horse collapses.
As I clumsily try to adjust the fire, the small fish I am
    cooking crumbles to pieces.[c]

. . .

The suffering carves at my flesh, carves at my bones, and
    renders me an inlaid sculpture of despair!
How could this hymn become anything but "A Song of Unhappy
    Fate."[d] [29]

Note:

a. The Cheng-ch'ü and Pai-ch'ü were irrigation ditches built by virtuous rulers
   and famous for irrigating and bringing prosperity to their surrounding territories. Kung Sui and Huang Pa were Han dynasty officials known for their
   encouragement of agriculture.
b. Buddhist allusions: to eat the fruit of the "sweet tree" guaranteed immortality; the "fields of blessedness" (*punya-kṣetra*)—in other words, good deeds—
   produce good fortune just as conventional fields produce crops.
c. Chinese allusions: in the *Shih-ching,* a tired horse's falling down is a metaphor for administrative collapse; according to *Lao-tzu,* a great nation must
   be governed with the same care required to cook a delicate fish. Because the
   meaning of the couplet that follows is obscure, it has been omitted.
d. A Chinese *yueh-fu* theme. *Yueh-fu* are said to have originated as folk songs
   collected during the Han dynasty, but later became standard poetic form.

The Buddhas do not seem to have been cooperative, and finally, Michizane turned to Japan's native deities and addressed a
prayer to the gods of Fortress Mountain (Kiyama). Fortress
Mountain, close to the provincial capital, acquired its name because its level top once had been fortified in ancient times. It
was also the site of a local Shinto shrine. By Michizane's day,
the fort had fallen into disuse, but the shrine remained an important place of worship.

A Prayer to the Gods of Fortress Mountain

On the sixth day of the fifth month in the fourth year of the
Ninna era [888], the Governor of Sanuki, Senior Fifth Rank Lower,
Lord Sugawara reverently prays to the gods of Fortress Mountain
with offerings of wine, fruit, incense, and cloth. Since the fourth
month, week after week hardly any rain has fallen. Officials and subjects are troubled. Sprouts and seeds cannot be planted. I carefully
divined with tortoise shells to seek auspicious signs and faithfully
tried to follow the five constant virtues. A governor shares the grief
of his people and their dismay over this calamity. What a misfortune
to meet with such unseasonable weather! Perhaps my administration
is not virtuous or my intentions are not being conveyed?

Of the many mountains in the province, this one is the grandest, and of the numerous shrines, this one is the holiest. I have chosen an auspicious time to make this reverent plea. The gods can judge my sincerity. Sanuki contains eighty-nine villages with two hundred thousand inhabitants. If not one village experiences calamity and if not one mouth voices complaint, then the holy offerings of food, cloth, and jewels will be pure and plentiful. The people will surely respond to the gods' generosity with prayers of thanksgiving and respect for divine power. But if the benevolent rains are few and the dry clouds of drought gather, the power of the gods will be as if hidden, and the people's prayers will remain unanswered. Thus, the gods will lose their luster and the people will be filled with anger. Both gods and men will suffer. The rites of worship will fall into disuse. As gods, you may judge this. Do not begrudge us your divine assistance. I beg you to accept this prayer.[30]

This prayer, with its threat that offerings might have to be abandoned, apparently proved more effective than the deferential Buddhist rites, and it is said that rain fell the next day. Today, a golf course occupies the top of Fortress Mountain, and the site of the shrine is marked only by a small rude altar. However, at a nearby Tenjin shrine, local believers still annually perform a dance to commemorate Michizane's prayer and the rain that ended the drought.[31]

Always, both in Sanuki and the capital, Michizane took his official responsibilities seriously, but despite his success in summoning the divine assistance needed to alleviate the drought, his overall effectiveness as governor is open to question. Before he arrived in Sanuki, his immediate predecessor, Fujiwara no Yasunori (825–895), reportedly commented, "The new governor is indeed a great scholar whose knowledge is far beyond my ability to measure. But consider his intentions! Truly he is a dangerous man."[32] Since Yasunori's remarks appear in a biography written by Michizane's rival Kiyoyuki, they can probably be dismissed as an attempt by Kiyoyuki to substantiate his own personal prejudices by attributing them to Yasunori, a highly regarded official. Contrary to the statement put into Yasunori's mouth, Michizane's intentions were good. Yasunori, however, may have had legitimate doubts of a different sort, for despite his learning, Michizane indeed was not well suited in temperament or training to the duties of a governor.

Japan's ritsuryō codes were based on the Confucian view that

5. *Governor Michizane praying for rain*
   Source: Sugawara jikki.

government ideally was to be entrusted to men of ability and virtue, and that training in the classics provided good background for such men. Michizane had the requisite education and thought of himself as a scholar-official in the Confucian mold. Thus, ignoring the realities of court politics, one could view his appointment as an example of the Heian court's adherence to the letter and the Confucian spirit of the *ritsuryō* codes. But even if Michizane had been sent to govern Sanuki for idealistic rather than political reasons, his appointment was not a wise one. The problem was that Confucian theory was not very realistic, at least as the Japanese were applying it. Aristocratic poets from the court did not necessarily make effective governors. Michizane meant well, but his skills as an administrator did not equal his talents as a poet.

During the early Heian period, the court was troubled by the poor quality of the silk sent to the capital as tax goods. On one occasion, some of it was said to be "just like a spider's web in the autumn"; another time some was described as "woven from fibers of weeds." Over a year after Michizane's arrival in Sanuki, the court issued one of its frequent regulations intended to help correct this problem:

> The silk sent from nineteen provinces is exceptionally coarse and quite unlike that sent in the past. The governors are to be officially reprimanded. Silk of the old type shall be taken from the government storehouse and a bolt of it sent to each governor as a model for the silk that in the future shall be presented.[33]

Sanuki was one of the provinces criticized for sending inferior silk, a clear indication that Michizane's performance as governor was less than satisfactory. His problems continued after his term in the province ended. Before a new governor could assume office, the records of the previous administration had to be approved. In Michizane's case, the process would take a whole year, and until the matter was settled, he could not be appointed to a new office. During this wait he submitted his memorial stating that governors alone should not take full blame for provincial difficulties, that district officials too were partly responsible. Delays in reappointment following provincial service were common and do not necessarily mean that Michizane was guilty of any serious misconduct; however, scattered evidence does suggest that Michizane had not been as effective a governor as he would have wished.[34]

A JOURNEY HOME AND THE AKŌ INCIDENT

During Michizane's first year in Sanuki, he constantly expressed his loneliness:

> Autumn
> Whom can I ask whether I deserve this fate?
> Autumn comes and darkness lengthens; the man away
>   from home grows sad.
> Outside my window, the cold wind buffets the ancient
>   pine,
> Above the shabby bamboo fence, the moon descends.
> I know not the comforts of playing the koto or
>   drinking wine.
> I am able only to praise the Buddha and recite
>   poems.
> As night deepens, on the mountain road the songs of
>   woodcutters cease.
> Alas, will the neighbor's cock never announce the
>   dawn?[35]

> Winter Night Away from Home
> In my traveler's lodgings, autumn has passed and
>   winter arrived.
> My face grows haggard from sleeping alone night
>   after night.
> The guards at the gate coldly blow their horns.
> I am startled by the morning bell of Kaihōji.[a]
> Our enjoyment of pleasures follows the position of
>   the moon.
> We recite poetry slowly or quickly in harmony
>   with the wind in the pine.
> Sleep long eludes me as I ponder the troubles of
>   this world
> And thus I am unable to meet my friends even in
>   dreams.[36]

Note:
a. Michizane noted that Kaihōji was a monastery to the west of the provincial capital.

During Michizane's second year, however, he discovered that Mototsune had not been totally mistaken in suggesting he might enjoy the scenery of his temporary home. He continued to miss his family and friends, but his loneliness was mitigated somewhat by taking excursions to enjoy Sanuki's natural beauties:

> Visiting the Mountains on a Spring Day
> Some afternoons, I find a lull in my official
> duties,
> And go two or three leagues to visit the mountains.
> By the edge of the valley stream, I listen to the birds' gay
> songs.
> From my horse, I pluck the flowers that weigh the branches
> down.
> To appreciate the clouds of ivy, I enter deeply into the
> mountains.
> Hating the bother of public duties, I am reluctant to
> return.
> Since first arriving at this post, I have felt weary and
> depressed,
> But encouraged by the spring breeze, my face breaks into
> a smile.[37]

After his second autumn in Sanuki, Michizane was granted permission to return home briefly and spend the winter in the capital. His subordinates feared that he might choose to remain there, and one of them wrote inquiring about his plans. Michizane responded with:

> In Reply to a Message from Clerk Kura:
> Reassuring the People of Sanuki Who Worried I Might Not Return
> When the oars came to rest at an isolated island, I
> received a letter.
> I could see it contained your deepest feelings.
> How sad that today we tearfully parted!
> How fortunate that last year we were able to meet!
> My voyage home should take only six days.
> I grieve that your term of office ends this winter.
> If I did not expect to see you again in this province,
> Why would I have planted the small pine by our office?[38]

Michizane's frequent complaints of loneliness may have caused the people of Sanuki—or at least his fellow officials—to worry that their governor might prefer to remain at home.

Certainly one would expect him to have rejoiced at the opportunity to visit family and friends. Yet his journey to the capital was filled with uncertainties:

> Spending a Night on Board the Boat
> My temporary lodgings are on a solitary boat.
> The east wind does not speed my journey.
> Amidst my travels, once again a traveler.
> My lot in life, always to live adrift.
> I now speak of profit like the salt merchant,
> But I would rather sound like the old fisherman.
> Here I have escaped from the dust of the world
> And have even neglected to inquire about conditions at
>   home.[39]

Later on his voyage, he wrote a series of five poems expressing Taoist sentiments. They include:

> On the shore grows a single pine
> Amidst layers of rocky cliffs.
> The pine stands there in complete isolation:
>   the shore is cut off in all directions.
> Thus confined, the short branches grow old,
> And following their nature the delicate needles densely
>   flourish.
> Insentient clouds spontaneously gather
> And lightly cover its joints with snow.
> Although attacked by fierce winds,
> Its roots hold firm; it is not defeated.
> Even the famed carpenters of old
> Would find its gnarled wood useless.
> Red trees grow in the southeast island.
> Yellow willows flourish on the northwest peaks.
> The wealthy always love to use them,
> And greedy officials sometimes gather them.
> They are cut with knives and chopped with axes.
> Born in spring, they do not last through winter.
> Elegance is truly to be feared.[a]
> I too would like to dwell on the isolated shore.

Note:
a. The word here translated as "elegance" (*monjō*) also means "literature."

> The white-haired man has abandoned fishing;
> Tears now fill his boat.
> Last night he possessed it,

But today he gazes in vain at his hands.
Although he would like to search, defying the waves,
He is too old and feeble to endure the winds.
This hook, handed down through generations;
How sad, his suffering knows no end.
What shall he leave to his descendants?
How shall he pay for food and clothing?
Try wielding the plow? He would feel ashamed before farmers,
Try raising sheep? He would be embarrassed before shepherds.
Not reluctance to change calling,
But regret because of former success.
Should a monk return to the laity,
In the monastery he is despised and barred entry.
When a Confucian scholar becomes an official,
The world laughs at his following the ambitious crowd.
At last I understand the old man's weeping.
He laments that he cannot persevere to the last in his trade.

Amidst the sea, an untethered boat
Drifts north, south, east, and west.
Its original master is unknown,
But an old man weeps on a nearby strand.
He had heard the price of salt was rising
And into an ill wind boldly set forth.
At night he proceeded three or four leagues,
Struck a rock, and was thrown into the darkness.
His broken rudder was washed away in the tide.
His emptied baskets float about in the waves.
He had sought tenfold profit,
But instead lost his chance of a lifetime.
Although the old man's tears are painfully sad,
His empty boat seems to enjoy its freedom.
When a man faces troubles before him,
Afterward everything causes him grief.
Those who seek unfair advantage are always thus,
But men with no ambitions are truly free.
Affairs ceaselessly begin and end;
I had best learn from *Chuang-tzu*. [40]

The two poems not translated describe a herd of deer struggling to swim through the sea and a monk who claimed to have renounced food but greedily took some rice Michizane offered. This whole sequence is distinctly different from the Taoist poems Michizane had written when visiting his aristocratic friend Masanori. Michizane was no longer romantically describing the tranquil pleasures of an idealized fisherman. Instead, he imaginatively and vividly portrayed things he apparently witnessed on a real voyage through the Inland Sea. These poems hint that Michizane had come to feel real doubts about the value of his official career. He had been an ambitious and successful young man, but had been frustrated in his career by a provincial post that he did not consider suitable. [41]

Michizane was troubled not only by his own fate, however, but also by rumors of problems at court that were soon to develop into the so-called "Akō Debate." Michizane himself played only a minor role in the incident, but many of his scholarly friends were intimately involved and it would have important consequences for his own career. Furthermore, it helps illustrate the political implications—and potential dangers—of seemingly academic squabbles. The origins of this incident lay in another unprecedented succession in the imperial line. Four months after Kōkō had become emperor, he gave the surname "Minamoto" to all his twenty-nine children, thereby technically removing them from the imperial family and the line of succession. Kōkō had been named sovereign only through the grand minister Mototsune's intervention, and Mototsune did not wish Kōkō's descendants to become emperors. Instead, he intended that the next sovereign should be one of the princes whom he had temporarily by-passed because of their youth but who were more closely related to him. Although Kōkō was in no position to oppose Mototsune's desires, privately he would have liked to revive the practices of his father Nimmyō's day when the imperial family had not been dominated by the Fujiwara. His appointment of many imperial relatives to high office is one indication of this desire, but on the whole, he could do little to make his wishes felt. [42]

In the eighth month of 887, only three and a half years after becoming emperor, Kōkō fell mortally ill. A crown prince still had not been named and so fourteen of the highest court officials, including Mototsune and the scholar Hiromi, presented a petition requesting that the matter be settled promptly. Three days later, on the twenty-fifth of the month, an edict stated that Kōkō's seventh son Sadami, a young man of twenty-one, was to have his surname Minamoto taken back so he could return to the imperial family. The next day he was proclaimed crown prince just as Kōkō passed away. Sadami then became Emperor Uda. This was an unprecedented event. Previously, when a successor to the deposed Emperor Yōzei was being sought, another former prince who had been removed to the Minamoto family expressed a desire to resume his status and be named the next sovereign. Mototsune rejected the suggestion because, he argued, a man who had been given a surname and made a subject could not return to the imperial family. That, however, is precisely what now took place, and even the mentally deranged Yōzei was displeased by his former retainer's becoming emperor.[43] Why then did Mototsune not object to Uda's selection?

The answer can be pieced together from surviving fragments of Uda's diary and a few other sources. The delay in naming a crown prince had resulted from the desire of both Kōkō and Mototsune to retain the appearance of harmony, for to select a successor would bring into the open their conflicting interests. Privately, however, Kōkō favored his son the future emperor Uda, a promising man who was just entering his prime. Two people helped convey the emperor's views to Mototsune. The first was Mototsune's sister who served as principal handmaid (*naishi no kami*) and had helped raise Uda. The second was Hiromi, a man personally close to Uda, as subsequent events would reveal. After Kōkō had received the petition requesting him to name a successor, the ailing emperor summoned Mototsune to ask his advice, and Mototsune himself is said to have recommended Uda. He had been apprised of the emperor's wishes and could hardly go against them in the dying man's presence. Moreover, since he had been able to dominate the court even during the reign of Kōkō, a mature man to whom he did not have close familial ties, he reasoned that he would be able to continue to do so during the new reign.

The emperor was pleased with the choice and summoned Uda. As he grasped his son's hand in his left hand and his chancellor's in his right, tears of gratitude filled his eyes. "I have become infirm, although I do not know the cause," he said to Uda. "Since Mototsune is truly noble, he should be made your principal minister," After Kōkō had passed away, Uda followed these instructions and said to Mototsune, "Now I have no parent on whom I can rely; I am indeed alone. I have not yet mastered the ways of government and am uncertain to whom I should turn. . . . You were regent during the previous reigns and your relation to me is as close as that of father to son. Please be my regent." "Should I be so ordered," Mototsune responded, "I will do my best to serve you."[44] The new reign appeared to be off to an auspicious start.

The new emperor's position, however, differed from that of his father, a fact that made Mototsune increasingly uneasy. Whereas Kōkō's mother had been a Fujiwara, albeit one only distantly related to Mototsune, Uda's mother was a member of the imperial family. Also, in contrast to Kōkō, who became emperor only after years of service in the court bureaucracy, Uda was a vigorous young man with little experience in government, as he himself admitted. His actions might be hard to predict. Therefore, assurances of cooperation to the contrary, the Fujiwara leader came to harbor doubts concerning Uda's intentions.

Mototsune's reaction to his new sovereign was in keeping with his usual political style. His predecessor, the first Fujiwara regent Yoshifusa, had been a forceful man who on occasion had driven his enemies from the court to mysterious deaths in the provinces. Mototsune, on the other hand, avoided such brazen maneuvering, even though his powers were as great. When affairs at court were not to his liking, he preferred to withdraw temporarily rather than actively interfere. Under Yōzei, he had gone into a brief retirement until the misbehavior of his nephew the emperor had become so intolerable that he was obliged to replace him. When Uda became emperor, Mototsune again withdrew to his mansion to await the promised edict asking him to run the government as he had during previous reigns. On the twenty-first day of the eleventh month, only four days after formally becoming emperor, Uda duly requested Hiromi to draft such an edict; it contained the first use of the term "*kampaku*." On the twenty-sixth day of the following month, Mototsune declined the appointment with a reply drafted by Michizane's protégé Haseo. This was a formality and in no way reflected Mototsune's true intentions. The next day, Hiromi drafted another edict expressing the same intent as the previous one, but this time, instead of using the term "*kampaku*," he referred to Motosune as "*akō*," a title that had previously been used by

Kōkō when granting Mototsune the powers of chancellor. At first, Mototsune did not respond.[45]

The new year, 888, began with the emperor and the chancellor still on reasonably good terms. Affairs were not, however, going as smoothly as they appeared to be. Mototsune had come to suspect that Uda indeed was showing signs of wanting to rely less on his chancellor than on men directly loyal to the imperial family, one of those men being Hiromi. Mototsune's displeasure was further aroused when the Fujiwara scholar Sukeyo informed him that, in ancient China, the title *akō* was strictly honorary and brought with it neither duties nor powers.[46] The issue was similar to the earlier questions concerning the status and duties of a grand minister, and again Mototsune was not interested in purely honorary titles. From some time in the second month, he refused to participate in court business. In the fourth and fifth months, scholars were commanded to offer opinions on the meaning of the term *akō*. All the opinions presented followed Sukeyo's interpretation that it was an honorary title.

Mototsune informed the emperor that as *akō*, there was no need for him to take up any responsibilities, but if summoned— presumably with a more suitable title—he would gladly resume his duties as chancellor. Uda then ordered Sukeyo and Hiromi to the palace to debate the matter. Afterwards, he lamented in his diary:

> Today I summoned to court the individuals involved. Both presented their arguments and on hearing them, I thought both quite reasonable. But the day was very hot, and my heart was filled with anxiety. Thus I could come to no decision. All affairs of government, great and small, have stagnated. All the provinces and all the ministries complain ceaselessly.[47]

Eventually, the emperor noted in his diary that, as a result of his distress and emotional exhaustion, he had come to suffer from impotence. Fortunately, that difficulty was alleviated by a drug one of his ministers recommended.[48] Uda's political problems, however, were not so easily solved. The high court officials were all claiming illness and refusing to do their duty, in fear of Mototsune's wrath should they appear to be siding with his opponents.

Without Mototsune, the court could not function, and steps had to be taken to placate him. On the seventh day of the sixth month, Uda proclaimed that Hiromi's choice of the term *akō* had been contrary to his wish and formally requested that Mototsune resume his duties. This was to no avail. The incident finally quieted down in the tenth month. On the second day of that month, Uda took a daughter of Mototsune as consort, and on the thirteenth, legal experts were ordered to consider Hiromi's punishment for having acted contrary to the emperor's will.[49] At last this seems to have satisfied Mototsune, and, by the time punishment was determined two days later, Hiromi had been pardoned. On the twenty-seventh, Mototsune and Hiromi resumed their duties. Thus ended the Akō Debate. Its overt cause was a seemingly minor question of terminology, but in reality it was a power struggle between emperor and minister. The issue was sufficiently important to bring court business to a standstill for almost a year.

Probably Uda had not originally planned to restrict Mototsune's authority by naming him *akō;* however, once the issue was raised, he felt obliged to support his friend Hiromi, whom in his diary he called "my professor." Whatever Uda's original intentions may have been, later events would prove that Mototsune's fears were justified. Uda would indeed attempt to limit Fujiwara power. Thus, the significance of the ancient Chinese title *akō* was not the ultimate issue, despite the protracted scholarly debate that ensued. The real question was whether Uda could rule without relying on Mototsune. Uda had asked Mototsune to continue in his role as chancellor, but at the same time had turned to personal associates for advice. This was cause enough for Mototsune to retire from government and thereby prove through his departure that court administration could not function without him. Mototsune clearly demonstrated who was the more powerful man.

Although Michizane's direct involvement in the Akō Debate was limited, it would have a profound influence on his subsequent career. Michizane arrived in the capital late in 887 and was present at Uda's formal accession ceremony on the seventeenth day of the eleventh month. This was the occasion of his promotion to the senior fifth rank lower. By the second month of the following year when Mototsune grew adamant about the term *akō*, Michizane was already back in Sanuki. Still, Michizane was deeply concerned about the issue. It split his scholarly faction in two. Both Hiromi and Sukeyo, the two principal scholars involved, had been students of his father's and were friends of his. Worse, Sukeyo and Haseo joined with Michizane's enemy Kiyoyuki when they criticized Hiromi. All the scholars at court, except Hiromi, seem to have realized where ultimate political power lay and sided with Mototsune. Michizane was distressed to see his friends thus quarreling with each other. In more general terms, he also worried that this commotion, masquerading as debate over a pedantic trifle, was a detriment to the whole academic community because it made a farce of scholarship. His anxiety while journeying back to the capital was probably the result of rumors that Mototsune was not actively supporting the new emperor. While in the capital, Michizane joined with his friend, Taira no Suenaga—Masanori's brother—and sent a letter to Mototsune, admonishing him for his behavior.

After his return to Sanuki, Michizane followed the Akō Debate as closely as he could, and with obvious distaste:

> Saddened by a Letter from Home
> A letter arrives from my home in the capital.
> On borrowed paper, it mixes public and private:
>   I read it facing the corner.
> A child is ill, and I first lament my duties in a distant
>   province
> But ugly disputes then make me glad I am not a Confucian
>   scholar at court.
> Why should I grieve that summer and winter my family is poor?
> I only fear the dangerous wind and waves on my way
>   through this world.
> Away from home, I quietly discuss the way of kingly
>   government.
> But the mountains are nearby and I shamefully admit I
>   have come to resemble a woodcutter.[50]

> Thinking of All My Poetic Friends:
> Sent to the Former Lieutenant Governor of Mino,
> Shimada no Tadaomi
> Only few of our nation's poets remain in the capital,
> And they all exhaust themselves arguing about *akō*.[a]

Kose's tenure in his busy provincial office is almost
   complete,
But Abe's vexatious duties are not yet ended. [b]
Nothing can alleviate the drought here in the south,
And what are the sentiments of the coarse barbarians in
   the east?
Your term in the province over, surely you have ample
   leisure;
The sun and moon, the misty view, appreciate them
   as you like. [51]

Notes:
a. Here, Michizane noted, "I hear that the court has ordered all scholars to
present opinions on the duties of an *akō*."
b. Kose no Fumio was serving as governor of Echizen, and Abe no Okiyuki as
lieutenant governor of Kōzuke.

It was small comfort to Michizane that he was safely removed
from the Akō Debate. Some of his best friends were all too involved in a rather unseemly way, while others, like himself, were
isolated in the provinces. He envied Tadaomi who was now in
the capital without official position or involvement in the incident.

As the Akō Debate was about to reach its climax, Michizane
received a letter from Hiromi. All of Hiromi's scholarly associates at court had turned against him, and he too, like Mototsune,
had retired to his mansion. He requested that Michizane come
to his aid. [52] Michizane promptly returned to the capital for a
second time and presented Mototsune with a long letter giving
his opinion on the matter. In contrast to his more timorous
colleagues, Michizane did not hesitate to strongly support
Hiromi and point out Mototsune's folly.

Michizane stated that the *akō* affair caused him great anxiety,
first, out of concern for the fate of his own scholarly calling and,
second, out of concern for Mototsune's standing as a loyal minister. Michizane proceeded to defend Hiromi as a conscientious
scholar. Writers could not possibly quote entire classics, Michizane pointed out, but instead borrowed appropriate terms to
convey their meaning. Such practices were necessary if one
wanted to write elegantly. The term *"akō"* as used in the *Book
of Songs* and the *Classic of History* indeed referred to an honorary title; however, as used in later works, it described an official

with duties comparable to Mototsune's—a fact other scholars had failed to mention. Certainly Hiromi had no intention of implying that Mototsune had no duties. If Hiromi were punished for such a trivial matter, later writers could hardly escape similar accusations, and the result would be to bring about the decline of literature.

Having defended Hiromi's scholarship, Michizane went on to point out the impropriety of Mototsune's actions. Michizane observed that Hiromi's status at court was in some ways even superior to Mototsune's. Hiromi had contributed to the selection of the new emperor, and his daughter had borne two of the emperor's children. Thus, in service and in personal ties to the emperor, Hiromi surpassed Mototsune. To punish such a learned and dutiful man would only bring shame to the Fujiwara. Since ancient times, the contributions of the Fujiwara had been great, but, according to Michizane, in recent years the family's fortunes had faded somewhat. Mototsune alone, with his superior virtue, could maintain the good name of his ancestors. Ominously, Michizane noted, "A single termite can destroy a thousand-foot tree; a mere ant can bring down a ten-thousand-yard embankment." In strong language, Michizane reprimanded the chancellor:

> You, Mototsune, occasionally served at the national shrine, but how can that service compare with the merit of Hiromi's accumulated days of worship? Because of your position, you are supposed to be a model of behavior, but how can being a model compare with Hiromi's active efforts as a teacher? Your office gives you the nobility of a great minister, but how can that status compare with his as the grandfather of princes? [53]

Michizane's letter was courageously outspoken. No other scholars at court had dared to disagree with Mototsune. Previously, Michizane had gone somewhat farther than his colleagues in pointing out the honorary nature of Mototsune's position as prime minister; however, he had qualified this view by also stressing the great prestige attached to the office. This letter was far less restrained, possibly because it was only a personal letter, not a public statement of opinion.

Despite its strong tone, the immediate effect of Michizane's letter is uncertain, for it appears to have been written in the eleventh month, well after the Akō Debate had been brought to a satisfactory conclusion. Perhaps because of poor communications, by the time Michizane had received Hiromi's letter and made his way to the capital, the affair had already ended, and Michizane's letter was simply a belated statement of his views. Alternatively he may have arrived in time to help mediate the settlement and then sent the letter afterwards as a summary of his opinions. A final possibility is that the date implied in the modern text of the letter is the result of a copyist's error and the letter was indeed presented in time to influence Mototsune's actions. Surviving evidence is inadequate to permit a definite conclusion. Ultimately, however, the letter probably contributed both to Michizane's rise to a position of political power and to his eventual downfall. Even if it did not affect the outcome of the Akō Debate, it brought Michizane to Uda's attention as one of the few able and learned men at court who had the courage to oppose the Fujiwara.[54] Unfortunately, it also must have put a severe strain on the good relations Michizane had been able to maintain with the Fujiwara. In the end, the quarrel between Mototsune and Hiromi had no long-lasting significance for either of the two principals. Just over two years after the two men had settled their differences and returned to work, both had passed away.[55]

THE GOVERNOR AS POET

Returning from his first visit to the capital, Michizane stopped at the Akashi Post Station and there, on the wall, he wrote:

> Leaving home four days ago, I now lament the spring.
> Why is it that everywhere the plum and willow are revived?
> You ask why the traveler is so melancholy?
> The governor of Sanuki is at heart a poet![56]

For Michizane the official, the years in Sanuki were often frustrating, but for Michizane the poet, they were both stimulating and productive. To "quantify" the matter, of the 514 poems in Chinese that Michizane included in his two anthologies, 134 were written during his term in Sanuki. Or, to put it another way, he wrote 26 percent of his extant poems in the space of only four years. Far more significant than such statistics is the fact that he composed some of his most interesting poetry while serving as a provincial governor.[57] The most distinctive feature of Michizane's poetry written in the provinces, including that which he would later write in exile, is its informal quality.

The terms "formal" and "informal" have been used to classify court poetry written in Japanese, and the distinction applies equally well to Japan's literature in Chinese. Formal poems were those on which were lavished more attention and care, whereas informal poems were freer from the constraints of social and literary decorum. Formal poems seem to express what circumstances demanded; informal poems to express individual thoughts and feelings. The distinction between formal and informal is closely related to that between public poetry written for a wide audience and private poetry addressed to individuals or an intimate group. Although all informal poems were essentially private, not all formal poems were public. One could write a formal poem addressed to a friend, but one could not write an informal poem at an imperial banquet.[58] Sometimes these distinctions are slightly blurred, at least in Michizane's poems in Chinese. For example, the poem that Michizane wrote at his last imperial banquet before departing for Sanuki begins in a properly formal tone, but ends on an unexpectedly personal note. His distress over his provincial appointment was such that it intruded somewhat inappropriately into a poem that ought to have merely praised an auspicious occasion.

In most cases, the difference between formal and informal poems in Chinese is readily discernible. The language of formal poetry in Chinese—particularly Michizane's—was often difficult, filled with erudite displays of obscure vocabulary and allusions to the classics. Unless extensively annotated, such poetry can only be read with ease by those thoroughly trained in the Chinese classics. Also, the subject matter of formal poetry was usually conventional and the themes either very lofty or very elegant. For example, when Michizane wrote a poem after one of the university's Memorial Rites to Confucius, as a matter of course he commented on the philosophical significance of the text on which the lecture had been delivered. A palace banquet, on the other hand, called for stress on the splendid elegance of the entertainment and the emperor's personal goodness. These

poems may be admirable as displays of technical and verbal in-
genuity, but their conventional themes and linguistic difficulties
make them unappealing to most present-day readers. Heian
courtiers, however, admired such exemplars of sinological lore,
and thus much of their poetry in Chinese that survives is distinctly formal. Perhaps this is because writing poetry in Chinese
was sufficiently difficult that Japanese rarely bothered to do so
except on the most solemn occasions, which required the effort.
Alternatively, informal poetry may have been written, but not
considered appropriate for inclusion in the imperial anthologies
that preserve much of early Heian literature in Chinese. Gradually, literature in Chinese lost some of its public character as an
expression of the court's commitment to Confucian ideals, and
the major mid-Heian anthology, *Honchō monzui* (Choice literature of this realm, compiled c. 1040), included lighter pieces in
addition to more formal works.

Michizane's works are often cited as the major exceptions
to the dry pedantry and banality of much Heian poetry in
Chinese.[59] The poems offered as evidence of his literary abilities
are usually his more informal ones, although his formal poems,
too, surpass in erudition most of those by his contemporaries.
When he was at home in the capital, Michizane wrote both
formally and informally, but the formal poetry predominated,
especially in his later years. His poetry written in Sanuki, on the
other hand, was virtually all informal. The reason for the sudden
change in his poetic manner is obvious. At court, he was regularly summoned to compose verse at a variety of formal occasions.
In Sanuki, such occasions were all but nonexistent. The one
conspicuous exception was a solitary Memorial Rite to Confucius that Michizane performed during his second year in
Sanuki.[60]

If the number of occasions demanding formal poetry was reduced, those inspiring informal poetry were increased. Michizane's responsibilities as governor may have been great; however,
his subordinates probably carried out most of the routine details
of administration. Michizane had more leisure than he had had
when in the capital, and he used the leisure to indulge in his taste
for literature. Bemoaning one's loneliness was a favorite theme
of Chinese poets away from home and perfectly suited Michizane's mood. Also, Sanuki opened his eyes to new experiences,

such as the beauties of rural Japan and the difficulties in the lives of its common folk. In some ways, the two poems he had written on his journey to Tsuruga ten years earlier presaged those he wrote in Sanuki. Then too, he began by describing his anxieties, but in the end came to admire the seashore he was visiting.

Michizane portrayed the natural beauty of Sanuki, at first in the melancholy mood of a man who was appreciating the view but would have rather been comfortably at home:

Late in the Spring
I Visit the Matsuyama Official Villa[a]
The crossed eaves of the Official Villa are pillowed on the
shoulders of the sea.
Advancing and retreating, the wind and waves do not let dust
accumulate.
Dangerous boulders have been moved to open a roadway,
And I have planted pine seedlings for my successors to enjoy.
On the beach a gull rests its wings as the tide recedes in
the evening.
Twisting streams of heat waves rise from the deep spring
grasses.
The fisherman's songs and fires are not my friends.
Clutching my knees, I recite a verse, then soak my
handkerchief with tears.[61]

Note:
a. A government office was located at Matsuyama, a village then on the beach not far from the provincial capital. Today a Tenjin shrine marks what is said to be its original site, and land has been filled in so that it no longer overlooks a nearby sea.

Michizane gradually came to appreciate his province's natural beauties. Especially after his return from the capital, where he had witnessed the beginnings of the Akō Incident, rustic Sanuki—far removed from court intrigue—came to seem quite attractive indeed:

Composed on an Excursion
When a bird escapes its cage, its wings do not tire.
Here, I can look up to the green mountains and down to
the blue sea.
In the capital, streams flow through the private lands
of princes and nobles.
In the surrounding provinces, flowers bloom in the
forests of great ministers.

6. *Composing a poem at the Matsuyama Official Villa*
   Source: Dazaifu Temmangū.

In jest they accuse others of greed, but slander
    trespassers on their land.
They steal the best views for their own eyes, but scold
    anyone peeking at their pavilions.
Although the marvelous countryside here does not have
    an owner,
Its reputation is gradually spreading and I fear meddlers
    may soon appear.[62]

Now, he claimed to enjoy the company of the fisherman, whose songs he had earlier found so alien:

    Three Poems Written on a Spring Excursion
Freed from work a single day, I regret that spring is
    soon to end.
Alone, I stand before a flower by the river.
Now and again, I fix my gaze northwest towards the
    capital.
Fellow officials point and stare, thinking me a fool.

The flowers have faded, the birds flown off, the feeling
    of spring has waned,
But my poetic ardor stirs me to step out for a
    moment.
Evening darkens, but still I do not return; loudly I chant
    a poem.
The people of the province say I have gone quite mad.

The days grow long, and shorten my night's sleep.
I go out with some local lads to teach them how to read.
Sometimes I meet the warm-hearted old fisherman.
Each of us tells of his aspirations: we do not talk of
    fish![63]

Invented conversations with the common people of Sanuki were a device Michizane occasionally used in this poetry; for example:

    A Question to "Old Man Rush Basket"
"White-haired old man," I ask,
"Why are you known as 'Rush Basket'?
How old are you and where do you live?
And please tell me how you came to be lame and
    stooped."

A Reply Written for the Old Man
"My name 'Rush Basket' comes from my craft.
Fully sixty years old, I live east of the mountain.
I suffered from festering boils and my legs were
   crippled.
Although I do not recall the year, it was when I was a
   small child."

Another Question
"Come forward. I wish to inquire, do you have further
   problems?
The infirmities of age are natural to a man of your
   years,
But the prices of baskets sold in the village must be
   low.
Surely you have not been able to avoid starvation and
   cold."

Another Answer
"I have two daughters, three sons, and one old wife.
Together they cry, both in and out of my thatched hut.
Today, however, we are comforted by your kind inquiry."
When he departed, leaning on his staff, I granted him a
   peck of rice.[64]

This poetic dialogue was not Michizane's only expression of
concern for the poor of Sanuki and their plight:

To whom does the cold come early?
To the man who fled and has been sent back.
Although I search the registers, I cannot find his name.
Asking for it, I try to determine his former status.
The land of his native village is barren.
His fate is to be always poor.
If men are not treated compassionately,
Surely many will continue to flee.

To whom does the cold come early?
To the child orphaned as an infant.
He knows his parents only through stories heard.
Still, he is not exempted from taxes and corvée duty.
His robe woven of kudzu vines is too thin for winter.
He lives on greens hardly adequate to sustain him.
Whenever he suffers from the wind and frost,
He recalls his parents during dream-filled nights.

To whom does the cold come early?
To the man who gathers medicinal herbs.

He sorts them out by their nature,
And thus he fulfills his corvée and tax duties
Although he knows just when to pick the herbs,
He cannot cure his own illnesses and poverty.
If he were found short just one blade of grass,
His brutal whipping would be unendurable.

To whom does the cold come early?
To the sailor employed on another's boat.
He cannot rely on farming or a trade,
But instead is forever a hired hand.
He owns not even enough land on which to stand an awl.
A man who pulls oars is naturally poor.
He thinks nothing of the dangers of wind and waves,
But hopes only for regular employment.

To whom does the cold come early?
To the man who sells salt.
Although boiling sea water may be simple work,
Engulfed by smoke, he cannot worry about his health.
When the weather is dry, the price everywhere drops.
In general, merchants are not poor.
Still he wishes to protest the monopoly of the rich,
And complains constantly to the harbor officials.

To whom does the cold come early?
To the man who gathers firewood.
He can never expect to enjoy any leisure,
But instead must always carry heavy loads.
He goes to the dangerous cloud-covered peaks
And returns to his poor hut.
When the price is low, he has trouble supporting his
    family.
His wife and children are always starving and ill. [65]

These poems come from a group of ten, all of which use the same characters as rhymes, as well as the same first line. The remaining four describe an old widower, a post station attendant, a fisherman, and a peasant who has fled to Sanuki. Michizane borrowed the form of these poems from a similar set of twenty poems by Po Chü-i's friend, Yuan Chen (779–831). Each of Yuan Chen's poems also consists of eight five-character lines, beginning with a repeated question, "Where does spring appear early?" Even the wording of the questions is similar: Yuan Chen and Michizane both begin with the same interrogative word and end with the same character for "early." The subject of the two sets of poems, however, could not be more different. Yuan Chen wrote of the beauties of early spring, Michizane of the suffering of the poor as winter approached.[66] Over a century earlier, Yamanoe no Okura (c. 660–733) had also written poems expressing concern for impoverished peasants, but since then poetic decorum had rejected such vulgar topics, at least in Japanese poetry. In China, however, poems commenting on social problems were more than merely acceptable. Po Chü-i in particular was proud of his socially committed works. If Michizane borrowed the form of his poems from Yuan Chen, their theme had been suggested by Po Chü-i.

Michizane's immediate inspiration, however, was not Chinese poetry but his surroundings in Sanuki. Inaccurate census registers and peasants who fled rather than pay their taxes were serious problems in Michizane's day, and eventually contributed to the decline of the *ritsuryō* land system. The specific occupations Michizane described were all common in Sanuki, which grew many medicinal herbs, was located on the well-traveled Inland Sea, and even today produces much salt.[67] Had Michizane simply been imitating Po Chü-i, he might well have written similar poems while living comfortably at home in the capital, but his only poems depicting the suffering of the poor were written while he was serving in Sanuki and had occasion to witness the problems described. Were Michizane merely following a fashion for things Chinese, he would have depicted his peasants in Chinese surroundings. Instead, the people in his poems are distinctly Japanese from Sanuki.

Michizane was of two minds regarding the people of his province. His ten poems on the suffering of the poor were written not during the years he came to appreciate Sanuki as a refuge from the conflict at court, but rather during his first year there, not long before he commented on his inability to speak with the fishermen. The attitudes expressed appear contradictory and reflect Michizane's ambivalence. As a conscientious governor with the best Confucian intentions, he was sincerely concerned with the welfare of his province's people. His first contacts with their sufferings may have been a shock to the well-bred court aristocrat, and he responded in the way he knew best, with poetic expressions of sympathy. Such expressions, however, did not necessarily mean he enjoyed his actual dealings with the poor. That was a different matter altogether. To his credit, Michizane showed concern over social problems that most of his contemporaries ignored, at least in their poetry. But he merely wrote poems describing the poor and did little to improve their conditions.[68]

In addition to describing Sanuki and its people, Michizane also wrote of more personal matters, such as the faith in Buddhism he had expressed at the time of the drought. His interest in Buddhism was not new. While still a student, he had been asked to compose the introduction to a Buddhist work that had been begun by the famous priest Ennin (793-864). The work was completed by a disciple who had requested Michizane's father to write the introduction. Koreyoshi, however, was busy, and finally Michizane fulfilled the request with an introduction that greatly pleased the disciple. Later, after passing his civil service examination, Michizane went to a monastery for a fifteen-day retreat, and throughout his life he would pray to Amida Buddha for the salvation of those who had died.[69] Although his belief was not new, he expressed it with new conviction while in Sanuki. For example, as governor he was expected to conduct a service of repentance at the end of each year. This custom had been begun at the palace in 838, and eight years later it was decreed that similar rites be performed in all the provinces. In 871, special images were provided:

The Service of Repentance
Suffering is the fate of all sentient beings.
Seeking pity and filled with repentance, we look up to
the Buddha.
Our sage Emperor Nimmyō of the Jōwa era [834-847] first
issued the edict,
And our virtuous ruler Seiwa of the Jōgan era [859-876]
prescribed the regulations for eternity.
Originating in the ninefold imperial palace, it spread
to the many provinces,
Beginning with an emperor's vow, it has been extended to
all his subjects.
As the year ends, for three full days, we restrain our
animal desires.
On this occasion, throughout the land, the Buddha's law
is preached.
Exactly fifty years have passed since this vow was uttered.

It seems ancient, and yet it is renewed.
I am now a provincial governor, dwelling in the south.
Morning and evening, I obediently gaze north toward the
  imperial palace,
But those rushing to offer respect at court are sometimes
  only sycophants.
Those who faithfully carry out their orders are truly
  loyal ministers.
I officially prohibit butchering before and after the
  service,
And give up strong-smelling vegetables during the period
  of worship.
Filled with the pleasures of meditation, I make offerings
  of cold food.
I present the holy water that I drew from the well at
  dawn.
Everyone within this province is filled with pious
  thoughts,
And all the land is swept clean of the dust of moral
  infection.
The fragrance comes from the repentant heart, not from
  the fire.
Hands clasped in prayer bloom without awaiting the
  spring.
We rely on the thirteen thousand Buddhas
To have pity on the suffering of the two hundred eighty
  thousand people.[a]
The dwellers of this far-off province always live in
  poverty,
And future generations too will surely also be poor.
It is not just fate from former lives that produces this
  misery,
But the deeds of one's lifetime also are a cause.
In this endless universe, where did we originate,
And why did we come to this human world?
Should one avoid paying his taxes, the crime is recorded
  by heavenly clerks.
When officials scheme for private gains, the guardians of
  hell take notice.
Unwittingly the fisherman may kill his brother,
And the hunter may enjoy slaughtering his former master
  or parent.
In hell, those who made needless appeals at court have
  their tongues used as ploughs.
Those who followed the mob and spoke foolishly have their
  lips dipped in boiling water.
According to the universal teachings of Buddha, it is sins

that first appear.
If one turns away from harmony for just one night,
  suffering then ensues.
Hacked by the knives of man-eating demons, the flesh
  will fly from the body.
The bones will be sent to hell to be used as firewood
  beneath the devils' cauldrons.
When filled with doubts or ignorance, there can be no
  enlightenment.
I hope to encourage those I govern, although they are
  benighted.
Who is fervently crying, "Be ashamed of your sins!
  Repent!"
The Bodhisattvas's disciple, Sugawara no Michizane! [70]

Note:
a. Here Michizane provided two interlinear notes, first explaining that there
  were 13,000 Buddhas in the *Butsumyō kyō* (Buddhas's name sutra) and then
  that the population of his province was 280,000.

This poem presents a curious blend of Michizane's public and
private concerns. The Buddhist rite described was very much a
public one, conducted in accordance with an imperial edict, and
one of its purposes was to pray for the well being of Sanuki's
people. If the rite was public, the poem itself had a very personal
tone, for the rite was performed shortly after the Akō Debate,
and Michizane's distress over the incident colored parts of the
poem. He favorably compares himself, faithfully obeying imperial orders, with those at court—presumably his less courageous
scholarly acquaintances—who prefer to flatter the influential
rather than tell the truth. It was no coincidence that Michizane
chose to specify the torments meted out to those who made
complaints or spread rumors; those were precisely the men
whom Michizane found most bothersome. Nonetheless, as the
final couplet in particular suggests, whatever Michizane's official
responsibilities or personal grievances, he was performing the
Service of Repentance not simply because it was an official
duty but more importantly because it was something in which
he deeply believed.

Michizane's personal concerns were not all so philosophical:

Noticing My First Scattered Grey Hairs
I am ten years older than P'an Yueh.[a]
Grey hairs, where have you been hiding?

> At first I did not notice you, but now I do!
> Surely it is because I live in sorrow here by the
> seashore. [71]

Note:
a. P'an Yueh of the Chin dynasty (265–317) was famed for his handsome appearance, but wrote that his hair started turning grey when he was only thirty-two, ten years younger than Michizane at the time of his appointment to Sanuki.

Chinese poets also wrote poems lamenting their grey hairs, but here again, even if Michizane's work may have followed Chinese precedents, it was also responding to an immediate problem. Toward the end of Michizane's term in Sanuki, he was forced to resort to strong measures in dealing with this misfortune: he took to pulling out his grey hairs with tweezers. [72] Other worries were not so easily taken care of. Michizane sorely missed his family in the capital, and was concerned about his children's welfare:

> Speaking of My Children
> My sons are foolish, my daughters ugly: such is their
> nature.
> I have already missed the proper times to celebrate their
> coming of age.
> If flowers bloom on an old tree, they will lack the
> crimson hue.
> If birds are nurtured in a dark valley, their wings
> develop slowly.
> My family is not rich in material goods; it must rely on
> me.
> Literature is my profession, but who shall inherit the
> craft?
> It is as pointless as lamenting one's old age,
> Yet when I think of my children, I am filled with grief. [73]

> Unable to Sleep
> Unable to sleep, I fitfully pass the night.
> I am pained by thoughts of my home in the eastern
> division of the capital.
> Its bamboo grove and flower garden are completely
> neglected.
> I hear that in the seventh month my daughter gave birth
> to my grandchild. [74]

Conventionally, wine was supposed to be an antidote to sadness. Michizane, on occasion, enjoyed drinking with friends, but increasingly as he grew older, he found that even though he sought distraction in drink, it offered no comfort. For solace, Michizane turned sometimes to religion, and sometimes to literature:

Quiet Thoughts on a Winter Night

Beneath the eaves of the white-thatched roof, I sit
   before the fire.
My personal serving boy leans against the wall asleep.
The calendar indicates only a single month of winter
   remains.
I have already completed three years of my term in this
   office.
Because I do not enjoy wine, my grief is not easily
   dispelled.
Reciting poetry is dear to my heart, but I have trouble
   concentrating on government.
While thinking of the countless problems that weigh upon
   me,
From my window I receive the message of the impending
   dawn.[75]

The Books in My Temporary Lodging

When I came, I tried to bring only the essentials,
But this did not stop me from bringing more than ten sets
   of books.
The One Hundred and One Methods helps me maintain my
   health.[a]
The five thousand characters of *Lao-tzu* nobly show the
   emptiness of words.
For reciting, I have Po Chü-i's latest collection of
   poems.
To prepare lectures, I refer to Pan Ku's old *History of
   the Han.*
When my term of office is over, I shall carry them back
   with me.
How embarrassing if I were to accidentally forget them
   and fill their boxes with clothing![76]

Note:
a. *The One Hundred and One Methods (Pai-i fang)* was apparently a medical work, although it is not mentioned elsewhere.

Throughout his years in Sanuki, Michizane constantly bemoaned his isolation, and again poetry provided one remedy. He exchanged poems with friends and family at home in the capital and also with friends serving in distant provinces. His students were also a comfort. He corresponded regularly with them and was able to meet with them when he wintered in the capital. Although he was no longer directly involved in their education, he remained concerned for their welfare and was greatly relieved when he learned that his rival Kiyoyuki had passed one of them on the civil service examination.[77] The students seem to have appreciated Michizane's concern, and two took the trouble to visit him in Sanuki:

> Thanking the Newly Accepted Student of Literature,
> Bunya no Tokizane, Who Has Left His Aged Mother
> to Visit His Former Teacher
> How unexpected! I heard your voice and laughter as if in
> a dream.
> Here in this lonely dwelling away from home, half the
> night has passed.
> Before the moons of spring had passed, you broke off a
> branch of the cassia tree.[a]
> The brisk autumn wind blows away the distant cloud.
> Your aged mother in the western division of the capital
> must be envious,
> But this man of leisure in the south is filled with joy
> upon greeting you.
> Perhaps you can get an appointment as a secretary,
> And stay a while to help me with drafting documents?[78]

Note:
a. Breaking a branch off the moon's cassia tree usually alluded to passing the civil service examination. Here it clearly refers to passing the university's entrance examination.

> I Present Paper and Ink to the Student Fujiwara,
> Thanking Him for Coming to Visit
> From across the waves and sands, I unexpectedly meet an
> an old friend.
> When I first saw you this morning, my eyes filled with
> tears.
> Please use this ink and paper
> To send me word in the spring breeze that you have broken
> off a branch of the cassia.[79]

Not all of Michizane's visitors were such pleasant surprises. A certain Miyaji no Tomoe happened to pass through Sanuki on business, and the night before he was to leave, he begged Michizane to write a prayer commemorating his mother's fiftieth year. In the capital, Michizane had written many prayers of this sort, usually for the highest-ranking courtiers, but Tomoe was no high-ranking courtier. In fact, no information about him survives except for this prayer. However, he was persistent. Tomoe made his request late in the evening after Michizane had already retired, and would not be put off. Finally, as Michizane lay in his bedding, he recited something appropriate for Tomoe to write down. Later, Tomoe sent him a copy, which he duly included in his collected works with an explanatory note.[80] Literary fame clearly had its drawbacks.

In some ways, Michizane's earlier career at court seems more typically Chinese than Japanese because his appointments were based as much on his learning as on his family ties. Similarly, his turn to poetry while in the provinces had good Chinese precedents. China's poets, too, when stationed in distant provinces, had sought comfort in their art. Michizane and his poetry are interesting, however, not because they simply followed Chinese patterns, but rather because, while adhering to Chinese patterns, they retained their individuality. Michizane's poems written in Sanuki do not simply reflect Chinese precedents; they reveal the province, its people, and Michizane's personal joys, or more often, his sorrows. At least during his years in the provinces, Michizane was indeed at heart a poet.

5 · The Rise to High Office

The years from 890, when he returned to the capital, until 901, when he was driven into exile, mark the third stage in Michizane's official career. In a remarkably short time, he attained a position of political power unprecedented in the Heian period for a man of his scholarly background. Michizane's academic abilities and, to a lesser extent, his administrative experience in Sanuki made possible his surprising political ascendancy, but a more direct cause was the patronage he received from Emperor Uda. Under Uda, Michizane served as one of the principal agents in the emperor's struggle to revive the political fortunes of the imperial family by means of the *ritsuryō* system. In addition, he became Uda's closest confidant and adviser. Although Michizane could be a difficult individual and had few intimate friends, he remained on the best of terms with the young emperor, perhaps because he was flattered by the unexpected attention he was receiving from Uda, a man who both needed him as an ally at court and also admired him as a poet. Michizane's rise to high office during Uda's reign illustrates how early Heian politics worked at the highest level and reveals a complexity beyond that suggested by later romances in which the principal question is whose daughter will produce the next crown prince. That was indeed a concern, but questions of personal allegiance and occasionally of policy were also considerations.

Having entered the path to political power, Michizane would

never return to a position at the university. He did, however, remain involved in scholarly and literary activities, for Uda turned
to him not only for political advice but also for assistance in
compiling important historical works. Moreover, not long before
his final exile, he gathered his own literary works, plus those of
his father and grandfather, into a anthology that he presented
to Uda's successor Emperor Daigo (885–930, r. 897–930).
Throughout his years in high office, Michizane also continued
to compose poetry, but he was no longer the prolific and colorful writer he had been in Sanuki. Now he wrote principally at
official functions in the learned manner expected for such occasions. The responsibilities of high office allowed him neither the
time nor the privacy to express himself freely in his poetry, and
so although his official career is well documented, his personal
feelings and opinions are largely unknown. Michizane the court
minister's proposals were accepted and some had lasting significance, most notably his recommendation that his mission to
China be cancelled. He compiled histories that remain valuable
sources for modern scholars. And he continued to write poetry
that his contemporaries admired, although most of it was in a
conventional and impersonal style that reveals more of his
technical skills than of his literary individuality. As a result, we
see a different side of Michizane during this stage in his career
than we did earlier.

AN IMPERIAL PATRON

In the summer of 889, as his four-year term in Sanuki was draw-
ing to a close, Michizane began to worry about a new problem:
the evaluation of his accomplishments as governor:

> A Small Banquet to Enjoy the Coolness
> We escape the heat to this leisure pavilion,
> Our complaints vanish, though we still long for home.
> On this southern shore our bodies are cooled;
> Our hearts are calmed by the breeze through the northern window.
> Gazing into the distance, we see the marvelously verdant shoots;
> Afar, the millet appears to be ripening everywhere.
> At times like this, what cares have I?
> Only that my term is almost over, but my achievements are few.[1]

Michizane had reason to be apprehensive. Although he returned to court in the spring of 890, just four years after his original departure, he was not appointed to a new office until one year later. As noted, problems often accompanied a change of provincial governors. Michizane's difficulties may have been largely the result of his own impatience. When a governor's term had ended, he was supposed to remain in his province until the records of his administration had been cleared and the new governor had arrived. In his haste to return home, however, Michizane departed Sanuki before these matters were settled.[2] As a result, he spent his first year back in the capital waiting for the complications to be unraveled. In addition to his uncertain official status, Michizane was also troubled by ill health:

> Resting at Home because of Illness, I Record My Feelings
> for Presentation to the Scholars at the University
> For years, I dwelt by the sea and was filled with frustration.
> Even more vexatious, my futile labors have brought on chronic illness.
> I left the provincial capital after burning painful moxa on my leg,
> And when once again I met my old friends, the boils on my face had
> not yet healed.
> My servants are troubled to find fish swimming in my pots.
> Guests return home laughing after seeing sparrows caught in the net
> over my gateway.[a]
> My body is not yet withered; my spirits are still strong.
> If the medical treatment proves effective, perhaps I can return to
> work.[3]

Note:
a. In other words, his pots had not been used for cooking during his years of
absence. A net hung over one's gate to catch sparrows conventionally suggested that one had few callers.

Michizane's first year back in the capital was not a notably happy one, but still he managed to find pleasures in his freedom from official duties. Once more he turned to Taoism, and this time wrote a sequence of three learned poems based on passages from *Chuang-tzu*. Also, he enjoyed his garden. He was especially pleased when a friend presented him with some new bamboo, and later when his chrysanthemums revived after their neglect during his absence. More significantly, once again he was being regularly summoned to compose poems at the palace. His immediate circumstances were not altogether cheering, but his future prospects seemed reasonably bright and he looked forward to resuming his teaching duties.[4]

Finally, on the twenty-ninth day of the second month, 891, Michizane was appointed head chamberlain (kurōdo no tō), and thus became the chief officer of the Chamberlain's Office, a special institution that had been created in 810 to assist the emperor in his public duties. It was not part of the regular bureaucracy as established by the codes, but because of its important responsibilities and proximity to the emperor, it became a powerful office. Only able men were appointed to it, and their chances of future preferment could be greatly enhanced by developing close personal ties with the emperor and acquiring a familiarity with the operations of the government at the highest level. This office was very different from the posts Michizane and other members of his family had previously held, for it could be a steppingstone to positions of real power at court that would far exceed in influence those theretofore occupied by the Sugawara within the academic community. This appointment was so great an honor that Michizane felt obliged to decline it twice.[5] Earlier, he had drafted documents for other officials going through the formality of declining their high offices, but this was the first time he had to compose such documents for himself.

Michizane's new post foretold the fact that in his remaining years at court he would not resume his academic duties, but would break with family tradition and become increasingly active in court politics. This change in Michizane's career came as a result of a shift in the relative power of the Fujiwara and the emperor. In the first month of 891, Mototsune had died. His heir Tokihira, despite high rank and office, was only twenty-one years old. Michizane's new appointment was made one month after Mototsune's death, and another month later there was a significant series of promotions among the high court nobles. Two Fujiwara were raised to minister of the right and great counselor respectively, but both were elderly men with little political influence. Three Minamoto were also promoted, one to great counselor and two to middle counselor. Among them was Uda's full brother, who was soon brought back into the imperial family as Uda himself had been earlier. These promotions left five vacancies for consultants, only two of which were filled, one by Tokihira and the other by an additional Minamoto.[6] Mototsune's death had finally given Uda the chance to govern as he wished, and he soon began to promote men who were either descendants of the imperial family or who had established reputations for their abilities. As a result, although Tokihira remained a powerful individual, the fortunes of the Fujiwara were clearly on the wane. Of the eleven senior nobles, only five were Fujiwara, and all of them were either very old and politically ineffective or very young and inexperienced.

The men Uda selected to counterbalance the Fujiwara regents' family were principally from Minamoto lineages. The most important of them was Minamoto no Yoshiari (845–897), a son of Emperor Montoku who had been removed from the imperial family by the grant of the surname Minamoto. In that respect, his background was similar to Uda's. In addition to his being of the most noble birth, Yoshiari was also an experienced official. He had been named a consultant in 872 when he was only twenty-eight. Ten years later, he was promoted to middle counselor, and in 888, he was given the key post of minister of popular affairs. Although he had close ties to the Fujiwara regents, he became an important ally of Uda. Michizane may have been responsible for bringing Yoshiari over to join Uda's side in the emperor's struggle with the Fujiwara, for Michizane and Yoshiari had long been friends. They were the same age and possibly even were cousins, since both of their mothers were from the Tomo family. Yoshiari was an experienced member of the Council of State, and after Mototsune's death, he became an active supporter of Uda's programs.[7]

In addition to members of the Minamoto family, two other men received special promotions from Uda. One was Fujiwara no Yasunori, Michizane's predecessor as governor of Sanuki. Yasunori was from the politically weak Southern House of the Fujiwara and had spent most of his career serving in a variety of provincial posts. He had acquired an excellent reputation as an administrator, and so in 892 he was named consultant, his first important post at court and a rare honor for a man with his background. At the time, however, Yasunori was already sixty-eight and three years later he died, before Uda had a chance to employ him in a position of real power.[8]

The other individual from outside the Minamoto family whom Uda specially favored was Michizane. Obviously, Michizane's abilities were very different from Yasunori's, but he too fitted very well into Uda's plans. First, during the Akō Incident, he alone had courageously supported Uda's favorite Hiromi and had criticized Mototsune's actions. Uda's humiliation in the Akō Debate influenced his subsequent decisions. For example, only seven days after Mototsune's death, Sukeyo and Kiyoyuki, scholars who had actively supported the chancellor, were named to serve as governors of Mutsu and Higo, two of Japan's most isolated provinces.[9] Michizane had demonstrated that he was no sycophant of the Fujiwara, and his attitude appealed to Uda. Moreover, Michizane was now a mature and experienced official, familiar with both the court bureaucracy and local administration. Even if he had not been as effective a governor as Yasunori, still he had acquired a better knowledge of provincial conditions than had men whose whole lives had been spent at court. Finally, many of Michizane's former students were now serving in the bureaucracy, and they could be counted on to support their teacher should he be placed in a position of authority.

In addition to these political considerations, Uda also had more personal reasons for supporting Michizane. The emperor was an enthusiastic patron of both Chinese and Japanese poetry. Perhaps he was influenced by the Confucian view that the government ought to encourage literature and scholarship, or possibly it was simply a matter of individual taste. Whatever the reason, Uda combined interests in government and literature as had Emperor Saga more than half a century earlier. Therefore, Uda revived court functions at which Chinese poetry was composed, and after his abdication he encouraged the compilation of the *Kokinshū*, the first imperially sponsored anthology of poetry in Japanese, completed in 905.[10] Michizane's literary skills may have been as important in bringing him to Uda's attention as had been his letter to Mototsune. Eventually a close personal relationship developed between Michizane and Uda. Michizane privately advised the emperor on political matters, lectured to him on Chinese texts concerning government, accompanied him on excursions into the countryside, placed one daughter as an assistant handmaid (*naishi no suke*), and ultimately married two others into the imperial family. One became a consort of Uda and another married his son, Prince Tokiyo (886–927).[11] Earlier Sugawara women had served at court and even produced children by emperors, but these were the first whose marriages had political implications.

Before being sent to Sanuki, Michizane had attained a powerful position in the important Ministry of Ceremonial. Now, under Uda's sponsorship, he was first appointed head chamberlain and soon after returned to his old post in the Ministry of Ceremonial. His subsequent advance to high office was rapid and involved frequent promotions. A comparison of his and Tokihira's careers, outlined in chart 2, reveals how Michizane gradually attained an official position all but equaling that of the Fujiwara leader. Many of the offices mentioned are classified as "left" or "right"; in all such cases, the "left" was considered superior.

At the beginning of 891, Michizane was forty-seven years old, held the senior fifth rank lower, and was out of office. At the same time, Tokihira, although only twenty-one, already held the junior third rank and was serving as honorary consultant. Later that year, Michizane was assigned three important posts, which he held simultaneously. Tokihira's promotions were less impressive. His title of consultant was changed from honorary to regular, and he was given a nominal military office. Two years later, he became a middle counselor, and on the same day four new consultants were named: Michizane, two Minamoto—of whom one was Uda's half-brother—and a Fujiwara not closely related to the regent's family. Thus, although Tokihira was promoted, the number of non-Fujiwara members in the Council of State increased considerably.[12]

When he became a consultant, Michizane attained the highest post ever held by a member of his family. He did so at the age of forty-nine. His father had not become a consultant until he was sixty-one, and his grandfather had only been an honorary consultant, a title he received at the advanced age of seventy. Michizane's status was still inferior to that of Tokihira, but his prospects had become far brighter than those of any of his ancestors. Between 893 and 897, Michizane was rewarded with a succession of increasingly important posts, while Tokihira was merely maintaining his already high position. A simple list of Michizane's offices does not fully reveal his status in the

CHART 2

The Careers of Michizane and Tokihira (891–901)

Year	Date	Michizane	Tokihira
891		(Age 47: Senior fifth rank lower)	(Age 21: Junior third rank, Honorary Consultant, Supernumerary Governor of Sanuki)
	2/29	Head Chamberlain	
	3/9	Junior Assistant Minister of Ceremonial	
	3/19		Consultant
	4/11	Middle Controller of the Left	Commander of the Right Gate Guards (Uemon no kami)
892	1/7	Junior fourth rank lower	
	2/21		Commander of the Left Gate Guards (Saemon no kami)
	5/4		Chief of the Imperial Police (Kebiishi no bettō)
	12/5	Mayor of the Left Capital District	
	?/?	Assistant Chief Investigator of the Records of Outgoing Officials (Kageyushi no jikan)	
893	2/16	Consultant and Supernumerary Senior Assistant Minister Ceremonial	Middle Counselor
	2/22	Major Controller of the Left	General of the Right Bodyguards (Ukon'e no taishō)
	3/15	Chief Investigator of the Records of Outgoing Officials	
	4/2	Assistant Master of the Crown Prince's Household (Tōgū no suke)	Master of the Crown Prince's Household (Tōgū no daibu)
894	8/21	Ambassador to the T'ang	
	12/15	Gentleman-in-Waiting (Ji jū)	

		Michizane		Tokihira
895	1/11	Governor of Omi		
	10/26	Junior third rank, Middle Counselor		
	11/13	Supernumerary Master of the Crown Prince's Household		
896	8/28	Minister of Popular Affairs		
897	6/19	Supernumerary Major Counselor and General of the Right Bodyguards	6/19	Major Counselor and General of the Left Bodyguards (*Sakon'e no taishō*)
			7/7	Superintendent of the Chamberlain's Office (*Kurodo no bettō*)
	7/13	Senior third rank	7/13	Senior third rank
	7/26	Master of the Empress's Household (*Chūgū no daibu*)		
899	2/14	Minister of the Right	2/14	Minister of the Left
901	1/7	Junior second rank	1/7	Junior second rank
	1/25	Supernumerary Governor General of Dazaifu (*Dazai no gon no sochi*)		

Sources: Data in this chart come principally from *KB*, Kampyō 3 (891) – Shōtai 4 (901). They have been supplemented and corrected by information from a variety of other sources; in the case of Michizane, from *KBKK, Kitano Tenjin goden, Kanke godenki*, and *Nihon kiryaku*; in the case of Tokihira, from his biography in *SB*.

bureaucracy. He was not merely being moved from one office to the next, but rather was adding to the total nu.nber of offices he held. He became a veritable Pooh-Bah, holding as many as six titles simultaneously. His complete signature to an 894 document gives some idea of his new stature in the court government: "Ambassador [to the T'ang], Consultant, Assistant Investigator of the Records of Outgoing Officials, Junior Fourth Rank Lower, Major Controller of the Left, Supernumerary Senior Assistant Minister of Ceremonial, and Assistant Master of the Crown Prince's Household, Lord Sugawara."[13] Michizane omitted his given name, but certainly no one could have had difficulty in placing him.

In 895, Michizane finally caught up with Tokihira when he too was promoted an extraordinary three grades to the junior third rank and appointed middle counselor. On the day of that appointment, three new consultants were also named, two of whom were Minamoto with experience in important court offices. Again, Uda was showing his preference for able men who had few ties with the Fujiwara. In 896, the minister of the left, who was the senior Fujiwara statesman, retired, and the following year, Minamoto no Yoshiari, by then minister of the right, died. Thus, the two highest regular posts at court were left vacant at a time when the two positions for major counselors had already been vacant for a year. Apparently, Uda was procrastinating in making appointments to the highest offices until he could fill them with men of his own choice. On the nineteenth day of the sixth month, eleven days after the death of the minister of the left, Tokihira was named major counselor and general of the Left Bodyguards. As Mototsune's heir, he could not be by-passed; but on that same day, Michizane was given the almost—but not quite—equal offices of supernumerary major counselor and general of the Right Bodyguards.[14] The power of the Fujiwara had not been eliminated, but they were forced to share it with a man who was a newcomer to the highest levels of the government.

Tokihira's position would appear to have been somewhat superior, but, in fact, Michizane had become the most powerful man at court. In addition to being a major counselor, Michizane was also minister of popular affairs, which, as noted earlier, was a position of great responsibility usually given to an experienced bureaucrat. Tokihira's only other office was that of general. Although such military titles were great honors, they involved no important duties. Another measure of Michizane's status was his activity on the Council of State in the approximately one and a half years since his appointment as middle counselor in 895. Almost twice as many regulations were issued under his name as under the name of any other noble. These regulations concerned a wide variety of problems, but did not necessarily reflect Michizane's personal policies, for an official could not approve a proposal that he himself had made. Still, only trusted officials were allowed to perform this function, and the number of regulations issued under Michizane's name indicates that he had become the principal figure in the Council of State.[15]

Uda's policies were not restricted to changes in personnel. In addition, as a means of showing his support for the *ritsuryō* system, he became a patron of cultural activities associated with Confucianism, its intellectual foundation. He was an enthusiastic supporter of poetry and he ordered the compilation of two historical works. Michizane was an important contributor to these literary endeavors. Uda also showed his commitment to the Confucian ideal of imperial benevolence in the seventh month of 896 when he called on Michizane to assist him in a special concern. Earlier, Uda had asked an official in charge of the imperial police to check the number of prisoners in the capital's jails, and now he stated to Michizane, "I myself ought go to the prison and consider their release, but my virtue does not equal that of the ancients; affairs today are not yet satisfactory. You are my close retainer, my great teacher. Investigate the prisoners, and based on the facts, release or retain them."

Michizane then went with three other officials to the south gate of the guards' office, where he had the prisoners brought forth and lined up in the street. After he had their records checked, he declared that sixteen were indeed guilty of serious crimes and ordered them returned to jail. The culpability of the remaining forty-six prisoners, however, he found to be doubtful. Some, he noted, had been in jail as long as three years while their cases were being investigated. Although among them were men who had been charged with crimes as serious as murder, rape, and arson, he announced that it was the emperor's wish to release them with a warning that they would not be so leniently treated should they commit crimes in the future. In their gratitude, some of prisoners prostrated themselves and sobbed; others looked to the heavens and sighed. Both the officials and even the passers-by who witnessed the event were moved to tears, according to Michizane's report.[16]

The Chinese frequently proclaimed broadly inclusive amnesties and conducted inspections of prisons to release those who were unjustly incarcerated. These acts served to demonstrate the emperor's benevolence and power to cleanse wrongdoers of their crimes. The Japanese also adopted the practice of issuing amnesties either to commemorate auspicious events, or as part of efforts to ameliorate misfortunes. For example, as noted earlier, Michizane's father had drafted the text for an amnesty that was proclaimed when Emperor Montoku lay terminally ill. Such amnesties were common in the Nara and early Heian periods. Imperial inspections of prisons, however, were rare in Japan.[17] Thus, Uda's decision to have his "close retainer" and "great teacher" Michizane review prison cases was an extraordinary gesture of considerable symbolic importance. It was a direct exercise of imperial power that demonstrated Uda's commitment to Confucian modes of government. His choice of Michizane to be his representative was highly appropriate.

In addition to symbolic acts, Uda also initiated more practical reforms. For example, under his leadership, the court embarked on a program of attempting to reinforce the *ritsuryō* system of local administration. Responding to petitions from provincial governors, the court issued new regulations prohibiting direct contacts between powerful families in the capital and district officials or peasants. Other regulations protected peasants' rights to land from encroachment by those same powerful families or by monasteries. A final concern was strengthening the court's control of provincial governors.[18] In 896, as part of that policy, the dispatch of rice-tax investigating officials (*kenzeishi*) had come up for consideration. These were officials periodically sent from the capital to insure that the provinces were collecting their proper amounts of tax rice. At first, Michizane was opposed to their dispatch because, on the basis of his experience in Sanuki, he felt that they merely created difficulties in the provinces. Two or three other nobles, including Uda's ally

Yoshiari, agreed and the matter was temporarily put aside. The second time the matter came up, Yoshiari presented a compromise proposal: of any extra tax rice that these inspectors might be able to collect, as much as half would be left with the provincial officials, thereby making extra income available for use both at court and in the provinces. This seemed reasonable to all—including Michizane—and special officials were duly appointed.

Later, however, Michizane began to have additional doubts and discussed the matter with others more experienced in provincial administration than he. Michizane finally reverted to his original view that the inspectors should not be sent. First, he observed that half the tax rice normally collected was in fact returned to the peasants as interest-free loans and therefore would not be found in the granaries by the inspectors. Any attempt to make up the resulting apparent deficiency would seriously hinder normal and just procedures. Second, any excess rice located would probably be of such poor quality as to be hardly worth the effort to collect. It would bring little benefit to the government, but its collection would cause the peasants unwarranted hardship. Finally, the officials selected to become investigators all had more important duties to perform at court. Michizane concluded by requesting that the dispatch of these officials be reconsidered. Michizane's views seem to have been accepted, for no further reference was made to this dispatch of investigators.[19]

As a result of his experiences in Sanuki, Michizane was able to see the issue from the point of view of a provincial official rather than that of a court noble. The court would probably have been able to gain additional revenue by means of these tax investigators, but it would have done so at the expense of interfering with those honest and efficient governors who had managed to accumulate a surplus and would have placed an excessive burden on the peasants, who would have had to pay additional taxes. The court did not abandon its policy of trying to control governors, but this particular proposal was put aside. Earlier Michizane had made proposals concerning government policy, for example, his suggested reforms of civil service examination procedure, but his ideas were not followed. Now he wielded sufficient influence that his recommendation was accepted. Ironically, however, it was a proposal that fit in more closely with the Fujiwara policy of modifying court practice to fit the current situation rather than with Uda's approach of returning to the spirit of the original codes.

In addition to his influential position in the Council of State, Michizane also became Uda's personal confidant. The first known instance of Uda's turning to Michizane for advice occurred in 893 when the question of selecting a crown prince arose. Years later, Uda stated that he had discussed the matter with Michizane and no one else. Recent experience had shown that the imperial succession could be easily manipulated by men like Mototsune. As part of the settlement of the Akō Debate, Uda had taken Mototsune's daughter Haruko (Onshi) as a consort, probably with the understanding that should she bear a son, he would be named crown prince. Mototsune, it is said, died praying that his pregnant daughter would bear an imperial grandson, but his prayers were not answered; fortunately for Uda, Haruko's child was a girl.[20]

After Mototsune's death, then, Uda was free to select a crown prince whom he himself favored. There were two candidates: his eldest son, Atsugimi (whose name is sometimes read "Atsuhito") and a younger son, Tokiyo. Primogeniture was not the rule, and Uda personally may have favored Tokiyo, a maternal grandson of Uda's scholar friend Hiromi, but finally Atsugimi was selected. His mother was indeed a Fujiwara from the powerful Northern House, but she was not closely related to Tokihira. Uda and Michizane had reasoned that, to select Tokiyo would arouse the ire of Fujiwara leaders, whereas Atsugimi would be acceptable, even though his succession would not be particularly beneficial to Tokihira. On the second day of the fourth month, Atsugimi was ensconced as crown prince; Tokihira was named master of the Crown Prince's Household; and Michizane was appointed assistant master. This was in keeping with their relative official status at the time, but not with the roles they had played in the crown prince's selection. In 895, after Michizane had been promoted to rank and office equaling Tokihira's, he was duly appointed supernumerary master of the Crown Prince's Household.[21]

Michizane also appears to have acted as the young Crown Prince Atsugimi's tutor, although he did not hold the title. On a number of occasions, he wrote poems nominally at the prince's command, but more likely for the prince's instruction. Once, in the third month of 895, when Atsugimi was only eleven, he presented Michizane with a challenge:

> I have heard that in T'ang China, someone wrote one hundred poems in a single day. I would like you to try composing ten poems in only two hours.[22]

The crown prince then gave Michizane ten conventional themes, including "Falling Leaves," "Purple Wisteria," and "Green Moss." Within an hour, Michizane proudly noted, he had completed the ten quatrains as commanded. Atsugimi was properly impressed, and some time later when Michizane was spending an evening on duty, the prince once more challenged him:

> Judging from the ten poems you wrote last spring, I know you write with both speed and skill. Now, I shall select twenty topics appropriate to this season [the summer] and make the same request.[23]

Twenty poems required the full two hours, but Michizane managed to complete the task between approximately 6:30 and 8:30. Later, one of his students borrowed these poems to make a copy and somehow lost three. Because Michizane had written them hurriedly with just one draft, he was not able to recall the missing poems but he included the remaining seventeen in his collected works. These poems were mostly on conventional themes; however, the following one does take a somewhat unusual subject and clearly reveals the didactic intent of all the poems in the series.

Money

How profitable for the nation is our elder brother.[a]
Put into circulation, it fills people's hands.
From the "elm pods" came the light seeds.[b]
And the "treasure spring" is the source of the merchant's business.[c]
The greedy devote themselves entirely to it,
But the truly noble do not deign to mention it.
Who can distinguish a forgery?
It is better to encourage propriety and moderation.[24]

Notes:
a. "The eldest brother of the household" was a standard Chinese euphemism for money.

b. "Elm pods" was a nickname given to light coins minted under the first Han emperor in response to complaints that Ch'in coins were too heavy.

c. "Treasure spring" was the inscription on coins minted at the beginning of the Later Han.

In the same year that he was displaying his poetic virtuosity to the crown prince, Michizane was again consulted by Uda on a private matter—the emperor was thinking of retiring. There are three explanations commonly given for Uda's desire to abdicate. Some scholars argue that he was not interested in governing, but wished instead to devote the remainder of his life to poetry and religion. Others suggest that the power of the Fujiwara was too great, and he had abandoned his ambition to rule as well as reign. Indeed, after his eventual abdication, Uda did turn to Buddhism and showed a great interest in poetry, but he also maintained an active concern for affairs of government. Moreover, at the time he was considering retirement, his policy of promoting men not related to the Fujiwara regents was proceeding successfully.[25] Neither of these theories seems altogether satisfactory.

Most likely, Uda wished to abdicate in an attempt to follow the precedent of Emperor Saga and control the government as a retired sovereign. If he voluntarily abdicated, he could be sure that his personally selected crown prince would succeed him and that Tokihira would not be able to become the all-powerful regent his father had been. Moreover, Uda could leave in a high position at court his friend Michizane, on whose loyalty he could rely—both because of their personal ties and because of Michizane's dependence on imperial patronage to maintain his status. This would be distinctly different from the situation when Kōkō and Uda himself had become emperors under Mototsune's sponsorship. Paradoxically, retirement seemed the most secure means of maintaining imperial power.[26]

In 895, Uda secretly discussed with Michizane his desire to abdicate, but Michizane warned him that the time was not yet right. The crown prince was only eleven and Michizane himself had just been promoted to middle counselor, an office that for the first time gave him authority to issue official regulations in his own name. Michizane reasoned that Uda's retirement would be premature. After Michizane had presented his views both orally and in writing, the emperor conceded that his minister's admonitions were just. Two years later, however, rumors of Uda's intentions to retire began to circulate, and they even included speculation on the date of his planned abdication. At first the emperor hoped to continue postponing the event, but Michizane warned him that to do so now would only cause people to wonder about his resolve. Since his plans had become known, it was best to carry them out. Although never stated, a more important consideration was that conditions at court had changed. Michizane had just been named major counselor and so had become, along with Tokihira, one of the two top-ranking officials at court. Thus, he was in a better position to look after Uda's—and his own—interests at court. Again, Uda accepted Michizane's advice and, as he noted, his "resolve became as unmoving as a rock."[27]

On the third day of the seventh month, 897, Crown Prince Atsugimi celebrated his coming of age at the palace. Together, Tokihira and Michizane placed the cap of adulthood on his head. Later that day, Uda announced his abdication, and ten days afterwards Atsugimi formally became the new Emperor Daigo. Again, Tokihira and Michizane played major roles in the ceremony, and both were rewarded with promotions to the senior third rank.[28] Uda left his thirteen-year-old son a "testament" instructing him in how to govern correctly. It was filled with practical advice on a wide range of matters and maxims expressing basic principles to be observed:

> When determining promotions and rewards for palace guards who have been on duty long hours and have good reputations, do not hold rigidly to precedents; just avoid the words of women and the advice of lesser men. . . . When foreign [literally, "barbarian"] guests must be received, greet them from behind a curtain; do not face upon them directly. I have already made an error with Li Huan [a Chinese summoned to court in 896]. . . . Do not select as provincial officials those who request appointment. Only allow to serve those who have experience in the various offices and are known to be effective.[29]

It also recounted the deeds of former emperors:

> When Emperor Kammu was suffering from the heat, he went to cool off in the imperial park after court business had been completed.

... Once, when the Rashōmon[a] was being constructed, he went to inspect it. After looking at it, he called the carpenter and said, "This gate ought to be lowered five inches." Later he went again, summoned the carpenter, and inquired how the work was proceeding. The carpenter replied, "It has already been lowered." The emperor sighed and exclaimed, "How unfortunate that you did not add five inches!" When the carpenter heard this, he fell to the ground in a dead faint. The emperor was startled. After a while, the carpenter regained his senses and explained, "Actually the gate has not been lowered. I lied because to lower it would have been very troublesome." The emperor pardoned his crime.[30]

Note:
a. The central gate was on the southern boundary of the Heian capital, and hence the principal entrance. It was said to have been two stories high, with a foundation of 26 feet wide and 106 feet long.

The most interesting part of the testament, however, is its recommendations of Tokihira and Michizane. Of Tokihira, Uda wrote:

The general of the left, Lord Fujiwara, is the descendant of meritorious officials. Although young, he is already well versed in governmental principles. Last year, he had an unfortunate affair with a woman, but I quickly put the matter out of mind. Since last spring, I have assigned him important official responsibilities and treated him as the first among my ministers. He can provide excellent advice and assist in all governmental matters.[31]

Uda had kind words for Tokihira but did not fail to point out his relative youth and his reputation as a womanizer. Tokihira's unfortunate affair of the previous year cannot be identified, but he is said to have run off with his elderly uncle's young wife some years later.[32]

Uda then described Michizane:

The general of the right, Lord Sugawara, is a scholar of great erudition who also has a deep understanding of government. I have taken him as my mentor and often received just admonitions from him. Accordingly, I have given him exceptional promotions as a reward for his merit.

At this point, Uda gives a detailed account of how Michizane had counseled him both on the selection of a crown prince and on his own abdication. Uda concluded:

Lord Sugawara is not simply my loyal retainer, but should also be accepted as a meritorious retainer to the new emperor. His contributions must not be forgotten.[33]

Uda praised Michizane without reservation, and by detailing Michizane's valuable advice, Uda devoted almost three times as many words to him as to Tokihira. Moreover, at a number of other places in the text, he recommended that the new emperor seek Michizane's guidance, and rely on his daughter, the handmaid, in matters relating to the women's quarters. In contrast, Uda did not mention Tokihira except in the passage quoted. Because Tokihira was "the descendant of meritorious officials," Uda had little choice but to treat him with respect; however, Michizane was the man in whom he placed greater trust.

Uda's testament is a fascinating revelation of his personal views, but an edict he proclaimed on the day of his abdication had far greater political implications. It stated:

Until the young emperor has matured, all affairs of government shall be conducted in accordance with the instructions of Major Counselor Lord Fujiwara and Supernumerary Major Counselor Lord Sugawara.[34]

Tokihira and Michizane were thus given powers comparable to those held by Mototsune when he was no longer formally regent but continued to dominate the court. They could not be named regents because Daigo, though only thirteen, had celebrated his coming of age and was considered an adult. Also, neither Tokihira nor Michizane were related to Daigo's mother in a way that would have entitled him to become regent. After his regency had ended, Mototsune had been named grand minister, but that title, too, could not be granted. It had never been shared by two men, and neither Tokihira nor Michizane was yet even a minister of state. To make them grand ministers would have been too abrupt a promotion. Thus, they were not given a specific office. Instead, they became the first men granted the power of "private inspection" (nairan), which meant that government documents had to pass through their hands before going to the emperor for final approval. In later years, this crucially important power would normally be granted to regents and chancellors. In fact, during most of the years that the famous minister

Fujiwara no Michinaga held sway at court, he was neither regent nor chancellor but minister of the left with the power of private inspection. Although Tokihira and Michizane lacked the title, they were, in effect, co-regents.[35]

Compared to his eminent forebears who had monopolized court power, Tokihira's status was not remarkable. As a Sugawara, however, Michizane's newly acquired political eminence was unprecedented. In their last years, both Michizane's father and grandfather had attained positions of great honor, but never before had a member of the family been actively involved in the Council of State. For a man previously known only for his scholarship and poetry to be given the powers of regent was unheard of, and his sharing those powers hardly diminished his glory. Michizane's rise was largely the result of a complicated series of events that had allowed an emperor to attempt governing personally without relying exclusively on Fujiwara regents. At the same time, his promotion can also be seen as reflecting a continued respect for the Confucian principle that men should be advanced on the basis of their ability. Although Uda relied extensively on his own relatives, the main exception to this practice was a man known primarily for his learning, a quality the emperor respected highly. Without Uda's patronage, Michizane would never have been able to reach so powerful a position; however, without his own years of study and exceptional talents, he would never have come to the emperor's attention. Michizane's promotion to high office was both a part of Uda's strategy, and also a reward for his abilities as a scholar and poet.

COURT SCHOLAR AND POET

In addition to promoting Michizane to high court office, Emperor Uda also called upon his abilities as a scholar, or, more specifically, as a historian. In 893 or perhaps 894, Michizane was named to a committee responsible for compiling the last of Japan's Six National Histories (Rikkokushi). As its name suggests, this chronicle, *Nihon sandai jitsuroku* (generally abbreviated to *Sandai jitsuroku,* Veritable records of three reigns) was to cover the previous three reigns: those of emperors Seiwa, Yōzei, and Kōkō; the years from 858 to 886. About the same time that he was placed on this committee, Michizane was also ordered personally to arrange by topic the entries from all the court chronicles into a work that came to be known as *Ruijū kokushi* (Classified history of the nation). Uda's interest in compiling these histories further demonstrates his respect for Chinese concepts of government. The Chinese had long considered the writing of histories an important duty of the state, and the Japanese historiographic tradition began under the stimulus of such ideas and in imitation of Chinese models. Also, again in keeping with Chinese practice, Japan's chronicles presented the emperor as the center of power at court, and so Uda may have hoped that a new history would offer ideological support for his political position, even though the reigns chronicled in *Sandai jitsuroku* were those in which the Fujiwara regents first gained power.[36]

Uda's choice of Michizane to carry out these important responsibilities was an appropriate one. At the university, Michizane had studied China's histories, and thus he was well qualified to assist in the compilation of a chronicle based on Chinese historiographic techniques. Moreover, this assignment gave Michizane yet another chance to maintain a family tradition. His father had helped compile the previous official chronicle, and Michizane himself had drafted its introduction.[37]

Uda's selection of the committee to compile *Sandai jitsuroku* reflects his political strategy as well as his interest in Chinese culture. Customarily, the leading Fujiwara statesman at court had served as the principal member of each of the committees responsible for drafting Japan's official chronicles. Although lower-ranking but more scholarly members of the committees did the actual work of putting together the histories, the names of eminent Fujiwara were listed first among the compilers. Uda, however, broke with tradition by naming his ally Minamoto no Yoshiari as the highest-ranking member of the committee for the *Sandai jitsuroku*. The remaining members of the committee were, in order of rank, Tokihira, Michizane, Ōkura no Yoshiyuki (832–921?), and Mimune no Masahira (853–926). Along with Michizane, the last two members of the committee were scholars, and, because Michizane was kept busy with the demands of high office, they were to be chiefly responsible for drafting the text.

Work on the *Sandai jitsuroku* did not progress rapidly, nor, as it turned out, did it proceed as Uda had intended. In 897, Yoshiari died, and one month later Uda abdicated. Compilation of the history was temporarily abandoned until Uda's successor ordered it resumed, and by then Tokihira had become the highest-ranking member of the committee. The final version of the chronicle was not formally presented to the emperor until the eighth month of 901, after Michizane had already been exiled, and Masahira, too, had been sent from court with a provincial appointment. Accordingly, only the names of Tokihira and his former tutor Yoshiyuki appeared as compilers of the finished work. Contrary to Uda's original intention, the Fujiwara were able to claim full credit for the *Sandai jitsuroku*.[38]

Ultimately, Michizane's contributions to the last of Japan's official histories were not formally acknowledged, although for six years he was a member of the committee, and traces of his influence can be discerned, for example, in the careful treatment given his father. Included was the full text of the long prayer Koreyoshi had written for the dedication of the newly repaired Great Buddha at Nara, and he was given an obituary not only flattering but also unusually detailed. Michizane also seems to have composed the obituary for the great monk Ennin, whose Tendai sect had long-standing ties with the Sugawara. Yoshiyuki was the only scholar who remained on the committee until its task was completed, and he managed to make many references to his own accomplishments, despite his relatively low rank. In contrast, Michizane received only the treatment due to a man of his position. There is no indication either that he tried to emphasize his own contributions or that they were expunged after he was sent into exile. Michizane did not exaggerate his own accomplishments, but as a filial son, he was concerned that his father's achievements be given respectful treatment, and he assisted with other parts of the project in which he had a personal interest.[39]

Just as Michizane's individual contributions to *Sandai jitsuroku* cannot be measured accurately, so his role in the compilation of *Ruijū kokushi* presents problems. There can be no question that, on Uda's orders, he was working on a topically arranged history of Japan, for around 893 he mentioned the project twice in his own writings, and a variety of other sources specifically attribute *Ruijū kokushi* to him.[40] Still, his authorship has been questioned. *Ruijū kokushi* contains entries from all of the six national histories, but as noted, the last of them was not formally completed until after his exile. A number of conclusions are possible. *Ruijū kokushi* could have been compiled later and attributed to Michizane, because he had in fact worked on a similar project. Or Michizane could have arranged the data from the first five of the national histories, and one of his students later could have added those from *Sandai jitsuroku,* while retaining Michizane's original scheme. Alternatively, Michizane could indeed have completed the whole work, using a draft of *Sandai jitsuroku* to which he had access as a member of the compilation committee.

None of these theories can be conclusively proven, but textual evidence tends to support the last of them. First, all the entries are treated identically, including those from *Sandai jitsuroku,* and second, the arrangement of the entries displays a certain historiographic sophistication. Thus, *Ruijū kokushi* seems to be the work of a single man who worked on it with great care and attention to detail. Michizane unquestionably was involved in a project of this sort, and he had the scholarly background needed to produce the refinements found in *Ruijū kokushi.* Had a later individual tried to fit the entries from *Sandai jitsuroku* into the original plan, some inconsistencies would probably have appeared. Yet there are none. The traditional attribution to Michizane is almost certainly accurate.

The sophistication of *Ruijū kokushi* is revealed not in the text, which is taken directly from the official chronicles, but rather in the arrangement of the entries. Michizane displayed his greatest originality in their dating. For each entry, he indicated both the era name (*nengō*) and the reigning emperor. His use of era names was more precise than that of the original chroniclers. They had treated all events that occurred in the year when a new era name was proclaimed as belonging to the first year of the new era, even though some of the events may have preceded the changes. In *Ruijū kokushi,* however, such years are divided in two, and entries prior to the proclamations are dated with the old era names. Only those from after such proclamations use the new names. This system is not only historically more accurate, but also demands greater attention on the part of the compiler. In addition, *Ruijū kokushi* is more systematic than the chronicles in its use of emperors' names. Different chronicles had used different methods for referring to emperors. Some employed native Japanese names, some Chinese-style names, and others had used appropriate titles. Michizane adopted what later became the usual practice of referring to all emperors by Chinese-style names.

The idea of a topically arranged history was not a new one. Such works already existed in both China and Japan, and occasionally Michizane copied their sequence of topics. For example, he followed the Japanese custom of placing a section on Shinto first. Here he again revealed his historiographic sophistication by beginning with the complete text of the first two chapters of the *Nihon shoki*, which cover the age of the gods. No attempt was made to classify the contents of these chapters, and in this way Michizane distinguished myth and legend from history. No other sections of the chronicles were treated similarly. *Ruijū kokushi* was intended as a practical reference work on court procedures and precedents. As such, it was widely used in the Heian period. As late as the Kamakura period, references to the Six National Histories were often not to the original texts but to Michizane's classified version of them. Even today, its surviving chapters remain valuable for historians. They fill in lacunae in some of the original texts, and Michizane's choice of classification for an item can be a clue to its meaning. For example, he included "government interest-bearing loans" (*suiko*) and "government interest-free loans" (*shakutai*) as separate categories. The original chronicles in some instances failed to specify the type of loan to which they referred, but, by placing them under one or the other classification, Michizane offers a reliable—or at least very early—interpretation of the texts. Although perhaps not a labor of original scholarship, the compilation of *Ruijū kokushi* was a monumental task. The completed text totalled two hundred chapters, of which unfortunately only sixty-two are now extant.[41]

Some twenty years earlier, as a minor official, Michizane had begun to compile a collection of administrative precedents. Administration, however, was not Michizane's forte, and the project was abandoned. History was more to his liking and proved to be the area in which he made his most valuable scholarly contributions. He helped compile what was to be the last of Japan's six official court chronicles, and alone he arranged by topic all the entries from those chronicles into a massive reference work that remains today a useful tool for historians. Both of these works were compiled at the command of Emperor Uda, whose sponsorship of historical writing revealed his concern for the Chinese intellectual traditions that lay behind the institutions of Japan's bureaucratic government. After *Sandai jitsuroku,* a seventh national history was drafted in the tenth century, but it was never formally completed. By that time, the court had largely abandoned its commitment to the Chinese modes both of statecraft and of scholarship. The draft was eventually lost.[42]

Over the centuries, many additional works have been attributed to Michizane, but most of them long since have been dismissed as forgeries. One anthology, however, remains the object of controversy. It is *Shinsen Man'yōshū* (Newly selected *Man'yōshū*), which consists of two chapters, each containing over one hundred *waka* by various authors, with every *waka* followed by a poem in Chinese on the same theme. The tradition that Michizane compiled *Shinsen Man'yōshū* is an old one. Already in the third imperial *waka* anthology, the *Shūishū* (Collection of gleanings, c. 1000), it is referred to as "*Kanke Man'yōshū,*" literally "The Sugawara Man'yōshū."[43] Some specialists still support this attribution, but recent scholarship has cast considerable doubt on it.

Critics have stressed the lack of evidence from contemporary documents to support the attribution and to problems within the text itself. In writings of unquestionable authenticity, Michizane never mentioned *Shinsen Man'yōshū,* although he did note his other editorial projects. Some scholars have construed the inroduction to the first chapter of *Shinsen Man'yōshū* as referring to Michizane, but that interpretation is based on what seems to be a corruption in the text. The *waka* in the anthology are clearly not Michizane's, but the matching *kanshi* were thought to have been provided by him. Detailed studies, however, have shown this to be highly unlikely. The *kanshi* in the first chapter show no characteristics of his style, and those in the second chapter are not even poems, but clumsy Chinese paraphrases of the *waka.* When the *Shinsen Man'yōshū* was first attributed to

Michizane around the year 1000, he was already worshiped as patron saint of literature, and the introduction was already being misread to suggest he compiled it. Hence, it came to be regarded as the *"Sugawara Man'yōshū."* The attribution is not totally inconceivable, for, in fact, the *Shinsen Man'yōshū* originally was compiled in 893 when Michizane was serving at court and actively involved in literary activities. But the evidence connecting him to it is weak, and the idea that he compiled it must be viewed as an aspect of Tenjin worship. The *Shinsen Man'yōshū* is an intriguing work, but Michizane probably had nothing to do with it.[44]

In 900, Michizane completed one last major editorial project to which his contribution cannot be questioned. That year, on the sixteenth day of the eighth month he presented to Emperor Daigo, Uda's successor, a collection of his grandfather's, his father's, and his own works. He also wrote an explanation of how he came to compile this anthology. First, as crown prince, Daigo had personally requested a copy of the poems Michizane had written in Sanuki. These became chapters three and four of the final anthology. After Daigo's accession, an unnamed courtier suggested that Michizane present to the emperor the poems he had written during Uda's reign. These would correspond roughly to chapter five of the anthology. While he had been in Sanuki, rain had severely damaged the drafts of his early works that he had left behind in his library. But Michizane learned that a certain Taira no Arinao, lieutenant governor of Kaga, was an enthusiastic collector of literature—although he was no writer himself—and he might have copied Michizane's now mutilated texts. Michizane made inquiries and a few days later was delighted to receive copies of several hundred works, probably the poems that make up the first two chapters of his anthology. Not surprisingly, many of these poems appear to be out of sequence. Michizane added his most recent poems and various works of prose, edited them, and arranged them into twelve chapters. The first six consisted of his *kanshi* in more or less chronological order, and the remaining six of prose classified by form. Finally, he acknowledged his filial debt by also compiling the works of his grandfather and father. The resulting anthology had twenty-eight chapters. The twelve that contain

Michizane's writings have come to be known as *Kanke bunsō*
(The Sugawara literary drafts).[45]
Daigo accepted the collection with a poem of his own:

From of old your family has been one of scholars.
The flowers of literature you present today are more precious
    than gold.
Reciting but a single couplet, one knows their worth.
How much more valuable when one can read to contentment the
    works of three generations!
Your voices are clear like polished gems.
Your phrases are colored like the red sky.
Truly the works of the Sugawara family surpass those of Po Chü-i.
His collection will now be left in its box covered with dust.[46]

Michizane modestly responded:

I owe a debt to my progenitors:
They bequeathed me not gold but a love of literary beauty.
In this box are twenty-eight scrolls.
How honored I would be if the emperor occasionally read them!
My humble loyalty is expressed with deeds.
The virtuous imperial poem touches me to the core.
May the limitless imperial beneficence reach to my father and
    grandfather.
It is deeper than the autumn sea![47]

In 1131, an obscure Fujiwara courtier offered a copy of *Kanke
bunsō* to Kitano Shrine, already the capital's principal center of
Tenjin worship. When he had copied the text seven years prior
to the presentation, he had added Michizane's later works to his
manuscript. His fortunes had not been the best, and, abandon-
ing hope for success in his present life, he hoped that his offering would serve as a prayer for an auspicious rebirth. All later
editions of Michizane's works derive from this text. The oldest
surviving manuscript dates from 1680, but despite the late date
its authenticity has not been questioned.[48] Modern scholars are
fortunate to have Michizane's works in Chinese in their original
form. Michizane's arrangement of his writings makes them particularly useful. First, he attempted to place them in chronological order; thus most of them can be dated with considerable

precision. Second, Michizane carefully added notes explaining contemporary events to which he alluded. Difficulties remain, but fewer than would be the case had Michizane himself not provided some commentary. Unfortunately, his *waka* do not survive in so reliable a format.

Of the many literary anthologies compiled during the early Heian period, most are now lost, among them the works of his father and grandfather that Michizane also had presented to Emperor Daigo. The survival of Michizane's own works can be explained in two ways. Most obviously, Michizane was deified and his writings were treated with special respect. Present texts all derive from a manuscript that had been offered to a shrine as an act of faith. Less apparent, but perhaps just as important, is the recognition that Michizane's contemporaries had of the literary excellence of his works. The praise in Daigo's poem may be exaggerated, but the respect he felt for Michizane's poetry was real. In 926 when he granted a Buddhist monk permission to visit China, Daigo placed Michizane's name at the head of a list of Japanese *kanshi* poets whose works he wished the monk to take with him and show to the Chinese.[49] The fact that an obscure courtier had taken the trouble to copy his early writings further suggests how widely they were admired by contemporaries. Michizane's poems might have survived because of their literary merit even if their author had not been deified.

During his ten years in high office following his service in Sanuki, Michizane produced a considerable amount of poetry in addition to his works as a compiler. This poetry, however, was very different from that which he had written only a few years earlier in Sanuki. There, his poetry had a distinctly personal, informal quality—despite its Chinese language. After returning to the capital, Michizane wrote almost exclusively in a formal style. The number of poems he wrote on imperial command is one clear indication of this change, for these circumstances demanded the highest degree of formality. Between his return from Sanuki and his exile, Michizane wrote 153 poems in Chinese. Forty-seven of them were written at court occasions on themes selected by emperors Uda and Daigo, and another 30 were written for Daigo while he was crown prince. Thus, almost half of his poems in these years were written to satisfy imperial orders. Of his remaining poems, approximately 20 were written for occasions comparably formal, such as the university's Confucian Memorial Rites and the reception of an embassy from Parhae. Michizane himself valued these works highly.[50] Their composition reflected his high status at court and his close ties with the imperial family. Also, the difficulty of their language demonstrated his linguistic virtuosity. To modern readers, however, they are less appealing.

The reason why Michizane wrote little formal poetry while in Sanuki is simply that the public occasions calling for it did not exist outside the capital. However, it is more difficult to explain why he came all but to abandon writing poems in a more personal style during his years in high office. As a young bureaucrat, he had vividly described his work in poems such as "Professorial Difficulties," and also his personal misfortunes in "Dreaming of Amaro" and similar poems. He had not restricted himself to formal poetry just because he was serving at court. As a high official, however, he rarely wrote of such personal concerns. Two notable exceptions were a poem lamenting the death of Tadaomi in 891 and another one written a year later describing a day off from his public duties.[51]

Possibly, when he was in high office, Michizane no longer had the freedom to make private comments about his official duties. As a professor he could safely complain about his students, but as a minister of state, he could not risk making unfavorable remarks about his high-ranking fellow statesmen. A second consideration was that Michizane's responsibilities increased with his rank. Formal poetry had to be written at public occasions as part of his official duties, but the writing of informal poetry required a certain amount of leisure. And Michizane must have been very busy during his last years at court, because, in addition to his official duties, he was also involved in various scholarly projects. Thus, in his poem describing a day off from work, he laments that he has little time to relax after spending the day tending to domestic chores and the evening working on *Ruijū kokushi*. A high official simply did not have time to indulge in poetry for its own sake.

Michizane never abandoned his vocation as a scholar and a poet; however, both his scholarship and his poetry changed in accordance with his new position. He no longer lectured to students at the university. Instead, he assisted in the compilation of historical works and literary anthologies. These projects reflected his close ties with the imperial family. The two histories to which he contributed were both compiled on imperial command, and his Sugawara family literary anthology he presented to Daigo. The formal nature of the poetry he wrote while in high office also can be attributed to his new status: he was writing poems on imperial command rather than for his own enjoyment. If imperial patronage meant unprecedented high office, it also resulted in a change of poetic style.

6 · Diplomat

Japanese relations with China had a long and noble history. Chinese histories record the arrival of representatives from Japan as early as the second century B.C., when the Japanese Archipelago was still inhabited by primitive tribes. In the following centuries, during which Japan was gradually being unified, its envoys were periodically noted by the Chinese, whose own land was divided after the fall of the Later Han dynasty in 221. By the time the Sui dynasty had reunited China in 589, Japanese culture had advanced to the point that its missions were now recorded in its own histories as well as in those of the Chinese. As many as six embassies may have been sent to the Sui before it was succeeded by the T'ang in 618. Twelve years later, the Japanese dispatched the first of their envoys to the T'ang (*kentōshi*), and in the following two centuries fifteen official missions went to China.

The Japanese were never completely comfortable in their diplomatic relations with the "Central Kingdom," for the Chinese expected their neighbors to maintain a subservient attitude. Instead of submitting, the Japanese chose to regard themselves as the center of their own diplomatic order. Despite the resulting awkwardness, Japanese missions to China continued because they brought back both material goods, and, more importantly, a knowledge of Chinese culture. This knowledge was not based merely on the superficial impressions gleaned during a few months' travel, for along with the diplomats, students and

227

Buddhist monks were sent, and some of them remained to study for decades in China before going home to Japan. The information they brought back was valued highly and their contributions to Japanese culture were incalculable.[1] The heritage of their activities influenced virtually every aspect of Michizane's career. He served in a bureaucracy inspired by Chinese models, studied Confucian and Taoist classics, believed in Chinese forms of Buddhism, and wrote most of his poetry in the Chinese language.

Michizane had a deep understanding and appreciation of Chinese culture, but ironically, a proposal of his in 894 led to the abandonment of Japanese missions to China. In that year, Michizane was named ambassador to the T'ang, and his friend Haseo, vice-ambassador. Michizane then recommended that the mission be canceled. His suggestion was accepted, and regular diplomatic contact with China virtually ceased until the Ashikaga shoguns sent their representatives to the Ming court more than five centuries later. When Michizane made his proposal, he was one of Japan's leading authorities on foreign affairs. His uncle and grandfather had accompanied the previous two missions to China. Michizane was then in the midst of compiling his historical works, and so even if he had not heard of his relatives' experiences in China directly, he had recently read of them in the chronicles. In addition to his knowledge of China, acquired principally from books, Michizane also had the experience of personally having helped to receive two missions from Parhae.

RELATIONS WITH PARHAE

Today, the Kingdom of Parhae seems little more than a footnote in the history of East Asia, but during the eighth and ninth centuries, it flourished on T'ang China's northeast border. Parhae's founders were men who earlier had been rulers of Koguryŏ, a relatively advanced nation located in northern Korea that in 668 had been defeated by the combined forces of China and Silla. The leaders of Koguryŏ were kept in captivity in North China until a local rebellion broke out in 696 and gave them the opportunity to escape eastwards to Manchuria. There they joined with more primitive but ethnically related tribes, and after fighting off a T'ang army, they proclaimed the creation of the Kingdom of Chin, circa 698–700. Despite initial resistance, the Chinese gradually came to accept the new state, and in 713 the T'ang court formally "enfeoffed" its ruler as "king of Parhae." This new name came to be accepted, and regular diplomatic relations were established. These relations were conducted in accordance with the Chinese scheme of diplomacy, and Parhae became nominally a vassal state. Its kings held Chinese titles and sent members of the royal family to the Chinese capital as de facto hostages. Formal missions were supposed to bring "tribute" to China annually and in fact were almost that frequent.[2]

Like Japan in the same period, Parhae enthusiastically adopted many forms of Chinese culture. A bureaucracy was created on the T'ang model; however, a curious innovation was that Parhae had not one but five capitals. One was indeed the primary capital, but the government occasionally was relocated to the others. These cities, like the Japanese Nara and Heian capitals, were copied from the plan of Ch'ang-an and laid out on a rectangular grid. Again as in Japan, Buddhism flourished; although archeological remains suggest Koguryŏ rather than T'ang styles.[3] Chinese literature was fashionable, but all that remains of Parhae's literature are nine poems in Chinese, all preserved in Japanese collections. For example, Ambassador Wang Hyo-lyŏm, who was in Japan in 814–815, wrote as he was about to return home:

> Expressing My Feelings while in Izumo Province:
> A Poem Presented to the Two Imperial Messengers
> A south wind over the sea stirs thoughts of returning home.
> Geese from the north cross the broad skies evoking weariness.
> Fortunately I am accompanied by the singing of mated phoenixes,
> And feel no grief over waiting many days in a distance province.[4]

Sadly, the optimism expressed in this poem proved unwarranted. The ambassador's boat was blown back after it had finally departed from Izumo, and Wang Hyo-lyŏm died before he could attempt another voyage home.

Between 719 and 738, Parhae's second king embarked on a program of national expansion that led to war with its neighbors, briefly including the Chinese. Surrounded for a time by unfriendly states, Parhae sought allies and turned for possible support to Japan, which had once sent military aid to Koguryŏ. Therefore, in 728 Parhae sent its first mission to Japan. Such missions continued on a fairly regular basis until even after Parhae's fall: in 929 a representative came asking help in recapturing the kingdom from the Khitan, who had defeated it three years earlier. This last mission was turned back by the Japanese, who by then had become observers rather than active participants in affairs on the mainland. In all, thirty-three missions from Parhae to Japan are recorded, although some were probably unofficial trading missions and a few were not received by the Japanese court, which did not always like the tone of Parhae's official communications. In return, Japan also sent thirteen missions to Parhae.[5]

Because both Parhae and Japan were at the time strongly under the influence of Chinese ideas, they both looked to Chinese precedents for guidance in their conduct of diplomacy. To the Chinese, relations between two equal nations were unknown, at least in theory. Foreign relations meant relations between a superior "Central Kingdom"—the Chinese—and various inferior nations—everyone else. This was the pattern that the Japanese adopted—except that they took for themselves the position of Central Kingdom and consequently Parhae appears in Japanese records as a vassal state. Its gifts to the Japanese court were considered tribute, and its emissaries were rewarded with Japanese court rank.[6] Unfortunately, Parhae court records do not survive, and consequently there is no way of knowing how emissaries from Japan were received in Parhae, although Japanese visitors perhaps followed the practice of their compatriots who in China discreetly adopted a more humble posture than they were willing to admit when they returned home, for at home Parhae too may have regarded itself as yet another Central Kingdom.

Relations between Parhae and Japan began out of political and military considerations. Parhae sought a military ally and Japan was flattered to have a new "vassal state." Gradually the motives behind the dispatch of missions changed. Trade became increasingly important, and Parhae's embassies increasingly large. When a mission of over a hundred men appeared in Japan in 828, they were denied permission to enter the Japanese capital, and private trade with foreigners was prohibited. Commerce had become a primary reason for the missions, and the Japanese court was less flattered by trade than by tribute.[7] The continuing exchange of emissaries also served a vital cultural function. Parhae evolved into a middleman between Chinese and Japanese culture. The emissaries from Parhae were sometimes learned men with whom Japanese scholars exchanged verse and learned of new trends in T'ang poetry. In 859 a Parhae mission brought to Japan a new Chinese calendar, which was adopted three years later and continued in use until the seventeenth century. These missions also provided valuable information about events in China. For example, a Japanese envoy returning from Parhae in 758 brought Japan its first news of the Rebellion of An Lushan, which then had just begun. Finally, on at least one occasion, Parhae served as an intermediary for cultural exchange in the opposite direction by sending eleven Japanese dancing girls as a gift to the Chinese court in 777.[8]

The first time Michizane was assigned to greet an embassy from Parhae in 872, his duties were interrupted by his mother's death. On two subsequent occasions, however, he took a more active role. The well-documented Parhae mission of 882–883 serves as a good example of how the Japanese treated their foreign guests, and of Michizane's own involvement.

On the fourteenth day of the eleventh month, 882, a mission of 105 men from Parhae landed in Kaga province, located directly across the Japan Sea from Manchuria. The court was notified of their presence thirteen days later, and preparations to receive them were begun immediately. The next day, the court instructed Kaga to treat the official visitors well and issued the usual ban on private trade with them. Then, three officials were appointed to escort the embassy from Kaga to the capital. Among them were Ōkura no Yoshiyuki, the scholar who would collaborate with Michizane in compiling the *Sandai jitsuroku,* and an obscure individual who was to serve as interpreter.[9]

Although preparations had been begun promptly, they proceeded rather slowly. A month after being notified of the mission's arrival, the court ordered:

Because of the planned entry of the Parhae guests into the capital, the provinces along the route—Yamashiro, Ōmi, Echizen, and

Kaga—are commanded to repair government buildings, roads, and bridges; and to bury corpses left by the roadside. Also, the provinces of Echizen, Noto, and Etchū shall send wine, meat, fish, fowl and garlic to Kaga in order to feed the visitors.[10]

Another two months later, winter clothing was sent to Kaga for the official guests. It was then the end of the second month, roughly corresponding to March, and Kaga would have been still rather cool even though the season was nominally spring. On the eighth day of the third month, the official escorts departed for Kaga to lead the mission to the capital.[11]

Meanwhile, the court was arranging a splendid reception. Already, 107 musicians had begun rehearsing to perform for the visitors. All officials, even the most menial, were given dispensation "to wear forbidden things," distinctive clothing normally worn only by aristocrats. Additional men were appointed to look after the envoys from Parhae during their stay in the capital and on their return trip to Kaga. Among these officials was Michizane's disciple Haseo, then still a graduate student of literature. An effort was being made to greet the guests with erudition as well as elegance: perhaps half the officials assigned to deal with them were men known as scholars and poets.[12]

The amount of literary activity accompanying the reception of representatives from Parhae varied, but on this occasion the ambassador was an enthusiastic poet. Poetic exchanges had already begun while he was in Kaga, and the court was anxious that they should continue smoothly at court. Accordingly, two of its best poets, Michizane and his former tutor Tadaomi, were given special temporary promotions. At the time, Michizane was serving as junior assistant minister of ceremonial and professor of literature. He was given the post of senior assistant minister of civil affairs, a higher position in the ministry directly responsible for entertaining foreign guests. Tadaomi, then employed in the provinces as a lieutenant governor, was summoned back to court and given the title "director of the Bureau of Buddhism and Aliens."[13] Since this bureau was part of the Ministry of Civil Affairs, temporarily, Tadaomi became a subordinate of Michizane. These appointments placed two of the court's most able *kanshi* poets in posts that made them directly responsible for the foreign guests. The Japanese thus sought to give the impression that theirs was a highly civilized state in the Chinese mode.

At last, on the twenty-eighth day of the fourth month, more than five months after their arrival in Kaga, the mission from Parhae entered the capital. It was escorted to the official Foreign Envoy's Quarters (Kōrokan) by Michizane's friend Taira no Masanori. The guests were allowed a few days to rest, and then Ambassador Pae Chŏng formally presented the message and gifts from the king of Parhae in a magnificent ceremony. Everyone in the capital who held court rank was present. The message is not preserved, but it probably resembled earlier ones that had been couched in rather humble, even obsequious language. The following day there was a banquet at which the emperor personally granted Japanese court rank to all members of the mission and bestowed on them appropriate Japanese court costumes. This was essentially the same way that the Chinese received their envoys from "vassal" states. The guests left to change into their new clothing and returned for an elaborate entertainment. Fully 148 women danced. After several rounds of wine, the envoys were offered a silver bowl of loquats from the emperor's table, and before departing they were given additional gifts in accordance with their rank. Again, all the officials at court were present.[14]

The fifth day of the fifth month was important in the calendar of annual events borrowed from China. The day was considered inauspicious and originally had been devoted to gathering medicinal herbs to ward off unhealthy influences, but in ninth-century Japan the practices had been modified somewhat. Nobles appeared at court with garlands of irises adorning their heads. There, they were given sacks of medicinal herbs and joined the emperor in watching the imperial guards perform feats of mounted archery and horsemanship. This year, with a foreign mission at court, it had been decided that the festivities would be rescheduled in the event of rain, which was likely to fall since it was the rainy season. As feared, there was a downpour. However, someone had mistakenly led the Parhae envoys to court before the postponement could be formally announced. They were hurriedly led indoors, given garlands of irises, and the ceremonies were conducted despite the rain.[15]

That evening, Michizane and Tadaomi visited the Envoy's

Quarters. Although the rain had ceased, the weather remained unpleasant; Michizane wrote:

"Heat after the Rain"
Composed in the Ambassador's Room
The wind's coolness meets the dense heat and is consumed.
We never saw the blue sky, yet the sun has already set.
I wipe away perspiration, as my subordinates ply me with questions,
But your ship will have ice from which to drink, so you need not
    worry.
Yearn not for the cold plains of your home a thousand leagues away.
Instead, let the flow of this stream encourage you to imbibe freely.
Filled with talk and laughter, this night should never end.
Thus we can prevent sad dreams of your native land.[16]

Tadaomi too contributed a poem on the same theme:

Braving the heat, we came to visit and approached the curtained
    doorway.
Our guest's room is tranquil, now that the rain has ceased.
If we could meet but another night!
Rare are such occasions for the exchange of true sentiments.
This humble official is not unable to express himself,
But is awed by the ambassador's eloquence.
If we record our feelings, though apart, we can long remember each
    other.
Let us never forget how we drank and relaxed tonight![17]

On the seventh and eighth day of the month, the envoys exchanged their "special tribute" (bekkō)—trade goods—with officials of Japan's Imperial Storehouse Bureau (Uchi no Kura no Tsukasa). Private trade had been forbidden at least in part so as not to interfere with the official trade. Details were not recorded on this occasion, but Parhae usually brought furs—including tiger, bear, and leopard—along with honey and ginseng. In return, the Japanese offered various types of silk and brocade.[18] This exchange of unfinished goods for finished and probably very elegant fabrics suggests that Japanese craftsmanship was more sophisticated than that of Parhae. However, the banning of private trade indicates that Parhae's products were nonetheless highly prized.

After this commercial exchange had been completed, the

court held a lavish farewell banquet at court, to which it appears only high-ranking courtiers were invited. There, a curious incident occurred. At the last moment, the official who had been delegated to serve as personal attendant to the foreign guests had had to withdraw. Fujiwara no Yoshitsumu, a man known for his grace and good manners, was quickly summoned to perform those duties. Ambassador Pae Chŏng was impressed with him, and during the course of the banquet suddenly reached for his brush and inkstone with the intention of presenting him a poem. Yoshitsumu, however, was either not skilled at composition or had not had time to prepare any poems for the occasion. In any event, he was not ready to exchange verses and hastily absented himself. The ambassador, realizing his indiscretion, immediately put aside his writing implements. When the emperor saw this, he was impressed and privately presented Pae Chŏng with an outfit of clothing in recognition of his tact.[19]

This seemingly minor incident, carefully recorded in Japanese official chronicles, reveals the importance of *kanshi* as a part of diplomacy. To be caught without a poem in Chinese was a great source of embarrassment. The Japanese had gone to great lengths to entertain their guests magnificently and were anxious also to display their literary accomplishments. Such efforts were essential if Japan was to maintain the fiction that it was a superior nation to which Parhae was a mere vassal. Michizane and Tadaomi were, in effect, officially designated poet laureates whom the court hoped would represent Japan well in a sort of poetic competition with Ambassador Pae. Their position was an important one, for the Japanese did not want Pae Chŏng to think Yoshitsumu's performance typical. Some years later, Michizane's grandson Fumitoki (899–981) made this connection between poetry and diplomacy more explicit. In 957, he presented a memorial recommending, among other things, that the Foreign Envoy's Quarters, then in ruins, be rebuilt. His reasoning was that foreign guests of state were always received by men of learning, and so a new building would inspire poets to study literature in Chinese.[20]

When the formal exchanges of poetry had been completed, Michizane gathered together the poems he and his colleagues had composed and provided an introduction for them:

I, as assistant minister of civil affairs, and Shimada no Tadaomi, as director of the Bureau of Buddhism and Aliens, together went to our guests' quarters. As the venerable regulations state, officials of two departments should not enter public buildings except when on government business. The director and I had observed that Ambassador Pae is a skilled poet, and we suspected that the others present might wish to prepare their poems in advance. We, however, resolved that although while present here we would exhaust ourselves in the effort, at other times we would not compose poetry. This idea was discussed and all agreed to it. Each time we joined together to exchange poems, we loosened our belts and collars, and traded many cups of wine. We composed poems without prepared drafts. Some had five-character lines, others seven-character lines. Some had six couplets, others four. All, however, were composed spontaneously without punctuation.

We began on the twenty-ninth day of the fourth month with poems using the character "to go" [Chinese *hsing*, Japanese *kō*] as the rhyme, and concluded on the eleventh day of the fifth month with poems of gratitude for the imperial gifts of clothing we had received. In addition to myself and Tadaomi, two other officials from the Bureau of Buddhism and Aliens were present, and we all exchanged poems harmonizing with those of our guests. Altogether there were fifty-eight poems. Lord Ōe contributed one more, making a total of fifty-nine. We five poets joined in this official duty and accordingly have decided to arrange these works into a single scroll so that they will not be forgotten. Hosts and guests are like rivals who must come to each other's aid. The sentiments of our guests are elegant; our own are crude. Placed together, they are like fragrant grasses and rank weeds growing in the same field. Those who were not involved with our endeavor would laugh if they see this and ridicule us if they hear of it. Alas, writers always belittle each other and only the wiser men of the future will be able to rectify this.[21]

Michizane's introduction emphasizes a number of important facts. First, his visits to the Foreign Envoy's Quarters where he exchanged poems with the ambassador were considered official business, not merely a pleasant pastime. Second, the exchanges were a form of friendly rivalry for which rather explicit rules were laid down: out of a sense of fairness, Michizane and his friends agreed not to prepare their poems in advance. In addition, Michizane proved himself a rather accurate prophet. As he feared, his poems were indeed faulted, and his chagrin has been described in an earlier chapter. Perhaps even a man less sensitive than Michizane would have been upset if such public and diplomatically significant contributions of his were criticized.

The poems Michizane presented to Ambassador Pae may have had an underlying political motive, but they expressed the warmest personal sentiments. Regardless of his government's ulterior motives, Michizane felt flattered to be selected as the poetic representative of the Japanese court and genuinely enjoyed the opportunity to display his virtuosity to an appreciative foreign guest, who may not have been Chinese himself but who did come from a land that was close to the source of Michizane's poetic language. The night before the ambassador's departure, Michizane wrote:

> On a Summer Night at the Foreign Envoy's Quarters:
> Parting with Our Guest from the North
> who is about to Return Home
> You are about to return, over the white waves to the distant green mountains.
> I regret that I am not able to see you off to the border.
> I am tormented by anxiety over your long journey ahead,
> And look forward to your coming again in the distant future.
> In the shade of a solitary cloud, the sails will soon be unfurled.
> If only you could stay a few more days here in our Envoy's Quarters!
> At this farewell gathering, why does nightfall seem so slow in coming?
> Because only then will we be able to shed tears in the privacy of darkness. [22]

Somewhat later, months after the mission had departed, he recorded:

> My Thoughts on Seeing a True Portrait
> of Parhae's Ambassador Pae
> Since seeing Lord Pae off on his ten-thousand-league journey,
> I have thought of him every night and not been able to sleep.
> Although this "true portrait" is facing me, I am not inspired to poetry.
> Alas, his clothing has been copied, but not his heart! [23]

On the twelfth day of the fifth month, two days after the final banquet, the envoys prepared to leave the capital. Again, officials were appointed, this time to see the visitors off from the capital. They brought to the Envoy's Quarters an imperial edict addressed to the king of Parhae. The Japanese message, like that brought from Parhae, is lost; however, one that Michizane had drafted for a previous mission in 872 was probably typical. Although it never specifically refers to Parhae as a vassal,

真圖
對我
無詩與恨
寫衣冠
不馬情

7. *Expressing his thoughts on seeing a portrait of Parhae's ambassador*
Source: Sugawara jikki.

自送㆑裴公

萬里行

相思㆑每夜

夢難成

it has a polite but condescending tone distinctly different from the deferential quality of the messages received from Parhae. Two days after the mission's departure, the women who had danced at the banquet were rewarded, "in accordance with the precedent of 842," when earlier visitors from Parhae had been in Japan.[24] This is the last specific reference to the 882–883 mission; however, it may have met with difficulties in readying its boats for the return voyage. Five months after the envoys had left the capital, an edict was proclaimed:

> The cutting of trees on Mount Tomari in Fukura village, Hagui district, Noto province, shall be prohibited. When missions from Parhae arrive in the north, they must make boats for their return home at this mountain. If the local people cut and gather the trees, sufficient lumber will not be available. Therefore, it shall be forbidden for the people to cut large trees. This should not interfere with their livelihood.[25]

The Japanese were determined to make a good impression on their foreign guests.

A DIPLOMATIC MISSION ABANDONED

By Michizane's day, receiving embassies from Parhae had become Japan's most common form of diplomatic contact with foreign states; however, historically Japan's own missions to China had been far more important. Michizane may have been Heian Japan's greatest authority on Chinese culture, but ironically, his most lasting contribution as a statesman was his proposal that his mission to China be canceled, for it brought to a close the period of over two centuries during which the Japanese had actively imported many elements of Chinese culture. Afterwards, Chinese culture retained much of its prestige among Japanese courtiers, but it was accepted more passively and its preeminence was no longer beyond question. The acceptance of Michizane's proposal did not cause the cultural and political changes that were taking place in ninth-century Japan. They had begun decades earlier. The abandonment of the mission, however, was an important symbolic gesture demonstrating that the Japanese government no longer felt the need to sponsor long, dangerous, and expensive journeys to China, journeys that also compromised Japan's diplomatic stance as a central kingdom comparable to China.

When Michizane made his proposal, he did not have in mind broad shifts in Japanese cultural history, but his exact intentions and those of the court are not at all clear and have become the subjects of considerable scholarly controversy. The debate revolves around the interpretation of a few directly relevant historical sources. The first is an official message drafted by Michizane in 894, just over four years after he had returned from Sanuki and one year after he had joined the Council of State as a consultant:

> In reply to the Monk Chūkan's Message from China;
> Written for the Council of State by Imperial Command
> By imperial command, I have read your message carefully. I was first saddened to find out that communications were long interrupted by rebellions, then pleased to learn that now you are enjoying a moment of tranquility. We have received the rare tea and the letter that you sent. Compared to the depths of your loyalty, the vast ocean seems shallow indeed! According to your report, Governor Chu Pao of Wen province [the modern Chekiang] has specially dispatched a messenger to visit our nation far to the east. We are deeply touched by his courageous attempt to cross the sea's endless waves, but after thoroughly investigating our ancient records, we have concluded that we cannot receive him. This cannot be doubted. Your letter states that he has already been sent, so we are not able to stop him.
> Many merchants have told us of conditions in China. They state that since the rebellions began, for over ten years Chu Pao alone has secured his territory, and the emperor respects his loyalty and industriousness. This seems to be the case. Although we receive only rumors, what ruler could hear them and not rejoice? Still, because of restrictions placed upon us by propriety, a message from the governor would not achieve its aims. If you should meet him in your travels, inform him of this.
> Furthermore, despite recent calamities and difficulties in obtaining necessary materials, our court has decided to send a mission to China. The time-consuming preparations may delay its departure, but if Chinese officials inquire, explain our intentions to them. This message has the authority of an edict and will be believed. In addition, we wish to present you 150 small ounces of gold dust to be used to purchase shelter, clothing, and food during your travels.
> The twenty-second day of the seventh month in the sixth year of the Kampyō era [894] [26]

Dated just under one month later, the following item appears in two sources with only minor variations in the text:

> The twenty-first day of the eighth month [894]: Consultant and Major Controller of the Left Lord Sugawara was named ambassador to the T'ang. Lesser Controller of the Left Lord Ki no Haseo was named Vice-ambassador.[27]

The names of three other officials presumably appointed the same day survive. A member of the Council of State, who would not have actually joined the mission, was placed in charge of preparations. Assigned to make the perilous journey were a scribe (rokuji) and an administrative officer, Fujiwara no Tadafusa (d. 928), who wrote, in Japanese:

> In the Kampyō era [889–897], I was named administrative officer for a mission to China. One evening when serving at the crown prince's quarters with other officials, we received some wine. I recited:

Nayotake no	On this long night,
Yo nagaki ue ni	The first frost settles
Hatsushimo no	On the graceful bamboo.
Okiite mono o	It is a time
Omou koro kana	When I am filled with cares![28]

Then, Michizane made his famous proposal:

> A Request That the Members of the Council of State
> Determine Whether or Not to Send a Mission to the T'ang
> Last year in the third month, the merchant Wang No brought a letter from the monk Chūkan who is in China. It described in detail how the Great T'ang is in a state of decline, and reported that the emperor is not at court [because of the rebellion] and foreign missions have ceased to come. Although Chūkan is merely a wandering monk, he has shown great loyalty to our court. When removed from their native lands, even the horses of the north and the birds of the south long for their homes. Is this not all the more true of men?
> Investigating records from the past, we have observed that some of the men sent to China have lost their lives at sea and others have been killed by pirates. Still, those who arrived safely in China have never yet had to suffer there from hunger and cold. According to Chūkan's letter, however, that which has never yet happened now seems likely to occur. We humbly request that his letter be distributed to all the members of the Council of State and the professors at the university so that they may carefully read it and consider the

merits of this proposal. This is a matter of national importance and not merely of personal concern. We present this proposal with deep sincerity and humbly hope that it will be given due consideration.
The fourteenth day of the ninth month, in the sixth year of the Kampyō era [894][29]

This is the document that Michizane signed with his six official titles mentioned earlier. In the text, however, he uses the plural "we" (*shintō*) to indicate that he was writing as a representative of all the men appointed to go to China. The opinion expressed was not his alone. Next, a chronicle reports:

The thirtieth day of the ninth month [894]: On this day the mission to the T'ang was canceled.[30]

However, an early and generally reliable biography of Michizane presents a slightly different sequence:

The fourteenth day of the ninth month [894]: A request was made that the Council of State determine whether or not to send a mission to China.
The fifteenth day of the fifth month [895]: There was an edict calling for the cancellation of the mission.[31]

From the above items, a few basic facts are clear. Michizane was named ambassador to the T'ang and his friend Haseo was appointed vice-ambassador, but as a result of a proposal presented by Michizane, the plan to send a mission to China was abandoned. Unfortunately, however, surviving sources suggest more questions than they answer. Why was Michizane named ambassador just one month after the court acknowledged receiving a letter that had described the chaotic conditions in late T'ang China? If the decision had been made to send the envoys despite the danger, why was this plan dropped only two weeks after Michizane had made his proposal, which was based on information presumably already well known? Or, was the decision not made until the following year, as another source indicates? The data are too scanty to allow any definite conclusions, although they have been the basis for considerable speculation. None of the many proposed theories alone can answer all the questions raised, but elements from various of them help to explain why Michizane's mission was canceled.

8. *Michizane and Haseo being named envoys to the T'ang*
Source: Sugawara jikki.

菅公
長谷雄
遣唐使館
宣下乎
賜布
之
圖

The problem is complicated by the fact that in places the meaning of Michizane's letter to Chūkan is not clear. The translation given is but one possible interpretation. According to another reading of the text, the message from the Chinese governor had arrived in Japan several years earlier, and although the Japanese had refused to acknowledge an envoy from a mere governor, they were encouraged to dispatch their own mission to China. Chūkan had learned of the plan and advised them to abandon it because of conditions in China. He may have also informed them that, contrary to what they had heard, in China the governor was viewed as a rebel.[32] This interpretation would explain why the Japanese first decided to send the mission and then soon cancel it, but it requires a very strained reading of the text.

One old explanation of the curious sequence of events was that Michizane's appointment was yet another attempt by the Fujiwara to dispose of him. They had him named ambassador in the hope he would be gone from the capital for a long time—perhaps forever, but Michizane outwitted the Fujiwara with his proposal that the mission be abandoned. This view finds little support among scholars today because there is no indication of a Fujiwara conspiracy, whereas ample evidence testifies that in 894 Michizane was on good terms with the Fujiwara.[33] The idea of sending envoys to China probably originated with Uda, not the Fujiwara. The emperor was trying to revive the practices of early Heian rulers, and a mission to the T'ang court was an appropriate part of his program. Michizane was the logical choice as ambassador, for he was Japan's leading authority on Chinese culture and his family had a long history of diplomatic experience. Another theory, also no longer widely accepted, is that Japan had advanced to the point that it no longer needed to learn from China, and Michizane's proposal indicates that he was the first to come to this realization. As noted, Michizane was an admirer of Chinese culture. Moreover, the Japanese court continued to respect China long after it had ceased to send official missions there and long after interest in native culture had revived.[34]

Economic elements provide at least a partial explanation for the abandonment of the mission. First, the missions were without question very expensive. Customarily, four ships were sent,

and often ships were wrecked and had to be rebuilt, as had been
the case with Kiyokimi's mission. Cost was one reason that
preparations usually required a number of years. By the late
ninth century, as Michizane noted in his letter to Chūkan, the
court was experiencing financial difficulties and could ill afford the expense of fitting out an elaborate diplomatic mission. Moreover, these missions were not exclusively diplomatic,
but also involved a considerable exchange of exotic goods, as
was also the case when Parhae representatives came to Japan.
In the ninth century, however, private Chinese traders were
appearing in Japan with increasing frequency, and they brought
with them the Chinese luxury goods admired by courtiers. Also,
they took pious Buddhist priests to China for study, another
function that had previously been performed by the official
missions. Thus the needs of the court were being met in a far
less costly—and less dangerous—manner.[35] This interpretation
certainly explains some of the reasons why the Japanese court
ceased sending embassies to China, but it does not deal with the
question of why Michizane was named ambassador.

Another view, dubbed by one Japanese scholar "the gesture
theory," focuses more specifically on Michizane's appointment.
By 894, no envoys had been sent to China for over fifty years.
Thus, in practice, the missions had long since been abandoned.
The reasons Michizane gave for canceling his mission were based
on information that had been known since his grandfather's
visit to China ninety years earlier. Therefore, the court may
never have intended to send Michizane to China, but rather,
Uda was hoping to raise the prestige of his favorite by giving
him the added title "ambassador to the T'ang." The post was
intended to be ornamental. Additional evidence to support this
theory is that Michizane continued to use the title "ambassador
to the T'ang" until he was promoted to great counselor three
years after the mission had been canceled. Haseo signed himself
as vice-ambassador for seven years. Clearly these titles were a
source of pride.[36] The problems with this theory are that the
planning mentioned in the letter to Chūkan would hardly have
been necessary for an embassy that was not meant to be dispatched, its administrative officer would not have suffered
from sleepless nights over an empty title, and mere scribes
would not have been appointed unless their services were

thought to be needed, for little honor could have been attached to so minor a post.

A recent interpretation suggests that the court appointed the envoys with every intention of dispatching them to China. However, an additional problem arose. Although they are not mentioned in the documents concerning the mission to China, pirates from Silla, Japan's old Korean enemy, began to ravage the Japanese coast late in 893. This was indeed a new problem that made an ocean voyage more dangerous than it had been in previous years. According to this view, most courtiers were not well versed in foreign affairs or even the problems with pirates, and so, ignorant of the difficulties, they proceeded to plan the mission. Even Michizane, who was better informed than most of his peers, at first did not object. But upon being named ambassador, he finally began to have doubts about the wisdom of attempting a journey to China. When he proposed canceling the mission, there was little opposition because his arguments were reasonable and clearly based on facts. The officers appointed kept their titles in the hope that they might later fulfill their duties. Michizane had not intended that relations with China be permanently ended, but such was the result of his proposal.[37]

This theory contains some truth. Not only did Michizane and his fellow envoys continue to use their titles, but *Engi shiki* (Regulations of the Engi era), completed in 927, included detailed provisions for the dispatch of missions to China, even though none had been sent for over ninety years and Michizane's had been canceled more than three decades earlier. Apparently, the Japanese had not precluded the possibility of further embassies to China. The court's presumed ignorance of the pirate attacks, however, is highly questionable. It assumes that ninth-century Japanese statesmen were remarkably uninformed even about such domestic problems as pirate attacks. Some courtiers may have devoted themselves to aesthetic pleasures and neglected their governmental duties, but others were busily keeping the records now used by modern scholars. Heian officials too must have read these documents. More concretely, only a month after the first report of pirate attacks, the court held a special Buddhist service to ward off disaster, and Michizane wrote a prayer for the occasion. After begging for relief from the droughts and epidemics that also plagued Japan, he asked that the pirates be destroyed.[38] This was over a year before he was named ambassador and indicates that the court was well aware of the pirates when it decided to send the envoys.

One further possibility is that the court did not change its mind quite so suddenly as is generally assumed. As noted, two sources for the cancellation of the mission give different dates for the event. The earlier date, which is accepted by most scholars, appears in a widely used and normally reliable chronicle. On the other hand, the biography of Michizane, which gives the later date, differs not only in the date, but also adds that there was an edict calling for the abandonment of the mission. Both sources may contain elements of truth. After Michizane presented his proposal, a preliminary decision could have been reached not to send the mission while the matter was under discussion. Only much later was the issue finally settled with an imperial edict, and thus a crucial decision was not made with quite the haste that first appearances suggest. Unfortunately, the evidence for this interpretation is too limited for it to be considered more than another possibility.

One important element has been generally overlooked when discussing the abandonment of official relations with China: the role of Parhae. In the court's view, the primary reasons for sending missions to China were political and cultural. They were intended to demonstrate that Japan was a civilized member of the East Asian community of nations and to bring back additional learning from China. The exchange of goods was, in theory, a distinctly secondary concern.[39] If this economic function of the missions was taken over by private traders, then the more important political and cultural function came to be largely performed by the envoys that Japan received from Parhae. Of the thirty-three embassies that Parhae sent to Japan, twenty arrived between 794 and 929. During this period, Japan sent only two missions to China, the ones on which Michizane's grandfather and uncle had gone. Thus, Japan remained a participant in East Asian diplomacy, even though it was no longer sending regular embassies abroad. In some ways, Japan's ties with Parhae were more gratifying than those with China, for Japanese attitudes toward diplomatic relations with China were ambivalent: the Japanese government sought recognition from the Chinese but also desired equality. Parhae seems to have been quite willing to place itself in a nominally inferior position, whereas in China, the Japanese had on occasion gotten into trouble for refusing to take a properly subservient attitude. Moreover, the missions from Parhae were an adequate—if perhaps less than ideal—means of following political events and cultural developments in China. Finally, as with private instead of public commerce, it was much safer to receive than to send missions. The court's lavish expenditure in entertaining its guests from Parhae illustrates how seriously it viewed them. The regular appearance of envoys from Parhae was a further reason why the Japanese came to see little need for sending their own missions abroad.

The arrival of the last embassy from Parhae that Michizane would receive may have been a direct consideration in the final decision to cancel Japan's diplomatic missions, although the evidence again is not conclusive. Here too the problem is one of chronology. Two different dates are given for the arrival of the guests from Parhae: the fifth month of 894 and the twenty-ninth day of the twelfth month of that year. If the former date, two months before the letter to Chūkan, is correct, the presence of an embassy from Parhae may have reinforced the feeling that there was no need for Japan to send its own envoys abroad. Also, the fact that Pae Chŏng was once more the ambassador would have caused the court to doubt the wisdom of risking the loss of Michizane's poetic talents. However, the later date probably is more accurate, for it would make the scheduling of the visit almost identical with that of the better-documented earlier mission Michizane had greeted. On the previous occasion, the embassy had arrived at the end of the eleventh month and entered the capital just five months later. Since this mission entered the capital in the fifth month, most likely it had arrived in Japan in the previous twelfth month, by which time the preliminary decision to abandon Michizane's mission had been made.[40] Even so, a connection may exist between Japan's receiving this mission and cancelling its own, for if in fact an edict was issued on the fifteenth day of the seventh month, 895, that would have been precisely when the Japanese were engaged in entertaining their foreign guests, who may have reminded them of the unstable conditions in China, the difficulties of the journey, and the advantages of receiving envoys from Parhae instead of sending them to China.

This latter embassy was Michizane's final chance to display

his talents as a poet-diplomat. By now, he was a member of the Council of State and so did not require a special promotion to give him the status needed to properly entertain the ambassador. The embassy arrived on the seventh day of the fifth month, 895, just missing the festivities that on their previous visit had been conducted in the rain. Four day later, Michizane and Haseo, both of whom retained their titles as ambassador and vice-ambassador to the T'ang, were sent to Pae Chŏng's quarters for a poetic exchange.[41] An appropriate character meaning "to associate" or "friendship" (Chinese *chiao*, Japanese *kō*) was selected as the rhyme, and they all composed poems expressing in the most elegant language their joy at the unexpected reunion. Michizane alone wrote a total of six poems, all with the same rhyme. His first was:

> Recording My Thoughts at the Envoy's Quarters
> I recall the past when we took hands and sealed our friendship.
> Seeing you again I am deeply moved and will regret having to
>   part once more.
> Our snow-white hair is of equal years, although we grew old on
>   opposite shores.
> One in our love of beauty, we gazed at the clouds and thought of
>   each other.
> A white colt once again eats the greens in our garden![a]
> The noble phoenix returns to nest atop our pavilion![b]
> I wish to inquire: with your great talent, are you not yet a minister?
> Please remember that Yang Hsiung[c] understood when mocked by
>   the uncouth.[42]

Notes:
a. An allusion to the *Shih ching*, meaning that an honored guest has come and we would be pleased if he stayed.
b. The phoenix is Pae Chŏng.
c. During the Han dynasty, Yang Hsiung was ridiculed for declining official appointments, but wrote an essay sympathizing with those who made fun of him. Michizane's line means, "please understand why I ask so vulgar a question."

As Pae Chŏng was about to depart, Michizane for a second time wrote a farewell poem:

> Parting with the Ambassador from Parhae on a Summer Day
> At first I was overjoyed that you were attracted by our great ruler's
>   virtue,

But what can I say, now that you again set off on your long journey?
Each time I see you off or greet you, it is with affection,
But between your previous departure and this encounter, our hair
  has grown grey.
In twelve years, the next mission comes: we are not likely to be
  writing together.
In your native land, do not forget this distant shore.
We have exchanged fine gifts with each other:
You leave me pearl-like poems; I offer pearl-like tears.[43]

As Michizane suspected, he would not meet again with his friendly poetic rival; however, this was not the end of relations between the Sugawara and Pae families. When the next mission from Parhae came to Japan in 908, it was headed by Pae Chŏng's son Pae Ku. Michizane's son Atsumochi (d. 926) was one of the Japanese who greeted him, and he composed a poem duly noting their fathers' friendship.[44]

Michizane had maintained his family's diplomatic traditions by actively participating in Japan's relations with Parhae, but he is better known for his proposal that his mission to China be stopped. This is often considered a major turning point in early Japanese history, but, in fact, it was only one in a long series of events that led Japan to interrupt its diplomatic ties with China for a period of over five centuries. The Japanese had known of the unstable conditions in China as early as 805 when Michizane's grandfather and his fellow emissaries had brought back reports of internal rebellions and foreign invasions. Following the return of the last mission to China in 839, Japanese enthusiasm for further overseas adventures diminished because the frequent arrival of private traders from China and official envoys from Parhae rendered the Japanese embassies largely superfluous. The court's straitened finances added to its difficulties. Then, because Emperor Uda wanted to revive earlier traditions, he decided to dispatch a mission, regardless of the problems. The court's most able men, among them Michizane, were selected as envoys. But first a new report on deteriorating conditions in late T'ang China and then the ravages of Korean pirates led Michizane to recommend that his mission be postponed. The envoys kept their titles in the hope that they might make the journey later if conditions in China improved. Disorder persisted, however, until after the founding of the Sung dynasty in 960, by which time the Japanese court had lost interest in sending embassies to China. The consequences of Michizane's proposal thus proved more lasting than he had intended.

Overall, Japan's position in the ninth-century East Asian community of nations largely anticipated what it would again become eight centuries later. Early Heian Japan abandoned its diplomatic ties with China, principally because they had proved too dangerous, but also because they conflicted with Japan's sense of itself as China's equal, a central kingdom. The Japanese, however, were pleased to allow Chinese merchants to bring their goods, for trade was safer and less awkward than diplomacy. Meanwhile, Japan's national pride was being flattered by the arrival of periodic missions from Parhae. In the early years of the Edo period, again Japan chose to maintain only trade relations with China. By then, Japanese seamanship had improved and the journey to China was no longer fraught with danger, but the Ming dynasty was in decline just as the T'ang had been when Japan earlier had broken off relations. Once again, Japan preferred receiving envoys from a Korean state, this time the Yi dynasty of Korea proper rather than Parhae, a Korean kingdom in Manchuria. To be sure, the situations in the ninth and the seventeenth centuries were not identical. For example, the newly established Tokugawa shogunate regarded diplomatic recognition from Korea as an essential element in confirming its legitimacy, a problem that did not concern Heian emperors. Moreover, such events as Hideyoshi's invasions of Korea and the appearance of Europeans further complicated the situation in the later period. Still, the parallel situations are not simply coincidence. They reflect a continuity in Japan's diplomatic posture: Japanese leaders persistently resisted allowing their nation to appear subordinate to others. In the fifteenth and sixteenth centuries, the Ashikaga shoguns had violated that rule when they permitted themselves to become nominally vassals to the Ming, and one of the reasons why the Tokugawa subsequently chose not to restore diplomatic ties with China was to avoid the criticism to which the Ashikaga had been subjected.[45]

7 · From Minister to Exile

Michizane's years in high office, the third stage in his official career, began with a rapid rise to the highest rungs of officialdom, but after his patron Emperor Uda abdicated in 897, his situation became increasingly precarious. Uda remained an important power behind the throne, and Michizane was still his favorite. He employed Michizane as his representative when he was monitoring affairs at court, and he sought Michizane's company when he took advantage of his newfound leisure by visiting scenic spots in the provinces around the capital. Michizane kept a record of one such excursion: it shows the elegant courtiers first enjoying the manly pastime of falconing and later turning their attention to poetry, especially to *waka*, which was becoming increasingly accepted, even in formal situations.

Michizane could not long enjoy the pleasures of fashionable aristocratic recreations, for he quickly discovered that even the support of a retired emperor was not enough to allow him, a bookish outsider, to maintain his unprecedented status at court. His enemies came from two camps: established political powers, notably the regents' line of the Fujiwara family personified by Tokihira, and academic rivals, particularly Miyoshi no Kiyoyuki. Together they succeeded in slandering him and driving him into exile. Whereas Michizane's rise had been in part related to questions of policy—Uda's attempt to revive the *ritsuryō* system—his

255

downfall was the result of purely political machinations. Toki-hira, who would replace him as the most powerful man at court, in fact, was to adopt a program of strengthening the established institutions of court government. This was in keeping more with Uda's ideas than with the usual Fujiwara policy of modifying official procedures to benefit their family's interests. Tokihira did not oppose Michizane for ideological reasons; he simply did not care to share power with him. Kiyoyuki's objections were more personal, for he and Michizane had a long-standing scholarly feud. Traditional accounts may exaggerate Tokihira's villainy, but they are correct in treating Michizane's downfall as the result of purely personal rivalries.

Michizane spent his last years, 901 to 903, under close watch as an exile in Kyushu. Once again, as when he had been governor of Sanuki, he turned to poetry to express his frustration over an unforeseen and unwanted sojourn in the provinces. In its highly personal and informal quality, the *kanshi* Michizane wrote in exile resemble those that he had composed in Sanuki, but with one significant difference. Michizane's reaction to Sanuki was mixed: occasionally he admitted to enjoying the province's natural beauty and unaffected populace. In Kyushu, however, his afflictions and grief were mitigated only by the solace that Chinese literature offered in its many examples of poets who had suffered fates similar to his and its tradition of lamenting personal misfortunes, notably absence from home. Michizane was able to comfort himself by composing poems that protested his innocence and, through appropriate allusions, demonstrated that he was not alone in his misery, for some of China's greatest poets—including Po Chü-i, Michizane's favorite—had been also unjustly banished to distant provinces. Michizane's exile was thus an example of life unintentionally imitating art, and just as his career had begun in the Chinese manner by his passing a civil service examination, so it ended with a misfortune shared by many Chinese literati. Michizane's downfall, however, was more than a personal disaster, for it also was one of the events that marked the end of an age in which the Japanese court habitually looked to Chinese example for guidance in both government and culture.

AT THE HEIGHT OF HIS POWER

Following Uda's abdication in 897, affairs at court seemed to be proceeding as he had planned. Michizane and Tokihira together dominated the court. All orders from the Council of State were signed by one of them, and together they formally issued appointment lists. Despite his retirement, Uda continued to exert a strong influence on court decisions, most notably promotions. Michizane was but one of his many favorites who were placed in important offices, presumably on his recommendation.[1]

A minor incident that occurred in the fourth month of 898 reveals both Uda's interest in court politics and his reliance on Michizane:

> On the twenty-third day, appointments were made. After the discussions had been completed, Lord Sugawara was sent to the Suzakuin [where Uda was residing]. Then the names were written on the appointment form. After Michizane had returned, the list was presented to the two ministries.[2]

As part of the procedure for making new appointments, a form was prepared listing the vacant offices, with spaces left blank for writing in the names of those selected to fill the positions. In this case, apparently the new appointments were discussed in the Council of State, but before the names were written on the form, Michizane was sent to inform Uda of the decisions that had been reached. Although the source quoted is not altogether clear, Uda himself may have written in the names. Even if he did not, the appointments were not finally settled until he had approved them. In this way, he was taking an active part in a vital court procedure and was doing so with Michizane as his intermediary.

Various other events demonstrated the continuing close personal relationship between Michizane and the imperial family. For example, in the third month of 899 when Michizane's wife Nobukiko celebrated her fiftieth year, an imperial messenger, Lesser Controller of the Right Fujiwara no Yukimichi—of whom more will be said later—came to Michizane's mansion and formally granted Nobukiko the junior fifth rank lower. Later that day, the retired emperor himself personally commemorated the occasion by visiting the Sugawara residence. For his part, Michizane continued to draft documents for Uda and individuals closely associated with the retired emperor, even though by now he was rarely performing such services for others.[3]

Michizane was also enjoying the favor of the reigning Emperor Daigo, as is illustrated by an incident that occurred in 900 and later would become a standard element in popular accounts of Michizane's life. As was customary, the ninth day of the ninth month was celebrated at the palace with poets gathering to compose *kanshi* on a theme selected by the emperor. This year it was "The Dew Freezes in the Cold." The following day, poets were again summoned and ordered by the emperor to write a "Poem on Autumn Thoughts." Michizane's was:

> Over the years, your minister has experienced joys,
> But tonight everything seems to stir only sadness:
> The cold voice of the cricket in the blowing wind;
> The falling leaves of the Chinese paulownia, struck by the rain.
> You are at your peak; I am growing old.
> Your generosity is boundless; my repayment is slow.
> How can I relieve such feelings?
> I drink wine, listen to the koto, and recite poems.[4]

At the time, Emperor Daigo was only sixteen years old and Michizane was fifty-six. The young emperor was so touched by this poem that he gave his senior minister a robe. One year later, Michizane was in exile and recalled the event with his most familiar poem in Chinese:

> Ninth Month, Tenth Day
> This night last year, attending at the Seiryō Palace,
> I spoke my sorrow in a "Poem on Autumn Thoughts."
> The robe His Majesty bestowed on me, here with me now—
> each day I lift it reverently, bow to its lingering fragrance.[5]

The story of these two poems became another standard element in traditional retellings of Michizane's life. Unlike other elements in the legend of Tenjin, however, this anecdote was true; its poignancy required no further embellishments. Traditionally, it was used to illustrate Michizane's abiding loyalty to the

9. The robe bestowed by the emperor evokes memories
Source: Dazaifu Temmangū.

emperor, but the story also demonstrates that as late as the ninth month of 900, Michizane was enjoying the favor both of Retired Emperor Uda and of his son Emperor Daigo. One year later, he was in exile.

Although Uda abdicated primarily for political reasons, with the intention of controlling the court from retirement, he also took advantage of his newly gained leisure to enjoy frequent visits to famous scenic spots. Both Michizane and Tokihira occasionally accompanied him on these excursions. One of the most elaborate—and well documented—was a twelve-day journey through the provinces south of the capital in the tenth month of 898. Michizane went along and, starting from the second day, kept a record of the trip.[6] It not only reveals the close friendship between Uda and Michizane, but also provides a vivid picture of Heian court aristocrats enjoying the beauties of the countryside and expressing their pleasure in *waka,* which had become an important part of such occasions. Although Michizane composed *kanshi* too, he was the exception. His companions wrote in Japanese. In part, this was because the occasion was not as formal as court rituals, and the participants, mainly nobles rather than scholars, may not have been adept in their use of Chinese. Another reason was that the *waka* had come into its own as a literary form worthy of serious attention.

On the morning of the twentieth, the participants lined up for their departure from the capital. The first two days of the excursion were devoted primarily to falconing, a popular sport among Heian noblemen. The hunters—including some of the highest-ranking aristocrats—were divided into two teams of nine men each, as were the referees. These four groups wore carefully specified and very elegant matching costumes. Other courtiers, including Michizane and Haseo, accompanied the party, although they did not join in the first day's sport. As the time to depart approached, all mounted their horses and around ten they set off in a magnificent procession with the retired emperor in the lead. As they paraded south down Suzaku Avenue, the main thoroughfare of the capital, people thronged to see the spectacle. Women, in their efforts to catch glimpses of the retired emperor's face, ignored propriety and leaned from their carriages. The color of their robes further adorned the occasion.

An hour later, the men had arrived at Kawashima, a plain

southwest of the capital, and began falconing. They pursued their sport with great vigor until midafternoon, by which time they were all exhausted. An elegant repast was provided; Michizane personally looked after Uda's meal. Afterwards, the group proceeded to the imperial stables at Akame. Michizane, armed with bow and arrows, accompanied the retired emperor. When they arrived at Akame, the catch was counted. The winning team had managed to capture 122 small birds, their rivals only 96. The evening was devoted to more eating and drinking, with song and dance as entertainment. Several courtesans were present to further enliven the occasion. Uda observed that Michizane had never before tried falconing and invited him to join the hunt the following day. On the twenty-first, most of the party had to return to the capital to resume their official duties. Haseo, who had recorded the events of the first day, also left, although for a different reason: his right foot had been hurt when a horse stepped on it. Seventeen courtiers, among them Michizane and four retainers, continued with Uda to Katano, roughly halfway between the modern cities of Kyoto and Osaka. There, once again they hunted with their falcons, and presumably this time Michizane was given a chance to try his luck. How he did was not recorded.

In the following days, the courtiers' interest shifted from sport to aesthetic pleasures: visiting scenic spots and composing poetry. On the twenty-third, they passed through the old capital of Nara where they lamented the dilapidated condition of the Hokkeji Monastery and viewed the remains of the former palace. As they were leaving they found some wine and sweets left by the roadside. No owner seemed to be present and so they freely ate and drank. Someone suggested that a monk from another Nara temple had heard Michizane would be passing by and set out refreshments for him; however, seeing not only Michizane but also the retired emperor, the monk was so startled that he hid in the dense foliage.

At this point, Uda remembered that the famous poet-monk Sosei (d. c. 910) was residing at yet another nearby monastery. A messenger was sent to summon him and he came to join the group. Feeling that his religious name, Sosei, was not appropriate for the occasion, Uda decided that he should be referred to by a secular name, Yoshiyori, a Japanese reading for the name of the temple, Ryōin'in, in which he resided. With Sosei a member of the party, everyone's interest turned to composing *waka,* the form at which Sosei excelled. Soon they came to Mount Tamuke, literally "Offering Mountain," at which gifts were presented to the gods. There, Michizane composed a *waka* that has become one of his best known because of its inclusion in the popular anthology *Hyakunin isshu* (One hundred poems by one hundred poets, compiled c. 1200):

Kono tabi wa	This time, for the journey
Nusa mo toriaezu	I was unable to prepare offerings.
Tamukeyama	Gods of Mount Tamuke,
Momiji no nishiki	May the brocade of autumn leaves
Kami no manimani	Serve as a gift for you to enjoy.[7]

Sosei then contributed:

Tamuke ni wa	As an offering,
Tsuzuri no sode mo	I might cut off a sleeve
Kirubeki ni	Of my priestly robe.
Momiji ni akeru	Sated with the autumn leaves,
Kami ya kaesan	The gods, how could they refuse it?[8]

Both of these poems are based on a conventional metaphor comparing the red autumn leaves with brocade. Michizane's poem suggests that in his hurry to depart, he did not have time to prepare suitable offerings for the gods of Mount Tamuke, but that the natural beauty of the crimson leaves made an excellent substitute. Sosei presents an alternate view that the gods may have had their fill of autumn leaves and might prefer a piece of his somber robe. Such literary conventions and conceits were fashionable in Michizane's day, and came to be associated with the *Kokinshū,* Japan's first imperially sponsored anthology of poetry in Japanese, compiled just eight years later. In fact, the two poems quoted appear together in that anthology in the section on travel poems. Of the *waka* composed on this excursion, thirteen were eventually included in imperial anthologies, and two more were preserved in other collections. Six poets were represented.[9] This short journey through the countryside became a noteworthy event in the history of Japanese poetry.

Not all members of the entourage were outstanding poets, however. After passing Mount Tamuke, the party proceeded to Michizane's mountain villa in the Takechi district of Yamato province, about fifteen miles south of Nara. There they spent the night. Uda proposed that, because Sosei was famous for his *waka*, everyone should compose one to dispel his travel weariness. After each had presented his poem to the retired emperor, one of the "poets," Fujiwara no Yukimichi—the man who would bring word of Nobukiko's promotion the following year—went off by himself and sat in a corner facing the wall. There he did some calculations on his fingers. After some time, he returned to Uda and said, "My poem does not follow the proper form. I wish to remove three syllables." The retired emperor would not allow this and Yukimichi's predicament caused much comment. A late Heian scholar, Fujiwara no Kiyosuke (1104–1177), recounted another incident that occurred on this journey and gave further evidence of Yukimichi's poetic ineptitude. At one point, a singularly difficult theme was presented, and some of the best poets in attendance were not able to compose poems on it that satisfied them. No matter how hard they tried, they were not pleased with their efforts. This was because they could distinguish good poetry from bad. Yukimichi, on the other hand, had no trouble at all writing a poem he himself considered quite good. Such is the way with those who do not understand poetry, Kiyosuke lamented.[10] No examples of Yukimichi's poetry survive.

Two days after spending the night at Michizane's villa, the party arrived at Miyanotaki, "The Palace Waterfall." The falls were not remarkably high, but they were very broad and made a thunderous sound. The courtiers were so awed that they forgot the passage of time. Again, Uda commanded everyone to compose *waka*. His own contribution was

Miyanotaki	"The Palace Waterfall":
Mube mo na ni oite	Yes, true to its name
Kikoekeri	Can be heard
Otsuru shiraawa no	The jewel-like resonance
Tama to hibikeba	Of the falling white foam.[11]

Michizane wrote:

10. On an excursion with the retired emperor at Mount Tamuke
Source: Sugawara jikki.

Mizuhiki no	Will these white threads,
Shiraito haete	Drawn out in the water,
Oru hata wa	Be woven on a loom
Tabi no koromo ni	To make the many layers
Tachi ya kasanen	Of a traveler's robe?[12]

Although Michizane never mentions the waterfall, his poem uses appropriate images. The "white threads drawn out in the water" point to the falls, just as "jewel-like resonance" in Uda's poem suggests a palace.

After viewing the falls, the courtiers headed west. They stopped at Ryūmonji, a monastery that seemed to transcend the mundane world, surrounded as it was by pines, ivy, streams, and rocks. There they prayed and visited the site of a hut where a great sage had once lived. As they proceeded single file on their horses, it grew dark, and Sosei asked where they would stop for the night. Michizane responded with a couplet in Chinese:

> The road ahead is uncertain: where shall we spend the night?
> White clouds and crimson trees provide a traveler's lodging.

Although many of the men on the excursion were able *waka* poets, they were less skilled at *kanshi*. None was able to cap Michizane's couplet and complete the quatrain. "If only Haseo were here!" Michizane cried out repeatedly, for his friend surely would have been able to finish the verse.

Afterwards, the party rested for two days, during which time a messenger arrived from the capital to inquire about Uda's welfare. Then, on the twenty-eighth, the party continued its journey in the direction of the modern Osaka. That day, near the border of Kawachi province, they crossed Mount Tatsuta, another famous spot that once again called for a round of poems. It was raining and so Uda chose to pick up on the water imagery and write of the river there rather than the mountain:

Yo no naka ni	Throughout our land,
Iinagashiteshi	Word of its splendor has flowed:
Tatsutagawa	The Tatsuta River,
Miru ni namida zo	When I now see it,
Ame to furikeru	Tears fall like rain.[13]

Michizane, however, chose to write in Chinese this time:

> The mountain covered with crimson leaves breaks the loom of my
> heart,
> All the more so when I meet the drifting clouds that seem to leap from
> my feet.
> The cold trees do not know where I am going.
> In the rain, wearing brocade, I am returning home.[14]

This poem is distinctive for two reasons. First, it is the only
surviving complete *kanshi* of Michizane's that does not appear
in the anthologies he compiled. Along with the couplet he
wrote three days earlier that no one was able to cap, it is preserved in Michizane's account of this excursion that was abridged
and included in a later court chronicle. A more important feature is that Michizane seems to have employed a native Japanese
literary convention in this Chinese-language poem, a practice
he normally shunned. Although the poem's first line could
mean simply that the autumn leaves caused his heart to break,
probably it refers to the conceit he had used at Mount Tamuke:
that the red maple leaves formed a brocade, in this case a brocade vast enough to overwhelm the poet's "heart-loom" (*shinki*).
On this excursion, Michizane was visiting sites that had deep
associations with Japanese poetry, and he was accompanied by
a group of poets who preferred to compose *waka*. These influences led Michizane for once to mix his literary traditions. In
his *kanshi* he often described scenes and events peculiar to
Japan, but this is the only instance in which he employed a conventional conceit derived from *waka*. Perhaps he later thought
better of the experiment and so omitted the poem from his
anthology.

The day after the courtier-poets had visited Mount Tatsuta,
they arrived at the beach of Sumiyoshi, now part of Osaka. Because Sosei had to leave the rest of the group and return to his
temple, Uda now commanded everyone to write poems on parting. Fujiwara no Tsunesuke (879–938) wrote:

> *Kaminazuki*   A privilege as rare
> *Mare no miyuki ni*   As snow in the godless month:[a]
> *Sasowarete*   To join the imperial progress.

| *Kyō wakarenaba* | If today we part, |
| *Itsuka aimin* | When shall we meet again?[15] |

Note:
a. The tenth month, which Shinto deities from throughout Japan spent in Izumo, thereby leaving their native provinces "godless."

Uda bestowed on Sosei an outfit of clothing and a horse. The monk changed into his newly received robes, mounted the horse, and rode off. As the courtiers watched him depart they felt that with him went their inspiration to write *waka.* On the thirtieth, however, they visited Sumiyoshi Shrine, dedicated to the god of poetry, and one last time they all composed poems in Japanese. Around noon on the following day, they began their return trip home and finally they arrived at a small villa, belonging to one of the party, which was just outside the capital. There they waited for the sun to set and then proceeded to the mansion of the retired emperor. All who had accompanied Uda were rewarded with wine and silk; in addition, three of his most honored attendants, one of them Michizane, were also given horses from the imperial stables.

On this excursion, Michizane revealed that his poetic skills were not limited to verse in Chinese. He had written *waka* in his earlier years; however, it was only now, as a high official and confidant of Uda, that he began regularly to compose poems in Japanese on elegant public occasions such as this trip. This was largely because Uda had elevated *waka* to a status approaching that of poetry in Chinese. And, if verbal dexterity is taken as the measure of excellence, Michizane proved himself a capable poet in his native language. Although Michizane's *waka* are not as distinctive as his *kanshi,* he nonetheless participated in the ninth-century revival of poetry in Japanese.

Through most of his years in high office, Michizane was not only a close friend of the retired emperor and a companion to the reigning emperor; he also maintained good relations with the leader of the Fujiwara family, Tokihira. Tokihira did not go on the excursion just described; however, both he and Michizane earlier had accompanied Uda on a visit first to Kitano and then to the Unrin'in Monastery where together they joined in an exchange of poems in Chinese.[16] That was Michizane's only known visit to Kitano, the site where he would be enshrined fifty-one years later. In 893, when Michizane was appointed consultant, Tokihira congratulated him by presenting a Chinese jeweled sash imported from Cheng province, part of modern Honan. Michizane responded with a poem:

> Burdened by official duties, still I must take time to thank a man of great talent.
> Your gift glistens brightly; its jewels are not mere dust.
> Although it has no legs, first it arrived from Cheng province;
> And now, expressing kind thoughts, it comes here from your mansion.
> Abashed before your virtue, the snow forms only after you have formed your dress.
> Deferring to your glory, the flowers blossom in the wake of your progress.
> When I look at the design of this sash,
> I realize who was responsible for this scholar's promotion.[17]

Michizane's poem modestly suggests that his new office was the result of Tokihira's friendly assistance. That was a polite fiction, but Tokihira's generous gift and Michizane's humble reply were concrete signs of friendship between men who would come to be regarded as arch enemies.

Shortly following Uda's abdication in 897, however, another poem Michizane sent to Tokihira hints at growing tensions:

> In Response to a Poem by Tokihira,
> Written When He Accompanied the Retired Emperor
> on a Boating Excursion
> Reciting your poem makes me feel just as if I too were on the boat.
> Although I do not see you floating in the current, I can perceive your feelings.
> Blessed by our ruler's limitless beneficence, I know contentment.
> My heart is pure like water; why should I thirst with ambition?[18]

Four years earlier, Michizane had thanked Tokihira for a kind gift, but now he had come to feel a need to assure Tokihira that he was content with his position and did not wish to become a rival. As Michizane rose to high office, people began to see him as a threat to the Fujiwara domination of court politics. Michizane addressed this poem to Tokihira in an effort to demonstrate that he had no wish to displace the Fujiwara leader. His later actions would show that indeed he felt uncomfortable in his new high position. The sentiments he expressed were real. And even if Tokihira may have had some doubts about Michizane, as late as 899 he turned to him to draft a petition requesting an official charter for a monastery founded by Mototsune.[19] Such a favor would not have been requested of someone perceived as the family's arch rival. Tension was beginning to appear, but Michizane was successfully maintaining his official position and remaining on at least polite terms with the two principal powers at court, the imperial family and the Fujiwara.

DOWNFALL

Despite the support Michizane received from Uda and his attempts to maintain good relations with Tokihira, Michizane's position at court was not secure. The first indication of this was an incident that occurred in the ninth month of 898, just over a year after Uda's abdication. Because Uda had instructed his young son Daigo to follow the advice of Michizane and Tokihira, the two major counselors, all the other counselors concluded that their own advice was not required and ceased appearing at court to perform their duties. Probably they were jealous of the special prerogatives granted Michizane and Tokihira. Tokihira by himself might have been tolerated, for he was the scion of a family of regents, but Michizane, a descendant of scholars, could not be accepted, and so the two men were left to carry out the business of the Council of State unassisted. In a petition to the retired emperor, Michizane protested that he was a scholar and wished to devote at least some time to his teaching, but if he were to do so, Tokihira would have to handle the affairs of government alone, which would be quite impossible. Therefore, Michizane requested that Uda order the other counselors to resume their duties. Fourteen days later, Uda issued an edict as suggested—despite the fact that he was now retired—and the following day Michizane was able to report that it had immediately solved the problem.[20]

At the time, the highest offices in the Council of State were vacant. Uda hoped that by further promoting his hand-picked de facto regents he could increase their prestige and thereby avoid similar problems in the future. Accordingly, in the second month of the following year, 899, he had Tokihira and Michizane named ministers of the left and right respectively.[21] This gave them the highest regular posts in the Council of State and should have eliminated any need to rely on special edicts to shore up their position.

Another source of conflict, in this instance between Tokihira and Michizane, was their respective marital ties with the imperial family. As already noted, one of Michizane's daughters had become a consort of Uda's in 895. Uda came to favor her and in his testament, he recommended that she be entrusted to solve problems in the palace women's quarters. In addition, another of Michizane's daughters was serving as principal handmaid, the highest woman official at court. Finally, when Uda's son Prince Tokiyo celebrated his coming of age in the eleventh month of 898, he took yet another daughter of Michizane's as his wife.[22] Members of the Fujiwara regents' family sometimes had even closer and more intricate marital connections with the imperial family. For example, four of Mototsune's daughters married into the imperial family, and over a century later five of his descendant Michinaga's daughters were to do so. For a Sugawara, however, such close ties were unprecedented. Not only because of his high office, but also because of his special ties with the imperial household, Michizane had attained a position that made him an object of envy.

In contrast, Tokihira's relations with the imperial family were less than ideal, at least when compared to those of his predecessors Yoshifusa and Mototsune. At the time of the Akō Incident, Mototsune had forced Uda to marry his daughter Haruko, who was Tokihira's elder sister. Although she did not produce a son, she was named Daigo's adoptive mother, probably on the day of his accession. This fabricated relationship alone was hardly satisfactory to Tokihira. That same day, Tokihira attempted to have his younger sister Yasuko (Onshi) accepted as a consort of the new emperor, but Uda's mother, Princess Nakako (Hanshi), objected. Instead, she arranged to have her own daughter Tameko (Ishi) selected as consort: Daigo was married to his own aunt. Less than two years later, however, Tameko died in childbirth. Her mother heard rumors that this death was the evil doing of Yasuko's "angry spirit"—such beliefs were then common—and once more Nakako blocked an attempt by Tokihira to have his sister named Daigo's consort.[23] Thus, whereas

Michizane developed closer marital ties with the imperial family than any previous Sugawara, Tokihira was not able to retain what for the Fujiwara had become their customary close relationship with the reigning emperor. At the time, the rule of primogeniture was not followed, and the imperial succession usually went to the prince with the most powerful backing. A grandson of Michizane could possibly have become emperor, whereas Tokihira would have had trouble manipulating a blood relative into the imperial line. Tokihira's comparative weakness in this respect gave him all the more reason to be suspicious of Michizane.

From 897 to 901, the years immediately following Uda's abdication, Michizane's political strength is difficult to gauge precisely. Officially, in 899, he came to hold the second highest regular office at court, minister of the right, and so in status was inferior only to Tokihira, the minister of the left. They were in fact, if not in name, co-regents. In some respects, Michizane may have been the more powerful man. He had close marital ties with the imperial family, and clearly he, not Tokihira, had the support of Uda. Michizane also retained much of his influence in the academic world. He continued to teach at his private school. His eldest son Takami had become president of the university, another son was serving in the Ministry of Ceremonial, and a third was a graduate student of literature. Moreover, it was said that by 901, half the men employed in the court bureaucracy were his former students. One of them was his close friend Haseo, who also had come to hold high rank—junior fourth lower—and office—major controller of the left and gentleman-in-waiting.[24] Michizane was not lacking in supporters.

His powerful position, however, had aroused the envy of other high court nobles whom he had surpassed despite the relatively modest social prestige of his family. A significant measure of the fundamental precariousness of Michizane's status is the declining number of regulations issued by the Council of State under his name. During the last years of Uda's reign, he had been the most active high court noble in the Council of State, but the situation changed after Uda's retirement. Indeed, as Uda had ordered, Michizane and Tokihira completely dominated the council and no other noble issued any regulations. However, now Tokihira was by far the more active, and presumably influential, man. In the first three and a half years of Daigo's reign, twenty-one regulations were signed by Tokihira, compared to nine by Michizane. Of those nine, only three were issued during his final two years at court as minister of the right. Despite his promotion to that high office, his influence declined. The last regulation he signed was in the sixth month of 900. It ordered his old scholarly rival Kiyoyuki, who had recently become professor of literature, to resume a series of lectures on the *Shih-chi*. [25]

By the time Michizane was appointed minister of the right, he had risen to a position higher than was considered appropriate to his original status as a court scholar, and he petitioned three times declining the title. Although such petitions were customary and usually had meaning only as ritual, Michizane's may have been an exception. [26] The first of them presents an accurate assessment of his position:

> I, Michizane, wish to report:
> On the fourteenth day of this month, I was appointed minister of the right by imperial edict. The emperor's beneficence has been bestowed on me, but I do not feel I can accept it. Humbly, I must state that I am not of noble birth; my family is one of scholars. Through the generosity of the retired emperor, I attained the status of a high court noble, but as a result of today's promotion I can neither sleep nor eat because of my apprehension. People's hearts are not filled with tolerance. Demons gaze with envy and bring misfortune to those who prosper. I beg his majesty to consider my position and permit me to decline this office. It is not simply a matter of a lowly man's will being unshakable, but this is the desire of the populace. I am not equal to the great honor that has been granted me and with deepest humility make this request.
> The twenty-seventh day of the second month in the second year of the Shōtai era [899].
> Minister of the Right and General of the Right Bodyguards, Senior Third Rank, Lord Sugawara. [27]

Although the "populace" may not have cared about Michizane's promotion, individuals in high office certainly did. Michizane was not altogether comfortable with his new and somewhat too exalted office, but his petitions declining it, regardless of their sincerity, were politely rejected in the usual manner.

In the second and tenth months of 900, Michizane further petitioned to be relieved of another of his titles, general of the

第二表曰
伏願　階下追迴
寵命賜解臣官
改授其人俾賢
得路

第三表曰
伏望虛賢降
臨宸衷曲鑒
削臣官以全
臣福拾臣罷
以保臣身

11. *Declining the office of minister of the right*
Source: Sugawara jikki.

Right Bodyguards, which he had been awarded three years earlier. Once more he stressed that he was a scholar and this was an inappropriate appointment. The duties were in fact purely nominal, but the title was a great honor usually given only to men of the most noble birth, and, Michizane noted, five or six other men at court deserved it more than he. Because of their envy, after holding the title for three years, Michizane belatedly tried to relinquish it. Again, the language of his petitions declining office seems sincere. In more concrete terms, his attempt to resign from an office three years after being appointed to it was an extraordinary step, not simply a matter of following custom. After being named minister of the right, Michizane began to worry about the precariousness of his position and the jealousy of more nobly born courtiers. However, he was not allowed to withdraw from that office because to do so would have weakened Uda's position in the Council of State. Instead, Michizane hoped to mollify envious aristocrats by stepping down from an elevated but purely honorary post. Even this, however, was not permitted. On the contrary, in 900 Uda is said to have tried to strengthen Michizane's position by offering him the title of chancellor, which Michizane firmly refused, claiming he lacked the necessary aristocratic status.[28] The retired emperor was confident of his ability to support his favorite minister, but Michizane did not share Uda's optimism.

In the tenth month of 900, just one day after Michizane presented his second petition declining the title of general, he received a letter from Kiyoyuki, whom he had ordered to resume lecturing only four months earlier. The letter offered disturbing proof that his concern was justified:

Humbly, I, Kiyoyuki, wish to state:
Superficial acquaintances who speak with familiarity are false. Those who today talk of the future are dishonest. No doubt I will have to endure accusations of falsehood and dishonesty, but I feel I must warn you to be cautious.
While a student at the university, I secretly immersed myself in the occult sciences. Since ancient times, diviners have investigated the occasions when the mandate of heaven changes and retainers overthrow their lords. Most recently, the *Classic of the K'ai-yuan Era* (*K'ai-yuan ching*)[a] has presented their theories in detail. Determining the years of such momentous events is as easy as pointing to the palm of one's hand. This is something you surely know and I

need not further explain. However, even Li Chu could not see the dust above his eyebrows and Confucius could not guess what was in a box.[b] Thus, even my poor knowledge may be of some aid to your understanding.

It is my observation that next year will be indicated by the conjunction of the signs of the metal younger brother (*shin*) and the bird (*yū*), a combination foretelling a change in the mandate of heaven. The second month, indicated by the sign of the hare (*bō*),[c] will be particularly inauspicious, and military insurrections will certainly occur. I do not know who will suffer misfortune or meet with disaster, but if one were to shoot a crossbow into a marketplace, the person hit by the quarrel would surely be one who was already ill-fated.

The will of heaven is mysterious and difficult to perceive, but the words and deeds of men are easily known. It is my humble observation that you have risen above your status as a scholar and surpassed others to become a great minister. You have received imperial favor and flourished in your scholarly endeavors. There is no one whose virtue can compare with yours, except for Lord Kibi.[d] It is my hope that you will know contentment and recognize your proper status. You ought to retire to the mountains and devote yourself to the beauties of the clouds and mist. Would it not be splendid for later generations to admire you for this?[29]

Notes:
a. A work on divination that was compiled in the K'ai-yuan era (713–742) of the T'ang dynasty.
b. Li Chu was a legendary figure famed for his keen sight. Confucius's inability to guess the contents of an unfamiliar box is taken from *Pao-p'u tzu*, a Chin dynasty (265–317) Taoist work.
c. These were signs in the Chinese sexagenary cycle used to designate years and months.
d. Kibi no Makibi (see p. 74).

Kiyoyuki appeared to be giving Michizane a friendly, almost obsequious, admonition, but at the same time he ominously hinted at the most dire consequences if Michizane failed to resign promptly. Much of the letter's contents were already familiar to Michizane. In his second petition declining his military title, Michizane had noted that there had been complaints about his promotions and that he wished to devote himself to "serving the flowers and moon." When Kiyoyuki suggested that Michizane was overly ambitious, he employed the same phrase—"to know contentment"—that Michizane had used three years earlier in his poem reassuring Tokihira that he was not ambitious. The phrase was adopted from *Lao-tzu* and would soon reappear to plague Michizane. Michizane did not need to be reminded that his high position had aroused the envy of others.

By predicting that the second month of the coming year would be particularly inauspicious, however, Kiyoyuki gave Michizane a new reason to feel insecure. Ten days after sending Michizane the above letter, Kiyoyuki presented to the court his prediction that a "revolution" (*kakumei*) was imminent. He was using the term in its Confucian sense of a change in the mandate of heaven, a disruption of the imperial succession. His argument was essentially the same as in the letter to Michizane, but it was presented in far greater detail. He reiterated the date when insurrection would break out and a retainer would overthrow his lord, causing a change in the imperial line. Then he elaborated the Chinese theories of numerology and astrology that supported his prediction and maintained that the facts of both Chinese and Japanese history proved his case. In a later document on the same topic, he carefully demonstrated how, in each year that his theory would have predicted "revolution," indeed, terrible events such as the deaths of emperors had occurred. Occasionally he had to alter dates slightly or was forced to admit that the chronicles appeared to be incomplete for certain periods, but superficially, his evidence seemed convincing. In order to prevent these terrible developments, he recommended that the emperor carefully consider the matter and order his ministers to be on their guard, for with his benevolence and right conduct, the emperor could prevent the evil plot. In particular, Kiyoyuki encouraged the emperor to keep careful watch on those serving close to him.[30]

Kiyoyuki's theory must have impressed his contemporaries. His use of a complicated numerological scheme and astrological evidence was further enhanced by their basis in Chinese works that had only recently become known in Japan. In an age that believed deeply in various types of fortune-telling, he was using the latest, most up-to-date, Chinese methods of divination. Moreover, he was able to support his prognostication with detailed, although not altogether accurate, historical data. Kiyoyuki did not mention the name of the retainer who could be expected to overthrow his lord, but it must have been obvious to everyone at court that one minister in particular seemed somewhat out of place in the highest circles of the government.

Despite Kiyoyuki's dire predictions, the new year 901 began auspiciously for Michizane. On the seventh day of the first month, he and Tokihira were both promoted to the junior second rank.[31] Only in special cases were higher ranks awarded to exceptional individuals such as Yoshifusa and Mototsune. But on the twenty-fifth day of the month, just eighteen days after Michizane had reached this pinnacle, the following edict was proclaimed:

> For the past five years since we first became emperor, the Minister of the Left Lord Fujiwara [Tokihira] and others have assisted us with the affairs of government, in keeping with the instructions of the retired emperor. The Minister of the Right Lord Sugawara, however, who suddenly rose from a humble family to become a great minister, does not know contentment and hopes to dominate the court. He deceived the former emperor with flattery and now intends to disrupt the imperial succession. He would shatter the feelings of benevolence between father and son, and destroy the love between older and younger brother. His words are obedient, but his heart is rebellious. This is known by all in the nation. He is not a person who should serve as a great minister but deserves punishment under the law. However, out of special consideration for his position, he shall only be removed from his present office and be appointed supernumerary governor general of Dazaifu. Major Counselor Minamoto no Hikaru [845-913] shall be promoted to minister of the right, and offerings shall be made to placate the spirits of our ancestors.[32]

Suddenly, although perhaps not altogether unexpectedly, Michizane was removed from the second highest office at court and politely but firmly sent into exile in the form of a strictly nominal provincial office.

This edict came as a shock not only to Michizane but also to Uda. The retired emperor immediately rushed to the palace, but the guards would not let him pass. Uda is said to have rolled out a grass mat and sat all day in a garden by the eastern gate to the palace. When it grew dark, he finally gave up and returned to his own residence. The man responsible for barring Uda from entering the palace was Fujiwara no Sugane (855-908), a scholar whom only three and a half years earlier Michizane had taken the trouble to specially recommend for promotion. Although

Uda's entry into the palace was blocked, he was not without influence, and the day after this incident, Sugane, too, was exiled to Kyushu. Sugane's friends, however, were in control of the court and they immediately had him pardoned.[33]

On the twenty-seventh of the month, four of Michizane's sons were removed from their positions at court and banished to various distant provinces, far from both their home in the capital and their father in Kyushu. Nine other men were also exiled. None held even moderately important offices, but presumably all were closely associated with Michizane. Also on the same day, officials were appointed to guard Michizane on his journey to Kyushu. Their instructions were that he was not to be provided with either food or horses at the post stations along the way.[34]

On the thirtieth, Uda is said to have once again gone to the palace to protest, but as before he was refused entry. This time he spent the night outside the gate, and finally, on the morning of the first day of the second month, he gave up and returned once more to his residence. Later that day, Michizane was escorted from the capital. His family was scattered: his adult sons were sent into exile, his wife and older daughters remained in the capital, and his youngest children accompanied him to Dazaifu. The following day, Prince Tokiyo, who was married to one of his daughters, was forced to become a monk. In accordance with the edict exiling Michizane, on the fourth and fifth days, offerings were made at various shrines where his banishment was announced.[35]

Kiyoyuki continued to take an active interest in events. A rumor had begun to circulate that all of Michizane's former students were to be exiled. On the ninth day of the second month, Kiyoyuki sent Tokihira a letter objecting to such a strategy. Michizane's students had only studied, not plotted with him, and if all were sent away, some good men would inevitably be lost.[36] If Michizane's students were anywhere near as numerous as they were said to be, the court would have had trouble functioning without them. Kiyoyuki's views probably reflected less a concern for the possible loss of some able men than a realization that to exile all of Michizane's former students would have been totally impractical. On the twenty-second day of the month, Kiyoyuki proposed that the era name be changed, once

*12. The retired emperor rushing to the palace
in an attempt to save Michizane
Source: Sugawara jikki.*

太上法皇
宮中江
御幸之図

again referring to his theories on divination. This time he hinted that Michizane's "plot" was further proof of their accuracy. On the fifteenth day of the seventh month, Kiyoyuki's proposal was accepted and the era name was changed from Shōtai to Engi (literally, "Increased Joy").[37]

By the time the era name was changed, Michizane had long since arrived in his place of exile. He wrote:

Reading the Edict Announcing
the Beginning of New Era
The yellow paper of the edict announcing a new era
Brings "Increased Joy" unto all the people.
One reason was unfavorable signs;
Another reason, an auspicious star.[a]
All but capital crimes are pardoned
To purify the realm.
Reduced corvée duty brings strength to working men;
Bestowed gifts comfort the elderly.
In this vast ocean of imperial generosity
Dwells a solitary giant whale.[b]
Why does this fish appear here?
Because people say, "It is your new name."
But my mouth cannot swallow boats,
Nor does my voice stir up waves.
Alas, how pitiful the man who is exiled!
The times are against me; my spirit destroyed.[38]

Notes:
a. Both auspicious and inauspicious events were common reasons for selecting a new era name. The signs were those of the zodiac to which Kiyoyuki had referred. An auspicious star was also reported at this time.
b. Whales, said to swallow small fish and even boats, were a standard Chinese metaphor for evil ministers. Michizane noted that the term appeared in the edict, which is now lost.

Michizane's punishment was the most severe one that his contemporaries saw fit to inflict on a man of his station. In 923, only twenty-two years after he was exiled, however, he was posthumously pardoned and returned to his former offices. Ever since then the all-but-unanimous opinion has been that he was unjustly slandered and innocent of any wrongdoing.[39]

Specifically, Michizane had been charged with two offenses. One was the rather vague assertion that he "did not know contentment and hoped to dominate the court." Aside from its lack of precision, this charge clearly was untrue. Michizane had repeatedly tried to step down from his high offices when he realized they were arousing the envy of other powerful men, and he refused the title of chancellor that was offered him. The more specific charge was that he was plotting to depose the emperor. The edict suggests that he had tricked Uda into cooperating with him in a plan to replace Daigo with Tokiyo, his own son-in-law. This certainly would have "shattered the feelings of benevolence between father and son [Uda and Daigo], and destroyed the love between older and younger brothers [Daigo and Tokiyo]." Such a scheme indeed would have placed Michizane in a dominant position, but considering Michizane's often expressed desire to avoid further political involvement, this accusation, too, seems improbable.

Further evidence of his innocence is the fact that, after Michizane was pardoned, Daigo burned the records relating to his banishment. Presumably Daigo did so to hide his own culpability for having participated in the impeachment of an innocent man. Had Michizane been guilty, he would not have needed to destroy evidence.[40] In fact, the whole process of Michizane's deification can be seen as the result of a collective guilty conscience for having sent a virtuous man into exile. The usual reason, however, for believing in Michizane's innocence is that he himself repeatedly asserted it in poems written while in exile. These poems convey a feeling of sincerity and truthfulness, even if their honesty cannot be proven.

An occasional iconoclast has argued that Michizane was not so guileless as he would have had readers of his poems believe. This view is supported principally by the report of Fujiwara no Kiyotsura (867–930), an imperial messenger who saw him in Dazaifu and who would later figure conspicuously in the story of Michizane's deification. In the seventh month of 901, Kiyotsura returned to the capital and stated that Michizane seemed distressed but resigned to his fate. Then Kiyotsura further claimed that Michizane had told him:

> I did not plot anything, but I could not avoid being drawn in by Minamoto no Yoshi. Also, the retired emperor often told me of events in the former Jōwa era [834–848].[41]

During that era, Fujiwara no Yoshifusa had accused some of his rivals of plotting against the throne, drove them into exile, and had his cousin named crown prince. Therefore, a few scholars interpret the statement as meaning that Michizane reluctantly had been drawn into a similar plot, which was this time discovered by Tokihira.[42]

If indeed it is authentic, however, Michizane's statement is open to other interpretations. It could also mean that he had had private discussions that were mistakenly seen as conspiratorial. He did not specify into what Yoshi had drawn him. Although Yoshi was among the men exiled with Michizane, the innocence of his activities is suggested by the fact that all other surviving information about him points to his having been more a literary than a political figure. The reference to the Jōwa era is also ambiguous. Through most of that era, Saga had controlled the court as a retired emperor and sponsored many literary activities. Yoshifusa's famous coup came only after Saga's death. Uda was inspired by the earlier part of the era, which offered a model for his own programs, and so he probably discussed it with Michizane. A further consideration is that Michizane is not likely to have publicly admitted his guilt to an imperial messenger while privately proclaiming his innocence in his poetry.[43] The first part of Michizane's statement that he did not plot anything is more significant than the remaining ambiguous portion. The popular belief in Michizane's innocence is justified, even if in places the evidence can be twisted to suggest otherwise.

If Michizane was not guilty of plotting against the throne, then who slandered him? Traditionally, the blame has been placed on the Fujiwara family and on Tokihira in particular. This view was already expressed in *Ōkagami* (The great mirror), written around the year 1100, and became a standard element in later accounts of Michizane's downfall. Details of Tokihira's involvement in the plot against Michizane, however, are surprisingly few. The best evidence of his participation is found in his subsequent status and activities. Following Michizane's banishment, Tokihira no longer shared his power with a scholarly outsider and was able to dominate the court in much the same manner as his father Mototsune had. The month after Michizane was sent from the capital, despite Uda's continued disapproval, Tokihira managed to have Daigo take his sister Yasuko as a consort. In 903, she gave birth to a son who was named crown prince the following year.[44] Then at last, Toki-hira's position seemed secure. Because Tokihira profited most conspicuously from Michizane's exile, he has been accused of being the principal plotter and for many years was portrayed as a villain, even by members of his own family. Tokihira no doubt was part of the scheme to remove Michizane from power, but he was not an evil tyrant as worshipful partisans of Michizane have portrayed him. During most of the years they shared power, Michizane and Tokihira maintained reasonably cordial relations with each other. Subsequently, when he alone held sway at court, Tokihira proved an able administrator whose policies were aimed more at strengthening the court government than enriching the private fortunes of the Fujiwara family.[45]

A second man who aided in the plot against Michizane was his old scholarly rival Kiyoyuki. Michizane had long been on bad terms with Kiyoyuki, who had good reason to feel bitter. While Michizane and his academic followers were flourishing, Kiyoyuki had only managed to attain the post of professor of literature at the age of fifty-four after many years in insignificant, often provincial, offices. Kiyoyuki recognized both that Tokihira was dissatisfied with having to share his political power, and that Michizane's position was fundamentally insecure. Whether Kiyoyuki or Tokihira originated the idea of driving Michizane from court cannot be known, but both men stood to benefit from the scheme. To put it into effect, Tokihira provided the political influence; Kiyoyuki, the intellectual justification. Other men joined in, most notably Fujiwara no Sugane, the scholar whom Michizane had once supported but who blocked Uda from entering the place, and Minamoto no Hikaru, a son of Emperor Nimmyō who was on good terms with the Fujiwara and who would replace Michizane as minister of the right. A final participant in the plot was said to be Fujiwara no Sadakuni (866–906), who came from the Northern House of the Fujiwara family, but was somewhat removed from the regents' lineage. Since the beginning of Daigo's reign, he had been promoted rapidly, and the day after Michizane was banished, he was awarded Michizane's old office of general.[46]

In secret, they developed their plans. By some means they managed to gain Daigo's support. Daigo, like his father Uda, admired Michizane's erudition; however, he may have also resented Michizane as representative of his father who restricted his ability to act independently. Perhaps the plotters were able to convince him that Kiyoyuki's fearful prognostications were true. Or, alternatively, Daigo may have been attracted to Toki-hira's younger sister and saw this scheme as a means of taking her as a consort. As long as Uda was carefully supervising affairs at court from retirement, however, Michizane—whether he him-self liked it or not—could hardly be removed from high office. Then, in the tenth month of 900, Uda took another of his lei-surely excursions, this time to Mount Kōya, a Buddhist center south of the capital, and to Chikubu Island in Lake Biwa to the north.[47] Kiyoyuki seized the opportunity provided by Uda's absence to announce his prophecy that would soon become the justification for sending Michizane into exile.

Today there is no way of knowing whether Kiyoyuki believed the esoteric theories on which he based his prediction or whether they were merely a convenient rationale for making Michizane appear a source of imminent danger. Whatever his motive, the prophecy must have seemed quite reasonable to those who did not like Michizane anyhow. The importance of Kiyoyuki's con-tribution to the plot can be seen both in the language of the edict charging Michizane and the timing of his departure from the capital. The edict borrowed not only the idea that a retainer would overthrow his lord but even the phrase that Michizane did not "know contentment." To depose an emperor would have been a "revolution" in the sense that Kiyoyuki was using the term. Moreover, Kiyoyuki had predicted that his "revolu-tion" would occur in the second month of 901. That year, on the twenty-fifth day of the first month, Michizane was accused of his "crimes." Before Uda could come to his rescue, Michi-zane was duly sent from the capital on the first of the second month. Obviously, the timing had to be carefully planned so that Uda would not have an opportunity to interfere and the plotters could claim credit for having averted the terrible events that Kiyoyuki had predicted but that naturally did not occur. Tokihira must have handled the political arrangements, but Kiyoyuki had provided the excuse for sending Michizane into exile. The two were co-conspirators. Eventually, principal blame would come to be placed on Tokihira, the more con-spicuous figure, but he had received necessary intellectual support from Kiyoyuki.

Michizane's downfall was the result of many related causes. Clearly he had enemies at court. In part this was because he had risen above what his contemporaries would have considered his appropriate station in life. Men from traditionally more noble families scorned him as a parvenu. Earlier, when Mototsune had retired to his mansion because he was dissatisfied with the title "Akō," his fellow senior nobles followed suit and refused to perform their regular duties. When Michizane became a de facto regent, the senior nobles again abandoned their official responsibilities. In the first instance, Mototsune, scion of the court's most noble family, was being supported by his fellow aristocrats. In the second, the court's aristocratic leaders were refusing to cooperate with a scholar of more modest origins. To be sure, the Sugawara were not commoners. For centuries, they and their ancestors the Haji had held the ranks and titles of nobility, but they represented the lower strata of court families whose men typically did not attain the fifth rank. Because of their exceptional talents, Michizane's father and grandfather had risen to high rank and positions of influence in scholarly circles. Michizane then followed in their footsteps; however, that did not make him an aristocrat in the sense that the Fujiwara were. They could boast of close ties to the imperial family that dated back to the age of the gods.[48]

Economic considerations too were probably involved. The regents' lineage of the Fujiwara was the principal "powerful family" whose activities in the provinces Uda had sought to restrict. Men such as Mototsune and Tokihira had independent sources of income with which they could reward their loyal followers. The Sugawara probably did not. For a man like Kiyoyuki, whose obscure family could not have been wealthy, a close alliance with the Fujiwara offered more security than the modest court offices he normally might have held. Other ambitious men must have recognized the precariousness of Michizane's position. He had fewer private means at his disposal. Instead, he had to rely on the support of a retired emperor and on Japan's flagging commitment to the Confucian ideal of promotion based on intellectual merit.

Michizane's personality tended only to exacerbate his problems. He always had been proud of his own learning and did not hesitate to criticize those whom he felt did not meet his standards. At the same time, he could be swayed by factional

288 · From Minister to Exile

considerations and was not as objective as he claimed to be. Moreover, he had no tolerance for those who criticized him. It is no wonder, then, that during his years in high office he lamented having few friends.[49] He was not the sort of man who would have easily deferred to or compromised with the better-born but less-educated men who became his colleagues in the Council of State. Tokihira, the political rival, and Kiyo-yuki, the old enemy whom Michizane had failed in the civil service examinations, had little trouble finding others who shared their feelings towards the somewhat too learned minister of the right. If Michizane's social superiors disdained him, men of more comparable backgrounds saw little advantage in supporting him or were jealous of his success.

Another serious problem was that Uda misjudged his own influence at court. At a time when Michizane had come to sense the weakness of his own position and wished to step down, Uda countered by offering him the highest office at court—short of emperor. As events proved, Uda's position was not nearly so powerful as he had imagined. Uda could not simultaneously enjoy his leisure and also control the government. He discovered this too late, however, to save Michizane. In frustration, Uda abandoned his interest in court politics, and during the years immediately following Michizane's exile, he devoted himself to religion.[50]

A final cause for Michizane's failure in high office was one that he and his contemporaries surely could not have perceived. Michizane represented the ideals of an earlier age when Japan was enthusiastically borrowing Chinese culture. His training had been in Chinese literature. He was known principally for his poetry in Chinese. Most of his adult years were spent serving as a middle-ranking official in a bureaucracy adopted from Chinese prototypes. Even his rise to high office can be explained partially in Confucian terms: Uda promoted him in recognition of his great talent. Despite Chinese appearances, however, the court was gradually turning to more typically Japanese patterns, and even Michizane contributed to this change. It was he who proposed that missions to China be abandoned. Michizane may have intended the move to be temporary, but it proved long lasting indeed. Also, he joined in the new vogue for poetry in Japanese. Literary fashions may not have influenced court politics, but they did reflect new attitudes. High-ranking aristocrats had come to feel less obliged to admire a mere scholar who had unexpectedly risen to high office simply because Confucian theory indicated they should. Japan was reverting to an earlier political style in which the principle of hereditary status was more highly regarded. Michizane's downfall was one of the events that marked the end of an age.

THE YEARS IN EXILE

According to law, punishment for crimes varied according to the offender's status. A man of Michizane's exalted position, when judged guilty of wrongdoing, often was allowed to maintain a vestige of his honor in the form of a nominal official title signifying that he was a noble, not a common, criminal. So it was that, even during Michizane's final years of disgrace and banishment, he was in name the supernumerary governor general of Dazaifu. A few critics have suggested that his lamentations over his unhappy fate were unwarranted, for as supernumerary governor general, his salary should have been generous, and in addition, Dazaifu should have been an agreeable place to live, a sophisticated center for foreign diplomacy and local administration.[51] Michizane's office, however, was one commonly given deposed aristocrats, and no salary seems to have been attached. He was not even able to obtain adequate food supplies. Since he was kept under house arrest, he could not enjoy Kyushu as he had come to appreciate Sanuki. The impressive title did not hide the fact that he was regarded as a dangerous felon, a traitor to the emperor.

Michizane's journey to Dazaifu was a hard one, lasting over a month. On the route he was treated like a criminal—closely guarded and not given fresh horses—and the final years of his life spent in exile proved equally trying. He was closely guarded and suffered from malnutrition.[52] In these, the unhappiest years of his life, Michizane once again sought comfort in poetry. As he often had done earlier in Sanuki, he constantly lamented his unhappy fate and miserable life, but now his complaints clearly were justified. Both in style and theme, the *kanshi* he composed in Dazaifu resemble many of those he had written in Sanuki. Expressing himself in informal language, Michizane constantly longed for home and vividly portrayed his daily life. In addition, he now protested his innocence. Today, Michizane's popular reputation as a poet is based mainly on works, *waka* as well as *kanshi*, he wrote after his downfall. Regardless of whether he was writing in Chinese or Japanese, he expressed similar sentiments; however, the *waka* present many problems because they have become encased in legend and their very authenticity is not easily established. Three of his *waka* illustrate these difficulties.

As Michizane was about to leave his home, he is said to have addressed the plum tree in his garden with what would become his most familiar *waka:*

Kochi fukaba	When the east wind blows,
Nioi okoseyo	Let it send your fragrance,
Ume no hana	Oh plum blossoms.
Aruji nashi tote	Although your master is gone,
Haru o wasuruna	Do not forget the spring.[53]

To the cherry tree he recited:

Sakurabana	Oh cherry blossoms,
Nushi o wasurenu	If you are ones
Mono naraba	Who do not forget your master,
Fukikomu kaze ni	Send me a message
Kotozute wa seyo	In the wind that blows my way.[54]

These poems are based on the same conceit: a tree should recall its owner by blossoming even when he is gone, and the wind will carry the fragrance to him.

They first appeared in separate anthologies, but the two *waka* had come to be linked together by 1194, the date of the oldest version of *Kitano Tenjin engi* (The origin of Kitano Tenjin Shrine), the standard traditional account of Michizane's life and deification. It explained that, as he was about to depart for Kyushu, Michizane was overwhelmed by fond thoughts of his home and recited the two poems as vows of fidelity that he exchanged even with the insentient grasses and trees. The text concluded by commenting that his writing of the poems was very touching. Just twenty-five years later, an important new element was added when the story was retold in the oldest extant illustrated text of *Kitano Tenjin engi*. The narrative is

largely identical, but after the poems appear, we are told that
the faithful plum tree was so affected by the poem that it flew
to Kyushu, where it joined its master.[55] Today, an old plum
tree growing in front of the Tenjin shrine in Dazaifu is identified as a descendant of the one that flew from Michizane's
garden in the capital. This story is another reason why the
plum became an icon associated with Michizane.

Originally, the reaction of the cherry tree was not recorded,
but later recensions filled in this gap. One simply revised the
second poem and made it too address the plum tree. Another
text dating from the early Edo period (c. 1600–1700) expanded
the story by stating that for three springs the cherry did not
blossom and finally it withered. Since Michizane addressed similar poems to both trees, one may wonder why the cherry withered instead of flying to Kyushu with the plum. The answer is
that a completely different version of the legend had been
forced, somewhat inconsistently, into the original narrative. In
the alternate telling of the story, after Michizane arrived in
Kyushu, he longed for his favorite plum tree at his home in
the capital and recited his familiar poem. The tree then flew to
Kyushu to join him. The cherry tree that grew beside it, however, felt so neglected that it immediately withered. This, we
are told, inspired the poet Minamoto no Shitagō (911–983) to
write:

Ume wa tobi	The plum flew;
Sakura wa karenu	The cherry withered.
Sugawara ya	Ah, Sugawara
Fukaku zo tanomu	How deeply I rely
Kami no chikai o	On your divine oath.[56]

In medieval times, the pine was added to the plum and cherry
to form a triumvirate of trees associated with Michizane. The
story of Michizane and the pine presents further complications,
and again may have been inspired by a *waka* Michizane is said to
have composed after being banished from the court:

Oinu tote	Although it is old,
Matsu no midori zo	The pine tree grows
Masarikeru	Ever greener,
Waga kurokami no	While my black hair
Yuki no samusa ni	Becomes frosted with snow.[57]

13. Saying farewell to his plum tree
Source: Temmangū goden.

The stories about Michizane and the pine are related to puns on the first word in the poem. There, *"oinu"* means "grown old" or "aged," but in addition it can mean "grown" in the sense of "a tree has grown," or also "followed."

Michizane was first connected with the pine in an oracle dated 947. It revealed that a servant named Oimatsu ("Old Pine") had accompanied him to Kyushu and that Michizane wished to be worshiped at Kitano, where pines would grow. Soon afterward, thousands of pine trees are said to have miraculously "grown" *(oinu)* there overnight, and hence it became the site of the still popular Kitano Shrine. By the early Edo, the pine had been incorporated into a new *waka* based on the one that earlier had been attributed to Shitagō. The new version was said to be by Michizane himself:

Ume wa tobi	In this world,
Sakura wa karuru	The plum has flown;
Yo no naka ni	The cherry has withered.
Nani tote matsu no	Why is the pine alone
Tsurenakaruran	So heartless?[58]

This poem is based on yet another legend: the pine at Michizane's home in the capital was so embarrassed by Michizane's poetic remonstrance that it "followed" *(oinu)* the plum and flew to Dazaifu. *The Old Pine Tree (Oimatsu)*, a noh play by Zeami (1363–1443) hints at this story, and it became the key to the elaborate plot of the puppet play, *The Sugawara Secrets of Calligraphy*, first performed in 1746.[59]

The original three *waka* about the plum, the cherry, and the pine thus became intimately tied to a series of popular legends, but in addition the original poems themselves present problems. The first two are generally accepted as authentic, for they appear in relatively early anthologies, and the poem about the plum is clearly identified as having been written as Michizane was about to depart to his place of exile. Only the story about the tree's flight to Kyushu is a later accretion. However, the original collection that included the poem about the cherry simply stated that it had been recited when Michizane "was about to leave his home for a distant place." Thus, it might well have been composed before he went to Sanuki, not Dazaifu. The poem about the pine is even more problematic. It is thought to have been composed during his exile, but the time of its composition is nowhere specified. Because Michizane noted his graying hair as early as his years in Sanuki, the poem could have been written anytime after that. Moreover, it first appears in the *Shinkokinshū*, which was not compiled until 1205, long after Michizane's deification. The authenticity of the poems attributed to Michizane in that anthology has been questioned, and this poem might even be a forgery inspired by the story of the pines at Kitano rather than the source of the story.[60] Other *waka* said to have been written by Michizane while he was in exile present similar problems. Their place in the legends of Tenjin is well established, but their authenticity is difficult to prove.

Michizane's *kanshi* present a more reliable picture of his thoughts and experiences during his last years. The example that follows is one of Michizane's most remarkable works. As in most of the thirty-nine *kanshi* Michizane wrote in exile, he vividly describes his suffering, protests his innocence, and looks to Buddhism and Taoism for solace. The poem is autobiographical. It details Michizane's experiences beginning with his removal from office in the spring and ending with his first autumn in Dazaifu. Interspersed are sections reminiscing about his earlier career and alluding to Chinese officials who had suffered similar fates. These are elements that recur frequently in Michizane's last poems. This particular poem's uniqueness lies in its length: two hundred lines. At the time it was probably the longest poem ever to have been written by a Japanese, either in Chinese or in the native language.

Michizane borrowed the form of this poem, and even some of its language, from similar works by Po Chü-i and Yuan Chen. The two Chinese poet friends had experimented with long forms, and in 817 after both had been simultaneously banished from the capital, Po composed a lament in one hundred couplets, which he sent to Yuan, who responded with a similar poem. Michizane was influenced by both of these works. For example, Po had complained that the local population was uncouth, people gawked at him, letters from home had ceased to arrive, and he was removed from his friends. Michizane too bemoaned all these tribulations. Po had emphasized his current hardships by contrasting them with flashbacks describing his happier days in the capital, a technique that Michizane also employed. Some of Michizane's phrasing is similar to that in Yuan's poem.[61] When writing in Chinese, Michizane naturally looked to China and adopted the forms, techniques and language of Chinese poetry. Nonetheless, the experiences he described and the emotions he expressed remain distinctly his own:

Recording My Feelings: A Hundred Couplets

In this life, one's position is never secure.
Fate is determined by heaven.
How could I have foreseen this office in Dazaifu?
Why should my title have been changed to "exile"?
Demoted, I carried less weight than a mustard seed.
Driven out, I was sent here with the speed of an arrow.
Blushing with shame, my face became inured to disgrace.
Enraged, I had not even time to turn my head.
Every mud-filled ox's footprint became a trap;
In the sky flew only the predatory hawks and falcons.

My old retainer continually leaned on his staff.
Time after time, I whipped my tired horse.
Parting easily breaks the heart;
With a fixed stare, I gazed back towards the palace.
Falling tears suffused in the morning dew.
Sobbing voice mingled with the wood thrush.
Village streets were veiled in dust,
And the fields were rank with weeds.
The post stations ignored my horse's wounded hooves.
At the harbor, I was met by a boat with damaged stern.
On the route were over fifty way stations.
The distance was half three thousand leagues.
The horses were finally unhitched at the southern pavilion.
The carriage stopped at the boundary of the Right District.[a]
Peering through the small gate,
Curious spectators filled the main avenue.
I was nauseated and my chest ached.
I was exhausted and my feet were weak.
My skin had come to be carved with wrinkles,
And my spirit was worn down.
Two nights there were a traveler's lodging.
Gloomy despair tortured me,
An aged villager came and spoke of past events,
And helped me forget my wanderings.
How could I escape from this disaster?
I hoped eventually to clear my name of slander.
Never yet had evil triumphed over good,
Although truth was sometimes confused with falsehood.

I moved into a deserted official residence,
And repaired its decaying pine rafters.
The paths around it were largely obliterated.
The small building filled its plot of land.[b]
Its well was clogged; I dug out the sand and repaired the walls.
Its fence was neglected; I split bamboo to weave a new one.
In the garden was one row of old horseradish plants,
And a solitary fist-like rock covered with moss.
The appearance of the place was as it had been in the past;
Although I came to dwell here, it did not change.
I feared that as time passed, it might seem cramped,
But eventually I thought I would get used to it.

I sought companions among those who had suffered similarly.
As solace for my troubles, I investigated the ancients.
Talent and ability lead to disaster;
Wealth and nobility are the roots of all difficulties.
Fu Yueh took his hammer and joined the laborers by the boulder.
Fan Li drifted about the lake in a small boat.[c]
The desert sands of Ch'ang-sha are low and damp.
The waters of the River Hsiang are wide and deep.[d]
High rank was of no value to me.
Who, I wondered, has filled my old office?
Old friends fed me a portion of their food.
Relatives washed my clothing for me.
Thus I resigned myself to the suffering of this life.
Why should I have resented that death was not swift?
For my daily sustenance I relied on heaven.
The judgment of motives, I entrusted to the divine.
Time passed and spring ended.
The early summer's red sun blazed.
I thought to accustom myself to local ways,
And learn to accept the practices of this place.

They burn wood to make bitter salt.
Seeking dishonest gain, they invest their money in cloth.
Killing and wounding are taken lightly,
And gangs of thieves calmly walk about.
"O-fish-als" think it their duty to go fishing.[e]
The dust shield from a carriage is used to pound a boat's gunwales.[f]
The greedy profit from dealings in rice,
But offer only shoddy cloth when paying their taxes.
The abalone shop leaves a vile stench.
The koto strings are not properly tuned.[g]

With whom could I speak?
I slept alone with a bent arm as my pillow.
Endless rains fell on hot humid days,
And blocked the smoke from cooking at dawn.

The hearth and pot became a temple for the fishes.
The frogs noisily chanted on the tile steps.
Farm children brought me vegetables,
And my kitchen helper made me a thin gruel.
I wasted away like a lonely crane breft of its mate,
And starved like a hungry owl that threatens helpless chicks.
The crumbled walls diverted a rushing torrent of water.
The garden mud became the bed of a murky stream.

After the rain, the crimson sun finally appeared.
That evening, the curtain of green clouds lifted.
On this occasion, emptiness gave birth to light.
Amidst idle talk, I entered the dark mysteries.
Lao Tzu is said to have been the Buddha reincarnated.
Chuang Tzu went through life with a single purpose.
One's character must not be contrary to the constant Way.
Fundamental matters should be entrusted to nature.
I deeply appreciated "Discussion on Making All Things Equal,"
And was calmed by his "Imputed Words."[h]
My feelings were fainter than a dream.
My addiction to beauty could not be cured.
The flowers of my literature, where would they fall?
Even here, my emotions were stirred.
I sought comfort in sympathizing with Feng Yen,
And dissolve my cares in the works of the enviable Wang Ts'an.[i]
I did not speak for fear of violating the restrictions.
My brush was worn out from my continual scribbling.
Who would admire my poems?
There was no one to cap my verses.
I wrote my thoughts on paper,
But after reading them, I burnt them in my lamp.
Why should I have lamented that fate is uncertain?
Suffering is predestined from former lives.
Little by little, I rejected love and pleasure.
Slowly I abandoned strong-smelling vegetables and meat.
I clasped my hands in prayer and took refuge in the Buddha,
And turned my heart to the practice of meditation.
I came to hate today's sinful world,
But revered the truly enlightened ancients.
The pure moon showed that all is void.
The lotus of the marvelous law blossomed out of the mud.
The Bodhisattva's great vow could not be falsehood.
His blessings are many; he would not abandon us.
The discomfort of the summer heat diminished slightly,
And I knew that coolness would soon return.
I judged the weather from the ashes blown in the wind,
And the months from the position of the North Star.

The gap separating me from society widened;
Letters from home ceased to arrive.
My sash grew loose; I cried over the faded purple of my official robes.
Looking into the mirror, I lamented my grey hair.
A traveler's thoughts: geese in a line amidst the clouds.
Cold humming: the unaffected cicada clinging to the bark.
Now the orchid is overcome by the chill.
Nine times, I have seen the cassia blossoms on the full moon.
When cleaning my chamber, I sooth myself by hanging a chime.
My door is closed because I am too lazy to open the latch.
A lame sheep whose legs moreover are bound,
A wounded sparrow who nonetheless is tied up:
They struggle to see outside their confines,
And furtively pace before a door or window.
I gaze at the distant blue-green mountains,
And think of the rushing water in the far-off river.
For a moment my weakened body is revived.
Perhaps my dreary life will be prolonged?
My soul rushes homeward in a daze.
My eyes remember and tears overflow.
On what day shall I return to the capital?
How many years before I see my old garden?

I remember when I first took office,
And I recall the old days when I studied the classics.
On tests, I always "hit the mark."
How could the small fish I was boiling fall apart?[j]
In the examination hall, I broke off a branch of the cassia tree,
And on the south shore of the Inland Sea, I governed a hundred
    towns.
I maintained my ancestors' scholarly traditions,
And the Ministry of Ceremonial observed my success in the provinces.
My glory shone ever more brightly.
My jeweled symbols of office competed in their glitter.
The responsibilities were as heavy as a thousand-pound stone,
The danger as deep as a ten-thousand-foot abyss.
Seeing me serve as general and great minister,
People said I lacked merit and wisdom.
I tried to govern well, but fear I brought only disorder.
I grasped my dull blade, but it proved inadequate.
Humbly I appeared before the imperial screen.
Deferentially I touched the emperor's sword.
Removing my shoes, I transcended the dusty world,
And brushed sleeves with courtly sages.
We spent nights at banquets delighting in the cherry blossoms,
Or gathered in the mornings after having enjoyed the chrysanthemum
    wine.[k]

Although my talents were few, I was entrusted with a great
  responsibility.
A clumsy boat had to cross the great river.

I have not yet repaid the beneficence of the state,
And fear I will die by the roadside before I may do so.
P'an Yueh did not forget his home.
How could Chang Heng make the nobles abandon their hunting?[1]
In a forest, the wind fells the highest tree,
And extinguishes even the oil-filled lamp.
Swarms of slandering flies linger at the court.
How can honesty prevail?
Hating the eggs, they turned over the nest.
They sought the holes of ants and locusts to crush the young.
The law applied was unduly severe.
My contributions will not be carved onto the stone monuments.
I regret that I served with only loyalty as my armor and helmet.
My punishment was more painful than being cut down with a spear.

This small thatched hut,
Lies near the dark blue sea.
It will suffice as a temporary dwelling.
Surely here I will meet my end.
Although my spirit may long for home,
My bones will be buried in exile.
I know that man's lot combines fortune and misfortune,
But who could have divined my fate?
I have told my feelings in a thousand words,
But is there even one person who will take pity on me?[62]

Notes:
a. Like the capital, Dazaifu was laid out on a rectangular grid and divided into left and right sectors. Apparently, before entering the city, Michizane spent a few days at an official inn just south of Dazaifu.
b. An area of approximately 360 square yards.
c. During the Shang dynasty, Fu Yueh had tried to disguise himself among a gang of convict laborers, but was found amidst their tools by Emperor Wu Ting and was made a minister. During the Warring States period, Fan Li helped the king of Yueh win an important battle, but rather than retain his high position, he fled on a small boat.
d. Chia I, who had been a lecturer to Emperor Wen of the Former Han, was slandered and banished to Ch'ang-sha. During the Warring States period, China's most famous poet-exile, Ch'ü Yuan, drowned himself in the upper reaches of the River Hsiang.
e. Michizane puns on the word "gyotai," which refers to a fish-shaped emblem of office, but is written with characters meaning "fish-sack." A more literal translation of the line would be: "Officials take their creels/emblems of office and go fishing."
f. That is, an elegent object is being used in a vulgar fashion.

g. Here, Michizane noted, "The above ten lines lament that the local customs would defy any attempt at improvement."
h. These are the titles of chapters 2 and 27 of *Chuang-tzu*, as translated by Burton Watson (*The Complete Works of Chuang Tzu* [New York, Columbia University Press, 1968]).
i. Feng Yen was a Later Han official who was accused of crime and punished. He returned to his native village and withdrew from society. Wang Ts'an was a Wei dynasty writer who rose to high office. Although he was not exiled, he once fled the capital during a rebellion.
j. For "hit the mark," see chapter 2 ("The Student Years"), p. 106. The reference to boiling fish alludes to *Lao-tzu:* "Governing a great nation is like boiling a small fish," in other words, a delicate operation.
k. Here, Michizane noted: "I regularly served at private palace banquets."
l. The same P'an Yueh whose hair turned grey early (see p. 192) was sent to the west in the course of his official duties and wrote a poetic essay on the subject. During the Later Han, Chang Heng wrote a poetic essay condemning the extravagant hunting expeditions of the rich, but apparently to little effect.

Despite his hardships, Michizane never completely lost hope of being exonerated and summoned back to court. In the beginning of 903, spring according to the Chinese lunar calendar but distinctly winter by the solar calendar, Michizane optimistically wrote:

Spring Snow in My Place of Exile
So many plum blossoms filling the city and its outskirts.
The clear wind blows the flowers of the new year.
Sticking to the legs of geese, perhaps there is a message
written on silk?[a]
The heads of crows are spotted: shall I soon return home?[b][63]

Notes:
a. Su Wu, after being captured by barbarians, tied messages written on silk to the legs of geese. The emperor shot one of the geese, read the message, and rescued him.
b. During the Warring States period, Prince Tan of Yen was captured by the king of Ch'in. Tan wished to return home, but the king said he would only release him if the crows' heads turned white and the horses grew horns. Tan looked up to heaven and sighed, whereupon the crows turned white and the horses grew horns. Tan was released and returned home.

As in his first *kanshi* composed almost fifty years earlier, Michizane wrote of the plum blossoms. His health had not been good and despite the hopeful tone of the poem, he must have realized he could not have much longer to live. After writing this poem, Michizane gathered the *kanshi* he had composed in

14. *The exile Michizane in his residence*
   Source: Temmangū goden.

exile and sent them to his friend Haseo in the capital.[64] This compilation has come to be known as *Kanke kōshū* (The later Sugawara collection).

The wish to return home that Michizane expressed in his last extant poem went unfulfilled. In 903, on the twenty-fifth day of the second month, shortly after having written it, he passed away at the age of fifty-nine. The cause of his death is thought to have been beriberi and its complications brought on by malnutrition, or perhaps even stomach cancer.[65] Michizane's last years had been spent in suffering, both physical and spiritual. Nonetheless, as an exile in Dazaifu, he wrote some of his most moving poetry. It convincingly pleaded his innocence and loyalty to the emperor, and his posthumous pardon may have been at least in part the result of these poems he had sent to Haseo. Michizane finally succeeded in persuading the court of his innocence, but only after he himself had died.

Michizane's death, not surprisingly, became the subject of legend. In fact, *Kitano Tenjin engi* contains two seemingly contradictory versions. The first must have appeared after Michizane had been deified. It states that he composed a prayer declaring his innocence, climbed Mount Tempai ("Revere Heaven") just south of Dazaifu, and beseeched the gods to acknowledge his rectitude. After seven days, his prayer floated up into heaven and he himself was transformed into Tenjin. In the play, *The Sugawara Secrets of Calligraphy,* Michizane also flies off, in this case to the capital seeking revenge. In the earlier account, however, his apotheosis is followed by his death. As his remains were being taken to the burial ground, we are told that the ox pulling the cart stopped just outside the northeast corner of Dazaifu. Since it could not be made to budge farther, Michizane was interred there, at what became the site of the Dazaifu Temman Shrine. The story about the ox is probably a later fabrication, but Michizane may well have been buried at what is now the shrine, for archaeological excavations suggest that as early as the Nara period, a Buddhist temple had been located there.[66] In his death as in his life, fact and legend are closely intertwined.

15. Michizane is buried where the ox refuses to move
Source: Dazaifu Temmangū.

8 · Michizane as Tenjin

At the time of his death, Michizane officially was regarded as a criminal, yet only a few decades later he was being worshiped as a god. The cult of Tenjin is a fascinating and important subject in itself, both because it is a vital part of Japan's religious and intellectual history, and also because it helps to clarify how popular images of Michizane arose. The study of Tenjin worship, however, presents complications of its own. For example, its terminology is sometimes ambiguous. Michizane and Tenjin were regarded as two aspects of the same individual, and so when later documents referred to "Tenjin," they sometimes meant the man and other times the god. Similarly, Tenjin worship was a product of Shinto-Buddhist syncretism, and thus most of its institutions were simultaneously Shinto shrines and Buddhist monasteries until the two religions were forcibly separated following the Meiji Restoration. Moreover, neither an accepted core of doctrine nor an extensive organizational structure ever developed. Instead, the cult consisted simply of reverence for a deified ancient hero who was worshiped throughout Japan at independent shrines, great and small. In these respects, Tenjin worship resembles other aspects of Japan's native religious heritage. Lacking both unified theology and institutional hierarchy, it is best described in terms of its historical evolution.

THE PROCESS OF DEIFICATION

Traditionally, the story of Michizane's transformation into the god Tenjin begins with a series of misfortunes that befell the men who had falsely accused him. In 909, his political rival Tokihira died in his prime at the age of thirty-nine. Thirteen years later, the crown prince, then only twenty-one, also passed away. He was Tokihira's nephew, the child of Emperor Daigo and Tokihira's sister, whose marriage had followed Michizane's exile. The crown prince's demise was blamed on the wrath of Michizane's vengeful ghost, and so one month later Michizane was belatedly pardoned. Still, this did not placate the wronged minister and troubles at court continued, particularly among Tokihira's descendants. One of his grandsons was named the new crown prince, but he died in 925, a mere child of five. In 930 Japan suffered a drought, and just when arrangements were being made to conduct prayers for rain, a black cloud suddenly appeared and thunder resounded through the heavens. Lightning struck the palace and killed four courtiers, among them Kiyotsura, the man who years earlier had reported Michizane's supposed "confession" to the court. Emperor Daigo, shocked by this incident, soon fell ill, and three months later he too passed away. The lightning was attributed to the workings of Michizane's ghost, who now came to be feared as a thunder god. In the following years, most of Tokihira's descendants died at relatively young ages. The only exception was his second son, Akitada (898–965), who lived modestly, worshiped Michizane's spirit every day, and so was able to enjoy a long and successful career at court. At Kitano, just north of the capital, a shrine was dedicated to Michizane in 947, and forty years later, it was formally recognized by the government. Already, Michizane was known by what would become his familiar appellation, "Temman Tenjin."

This account is not inaccurate, but it does oversimplify a highly complex sequence of events. Closer examination reveals that Michizane's deification was the result of an intricate synthesis of Shinto and Buddhist ideas, and an intermingling of popular and aristocratic cultures. This diversity of origins explains Tenjin's rapid acceptance as one of the most widely worshiped gods in Japan's pantheon of deities. In addition,

Michizane's descendants had reestablished themselves as court scholars, and they too contributed to their ancestor's rise to the status of a patron saint of literature. The process by which Michizane came to be identified as Tenjin can be divided into four stages. In the century before Michizane's death in 903, beliefs that provided the basis for his deification already had appeared. Then, during the approximately four decades immediately following his demise, his sons were summoned back to court and returned to their old offices, while Michizane himself came to be feared as an angry ghost and thunder god. In the brief span between 941 and 947, his identity as Tenjin was clearly established through a sequence of revelations, and his spirit was enshrined at Kitano. Finally, by the end of the tenth century, the court had succeeded in pacifying his spirit, and his apotheosis as patron saint of literature was complete.

The Japanese had long divided their native gods into the categories of Heavenly and Earthly Deities, "Tenjin" and "Chigi" respectively. These Tenjin—the sun goddess Amaterasu among them—had been worshiped since time immemorial. In 836, the government ordered that prayers be said at Kitano to the Heavenly and Earthly Deities. Thus, nine years before Michizane was even born, Tenjin in the ancient sense were already worshiped at Kitano. Moreover, during his lifetime, prayers were addressed there to Raikō, the Thunder Lord, another deity that would soon be associated with Michizane's spirit. In the early Heian period, Kitano was the site of a pasture where the imperial guards kept their horses and where emperors had gone hunting. Michizane, however, seems to have visited Kitano only once, despite a later oracle that claimed it had been one of his favorite spots. Probably it was not Michizane but the Heavenly Deities and Thunder Lord who had enjoyed Kitano, and since Michizane had come to be associated with those deities, his spirit too was assumed to reside there. The confusion of Michizane's spirit with the ancient Heavenly Deities also helps explain the great number of shrines dedicated to Tenjin. Some of them originally had been dedicated to ancient but ill-defined Heavenly Deities that later were mistaken for Michizane as the popularity of the newer Tenjin worship spread. Even today at a few shrines neither the priests nor the faithful are certain whether the Tenjin they worship is Michizane or an older Heavenly Deity.[1]

Fear of angry ghosts was another essential element in Michizane's deification that already was well established during his lifetime. In 863, the court for the first time had sponsored a Spirit-Pacifying Ceremony (Goryōe), consisting of lectures on two sutras followed by song and dance. Its purpose was to appease the angry spirits of six individuals who had been victims of court intrigue and as a result were thought to have rained pestilence on the nation. Curiously, the rites to pacify them had begun not among the aristocrats who had caused their demise, but among commoners far removed from political struggles at court. Eventually, Michizane's name would be added to an expanded list of eight angry spirits who were customarily propitiated to put an end to epidemics or other natural disasters.[2] Already in this earliest stage of Tenjin worship that preceded Michizane's death, the foundations for his deification had been laid. Shinto deities were worshiped at Kitano, and Buddhist rites were performed to pacify the angry souls of courtiers who had died in disgrace. The Spirit-Pacifying Ceremony in particular demonstrated a close tie between popular and aristocratic beliefs. These seemingly disparate threads would become increasingly intertwined as the new Tenjin worship evolved.

The calamities that followed Michizane's death are the most conspicuous events in the second stage of his deification, the years between 903 and 940, but two other developments were equally important. The first occurred not at court but at Dazaifu. There, in 905, one of Michizane's former servants built an altar at his grave site. Michizane had been dead only two years and was not yet worshiped as a god, but he had been buried in the precincts of a Buddhist monastery, and so the altar must have been for regular memorial services. Fourteen years later, Fujiwara no Nakahira (875–945), Tokihira's younger brother, was ordered to sponsor the construction of a more substantial building there. No mention was made of Michizane, but at the time the court was dominated by Fujiwara no Tadahira (880–949), another of Tokihira's brothers, who is said to have maintained close ties with Michizane. Possibly he had proposed building the new edifice as a memorial to the falsely accused minister. It evolved into Anrakuji, one of the major Buddhist monasteries in Dazaifu. Around 1100, influenced by Tenjin worship, it gradually began to incorprate Shinto practices.[3] Following the Meiji Restoration the original Buddhist elements were eliminated, and today it is known as Dazaifu Temmangū, which, along with Kitano Shrine, is one of the two most important centers of Tenjin worship. Kitano may be more famous, but the Dazaifu Shrine has the distinction of being the oldest institution dedicated to the worship of Michizane's spirit.

The second important development was the return of Michizane's sons to the capital, perhaps through the intercession of his loyal friend Haseo, who remained an influential figure at court. In 906, Michizane's oldest son was summoned back from his exile in Tosa, the most isolated province in Shikoku. He was promoted one grade and resumed his position as president of the university. Two years later, a younger son became the fourth Sugawara to pass the civil service examination and subsequently was named professor of literature.[4] Positions at the university, particularly in its literature program, were becoming a Sugawara family preserve. Although later generations did not quite equal Michizane's literary achievements, they did produce able men who helped restore the Sugawara family name through their accomplishments and at the same time actively contributed to maintaining the principal institutions at which Tenjin was worshiped.

The founding of Anrakuji in Dazaifu and the reprieve of Michizane's sons were important, but not nearly so dramatic as the catastrophes that followed: the deaths at court and the lightning that struck the palace. Of these misfortunes, only the death of the first crown prince was blamed on Michizane's spirit in the laconic early chronicles. Apparently, fear of the late minister's revenge and his identification with the thunder god did not develop quite so rapidly as later accounts suggest. By the end of the Heian period, however, the stories had been much improved. Tokihira's death in particular was elaborated to include colorful details of spiritual battle between esoteric monks and Michizane's angry ghost. These later accretions may be fanciful, but at least one of the details is highly significant. After Tokihira fell ill, he summoned the holy monk Jōzō to say prayers on his behalf. Jōzō's father—none other than Kiyoyuki, Michizane's old scholarly rival—then went to visit the ailing Tokihira. Suddenly, Michizane's spirit appeared in the form of two green serpents protruding from Tokihira's ears and

16. *Serpents appearing from Tokihira's ears*
    Source: Temmangū goden.

demanded that Kiyoyuki instruct Jōzō to abandon his incantations. The frightened Kiyoyuki did so and Tokihira's breathing soon ceased.[5] This anecdote, vividly portrayed in illustrated versions of Michizane's life and deification, probably contains at least a kernel of truth, for later well-documented events would reveal that just as Kiyoyuki had first contributed to Michizane's downfall, so he and his sons would later contribute to his deification.

The death of the first crown prince in 923 was the first incident unquestionably blamed on Michizane's ghost at the time it occurred. One month later, an imperial edict posthumously pardoned Michizane, returned his offices, and promoted him one grade to the senior second rank. The edict specified that its purpose was to pacify his ghost. It was drafted by another of Kiyoyuki's sons. In the death of Tokihira, the role of Kiyoyuki and Jōzō had been ambiguous; whereas Jōzō had prayed for his recovery, Kiyoyuki had demanded that the prayers cease. The ensuing events, however, clearly point to a guilty conscience—or fear of Michizane's posthumous revenge—on the part of Kiyoyuki's sons. Also, a comparison of the origins of Anrakuji in Dazaifu with the developments at court reveals a pattern in the reactions of men from different social strata to Michizane's unhappy end. Among those of humble estate, prayer for Michizane's salvation was begun by a man who sympathized with him, his own former servant, and some decades later, other people from outside court circles would turn to him for support in their quarrels with government. In contrast, among the nobility, concern was expressed principally by those who had reason to fear his wrath, for example, the son of a former rival. Similarly, when deadly lightning struck the palace in 930, frightened courtiers soon concluded that Michizane had become a thunder god seeking fiery revenge.[6]

The idea that Michizane's ghost desired to punish his former enemies spread rapidly and appeared next in a surprising context. In 939, when the warrior Taira no Masakado (d. 940) turned from quarreling with his neighbors in the Kantō region to outright rebellion, a prostitute is said to have received an oracle from Hachiman, the god of war, naming Masakado the new emperor. According to the oracle, Michizane's ghost had composed the proclamation. This incident is in keeping both with Michizane's mortal duties as a drafter of government documents and with his posthumous activities opposing the dominant political faction at court. It is recorded in *Shōmonki* (A chronicle of Masakado), an account of the rebellion thought to have been compiled in 940 by Buddhist monks in the Kantō region. Even though this particular anecdote may be a creation of *Shōmonki*'s compilers, it remains significant, for it shows that by 940 an awareness of Michizane's ghost as an enemy of the court had spread all the way to the then-remote Kantō plain. Several shrines dedicated to Tenjin there are thought to trace their origins to this incident.[7]

In the decades immediately following Michizane's death, the second stage of his deification, he had come to be regarded as a supernatural being. An altar was built at his grave site, and he was granted a posthumous reprieve after courtiers had come to fear his revenge. Because records from this period are encrusted with later legends they do not always leave a clear picture of events, but they do demonstrate that already less than four decades after his death, aristocrats in the capital and commoners from Kyushu to Kantō knew of Michizane's spirit, and at least some regarded him as a threat to the court. Michizane's angry ghost was feared as a thunder god, but he was not yet clearly identified as Tenjin, an established member of the Shinto pantheon.

The third stage in Michizane's apotheosis was short but eventful. It lasted from 941 until 947 and witnessed a series of miraculous episodes and oracles that revealed many colorful details of Michizane's posthumous existence. They identified him as the new deity Temman Tenjin and culminated in his enshrinement at Kitano. Contemporaries were so struck by these wonders that they left meticulous records. Although some of the stories seem fantastic, they were recorded as fact. The first and most awesome of the divine revelations were experienced by Dōken, yet another of Kiyoyuki's sons. Like Jōzō, he had turned to religion, taking Buddhist vows at Mount Kimbu, a cultic center for the mountain ascetics (*yamabushi*). In 941, after meditating and practicing religious austerities there for twenty-five years, he presented the court a startling account of his recent experiences.

At noon on the first day of the eighth month, after praying and fasting in a cave for twenty-one days, he had suddenly

17. Lightening strikes the palace
Source: Temmangū goden.

passed away. A meditation (*zen*) monk greeted him and escorted him to heaven, where he met Śākyamuni, who had assumed the form of Zaō Bosatsu, the god of Mount Kimbu. Dōken was also introduced to a less familiar deity, Nihon Daijō Itokuten, whose name might be translated roughly as "Japanese Chancellor Awesome Deva." This turned out to be Michizane, who revealed that earlier he had been filled with anger and had planned to destroy Japan. Subsequently, however, esoteric Buddhism had calmed his wrath by one-tenth, and so he no longer intended to do great harm. Dōken told him that in Japan, everyone, high and low, knew him as "Fire and Thunder" (Karai) Tenjin and revered him as they did the Buddha. Michizane, however, protested that Fire and Thunder Tenjin was only his number-three messenger. He further noted that unless he became a Buddha, he still intended to punish those who had wronged him, although he would answer the prayers of those who worshiped him. After his meeting with Michizane, Dōken learned that it was this number three messenger who had caused the lightning to strike the palace.

Dōken then visited hell, where he saw four men in torment. One wore only a shirt on his back; the other three were naked. The one with the shirt revealed himself to be the former Emperor Daigo. He explained that along with three of his ministers—the men who were naked—he was being tortured for his sins, one of which was driving Michizane into exile. Daigo begged Dōken to have the court offer prayers for their salvation. Finally, thirteen days after he had passed away, Dōken miraculously returned to life and reported this strange experience to the court.[8]

Dōken's account made important contributions to the process of Michizane's deification. It is the earliest source to assert that he was widely worshiped as the Thunder God, although it also claims the belief to be false and raises Michizane to the status of the Thunder God's master. This view of Michizane as superior to the Thunder God would be mentioned again in an oracle six years later, but it would not be stressed in subsequent narrations of the Tenjin legend. It represents an early attempt to portray Michizane as a somewhat less terrifying deity. Another contribution of Dōken's account was, for the first time, to place Michizane's spirit in a well-defined religious context, that of esoteric Buddhism. This too helped make Michizane less frightening, for it suggested that he could be appeased by Buddhist rites. Tenjin worship would long remain closely tied to Buddhism; however, esoteric beliefs do not figure conspicuously in later practices. By placing Michizane above the Thunder God and in a Buddhist context, Dōken helped establish him as more of a god than an angry ghost, although most of the specific details he reported failed to become major elements of Tenjin worship.

Dōken's personal background helps explain why he became involved in the process of Michizane's deification. As a son of Kiyoyuki, he may have felt a sense of inherited guilt because of his father's involvement in Michizane's downfall. Moreover, although his was a minor court family, he chose to join the mountain ascetics, men usually of dubious social status. Thus he had entered into the world of popular religion, where fear of angry ghosts had originated, and so he was able to serve as a bridge between it and the court.

In the seventh month of 942, just a year after Dōken's mysterious experience, a poor woman, Tajihi no Ayako, received an oracle from Michizane. He revealed that he was now known as Tenjin and wanted her to build a shrine at Kitano, a place he claimed to have formerly enjoyed visiting. Ayako was too impoverished to carry out this request and attempted to satisfy Michizane by worshiping Tenjin at a humble altar near her hut in the capital. Word of Ayako's oracle seems to have spread, for in 945 a report from Settsu province, just southwest of the capital, stated that hundreds of people—men and women, noble and base, young and old—had gathered and were heading for the capital, singing and dancing as they went. They claimed to be worshiping "Shidara" deities. The word *"shidara"* usually referred to the rhythmic clapping that accompanies a song, and so the name of the deities and the description of their worship suggest a popular religious movement, perhaps like the *"Ee ja nai ka"* ecstatic dancing of 1867. In the case of the 945 incident, the worshipers brought with them three portable shrines. The principal one, complete with a *torii* gate, was dedicated to Ayae Jizai Tenjin. "Ayae" probably was the woman Ayako who had received the oracle from Michizane, and a contemporary source specifically identified the "Jizai Tenjin" with him.[9]

Ayako's oracle and the incident of the Shidara deities present a very different aspect of early Tenjin worship than did Dōken's account. For the first time Michizane was referred to as Tenjin without the Fire and Thunder prefix that Dōken had used. Also, this new Tenjin clearly belonged to the Shinto tradition. These elements did become essential features of later Tenjin worship. On the other hand, at least in the case of the Shidara deities, the older image of Michizane as an angry ghost and enemy of the court was still preserved. The exact nature of those deities and why they were being brought to the capital were not specified, but they probably represented a popular reaction to government policies. Here again, the common people were regarding Michizane sympathetically as a divine ally in their protest against the established order in the capital, a role previously attributed to Michizane in the Masakado Rebellion. Further aspects of Tenjin worship had appeared, but Michizane's ghost was not yet considered fully pacified. He was still viewed as a potential threat to the court.

The third stage in Michizane's deification ended with the founding of Kitano Shrine in 947. Two completely different accounts of that event survive. According to one, in the sixth month of 947, Ayako finally was able to carry out Michizane's instructions and established a shrine at Kitano. A second version states that three months earlier, another oracle was received by Tarō, the seven-year-old son of Miwa no Yoshitane, a Shinto priest from Ōmi, a province just east of the capital. Portions of this oracle roughly paralleled what Dōken had reported previously. The thunder demons—105,000 of them—were Michizane's followers, and he had sent them to punish disbelievers. Michizane promised, however, that he would reward those who worshiped him. The most significant difference between Dōken's account and this oracle was that Dōken presented Michizane in a distinctly Buddhist context, whereas this new oracle was predominantly Shinto in tone. Michizane stated that he bore no grudge against the popular Shinto deities of Kamo, Hachiman, and Hie, but lamented that he was not similarly worshiped. For the first time, he appeared in the context of established Shinto cults. Once again he requested that a shrine be dedicated to him at Kitano and mentioned that pine trees would grow there, the earliest association of Michizane with the pine tree. The oracle concluded, however, on a Buddhist note with a request that a Lotus Meditation Hall (Hokke Sammaidō) also be established there.

After receiving this oracle, the Shinto priest Yoshitane went to Kitano, where he met the Buddhist monk Saichin whose monastery was located there. While they were discussing what should be done, suddenly a thousand pine trees miraculously grew overnight, just as Michizane had predicted. Since the oracle thereby was proven genuine, they established the shrine as requested. Ayako is not mentioned in the earliest record of this story, but later accounts attempted to fuse the two different versions by stating that she cooperated with Yoshitane and Saichin.[10] In its three founders, Kitano Shrine brought together three different elements of Japanese religion: folk Shinto as personified by Ayako, probably a shaman not associated with any religious establishment; institutional Shinto as represented by Yoshitane, a professional priest at a regular shrine; and Buddhism, as embodied by Saichin, a monk whose name points to an affiliation with Saichō, the founder of Enryakuji, the great Tendai complex on Mount Hiei, which later came to control Kitano Shrine. Anrakuji, the temple in Dazaifu dedicated to Michizane, was already over forty years old, and with the creation of the shrine at Kitano, the institutional foundation had been laid for the metamorphosis of Michizane's angry spirit into the benevolent deity Tenjin. Moreover, divine revelations had helped place Tenjin in the context of established religious beliefs.

During the final stage in Michizane's deification, beginning immediately after Kitano Shrine was founded in 947 and lasting until the end of the tenth century, the institutions dedicated to Michizane were brought under the control of the court, and Tenjin came to be officially recognized as a deity. Just two months after Kitano Shrine had been established, the head of the Sugawara clan appointed the monk Heichū to become the first intendant of Anrakuji. He was a grandson of Michizane, and so initiated the tradition, maintained to the present day, that the men in charge of the temple (or the shrine it later became) all have been direct descendants of Michizane. Anrakuji had been founded by a commoner, but it was now under the

18. An oracle at Ōmi: Michizane and the thunder demons
Source: Temmangū goden.

control of a court family. The same process would soon occur at Kitano Shrine. In 959, it was rebuilt and expanded by Fujiwara no Morosuke (908–960), the most powerful man at court and a son of Tadahira, the Fujiwara minister who had remained friendly with Michizane. Ironically, Morosuke prayed that Tenjin protect coming generations of Fujiwara regents. In the following years, the shrine's original founders began to quarrel over control of the institution. The feud was settled in 976 when the government ruled that, following the precedent of Anrakuji, the Sugawara family should have control of the shrine. Since they had long maintained ties with Saichin's Tendai sect, the Sugawara supported him. Ayako and her followers, who had their roots in popular religion, were expelled.[11]

Once Michizane's descendants had gained control of the religious institutions that enshrined his spirit, Tenjin began to acquire the civilized qualities of the historic Michizane. In 986, when a group of literati presented a collection of their poems to the shrine, one explained that they did so because "Tenjin is the progenitor of literature; the lord of poetry." The image of Fire and Thunder Tenjin gradually diminished, and Michizane no longer inspired cults of ecstatic dancing among the populace. He did remain one of the eight angry ghosts to whom Spirit-Pacifying Ceremonies still were performed sporadically, but aside from that context, Tenjin had come to be regarded as thoroughly pacified, and the places at which he was worshiped, although founded by obscure figures, were under the control of court aristocrats. As a result, in 987, Kitano Shrine was formally recognized by the government, and four years later it appeared on an exclusive list of nineteen principal Shinto shrines. The shrine's glory was crowned in 1004 when Emperor Ichijō (980–1011, r. 986–1011) formally visited it. Michizane himself was not neglected. In 993, he received two final posthumous promotions: first to minister of the left and then, five months later, to the highest court rank and office, grand minister with the senior first rank.[12]

Less than a century after he had died in disgrace, Michizane had been posthumously promoted and was worshiped as a god at a shrine that had been ranked among the most important in the land. Various causes contributed to the rapid spread and prompt official recognition of Tenjin worship. First, even before Michizane's death, Heavenly Deities, also known as Tenjin, were part of Japanese religion, and fear of angry ghosts was widespread. These beliefs provided a broad and secure foundation upon which later Tenjin worship arose. Second, from its inception, Tenjin worship combined elements from both of Japan's two major systems of belief, Shinto and Buddhism. The cult of Tenjin was thus an integral part of Japan's syncretic religious tradition. Only after the Meiji Restoration did shrines dedicated to Michizane become strictly Shinto. Third, although Michizane himself was very much a man of the court and Heian nobles are usually regarded as isolated from the lower classes, Tenjin worship grew out of a fusion of aristocratic and common cultures; it was not simply a phenomenon of a small elite. And fourth, the continuing admiration for Michizane's poetry among men of letters led them to hold an enduring reverence for Tenjin, an attitude promoted by Michizane's own scholarly descendants, who encouraged government sponsorship of Tenjin worship. As court patronage gew, the popular elements that had contributed to Michizane's deification became less conspicuous, and in the eleventh and early twelfth centuries Tenjin appeared most often as a benevolent god of literature.

THE EVOLUTION OF TENJIN WORSHIP

The decades of warfare and political instability that accompanied the establishment of the warrior government at Kamakura also witnessed a religious revival. Sects of Buddhism promising easy salvation appeared, and itinerant preachers spread the new doctrines throughout Japan. Men of more ascetic temperament turned to the teachings of Zen, which eventually found an audience among members of the samurai class. These new forms of Buddhism were the predominant force that molded the evolution of Tenjin worship in medieval times, as faith in the now benevolent Tenjin spread anew among the populace and reverence for Michizane's literary talents grew among men of letters associated with the Zen sect. Tenjin worship thus changed but did not lose touch with its origins. Michizane's desire for vengeance was no longer a banner under which commoners protested government policies, but Tenjin remained a popular deity. Chinese had lost its preeminence as a literary language, but poets still presented their compositions at Tenjin shrines.

During the Kamakura period, one way in which Tenjin worship was incorporated into the new Buddhist ethos was that Tenjin came to be regarded as the Japanese manifestation of Kannon, the bodhisattva of mercy.[13] This was an expression of the then-popular doctrine that Shinto gods were Buddhist deities reborn in Japanese form. Identifying Tenjin with Kannon reinforced Tenjin's benign image and helped Tenjin evolve into a compassionate deity who protected the falsely accused and rewarded the honest. The promise of reward to those who worshiped Tenjin resembled the prospect of salvation offered to believers in popular Buddhism.

The cult of Tenjin also adopted methods for proselytizing that were used by the new Buddhist sects. Japanese preachers employed illustrated scrolls as a means of impressing on their audience the history and marvelous powers of their doctrines. These texts, known as *engi,* recounted the lives of men who established sects and the stories of how principal religious institutions were founded. Among the earliest of them is *Kitano Tenjin engi.* The oldest surviving text, dated 1194, presents a colorful narrative of Michizane's life and deification written in the vernacular—Japanese—not the learned *kambun* that previously had been used to chronicle his achievements. The first illustrated version appeared twenty-five years later. Today, approximately thirty illustrated versions, along with many unillustrated ones, are extant, making this one of the most frequently copied of all *engi,* a fact which is one measure of Tenjin's popularity.

The scrolls, which are generally similar, combine fact and legend in recounting the story of Michizane's achievements, downfall, and posthumous revenge. They conclude with a series of anecdotes telling of how those who worshiped at Kitano Shrine were rewarded whereas the disrespectful were punished. These stories, relatively late additions to the Tenjin legend, reveal the missionary intent of the scrolls. *Kitano Tenjin engi* presents what came to be an orthodox version of Michizane's life and deification, and also constitute the most familiar expression of Tenjin worship in the graphic arts. Although these works originally had been the product of aristocratic hands, they were soon put to use in propagating belief in Tenjin's powers. Today, the most famous of them, the oldest illustrated version, has been designated a national treasure and is on display at Kitano Shrine.[14]

During the Muromachi period, Zen, a sect that appealed to the elite, replaced the popular Buddhist sects as the most significant influence on Tenjin worship. The ties to Zen Buddhism manifested themselves both directly and indirectly. During the medieval period, Zen monasteries became centers that preserved Japan's heritage of Chinese learning and produced a massive corpus of *kambun* literature. As admirers of Chinese literature, Zen monks revered Michizane's accomplishments and composed poems in Chinese praising him. They esteemed Michizane so highly that they converted him posthumously to their sect. A legend first recorded in 1394 stated that in 1241, just after a Japanese Zen master had returned from studies in China, Tenjin appeared before him and begged to become his disciple. The Zen master responded by suggesting that Tenjin go to be initiated directly by his teacher in China. Tenjin then miraculously crossed the sea and appeared in the garden of the Chinese master, where he identified himself with a poem in Japanese. The Chinese sage immediately recognized the great Michizane, instructed him in the secret teachings, and presented him a Buddhist robe. Tenjin then returned to Japan and reported his success to the Japanese master. Although the historic Michizane chose not to visit China as a diplomat, ironically, he was credited with journeying to China as a pilgrim over 300 years after his death. This story became a popular theme among Japanese painters, who often portrayed Michizane wearing the garb of a Chinese Taoist monk and carrying a plum branch.[15]

Zen was also associated with the cult of Tenjin indirectly through *renga,* or linked verse, a form of Japanese poetry influenced by Zen aesthetics that flourished during the Muromachi period. It consisted of a series of short verses, often written by a group of poets each of whom in turn contributed a verse that was linked to the preceding one until a set number of verses had been composed. Poetry in Japanese had been composed at Kitano as early as 1204. It was intended to be for the pleasure of the Tenjin. Other gods were treated to music or sutra readings, but since Tenjin was a patron of literature, he was entertained with poetry, and because Chinese was no longer fashionable except in Zen monasteries, the poetry was in Japanese.

Renga were first composed at Kitano Shrine in the early fourteenth century when the form was in its early stage of development, and as it matured during the following century, the shrine became its principal center. A Renga Hall (Rengadō) was established there and the Ashikaga shoguns placed in charge of it leading poets, among them the greatest of all *renga* masters, Sōgi (1421–1502). Sōgi did not relish the post and resigned before a year had passed. This, however, was not a sign of disrespect toward Tenjin, for in fact some years earlier Sōgi had made a pilgrimage to the shrine at Dazaifu and had written an elegant description of it. That shrine also became a major regional center for linked poetry, and even today, a neighborhood adjacent to it is known as Rengaya, literally, "*Renga* House," presumably because it was the site of an establishment comparable to Kitano's Renga Hall. *Renga* poets made Tenjin one of their own just as the Zen monks did. In 1373, a child was said to have brought a poem in one hundred links to the mansion of an aristocratic poet, who thought this strange and so had him followed. The child went to Kitano Shrine and suddenly disappeared. Obviously, it was a messenger of Tenjin, who himself had composed the poem. When *renga* poets assembled, they hung a portrait of Tenjin to lend the occasions sanctity and provide poetic inspiration. Some centuries later, writers of comic verse (*kyōka*) did the same to add an air of mock solemnity to their gatherings.[16]

During the Edo period, images of Tenjin again changed to reflect new trends in thought and society. If in the Muromachi period Tenjin had been a Zen monk and linked verse poet, in the Edo period he became an inspiration to secular scholars, a god of calligraphy to schoolboys, and a hero of popular dramas to the merchant class. Confucianism had come to replace Buddhism as the dominant intellectual tradition, and Chinese studies once again achieved a popularity comparable to that which they had enjoyed in the early Heian court. Edo period scholars thus felt an affinity not just with Tenjin as a god of learning but also with Michizane as an intellectual progenitor. A list of those who expressed their reverence for Tenjin would include most of the great Confucians of the day, among them Hayashi Razan (1583–1657), the founder of the orthodox Neo-Confucian tradition patronized by the shogunate; Kinoshita Jun'an (1622–1689), an early private teacher of Confucianism; Kaibara Ekken (1630–1714), a popularizer of Confucian thought; and Ogyū Sorai (1666–1728), a follower of the "Ancient Learning" (Kogaku) school.

In keeping with rationalistic Confucian ideas, some of these men criticized the ancient legends. For example, Kaibara Ekken denied the truth of such obvious fabrications as Michizane's miraculous journey to China and denounced stories of Tenjin's divine retribution as even more objectionable than Tokihira's slander. "Tenjin," he argued, was characterized by "the virtues of honesty, purity, and moderation," and so could not have been responsible for such violent deeds. By the early nineteenth century, Rai San'yō, the scholar whose name appears with Michizane's on the facade of the Boston library, went so far as to defend Tokihira, who he argued was only protecting his position as other Fujiwara ministers had. According to San'yō, the man responsible for Michizane's (not "Tenjin's") downfall was in fact Uda, who should have realized that after he abdicated, Michizane would no longer be able to protect himself. As long as Uda remained emperor, Michizane would command respect, but as soon as Uda retired, people would claim that a professor of literature was corruptly dominating the government. Moreover, it was only natural that a son should hate his father's favorite, who could use his connections with the father to restrain the son. A son, Daigo for example, would prefer to select as his own retainers men closer to himself in age and inclinations, such as Tokihira. This was true among commoners and all the more true among emperors. What an emperor feared most was having a sibling threaten his position, and so only a few words from Tokihira were required to arouse Daigo's natural fears. Uda was mistaken in thinking that his testament, a single sheet of paper, could restrain his son. San'yō concludes by suggesting that Michizane should have realized the insecurity of his own position, and so he must take partial responsibility for his own downfall since he personally had encouraged Uda to abdicate. In this last point, San'yō is clearly wrong, but otherwise his analysis is remarkably perceptive. It completely rejects traditional views of Michizane as a deity, Tokihira as a villain, and emperors as anything but ordinary mortals.[17]

The Confucians were not the only scholars to admire Michizane; respect for Tenjin also was expressed by representatives of other intellectual traditions. The monk Keichū (1640–1701), a pioneer in the National Learning (Kokugaku) tradition, and Hirata Atsutane (1776–1843), an anti-Chinese Shinto nationalist, both worshiped Tenjin. Even one specialist in Dutch learning, Maeno Ryōtaku (1723–1803), went to pray at Dazaifu before he began to assist in translating the first Western medical text into Japanese.[18] The catholic appeal of Tenjin worship transcended the boundaries of intellectual affiliation, which in the Edo period became more clearly marked than in Japan's earlier ages.

In addition to new intellectual traditions, educational institutions also expanded in the Edo period. Many schools were founded, some for the samurai elite and others for the commoners. In addition to educating Japan's youth, many schools also propagated faith in Tenjin. Those run by feudal domains for their samurai continued the ancient Confucian Memorial Rites that had been performed a thousand years earlier at the court university. A few schools, however, altered the rites by placing an image of Michizane next to a central image of Confucius. Schools for commoners did not hold Confucian Memorial Rites, but most conducted "Tenjin Lectures" (Tenjinkō), ceremonies that traced their origins to the late Kamakura period. As conducted in the Edo period, the lectures began with a school's pupils presenting offerings of food and drink before an image of Michizane while praying for success in their studies and especially in their calligraphy. Their teacher would then offer a lecture on Michizane's virtues and achievements. The service would conclude with a reading of a text known as the *Tenjin Sutra* (*Tenjin kyō*). It was only a few lines long and invoked Tenjin's name in language mimicking that of a Buddhist sutra. Rituals such as these were continued into modern times. In Japan's prewar higher schools, student assemblies were held before an image of Michizane, and at least as late as the 1960s Tenjin Lectures were conducted in a few rural communities.[19]

The popularity of Tenjin spread to the theaters as well. Earlier, noh plays had alluded to Michizane and to legends associated with him, but the first full account of his life in dramatic form was written in 1713 by the greatest of Edo period playwrights, Chikamatsu Monzaemon (1653-1724). Although Chikamatsu's play did not prove to be a lasting success, it became the model for *The Sugawara Secrets of Calligraphy*, completed in 1746 and still among the most frequently performed works in the puppet theater and kabuki repertoires. In part, the popularity of the work can be explained by the skillful way in which it blended elements of historical fact and ancient legend with values, customs, and events of the eighteenth century. For example, the play took the fact that one of Michizane's daughters had married a prince and improved it by having the daughter elope with the prince against parental wishes, thereby introducing the familiar dramatic conflict between duty (*giri*) and human feelings (*ninjō*). Another key element of the play was, as its title suggests, Michizane's attempts to pass on the secrets of his calligraphy. As noted, his contemporaries did not regard him as a great calligrapher, but in medieval times his writing was praised, and by the Edo period, when no authentic examples survived, he was revered as the supreme master of the brush. In the play, Michizane teaches his secrets to a humble retainer who runs a village school. The most famous scene, combining comedy and melodrama, takes place there and must have reminded most of its original audience of their own schools, where they had been first taught of Tenjin's noble deeds.[20]

During the Edo period, Tenjin worship attracted ever more followers, and the Meiji Restoration in no way diminished its popularity. At least one early Meiji leader, Ōkuma Shigenobu, was a devoted follower of the Tenjin cult, the story of Michizane's virtues continued to appear in textbooks, and the plays about his life remained staples in the playhouses. One important change, however, did occur: in April of 1868, just months after the Restoration, the new government embarked on a policy of eliminating Buddhist elements from Shinto shrines. For the first time, Tenjin and the shrines dedicated to him became purely Shinto. The official effort to separate the two religions proved so successful that today Tenjin's ancient ties to Buddhism have been largely forgotten. Although in one sense this represented a radical break with the past, in another sense it was typical of the history of Tenjin worship, which had always adapted itself

19. Children being taught to worship Tenjin in an Edo-period household
Source: Temmangū goden.

to changes in Japan's intellectual climate rather than adhere to immutable doctrines. As with other manifestations of native Japanese religion, the cult of Tenjin lacked systematic theology and elaborate institutional organization. It consisted instead of individual shrines—some famous, others obscure—all dedicated to the spirit of a man, Sugawara no Michizane, who had come to be revered as a god. Over the years, new stories of Tenjin's miraculous deeds appeared and popular images of Michizane changed. The deeds of the historic Michizane alone remained unaltered, providing a foundation upon which the elaborate cult of Tenjin grew.

Michizane was, of course, no god. Contrary to Kaibara Ekken's claim, moderation was not one of his virtues. He indulged all too willingly in the academic feuds of his day. Moreover, despite good intentions, he did not prove to be an outstanding administrator when he served as a provincial governor, nor was his record in high office one of remarkable accomplishments. Nonetheless, he remains a figure who was indeed deserving of admiration, if not necessarily deification.

More than any of his contemporaries, he was able to take advantage of the flexibility offered by Chinese poetry to treat, for example, social and philosophical themes, to present vividly detailed imagery in poems of considerable length, and to express his personal feelings and experiences. As a result, he produced a body of literature that remains worthy of serious attention. His best poems can be appreciated simply as works of literature, and other works offer valuable insights into his personality and the times in which he lived. Had he written only in Japanese, literary convention would have restricted his range of expression: the standard form of Japanese poetry in his day consisted of only thirty-one syllables, perhaps ten words, and decorum insisted that poets limit themselves to courtly themes and language. Writing in Chinese, however, he was able to graphically show his compassion for the suffering of the poor or his grief over a son who had passed away; he could comfort himself during his years in exile by recounting the events of his life. In addition, the use of Chinese had powerful symbolic value for it demonstrated Japan's commitment to the Sinocentric norms then accepted throughout East Asia. In more practical terms, it facilitated the conduct of diplomacy and thereby allowed Japan to keep abreast of developments in neighboring countries. Had men like Michizane not kept alive a tradition of Chinese learning, Japan would have been indeed isolated.

Michizane's official career, too, was noteworthy, even if he failed to make a lasting contribution to Japanese political history, except in the negative sense of being among the last of the rivals whom the Fujiwara expelled from the court. The very fact that he attained sufficient influence to threaten the Fujiwara, however, was in itself a remarkable achievement. His was an aristocratic age in which men customarily did not rise above their families' ascribed status. Success on the civil service examinations offered the best chance for an individual to improve his position at court. The efforts of his immediate ancestors had established the Sugawara as a family of scholar aristocrats, and starting from this foundation, Michizane advanced to enter the highest rungs of court government. By Heian court standards, he was a man of modest origins, yet for a short time he was the most powerful man in the government. He attained that position in part as the result of happenstance: he had returned from a tour of service in the provinces just as an energetic and culture-loving emperor was looking for political allies. But in part he had earned the recognition that the emperor bestowed on him. The Chinese values of the day recognized his classical training as properly qualifying him as a government leader. Moreover, he had years of administrative experience, both at court and in the provinces, and he had shown himself to be a forthright critic of Fujiwara attempts to abuse their prerogatives. His tragedy was that the Confucian ideal of the scholar-official was not a realistic one, at least in the context of Heian Japan. A sensitive yet outspoken poet like Michizane was temperamentally unsuited to the political struggles that went with high office.

Michizane's posthumous deification was in itself a complicated and fascinating process. It was an attempt on the part of those who had slandered him to purge their guilt, but it was also a natural outgrowth of existing religious beliefs and occasionally even an expression of antigovernment feelings. Today, he has been worshiped as a god for well over a thousand years, and the accumulated trappings of divinity occasionally have obscured our view of Michizane the man. He was, however, indeed a remarkable figure deserving the highest respect for his real achievements as a poet, scholar, educator, diplomat, and official. He did not need to be deified to be remembered.

Notes
Bibliography
Glossary
Index

Key to
Abbreviated Citations

DNS   *Dai Nihon shiryō.* In citations of *DNS*, roman numerals refer to the section number, arabic numerals to the volume number. This and other chronologically arranged works are cited by date rather than page.

GR   *[Shinkō] Gunsho ruijū*, comp., Hanawa Hokinoichi, 1928-1937.

KB   *Kugyō bunin.* (*KT*, vols. 53-57).

KBKK   *Kanke bunsō, Kanke kōshū.* (ed. Kawaguchi Hisao, *NKBT*, vol. 72). In this, the best edition of Michizane's two anthologies, individual works are numbered, and so they are cited herein by these "*KBKK* item" numbers. Page numbers are occasionally used to refer to Kawaguchi's valuable introduction and notes.

KT   *[Shintei zōho] Kokushi taikei*, comp., Kuroita Katsumi, 1929-1964. The volume numbers used are those from the complete printing of this set. Some items from it have been reprinted with different volume numbers but identical pagination.

MJ   *Montoku jitsuroku.* (In *KT*, vol. 3).

NKBT   *Nihon koten bungaku taikei*, 1957-1969.

NS   *Nihon shoki.* (*KT*, vol. 1).

SB   *Sompi bummyaku.* (*KT*, vols. 58-60), cited herein as *SB*, 1-4, the numbering used in recent reprints.

SJ   *Sandai jitsuroku.* (*KT*, vol. 4).

SN   *Shoku Nihongi.* (*KT*, vol. 2).

SNK   *Shoku Nihon kōki.* (In *KT*, vol. 3).

ZGR   *Zoku gunsho ruijū*, comp., Hanawa Hokinoichi, 1931-1933.

Notes

INTRODUCTION

1. The two most comprehensive studies of Tenjin worship are Endō Taisuke, *Temman Tenjin shinkō no kyōikushiteki kenkyū* (1966) and Takeuchi Hideo, *Temmangū* (1968). The latter focuses principally on Kitano Shrine. The present head priest at the Dazaifu shrine, Nishitakatsuji Nobusada, a direct descendant of Michizane, has written a book that provides more information about his own shrine: *Dazaifu Temmangū* (1970). He also sponsored the two-volume collection of essays, *Sugawara no Michizane to Dazaifu Temmangū*, ed. Dazaifu Temmangū Bunka Kenkyūjo (1975), which contains many useful articles, including a review of research on Tenjin worship: Watanabe Kan, "Tenjin shinkō kenkyūshi josetsu," II, 331–355. It also includes a thorough bibliography of Japanese publications, 1878 to 1974, on both Michizane and Tenjin worship: "Sugawara no Michizane, Temmangū, Tenjin shinkō kankei bunken mokuroku," compiled by Fujino Hideko, II, 381–407. Takatori Masao's beautifully illustrated *Sugawara no Michizane: onryō no kami kara gakumon geinō no kami e*, vol. 4 of *Nihon o tsukutta hitobito* (1978) contains much information about Tenjin worship. Two important collections of primary sources should be mentioned. *Kitanoshi*, ed. Kitano Jinja (1909–1910) consists of three volumes. The first is a detailed, although not complete, listing of Tenjin shrines throughout Japan. The second two reprint an extensive collection of documents pertaining to Michizane and to Tenjin worship. This collection, known as *Kitano bunsō*, was compiled by the monk Shūen (1786–1859), who had been born into a family of priests descended from Michizane and associated with Kitano Shrine. Shūen spent thirty years gathering documents relating to his famous ancestor. A second collection is *Kitano*, ed. Makabe Toshinobu, vol. XI of *Shintō taikei: jinja hen* (1978). Although less comprehensive than *Kitano bunsō*, it contains the best editions of many important sources plus an introduction with valuable notes on their textual history. In English, see Richard A. B. Ponsonby Fane's "Kitano Temmangū: Patron Deity of Learning," originally published in 1937 and reprinted in *Visiting Famous Shrines of Japan*, vol. 6 of the Dr. Richard Ponsonby Fane Series (Kyoto, 1964), pp. 194–220.

Ivan Morris's *The Nobility of Failure: Tragic Heroes in the History of Japan* (New York, 1975) includes a chapter, "The Deity of Failures," (pp. 41-66) that treats both Michizane's life and deification. Stanleigh H. Jones, Jr. has recently published a complete translation of *Sugawara denju tenarai kagami* as *Sugawara and the Secrets of Calligraphy* (New York, 1985).

2. Inoue Tetsujirō, *Sugawara no Michizane* (1936), p. 9. For other studies of Michizane published on the occasion of the anniversary, see Fujino, "Bunken mokuroku," pp. 381-383. Anniversaries of Michizane's death are calculated in the traditional manner with the year of his death (903) counted as the "first anniversary."

3. How Michizane's name came to appear on the facade of the Boston Public Library is something of a mystery. Since the library building was constructed during Fenollosa's tenure as curator of Japanese art at the Boston Museum of Fine Arts (1890-1895), the idea may have been his. Fenollosa definitely was familiar with Michizane's work (see chapter 2, note 41). Alternatively, some have suggested that Okakura Kakuzō (Tenshin) proposed Michizane's name, but Okakura was not employed at the Boston museum until 1904. He was in Japan when the library was built. The concept of *wakon kansai* is discussed in David Pollack, "The Informing Image: 'China' in *Genji Monogatari*," *Monumenta Nipponica* 38.4:361-363 (Winter 1983).

4. Sakamoto Tarō's *Sugawara no Michizane*, vol. 100 of *Jimbutsu sōsho* (1962), was the first "de-mythologized" book-length study of Michizane. Kawaguchi Hisao's meticulously annotated edition of Michizane's two anthologies, *Kanke bunsō* and *Kanke kōshū*, vol. 72 of *Nihon koten bungaku taikei* (1966) is invaluable. It has an excellent introduction and elucidates the obscurities of his poems. Abe Takeshi has written various items on Michizane, including a chapter in his book, *Heian zenki seijishi no kenkyū* (1974), pp. 173-227, and *Sugawara no Michizane: kyūseiki no seiji to shakai* (1979). They are similar in content and tend to emphasize the age more than the man. The first will be cited more often because it was written for a scholarly audience and hence is better documented. The works cited in note 1 (other than the first two) also contain useful information; the essays and bibliography in *Sugawara no Michizane to Dazaifu Temmangū* are particularly helpful. The most recent Japanese book on Michizane, Nakashima Nobutarō's *Sugawara no Michizane: sono hito to bungaku* (Kobe, 1981), is one of the most traditional in its approach. Burton Watson's *Japanese Literature in Chinese, Volume One: Poetry and Prose in Chinese by Japanese Writers of the Early Period* (New York, 1975) includes a short essay on Michizane and elegant translations of 38 of his works, including 6 *waka* (pp. 73-130).

5. Morita Tei, *Heian jidai seijishi kenkyū* (1978), pp. 99-226; and *Ōchō seiji* (1979), pp. 62-119; Sasayama Haruo, "Heian shoki no seiji kaikaku," in *Iwanami kōza Nihon rekishi 3: kodai 3* (1976), pp. 233-269; Kitayama Shigeo, *Nihon no rekishi 4: Heian kyō* (1965), pp. 2-157; Hayakawa Shōhachi, *Nihon no rekishi 4: ritsuryō kokka* (1974); George B. Sansom, *A History of Japan to 1334* (Stanford, 1958), pp. 175-225.

6. Morita Tei, *Seijishi*, pp. 13-50; and *Ōchō seiji*, pp. 30-60; Aoki Kazuo, "Ritsuryō kokka no kenryoku kōzō," in *Iwanami kōza Nihon rekishi 3: kodai 3*, pp. 23-30; Seki Akira, "Ritsuryō kizoku ron" in ibid., pp. 56-62; Tsuchida Naoshige, "Shōkei ni tsuite," in *Nihon kodaishi ronshū*, ed. Sakamoto Tarō Hakase Kanreki Kinenkai (1962) II, 574-578; Takeuchi Rizō, *Ritsuryōsei to kizoku seiken* (1958) II, 142-155.

7. Two detailed descriptions of the *ritsuryō* bureaucracy are available in English: Jean and Robert Karl Reischauer, *Early Japanese History* (originally published

1937, reprint Gloucester, Mass., 1967) and Richard J. Miller, *Japan's First Bureaucracy: A Study of Eighth Century Government,* Cornell University East Asia Papers no. 19 (Ithaca, N.Y., 1979). William H. and Helen Craig McCullough describe how it functioned at a slightly later but considerably different period in Appendix A, "Some Notes on Rank and Office," to their translation of *Eiga monogatari, A Tale of Flowering Fortunes* (Stanford, 1980) II, 789-831. A standard reference in Japanese is Wada Hidematsu, *Kanshoku yōkai* (1979).

8. Aoki Kazuo, "Kenryoku kōzō," pp. 11-21; Seki Akira, "Kizoku ron," pp. 38-55; Takahashi Takashi, *Ritsuryō kanjin kyūyosei no kenkyū,* (1970), pp. 12-13, 516-519; Murai Yasuhiko, *Heian kizoku no sekai* (1968), pp. 23-36; Murao Jirō, *Ritsuryōsei no kichō* (1960), pp. 48-59; Robert M. Spaulding, *Imperial Japan's Higher Civil Service Examination* (Princeton, 1967), pp. 9-19.

9. Nomura Tadao, *Ritsuryō kanjinsei no kenkyū* (1970), pp. 95-227; and *Kodai kanryō no sekai* (1976), pp. 6-171; Takeuchi Rizō, *Ritsuryōsei,* II, 156-182.

10. Hisayuki Miyakawa, "An Outline of the Naitō Hypothesis and Its Effects on Japanese Studies of China," *Far Eastern Quarterly* 14.4:538-539 (August 1955); Denis Twitchett, "The Composition of the T'ang Ruling Class: New Evidence from Tunhuang," in Denis Twitchett and Arthur F. Wright eds., *Perspectives on the T'ang* (New Haven, 1973), pp. 47-85; Edwin G. Pulleyblank, *The Background of the Rebellion of An Lu-shan* (London, 1955), pp. 47-49; Miyazaki Ichisada, *Kakyo* (Osaka, 1946), pp. 2-23; and *China's Examination Hell: The Civil Service Examinations of Imperial China,* tr., Conrad Schirokauei (New Haven, 1981), pp. 111-129; and David G. Johnson, *The Medieval Chinese Oligarchy* (Boulder, Col., 1977), pp. 126-152.

11. The concept of *wen-chang* (the original Chinese pronunciation of *monjō*) is discussed in James J.Y. Liu, *Chinese Theories of Literature* (Chicago, 1975), pp. 99-101.

12. Kigoshi Takashi, "Michizane no shi to *Hakushi monjū,*" in Yamagishi Tokuhei, ed. *Nihon kambungakushi ronkō* (1974), pp. 163-165. The most detailed study of Po Chü-i's influence on Michizane is Kaneko Hikojirō, *Heian jidai bungaku to Hakushi monjū: Michizane no bungaku kenkyūhen dainisatsu,* (first published in 1978, 30 years after its author's death). No other book-length studies of Michizane's literature have been written, but numerous articles can be found in Fujino's bibliography. The most complete account of Heian literature in Chinese is Kawaguchi Hisao, *Heianchō Nihon kambungakushi no kenkyū* (1964). Kojima Noriyuki's multivolume study of early Japanese *kambun* literature, *Kokufū ankoku jidai no bungaku* (1968-) is currently up to volume 3 (1978), a detailed analysis of the *Ryōunshū,* the first imperial anthology of literature in Chinese. General surveys of Heian literature offer convenient introductions; see, for example, Konishi Jin'ichi's chapter, "Kambungaku," in Hisamatsu Sen'ichi and Nishishita Kyōichi ed. *Heianchō bungakushi* (1965), pp. 888-905; and chapter 1 of *Nihon bungaku zenshi 2: chūko,* ed. Akiyama Ken (1978), pp. 28-60. In English, see Watson's *Japanese Literature in Chinese;* Robert H. Brower and Earl Miner, *Japanese Court Poetry* (Stanford, 1961); and Shuichi Kato, *A History of Japanese Literature: The First Thousand Years,* tr., David Chibbett (New York, 1979), in particular pp. 109-119.

13. The poems in *Shinkokinshū* are no. 1688-1699. Unless otherwise noted, *waka* will be cited with the name of the anthology in which they appear and the number of the poem from *Kokka taikan,* ed. Matsushita Daizaburō and Watanabe Fumio (1963). Also see Kojima Yoshio, *Shinkokin wakashū no kenkyū, zokuhen* (1946), pp. 200-203; and Sakamoto Tarō, *Sugawara no Michizane,* pp. 148-150. Michizane's *waka* have not received extensive scholarly treatment, but a few

articles have been written, for example, Sasaki Nobutsuna, "Kajin toshite no Sugawara no Michizane," *Kaizō* 15.4:232-239 (April 1933) and "Kankō no waka ni tsuite," in *Kankō shōtokuroku* (Kyoto, 1944), pp. 135-143; and Shimmura Izuru, "Kankō no 'Umi narazu' no outa ni tsukite," in ibid., pp. 144-153. Also see Nakashima, pp. 329-375. Collections of Michizane's *waka* appear in many sources, among them Shimmura, pp. 371-377. Six of his most familiar *waka* are translated in Watson, *Japanese Literature in Chinese*, pp. 123-130.

14. Donald Keene, *Landscapes and Portraits: Appreciations of Japanese Culture* (New York, 1971), pp. 26-39.

CHAPTER 1: A FAMILY OF SCHOLARS

1. Professors of literature were also commonly chosen from the Ōe family and from three politically weak Fujiwara lineages, see Hisaki Yukio, *Daigakuryō to kodai jukyō* (1968), pp. 98-101, and 196-198; Momo Hiroyuki, *Jōdai gakusei no kenkyū* (1947), pp. 312-318. Genealogies of the Sugawara and other lesser court families are found in vol. 4 of *SB*, where many are "abridged" ("*ryaku*"). Although the Sugawara genealogy too is listed as abridged, it is in fact fuller than some of those not so described.

2. *SNK*, Jōwa 9/8/11; *MJ*, Ninju 3/6/2; *SJ*, Jōgan 12/3/30.

3. *SN*, Ten'ō 1/6/25. For a detailed and fully documented study of the Haji family, see my article, "The Origins of the Sugawara: A History of the Haji Family," *Monumenta Nipponica* 30.4:405-422 (Winter 1975). Published by permission of *Monumenta Nipponica*.

4. *SN*, Enrayku 4/12/23; *SNK*, Jōwa 9/10/17.

5. *SN*, Enryaku 4/12/23.

6. The basic primary sources on Kiyokimi's life are his obituary, in *SNK*, Jōwa 9/10/17; the outline of his official appointments in *KB*, Jōwa 6-9; and his genealogy, in *SB*, 4:57. Unless otherwise specified, data in this section come from these sources. Kiyokimi is discussed in Iyanaga Teizō, "Sugawara no Michizane no zenhansei," in *Nihon jimbutsushi taikei*, ed. Kawasaki Tsuneyuki (1963), vol. 1, *Kodai*, p. 151; and Inoue Kaoru, "Sugawara no Kiyokimi nidai," originally written in 1964 and reprinted in the author's *Kodaishi no gunzō* (1980), pp. 250-261. Kiyokimi's name can also be read "Kiyogimi," "Kiyotata," "Kiyotada," "Kiyotomo," or "Kiyodomo."

7. *SN*, Enryaku 9/12/1,30.

8. *Keikokushū*, in *Kōchū Nihon bungaku taikei* 24:358-368 (1936).

9. For a detailed and fully documented study of Kiyokimi's journey to China, see my article, "The Japanese Mission to China of 801-806," *Monumenta Nipponica* 37.1:1-28 (Spring 1982). Published by permission of *Monumenta Nipponica*.

10. *Nihon kiryaku, KT*, vol. 10, Enryaku 22/3/29.

11. *Ryōunshū*, pp. 1730-1733 in Kojima's meticulously annotated edition of that anthology, which appears as vol. 3 of his *Kokufū ankoku jidai*. My interpretation of the poem is based on Matsuura Tomohisa, "Pu-fun ch'iung-yao hsieh; Lai-chan lü-k'e chin," *Kambungaku kenkyū* 11:12-21 (January 1963). The second couplet of the poem is given a rather different but still plausible reading in Konishi Jin'ichi, "The Genesis of the *Kokinshū* Style," tr. Helen C. McCullough, *Harvard Journal of Asiatic Studies* 38.1:145 (June 1978). Konishi's article offers an excellent analysis of the influence of *kanshi* on Japanese poetry, but Matsuura's interpretation of this particular poem is convincing. The relation of the poem to native Japanese verse is discussed also in Kawaguchi Hisao, *Seiiki no tora: Heianchō hikaku bungaku ronshū* (1974), pp. 113-115. The scholar cited below is Hayashi

Gahō (1618–1680), whose *Honchō ichinin isshu* is quoted in *Kanshi, kambun, Hyōron,* vol. 11 of *Kenkyū shiryō Nihon koten bungaku,* ed. Ōsone Shōsuke, Kubota Jun, Hinotani Teruhiko, Horiuchi Hideaki, Miki Sumito, and Yamaguchi Akiho (1984), p. 14.

12. *NK,* Enryaku 24/7/25, 8/20.
13. *NK,* Daidō 1/1/28; *SNK,* Jōwa 8/2/7; Yoshimura Shigeki, *Kokushi seido* (1962), pp. 58–121.
14. *NK,* Daidō 1/1/28, 3/5/21, Kōnin 1/9/2, 1/9/19, 10/2. Chapters 15, 16, 18, and 19, covering the periods Daidō 1/10 to 3/3 and Daidō 4/4 to 5/8, a total of 33 months, are among those missing from *NK.* For a discussion of lieutenant governors serving as de facto governors, see Tokoro Isao, "Kokuga 'kanchō' no gainen to jittai," *Nihon rekishi* 264.85–106 (May 1970).
15. *Ruijū kokushi, KT* vol. 5–6, II, 115. Court histories held up a number of model provincial administrators as "good officials" (*ryōri*), Kiyokimi among them. Today the significance of these "good officials" in early Heian politics is a subject of debate among historians. For a critical summary of the debate, see Morita, *Seijishi,* pp. 5–8, 156–164.
16. Hayakawa, 387–410; Kitayama, *Heian kyō,* pp. 104–157; Sansom, pp. 99–128; G. Cameron Hurst, III, *Insei: Abdicated Sovereigns in the Politics of Late Heian Japan, 1086–1185* (New York, 1976), pp. 10–17.
17. Burton Watson, *Early Chinese Literature* (New York, 1962), pp. 202–230; Liu, pp. 106–114.
18. The original Chinese text and an English translation can be found in *Confucian Analects,* tr. James Legge, in *The Chinese Classics* (Oxford, 1892), p. 190. The translation quoted is original. The Japanese grading standards can be found in *Ryō no gige, KT* vol. 22, pp. 165–166, and *Ryō no shūge, KT* vol. 23–24, p. 645. For discussions of the Japanese acceptance of China's pragmatic theories of literature, see Ikeda Genta, "Heian shoki no okeru monjō no keikokuteki seikaku," in *Kammuchō no shomondai,* ed. Kodaigaku Kyōkai (Osaka, 1962), pp. 1–24. A revised version of the essay that covers a shorter period (the later decades of the ninth century are excluded) can be found in Ikeda's book *Nara Heian jidai no bunka to shūkyō* (Kyoto, 1977), pp. 139–165. A similar point of view is presented in Akiyama Ken, "Kodai kanjin no bungaku shisō," *Kokugo to kokubungaku* 32.4:30–39 (April 1955). Kojima Noriyuki has countered by pointing to Japanese references to China's aesthetic theories of literature in an essay, "Monjō wa keikoku no daigyō," which is included in his *Kokufū ankoku jidai* II, 724–770. For a valuable analysis in English of the influence of Chinese literary theories on Japan at a slightly later date, see John Timothy Wixted, "The Kokinshū Prefaces: Another Perspective," *Harvard Journal of Asiatic Studies* 43.1:215–238 (June 1983).
19. The reference appears in the introduction to *Keikokushū,* p. 233. Also see Liu, pp. 63–67; Ikeda Genta, "Heian shoki," pp. 3–6; Akiyama, "Bungaku shisō," pp. 31–32; Kojima Noriyuki, *Kokufū ankoku jidai* II, 724–770.
20. According to Kojima Noriyuki, the quoted phrase was first used in the 1930s (*Kokufū ankoku jidai,* II, 598–608). He adopted it for the title of his book. Also see Brower and Miner, pp. 79–186.
21. For discussions of early Japan's anthologies of literature in Chinese, see Kanda Hideo, "Kambungaku," in *Shimpan Nihon bungakushi 1: Jōdai,* ed. Hisamatsu Sen'ichi (1971), pp. 652–662; Okada Masayuki, *Nihon kambungaku shi* (1954), pp. 72–125; Yamagishi Tokuhei, *Nihon kambungaku kenkyū,* vol. 1 of *Yamagishi Tokuhei chosakushū* (1972), pp. 72–201; Ozawa Masao, "Kambungaku," in *Shimpan Nihon bungakushi 2: Chūko,* ed. Hisamatsu Sen'ichi (1971), pp. 115–

125; Matsuura Sadatoshi, "Chokusen sanshū kenkyū oboegaki," *Kokugo to kokubungaku* 34.10:21-29 (October 1957); Kawaguchi, *Kambungakushi*, pp. 17-33; Konishi, "Kambungaku," pp. 888-900. Representative poems from these anthologies are translated in Watson, *Japanese Literature in Chinese*, pp. 17-26, 40-51.

22. KBKK, item 674; *Honchō shojaku mokuroku*, in *Honchō shojaku mokuroku kōshō*, ed. Wada Hidematsu (1940), pp. 386-389.

23. The quotation comes from an essay on literature, "Lun wen," the only extant section of a longer work, *Tien-lun*, by Ts'ao P'i (A.D. 187-226, r. 220-226 as Emperor Wen of the Wei dynasty) that appears in *Wen-hsuan*, ed., Obi Kōichi, vols. 26-32 of *Zenshaku kambun taikei* (1974-1976) VI, 774-782. The essay has been translated into English most recently by Donald Holzman in his article, "Literary Criticism in China in the Third Century A.D.," *Asiatische Studien/ Etudes Asiatiques* 28.2:128-131 (1974). It is quoted in the introduction to the *Ryōunshū*, pp. 1326-1328.

24. *Keikokushū*, pp. 247-248. A detailed analysis appears in Kojima Noriyuki, *Jōdai Nihon bungaku to Chūgoku bungaku* (1965), III, 1768-1774.

25. *Wen-hsuan*, II, 430-439. The Chinese *fu* has been translated by Douglass Alan White as a Harvard College honors thesis, "Ch'eng-kung Sui's 'Poetic Essay on Whistling: The *Hsaio-fu*'" (1964). The term translated as "whistling" (*hsiao*) could refer to various nonverbal human sounds, including also humming, howling, hissing, screaming, etc. Although its precise meaning is not altogether clear, Kiyokimi certainly seems to be referring to whistling rather than to the word's other meanings. For discussions of "whistling," see Aoki Masaru, "Shō no rekishi to jigi no hensen," originally pub. 1957 and reprinted in *Aoki Masaru zenshū* vol. 8 (1971), pp. 161-168; Sawada Mizuho, "Shō no genryū," *Tōhō shūkyō* 44:1-13 (October 1974); E. D. Edwards, "Principles of Whistling—*Hsiao Chih*—Anonymous," *Bulletin of the School of Oriental and African Studies* 20:217-229 (1957); Minakata Kumakusa, "The Art of Whistling," (1925; reprinted in *Minakata Kumakusa zenshū*, 1973), 10:349-351; and Donald Holzman, *Politics and Poetry: The Life and Works of Juan Chi (A.D. 210-263)* (Cambridge, Eng., 1976), pp. 149-152.

26. *Bunka shūreishū*, in NKBT vol. 69, Kojima Norikyuki ed. (1964), pp. 251-252. The other poems in the group are by Yoshimine no Yasuyo, Asano no Katori, and Fujiwara no Yoshio. Japanese interest in Wang Chao-chün is discussed in Pollack, pp. 365-368.

27. For reform of rituals and changing the names of the gates, see *Nihon kiryaku*, Kōnin 9/3/23, 4/26; Inoue Kaoru, *Kodaishi*, pp. 251-253 and *Nihon kodai no seiji to shūkyō* (1961), pp. 3-26; Saeki Arikiyo, *Shinsen shōjiroku no kenkyū: kenkyūhen* (1963), pp. 437-474. For *Wine Etiquette*, see *Honchō shojaku mokuroku*, p. 301. Excerpts from it are preserved in *Gōdanshō*, the best edition of which is *Kohonkei Gōdanshō chūkai*, ed. Gōdanshō Kenkyūkai (1978), see pp. 281-282; and also in *Seikyūki*, in 2 vols., *Zōtei kojitsu sōsho* vols. 37, 40 (1930), II, 58-59. The list of necessary references appears in *Seikyūki*, II, 133.

28. SNK, Jōwa 2/7/14, 3/2/7.

29. This anecdote appears in Kiyokimi's SNK obituary. Whether in deference to Kiyokimi or not, the rank of mayors was indeed raised about the time of his appointment; see *Ruijū sandai kyaku*, KT, vol. 25 (1936), p. 222.

30. *Ryō no gige*, pp. 1-4.

31. The principal source of data on Yoshinushi is his obituary, MJ, Ninju 2/11/7. One of his *kanshi* is preserved in *Keikokushū*, p. 335. For his journey to China, see SNK, Jōwa 3/7/17, 6/8/25, 9/28; and *Ennin's Diary: The Record of a Pilgrimage*

to China in Search of the Law, tr. Edwin O. Reischauer (New York, 1955), pp. 42, 95.

32. The principal sources of information on Koreyoshi are his obituary, SJ, Gangyō 4/8/30, the outline of his career in KB, Jōgan 14 to Gangyō 4, and SB, IV, 58. Data come from these sources unless otherwise noted. Koreyoshi's career is discussed in Hayashi Rokurō's chapter, "Ōe no Otondo to Sugawara no Koreyoshi: Jōganki no seikai to gakkai," in his Jōdai seiji shakai no kenkyū (1969), pp. 482–509. Kawaguchi also devotes a chapter to Koreyoshi in Kambungakushi, pp. 111–122.

33. SNK, Jōwa 11/1/7.

34. SNK, Jōwa 13/2/29, 14/4/10; Kajō 2/1/3; MJ, Kajō 3/4/17, 10/1; Ninju 3/1/16; Saikō 3/2/8; Tennan 1/5/8, 2/1/10, 5/21; SJ, Tennan 2/9/23; Jōgan 5/2/10, 6/1/16, 11/4/13, 12/1/25, 17/4/25, 18/5/4. In the introduction to a group of poems, Koreyoshi proudly noted that he held the same office as Po Chü-i, Honchō monzui, in Honchō monzui chūshaku, ed. Kakimura Shigematsu (1968) II, 228–231. Kawaguchi suggests that this appointment was made with the Chinese poet in mind, Kambungakushi, pp. 120–121.

35. SJ, Jōgan 12/2/14, 14/8/25; Gangyō 3/11/25.

36. The quotation comes from Koreyoshi's SJ obituary. Also see Hayashi, pp. 494–502; Iyanaga, "Zenhansei," p. 154.

37. MJ, Saikō 1/10/20; Tennan 2/8/24; SJ, Tennan 2/9/2, 11/5; Jōgan 2/intercalary 10/23, 3/3/14 (where the text of Koreyoshi's prayer can be found), 18/5/4, 10/5; Gangyō 1/2/24. A rubbing of Koreyoshi's bell inscription is reproduced in Kokyō ibun, ed. Yamada Takao and Katori Hozuma (1965), pp. 71–73. Koreyoshi's piety is also attested to in Michizane's prayer for his parents' salvation, KBKK, item 650.

38. SNK, Jōwa 11/8/5. For Yoshitada, see his obituary, SJ, Jōgan 12/2/19. His interest in Taoism and the occult is described in Kawaguchi, Kambungakushi, pp. 156–166. Heian views of ghosts, etc. are found in Ichiro Hori, Folk Religion in Japan (Chicago, 1968), pp. 40–44, 68–81, 111–127.

39. Sansom uses the phrase "rule of taste," p. 178. Also see Kitayama, Heian kyō, pp. 208–241; Hayakawa, Ritsuryō kokka, pp. 420–433; Sakamoto Tarō, "Fujiwara no Yoshifusa to Mototsune," in Rekishi to jimbutsu, ed. Nihon Rekishi Gakkai (1964), pp. 163–187.

40. Ikeda Genta, "Heian shoki," pp. 18–22; Akiyama, "Bungaku shisō," pp. 30–35. Yoshifusa was not completely anti-intellectual, and poetic gatherings continued while he was in power (Kawaguchi, Kambungakushi, pp. 89–102), although Ikeda argues that they had become perfunctory. Also during these years, many former university students did achieve high office, but these were men who had been students when Saga was in power and Confucian studies were being more actively encouraged. Hayashi, Seiji shakai, pp. 485–488.

41. Ruijū kudaishō, ZGR XIIa, p. 16. This anthology contains another poem (pp. 30–31) on a similar theme that might be by Koreyoshi, although only the first character of the name "Sugawara" remains to identify the author.

42. Ruijū kudaishō, pp. 3–4.

43. The Platform Sutra of the Sixth Patriarch, tr. Philip B. Yampolsky (New York, 1967). The translation appears on pp. 129–132; the original Chinese, on p. 4 of the appendix. Published with permission of Columbia University Press.

44. For Taoism in Heian Japan, see Ikeda, Bunka to shūkyō, pp. 208–211; for Zen, see Martin Collcutt, Five Mountains: The Rinzai Zen Monastic Institution in Medieval Japan (Cambridge, Mass., 1981), pp. 3–4, 25–36; and Heinrich Dumoulin, A History of Zen Buddhism, tr. Paul Peachey (New York, 1963), pp. 137–139.

A copy of the sutra cited by Koreyoshi was among the works brought back to Japan in 847 by Ennin, see *Nittō shingu shōgyō mokuroku,* in *Taishō shinshū daizōkyō* vol. 60 (1928), p. 1083b.

45. *KBKK,* item 674; *Honchō shojaku,* pp. 386–389; Kawaguchi, *Kambungakushi,* pp. 120–121.

46. *MJ,* Ninju 3/10/22; Nomura Tadao, *Kanjinsei ron* (1975), pp. 194–211; Hisaki, pp. 96–98; Momo, pp. 91–92; Hayashi, pp. 502–503.

47. Wada states that the work was named *Tōgū setsuin* because Koreyoshi compiled it when he was tutor to the crown prince, "tōgū no gakushi." (*Honchō shojaku,* pp. 366–368). However, according to an early commentary, the title derives from the fact that the character "*tō*" is the first rhyme and "*gū*" the first "sound" in the traditional Chinese system of arranging characters phonetically (quoted in Kawase Kazuma, *Kojisho no kenkyū* [1955], pp. 55–59). For a variety of reasons, the latter theory seems more probable (Kawaguchi, *Kambungakushi,* p. 117).

48. Surviving fragments are collected in Wada Hidematsu, *Kokusho itsubun* (1940), p. 273 and addenda, p. 19. References to the dictionary appear in *Taiki* (the diary of Fujiwara no Yorinaga for the years 1136–1155), in *Shiryō taisei,* vol. 23 (1982), Ten'yō 1/7/25; *Kanchūki* (the diary of Fujiwara no Kanenaka for the years 1268–1300) in *Shiryō taisei,* vol. 35 (1982), Kenji 2/7/25; and *Gōdanshō,* pp. 11, 141–143, 238. Also see Kawaguchi, *Kambungakushi,* pp. 113–118.

49. *Honchō shojaku,* pp. 351–352, 385, 390; *Honchō reisō,* in *GR* vol. 6, p. 209; *Midō kampaku ki* in *Dai Nihon kokiroku* (1952) I, 257; Hayashi, p. 499; Kawaguchi, *Kambungakushi,* pp. 119–120, in which Kawaguchi suggests an alternate meaning of the title of Koreyoshi's third anthology.

50. *SJ,* Jōgan 11/4/13, 13/5/25; *MJ,* "Jo" (Introduction); *KBKK,* item 554; Hayashi, p. 498; Sakamoto Tarō, *Rikkokushi* (1970), pp. 276–283.

51. *KBKK,* item 650, and *KB,* Kampyō 5 (893); *Kitano Tenjin goden,* in *Kitano,* p. 3; *Kanke godenki* in ibid., p. 84 (where the surname of Michizane's mother is given as "Ōtomo," the family's ancient name). Tsunoda Bun'ei has speculated that Michizane's mother might be Tomo no Tomoko (Yūshi), but offers no evidence to support that identification (*Ōchō no eizō: Heian jidaishi no kenkyū* [1970], p. 258). Hers seems to be the only surviving name of a woman from the Tomo family who would have been about the right age to have given birth to Michizane, but there is no direct evidence connecting the two. Heian marriage customs are described in William H. McCullough, "Japanese Marriage Institutions in the Heian Period," *Harvard Journal of Asiatic Studies* 27:103–167 (1967).

52. For material on Tomo no Yoshio, see *KB,* Jōwa 15 - Jōgan 8; *SJ,* Jōgan 8/9/22; and Saeki Arikiyo, *Tomo no Yoshio,* vol. 156 of *Jimbutsu sōsho* (1970). His ancestors, the Ōtomo, are discussed in Paula Doe, *A Warbler's Song in the Dusk: The Life and Work of Ōtomo no Yakamochi (718–785)* (Berkeley, 1982). For Ki no Natsui's connection with the Sugawara, see Iyanaga Teizō, "'Shunjitsu kakei' no shi: Ōtemmon no hen to Michizane o torimaku hitobito," *Shintei zōho kokushi taikei geppō* 25:4–5 (July 1965).

53. *KBKK,* item 21.

54. This story appears, with only minor variations, in many early accounts of Michizane's life. The version translated is thought to be the earliest. It appears as *Tenjin kegenki* in *Kitano,* p. 81. For a detailed textual study, see Makabe Toshinobu, "*Tenjin engi* ni okeru Michizane kegen dan no seiritsu," *Kokugakuin zasshi* 69.6:44–55 (July 1968).

55. This story, from an unidentified source, is quoted in Mashimo Goichi, *Sugawara no Michizane seitanchi no kenkyū* (1972), p. 14. Its relatively modern language suggests a late date.

56. *KBKK*, item 526; *Shūgaishō*, in *Kojitsu sōsho* vol. 11 (1982), pp. 401-402; Tsunoda Bun'ei, *Murasaki Shikibu to sono jidai* (1966), pp. 221-229. The locations in modern Kyoto of the three sites are shown on a map in the unpaginated appendix to Takatori.

57. *KBKK*, items 82, 87, 96, 98; *Kitano Tenjin goden*, p. 106; *Kanke godenki*, p. 503; *KB*, Kampyō 5 (893); Iyanaga, "Zenhansei," p. 156; Sakamoto Tarō, *Sugawara no Michizane*, p. 18.

58. *SNK*, Jōwa 5/11/29; 6/3/11; *SJ*, Jōgan 1/11/20, 3/4/25; Gangyō 8/2/26; Tsunoda, *Murasaki Shikibu*, pp. 219-229. For general discussions of court ladies, see Yokoo Yutaka, *Heian jidai no kōkyū seikatsu* (1976), pp. 6-116; *Kōkyū no subete*, a special issue of *Kokubungaku*, 25.13 (October 1980); Tsunoda Bun'ei, *Nihon no kōkyū* (1973); and *Eiga Monogatari*, tr. McCullough and McCullough, II, 818-822.

59. *KBKK*, items 521, 650.

60. The quotation appears in Koreyoshi's obituary in *SJ*. Also see *KBKK*, item 650.

61. There are two theories on the origin of this temple. The one presented here is based on data from the prayer Michizane wrote one year after his father's death (*KBKK*, item 650), and is supported in *Shūgaishō* (p. 438). The evidence, however, is ambiguous. In his prayer, Michizane seems to say that construction of the temple began in 879, whereas the inscription he wrote for the temple's bell is dated 875. The prayer could be referring to the construction of a new building at a temple Koreyoshi had established some years earlier. The alternate theory is that Kiyokimi, with Saichō's cooperation, founded the temple after their return from China. This version is based on Sugawara family genealogies from the fourteenth century that note that the annual ceremony at the temple was begun by Kiyokimi (*Sugawara shi keizu*, in *ZGR* vol. 7b [1932], pp. 1, 49-50).

CHAPTER 2: STUDENT YEARS

1. *Shūishū*, no. 473. Sakamoto Tarō has questioned the authenticity of this poem, although he acknowledges that his evidence is far from conclusive ("Sugawara no Michizane no shōgai," in *Michizane to Dazaifu*, I, 6-7). For Michizane's coming of age, see *KBKK*, item 674. Chronologies of his life can be found in most books about him; the best is Fujino Hideko, "Sugawara no Michizane nempyō," in *Michizane to Dazaifu*, II, 357-378. She gives sources for virtually all her entries. For the cassia tree metaphor, see Nakashima, p. 92.

2. John W. Hall, *Japan from Prehistory to Modern Times*, (New York, 1970), p. 51. Descriptions of early Japan's education and examination systems can be found in Sansom, pp. 474-476; and Spaulding, pp. 9-17. Both tend to stress the aristocratic nature of the university and the limited function of the examinations. Such views are also common among Japanese scholars; see, for example, Hisaki, p. 5; and Nomura, *Kanjinsei*, pp. 249-307.

3. Unless otherwise noted, material in this section is based on data from the *ritsuryō* codes. Because the original Taihō Codes are lost, those referred to are actually the Yōrō Civil Codes (*Yōrō ryō*), compiled in 718 and promulgated in 757. The regulations concerning the education and examination systems are thought to be virtually identical in the two codes (Takikawa Seijirō, *Ritsuryō no kenkyū* [1966], pp. 436, 485-488, 501-502). The texts of the Yōrō Civil Codes are preserved in two later commentaries, *Ryō no gige* and *Ryō no shūge*. The best modern annotated editions of the codes are *Ritsuryō*, Inoue Mitsusada, Seki Akira, Tsuchida Naoshige, and Aoki Kazuo ed., vol. 3 of *Nihon shisō taikei* (1976) and Aida Hanji, *Chūkai Yōrō ryō* (1964). Material on the education and examination

systems is found in the "Personnel Code" (*Shikiin ryō*), "Education Code" (*Gaku ryō*), and "Evaluation Code" (*Kōka ryō*). The Education Code has been translated by James Crump as an appendix to his " 'Borrowed' T'ang Titles and Offices in the Yōrō Codes," in *Occasional Papers: Center for Japanese Studies* (Ann Arbor, 1952), pp. 51-52.

4. *NS*, Ōjin 15/8/6; Hisaki, pp. 6-20; Momo, pp. 7-9.

5. Hisaki, p. 28; Taga Akigorō, *Tōdai kyōikushi no kenkyū* (1953), pp. 141-143.

6. Hisaki, p. 17; Momo, pp. 42-45. The names of three pre-Heian professors of phonetics survive—all Chinese immigrants, the only ones known to have held posts at the university. By the Heian period, native Japanese were teaching phonetics.

7. *Ryō no gige*, p. 131; *Ryō no shūge*, p. 451. Aida explains that this was "educational," not criminal, punishment (*Yōrō ryō*, p. 597).

8. As early as 706, the government seems to have required that sons of the highest ranking officials take civil service examinations, although the exact significance of this regulation is not clear (Nomura, *Kanjinsei*, pp. 278-296). The first order that they attend the university was issued in 739, and similar orders were also issued in the early ninth century (Hisaki, pp. 55-56, 89-98; Momo, pp. 32-33, 39, 51-55).

9. *SN*, Tempyō 2/3/27; *Ryō no shūge*, p. 80. Lists of all known Nara and early Heian students' names can be found in Momo, pp. 46-47, 64-67, 81-86, 92-97, 111-112, 117. For the family background of literature students, see Hisaki, pp. 54, 95.

10. For Makibi, see *Nihon kodai jimmei jiten*, ed. Takeuchi Rizō, Yamada Hideo, and Hirano Kunio (1958-1977) IV, 904-908, where all primary sources on him are summarized in an entry under his original surname, "Shimotsumichi." For Yoshitada, see chapter one, note 38, and Abe Takeshi, *Heian zenki seijishi*, pp. 93-104.

11. Hisaki, pp. 155-166; Momo, pp. 407-448.

12. The proposed sample question is found in *Ryō no shūge*, p. 645. Actual examination questions and answers are preserved in a variety of literary anthologies, including the *Keikokushū, Toshi bunshū, Kanke bunsō, Honchō monzui*, etc. I have not been able to locate a listing of all surviving examples.

13. The Rikkokushi (Six National Histories) contain only one clear reference to the classics examination (*SNK*, Jōwa 12/2/12), one to the *shinshi* examination (*MJ*, Ninju 2/2/10), and none to the law examination, although some references to examinations do not clearly state the nature of the examination in question. An additional evaluation of a *shinshi* examination can be found in *Toshi bunshū, GR* VI p. 338. Kakimura Shigematsu has suggested that 12 of the 13 examination papers in the *Keikokushū* are in fact for the *shinshi* examination (*Jōdai Nihon kambungakushi* [1947], pp. 102-103), but his evidence for this conclusion is not convincing.

14. The Chinese and Japanese institutions are compared in Taga, pp. 140-159; and Hisaki, pp. 23-39. The original T'ang codes have been largely reconstructed by Niida Noboru in *Tō rei shūi* (1964). Relevant material is found in the sections corresponding to those in the Japanese codes cited in note 3 above. Crump has translated the T'ang education code in "T'ang Titles," pp. 51-56. Robert des Rotours has translated into French relevant sections from the *Hsin T'ang-shu*. They are found in his *Le Traité des Examens* (Paris, 1932), pp. 127-205; and *Traité des Fonctionnaires et Traité de l'Armée* (1947), I, 442-458. For general discussions of T'ang society, see the works cited in note 10 to the introduction.

15. The five factors influencing Japanese modifications of T'ang institutions are suggested by Crump, p. 40. Also see Hisaki, pp. 20-26.

16. *Honchō monzui,* I, 212-218; Hisaki, pp. 93-96.
17. Maki Hidematsu, "Shiin kō," *Ōsaka Shidai hōgaku zasshi* 2.1:106-113 (January 1955).
18. Hall, p. 51.
19. Hisaki, pp. 50-62; Momo, pp. 24-38.
20. Hisaki, pp. 45-46, 64-66; Momo, pp. 24-38.
21. Lands were first granted to professors in 773, although the granting of office fields was not formalized until 791. Other than professors, the lowest-ranking officials were middle counselors, who held the junior third rank; professors rarely exceeded the junior fifth rank. See Hisaki, pp. 63-75; Momo, pp. 40-41, 55-60.
22. *Ruijū sandai kyaku,* p. 158; *Ryō no shūge,* p. 80; *SN,* Tempyō 2/3/27.
23. Taga, p. 159; Hisaki, p. 46; Momo, p. 27.
24. Hisaki, pp. 46-49; Momo, pp. 26-27, 79; Sakamoto Tarō, *Sugawara no Michizane,* p. 133.
25. *SN,* Hōki 3/4/20; 11/2/27; *Ruijū sandai kyaku,* p. 223.
26. Hisaki, pp. 89-98; Momo, pp. 79-111.
27. Momo lists the names of only 22 students of classics from the early Heian period in contrast to 67 students of literature, despite the fact that the university was supposed to have at least ten times as many students in classics as in literature (*Jōdai gakusei,* pp. 63-67, 81-86). This discrepancy probably results from the fact that most surviving data are from biographies in such sources as the Rikkokushi and *KB,* which provided information only on the highest-ranking officials. Most of the university's students, their names now lost, presumably studied classics and went on to careers as minor court functionaries.
28. *Ruijū sandai kyaku,* p. 223; Hisaki, pp. 59, 79-80; Momo, pp. 31, 105-109.
29. *KBKK,* items 129-138.
30. *KB,* Gangyō 8. *KB* lists, on an annual basis, the names of all senior nobles (*kugyō*). Seventeen men are listed for the year 884. In addition to the Fujiwara and Minamoto, there are two princes and Ariwara no Yukihira who, like the Minamoto, was the descendant of an emperor. Significantly, the one remaining high official is Tachibana no Hiromi, a scholar and former professor of literature, who will be discussed later. The Tachibana too claimed descent from an emperor, Bidatsu (r. 572-582), but by the ninth century they were a noble though not powerful court family.
31. *Gōdanshō* contains many stories of quarrels among early Heian scholars, particularly in its chapters (*kan*) 3 and 5. Also see Hisaki, pp. 98-101; Momo, pp. 126-132; Kawaguchi, *Kambungakushi,* pp. 126-130; and Akiyama Ken, "Sugawara no Michizane ron no danshō," *Kokugo to kokubungaku* 34.10:37-45 (October 1957); and "Sugawara no Michizane no shijin keisei," in *Michizane to Dazaifu,* I, 181-202. The suggestions of ideological conflict appears in Ōsone Shōsuke, "Sugawara no Michizane: shijin to kōju," *Nihon bungaku* 22.9:1-4 (September 1973); and Gotō Akio, "Bunjin sōkei: Michizane no shūhen," a chapter in his *Heianchō kambungaku ronkō* (1981), pp. 79-93. Michizane's commitment to Confucian scholarship and poetry is expressed in *KBKK,* items 38, 50, 58, 65, 76, 87, 98, 179, 243, 274, 526, 629, etc.
32. A well-known although somewhat later example is Minamoto no Shitagō (911-983) who, despite his scholarly and literary reputation, was not rewarded with appropriate offices. A poem lamenting his lack of suitable employment can be found in Watson, *Japanese Literature in Chinese,* pp. 65-67. Of the many men who were known for their literary abilities in the late ninth century (a list can be found in Kawaguchi, *Kambungakushi,* pp. 177-178), only a few came from

the more powerful families and held high office; most were from less influential families and served in modest posts at court or in the provinces.

33. Takeuchi Rizō, *Ritsuryōsei*, II, 284-304, 371-391; Murai, *Heian kizoku*, pp. 16-18; Kitayama Shigeo, "Sekkan seiji," in *Iwanami kōza Nihon rekishi 4: kodai 4* (1967), pp. 3-14.

34. *KBKK*, items 18, 24, 44, 72, 89, 103, 113, 143, 350, 351, 357, 459; Iyanaga Teizō, "Ninna ninen no naien," in *Nihon kodaishi ronshū*, ed. Sakamoto Tarō Hakase Kanreki Kinenkai (1962), II, 552-563. Despite this article's narrow-sounding title (literally, "The palace banquet in the second year of the Ninna era"), it is in fact a valuable study of the internal workings of the court bureaucracy. Tsurayuki described his return journey to the capital in *Tosa nikki*, the earliest of Japanese literary diaries.

35. Hisaki, 196-204; Momo, pp. 196-199, 340-352. Kobayashi Yoshinori gives a detailed description of the reading systems used by the professorial families, although he argues that the efforts by those families to keep their traditions secret were probably not very effective (*Heian Kamakura jidai ni okeru kanseki kundoku no kokugoshiteki kenkyū*, [1967], 1077-1304. For a study of the university that focuses on it in the tenth century, see Peter Michael Wetzler, "Yoshishige no Yasutane: Lineage, Learning, Office, and Amida's Pure Land," PhD dissertation, University of California, Berkeley (1977), pp. 8-59.

36. *Kanke den* in *Kitanoshi*, II, 557-558 (this relatively late source should not be confused with *Kitano Tenjin goden*, which is also commonly referred to as *Kanke den*); Hisaki, pp. 215-216; Ogata Hiroyasu, *Nihon kyōiku tsūshi* (1960), p. 50.

37. *Ruijū fusenshō*, in *KT*, XXVII, 250.

38. *Honchō monzui*, I, 515-524; *Keirin ihōshō*, in *GR*, XXI, p. 573; Iwahashi Koyata, *Jōdai kanri seido no kenkyū* (1964), pp. 53-54; Hisaki, pp. 183-193.

39. *Kitano Tenjin goden*, p. 5; Hisaki, p. 176; Momo, p. 465.

40. *KBKK*, items 82, 117; Momo, pp. 392-397; Nakashima, pp. 86-89.

41. *KBKK*, item 1. A discussion of this poem, plus a curious translation apparently by Ezra Pound, appear in an appendix to Ernest Fenollosa's classic essay *The Chinese Character as a Medium for Poetry*, edited by Pound (1936; reprinted in San Francisco, n.d., pp. 34-37). Fenollosa surely knew who wrote the poem, but in the published version of his essay no mention is made of the poem's authorship, and most readers probably have taken it to be the work of a Chinese poet rather than that of an eleven-year-old Japanese boy writing in Chinese.

42. Kawaguchi Hisao and Wakabayashi Tsutomu, *Kanke bunsō Kanke kōshū shiku sōsakuin* (1978). Michizane's purported love for the plum was first questioned in Naganuma Kenkai's classic study, "Temman Tenjin shinkō no hensen," pt. 2, *Shirin* 4.3:115-120 (July 1919). For a more positive view, see Burton Watson, "Michizane and the Plums," *Japan Quarterly* 11.2:217-220 (April-June 1964).

43. *KBKK*, item 2; *Wakan rōeishū, NKBT* vol. 73, ed. Kawaguchi Hisao, p. 384.

44. Primary sources on Tadaomi are gathered in *DNS* I.1. The usual place for such "biographies" is at the date of an individual's death; however, since only the year of Tadaomi's death is known, the material is placed at the end of that year, Kampyō 3 (pp. 901-914). A selection of his poetry is preserved as *Denshi kashū* (*GR* vol. 6, pp. 340-361). Kimpara Tadashi analyzes Tadaomi's *kanshi* and attempts to reconstruct his genealogy and career based on the scanty evidence available in a series of articles reprinted in his *Heianchō kanshibun no kenkyū* (Fukuoka, 1981), pp. 141-257. Tadaomi's writings are also discussed in Kawaguchi, *Kambungakushi*, pp. 183-189. Also see *SJ*, Gangyō 3/1/7, Ninna 3/1/7; *KB*, Kampyō 2, 5; *SB* I, 45.

45. *Denshi kashū*, p. 340; Yamagishi, pp. 201–202. Kawaguchi tries to put the matter in a more positive light, admiring Tadaomi's "simple clarity," (*Kambungakushi*, p. 189).
46. *KBKK*, item 6. Also see items, 4, 5, and 7.
47. *KBKK*, items 522, 197; *Kitano Tenjin goden*, p. 3; *Kanke godenki*, p. 84; *KB* erroneously notes that he entered the university in the spring (Kampyō 5).
48. *Kitano Tenjin goden*, p. 3; Sakamoto Tarō, *Sugawara no Michizane*, pp. 24–25.
49. *KBKK*, items 8, 197; *SJ*, Jōgan 4/9/9. For a comprehensive study of annual celebrations in the Heian court, see Yamanaka Yutaka, *Heianchō no nenjū gyōji* (1972). Their importation from China and influence on Japanese literature are discussed by Mushakōji Minoru in two chapters, "Tōka no arashi," and "Shinsen'en no bun'yū," that appeared in *Kyūtei saron to saijo*, ed. Yamanaka Yutaka and Akiyama Ken, vol. 3 of *Nihon bungaku no rekishi* (1967), pp. 36–69. Chinese literary precedents for this particular festival are analyzed in A. R. Davis, "The Double Ninth Festival in Chinese Poetry: A Study of Variations upon a Theme," in *Wen-lin: Studies in the Chinese Humanities*, ed. Chow Tse-tung (Madison, 1968), pp. 45–64. For the ceremonies under Yoshifusa, see Ikeda, "Heian shoki," pp. 18–22.
50. Of 9 students of literature mentioned in *SJ* whose status can be determined, 6 held rank (Jōgan 2/11/16, 3/9/26, 14/4/16, 15/5/29, 18/5/27; Gangyō 1/12/27, 4/1/26, 7/4/2; Ninna 3/1/7). The 2 students whom Michizane recommended for promotion to graduate student both already held rank (*KBKK*, items 634, 635). There is no evidence, however, that Michizane held rank until he became a graduate student.
51. *KBKK*, item 14. Also see, Iyanaga Teizō, "Kodai no sekiten ni tsuite," in *Zoku Nihon kodaishi ronshū*, ed. Sakamoto Tarō Hakase Koki Kinenkai (1972) III, 353–467; Kawaguchi, *Kambungakushi*, pp. 130–134.
52. *KBKK*, item 115; *Fusōshū*, GR vol. 6, 203; *Honchō monzui*, I, 949–953; *Chōya gunsai*, KT vol. 29, 237–238; Momo, pp. 153–170. Hisaki argues for the dormitory's having earlier origins (*Daigakuryō*, pp. 84–87). As he points out, the evidence for Kiyokimi's role is not conclusive; however, his own case is not completely convincing either.
53. *KBKK*, items 9, 43. *KB* (Jōgan 14) and *SB* (4:58) refer to Koreyoshi's lectures on the *History of the Han Dynasty*; however, Michizane's poem, written the year when the other sources agree Koreyoshi's lectures ended, is clearly on the *History of the Later Han* and is the more reliable source.
54. *Ryō no gige*, pp. 130–131; *Ryō no shūge*, pp. 449–450.
55. *Gengo geijutsu no hana hiraku*, vol. 3 of *Nihongo no rekishi*, ed. Doi Tadao (1964), pp. 16–18.
56. *KBKK*, items 128, 153–157, 431; Watson, *Japanese Literature in Chinese*, pp. 77–78; Konishi, "Kambungaku," pp. 889–891.
57. *KBKK*, item 31.
58. *KBKK*, item 237. The translation quoted is by Watson, from *Japanese Literature in Chinese*, p. 99. Published with the permission of Columbia University Press.
59. *Kitano Tenjin goden*, p. 3; *Kanke godenki*, p. 84; *KB*, Kampyō 5.
60. *KBKK*, item 634. Also see Hisaki, pp. 52, 191; Tokoro Isao, "Miyoshi no Kiyoyuki no zenhansei," *Geirin* 17.5+6:177 (December 1966).
61. Koreyoshi apparently served as professor until the eleventh day of the second month, 867, when two new professors were appointed (*SJ*, Jōgan 9/2/11). Although *KB* does not give a precise date, it corroborates this by noting that Koreyoshi was a professor until 867 (Jōgan 14).

62. *Kitano Tenjin den,* p. 3; *Kanke godenki,* p. 84; *KB,* Kampyō 5; *SB,* IV, 58; Iyanaga, "Zenhansei," p. 161.
63. *KBKK,* item 292. The term translated as "wife and children" could also mean simply "wife." The correct translation would depend on whether Michizane had children as a graduate student. His oldest son was not born until some years later, but since he is said to have had 23 children, perhaps he already had a few daughters.
64. *KBKK,* item 526. This work has been translated by Watson, *Japanese Literature in Chinese,* pp. 104-106; the translation here is my own.
65. *KBKK,* item 25.
66. *KBKK,* item 19. Also see items 32, 37, 42, and 45.
67. *SJ,* Jōgan 8/1/12; *Ruijū sandai kyaku,* pp. 593-594; *KBKK,* item 49 (introduction translated by Watson, *Japanese Literature in Chinese,* pp. 83-84); *Denshi kashū,* p. 344. Michizane's drinking habits have received a surprising amount of scholarly attention. Sakamoto Tarō wrote an essay on the topic, "Kankō to sake," that was reprinted in a book by the same name ([1964], pp. 3-10). The subject is also discussed in Wakamori Tarō, *Sake ga kataru Nihonshi* (1971), pp. 57-60, and "Sugawara no Michizane," in *Ōchō no bunka,* vol. 3 of *Jimbutsu Nihon no rekishi* (1976), pp. 146-148; and Murai, *Heian kizoku,* pp. 11-13.
68. *KBKK,* item 35.
69. *KBKK,* item 175. Also see an unnumbered introduction on p. 240 and items 174, 176-178, 386-390. For information on Kanaoka, see *Dai Nihon shoga meika taikan,* ed. Araki Tadashi (1934), I, 1068-1073.
70. Michizane's traditional reputation as an artist is described—rather uncritically—in Inoue Tetsujirō, pp. 104-106, 172-174. For more skeptical analyses of his calligraphy, see Sakamoto Tarō, *Sugawara no Michizane,* p. 164; Haruna Yoshishige, *Jōdai nōsho den* (1972), pp. 153-166; Wada Hidematsu, "Sugawara no Michizane no hisseki ni tsuite," *Kokka* 32.1:3-5, 32.2:39-45 (July and August 1921).
71. *KBKK,* item 38. This poem has also been translated by Watson, *Japanese Literature in Chinese,* p. 85.
72. *KBKK,* items 566-567; *Kanke godenki,* p. 84; *KB,* Kampyō 5. A chart with typical ages of examination candidates can be found in Tokoro, "Kiyoyuki no zenhansei," p. 180. The length of graduate study is discussed in Hisaki, p. 108.
73. Private secretaries (*naiki,* literally "inner secretaries") were employed in the Ministry of Central Affairs and drafted documents for the emperor. They are not to be confused with secretaries (*geki,* literally "outer secretaries") who were under the Council of State and were responsible for both composing documents for the Council and revising those drafted by the private secretaries. Those posts of "inner" and "outer" secretary were considered very important and were given only to men with considerable literary ability.
74. Brief biographies of Yoshika can be found in Kawaguchi, *Kambungakushi,* pp. 162-177, and *Honchō monzui,* vol. 2, appendix, pp. 104-109. Three of the original six chapters of his collected works, *Toshi bunshū,* survive. They primarily contain official documents, including those relating to various examinations. A few of his literary works survive in other collections, including one *waka* in the *Kokinshū* (no. 466).
75. This story is found in the earliest biography of Michizane, *Kitano Tenjin goden* (p. 3), and became a standard element in the many versions of *Kitano Tenjin engi,* the most familiar traditional account of his life; see for example the oldest surviving text, *Tenjinki,* in *Kitano,* pp. 105-106. The version presented combines elements from both sources.
76. *KBKK,* item 484 (translated in chapter 7); Iyanaga, "Michizane no zenhansei,"

p. 193; Sakamoto Tarō, *Sugawara no Michizane*, pp. 32-34; Makabe Toshinobu, "Kankō ni okeru shijitsu to denshō," *Shintōshi kenkyū* 21.2:18-21 (March 1973).

77. *Gōdanshō*, pp. 34-35. Primary sources on Hiromi can be found in *DNS*, I.1, Kampyō 2/5/16. *KB* states that although Hiromi was appointed professor, he did not choose to take the office (Gangyō 8); however, *SJ*, a more reliable source, indicates he was professor from 867 until 869 (Jōgan 9/2/11, 10/10/11, 11/2/1). Hiromi's having studied under Koreyoshi is mentioned in *KBKK*, item 65. Also see Iyanaga, "Michizane no zenhansei," pp. 159-160.

78. *KBKK*, item 567. Yoshika's questions are found in *Toshi bunshū*, p. 334; Michizane's answers, in *KBKK*, items 566-567. Both the questions and answers are exceedingly recondite, and my summaries rely heavily on Iyanaga, "Michizane no zenhansei," pp. 158-159.

79. *Toshi bunshū*, p. 337.

80. *Ryō no gige*, p. 132; *Ryō no shūge*, pp. 454-455, 505-506.

81. *Toshi bunshū*, p. 337; *KBKK*, item 185. Sukeyo is said to have been the first Fujiwara to take the examinations, and some scholars objected on principle to a Fujiwara's even attempting them (*Gōdanshō*, pp. 22-24). For data on Sukeyo, see *DNS*, I.2, Kampyō 9, pp. 530-541 and a chapter discussing him in Gotō Akio, pp. 184-198.

82. Sakamoto Tarō, *Sugawara no Michizane*, pp. 28-29; Tokoro, "Kiyoyuki no zenhansei," p. 179. For examples of individuals who failed the examinations and did not have their grades revised, see *SNK*, Jōwa 10/5/15 and *KBKK*, item 47.

83. *KBKK*, item 50.

CHAPTER 3: BUREAUCRAT AND EDUCATOR

1. *SJ*, Jōgan 12/9/11.

2. *Ryō no shūge*, pp. 505-506; *Nihon kiryaku*, Enryaku 21/6/17 (which is probably the wrong date: *Ryō no shūge*, an earlier source, dates the regulation Enryaku 21/6/8).

3. Nomura, *Kanjinsei*, pp. 299-303; Iyanaga, "Michizane no zenhansei," pp. 160-162; Sakamoto Tarō, *Sugawara no Michizane*, pp. 35-36. The Rikkokushi do include one instance of the fifth rank being awarded to an individual, Ōnakatomi no Kunio, from a minor family while he was still a student of literature (*SJ*, Jōgan 8/1/7). The Ōnakatomi were a family of Shinto ritualists and Kunio's subsequent career demonstrates that, although he studied at the university, he did not break with family tradition. Perhaps he was promoted while still a student on the assumption that, whatever his rank, he would not hold regular bureaucratic appointments. Data on more obscure individuals such as Kunio can be located by means of *Rikkokushi sakuin* (ed. Rikkokushi Sakuin Henshūbu, Yoshikawa Kōbunkan, 1963-1969), an index to all individuals, offices, incidents, place names, and religious institutions mentioned in the Rikkokushi. For Kunio, see III, 14.

4. *KB*, Kampyō 5; *Kitano Tenjin goden*, p. 3; *Kanke godenki*, p. 85; Iyanaga, "Michizane no zenhansei," p. 163.

5. *KBKK*, item 58.

6. *KB*, Kampyō 5; *Kitano Tenjin goden*, p. 3.

7. *KB*, Kampyō 5; *Kitano Tenjin goden*, p. 3; *Kanke godenki*, pp. 84-85.

8. *KB*, Kampyō 5; *Kitano Tenjin goden*, p. 3; *Kanke godenki*, p. 85; Iyanaga, "Ninna ninsen," pp. 533-549.

9. *KB*, Jōgan 16-17; Iyanaga, "Ninna ninen," pp. 533-534.

10. *KBKK*, item 69.

11. *KBKK*, item 74. A similar poem (*KBKK*, item 73) has been translated by Watson in *Japanese Literature in Chinese*, p. 88.

12. *KBKK*, item 553.

13. Michizane's prose works comprise chapters 7 to 12 of *Kanke bunsō*. Edicts and imperial replies to "edicts" from retired emperors are in chapter 8 (*KBKK*, items 568-582); petitions make up chapters 9 and 10 (*KBKK*, items 583-635), and Buddhist prayers make up chapters 11 and 12 (*KBKK*, items 636-673). Of the 53 petitions, 40 were drafted for other courtiers, as were all but one of the 38 prayers. Michizane's prose is discussed by Kawaguchi in his introduction to *KBKK* (pp. 55-59) and *Kambungakushi* (pp. 211-217).

14. Petitions drafted for Yoshifusa: *KBKK*, items 611-613; those for Mototsune: *KBKK*, items 615, 620, 623, 625, 644; both petition and replying edict: *KBKK*, items 572, 577, 622, 623; petition for the professor: *KBKK*, item 614. Also see Sakamoto Tarō, *Sugawara no Michizane*, pp. 36, 43-45, 61-66.

15. *SJ*, Jōgan 13/9/28, 10/4, 5; Gangyō 3/3/23, 25; *KBKK*, item 556.

16. *SJ*, Jōgan 14/1/6, 26; *KB*, Kampyō 5; *KBKK*, item 569; *Kitano Tenjin goden*, p. 3; *Kanke godenki*, p. 84; Nomura, *Kodai kanryō*, pp. 125-126.

17. *KBKK*, item 75.

18. *KBKK*, item 76.

19. *Tsurugashi tsūshi*, ed. Tsurugashi Kyōiku Iinkai (Tsuruga, 1956), p. 89.

20. *KB*, Kampyō 5; *Kitano Tenjin goden*, p. 3; *Kanke godenki*, p. 85; *SJ*, Gangyō 1/9/26.

21. *SJ*, Gangyō 1/10/18; *KB*, Kampyō 5; *Kitano Tenjin godenki*, p. 3; *Kanke godenki*, p. 85; *KBKK*, items 82, 87, 120; Momo, pp. 312-314; Hisaki, pp. 97-101; Sakamoto Tarō, *Sugawara no Michizane*, pp. 45-64.

22. *KBKK*, item 82. The conclusion of this series of lectures was the occasion for the customary banquet at which everyone wrote poems on themes taken from the *History of the Later Han*. Ki no Haseo's introduction to this group of poems is in *Honchō monzui*, I, 293-297; Tadaomi's poem is in *Denshi kashū*, p. 349; and Michizane's is in *KBKK*, item 91. According to Haseo's introduction, the lectures had been begun by Michizane's predecessor in 872 and were completed by Michizane in 881. The commemorative banquet was held early the next year.

23. *KBKK*, item 63; *Denshi kashū*, p. 345; Tokoro, "Kankō ryōke no kyōiku katsudō," in Yūki Rikurō ed., *Nihon kyōiku bunkashi* (1975) p. 58.

24. *KBKK*, item 100. This poem was sent to Tadaomi, whose reply is in *Denshi kashū*, p. 350. Also see *KB*, Kampyō 5; *Kitano Tenjin goden*, p. 3; and *Kanke godenki*, p. 85.

25. Momo, pp. 172-233; Hisaki, pp. 133-155.

26. The most important sources on Kanke Rōka are *KBKK*, items 19, 36, 114, and particularly 526 (translated by Watson, *Japanese Literature in Chinese*, pp. 104-106); and *Kitano Tenjin goden*, p. 5. Modern studies include Momo, pp. 459-470; and Hisaki, pp. 176-179. Hisaki argues that "Kanke Rōka" was only a nickname, and that the school's true name was San'intei (Mountain Shade Pavilion). San'intei, however, seems to have been the name of Michizane's personal study outside of which students gathered, not the name of the school.

27. Hisaki, p. 176.

28. *SJ*, Ninna 2/1/16, 2/21, 6/16, 21; *KB*, Kampyō 2.

29. *Kitano Tenjin goden*, p. 3; *KB*, Kampyō 5; *SJ*, Gangyō 3/2/25.

30. *KBKK*, item 597.

31. *SJ*, Gangyō 8/3/9, 5/26; *KB*, Gangyō 8. Sukeyo's familial relation to Michizane was a complex one. He fathered a child by Michizane's daughter, and his mother, like Michizane's, was a member of the Tomo family (*SB*, II, 521-522).

32. *KB*, Jōgan 19, Gangyō 8; *SJ*, Gangyō 5/4/9; *SB*, I, 31.
33. Appointments to the Ministry of Ceremonial are found in *Rikkokushi sakuin*, IV, 159.
34. *KBKK*, items 558-565.
35. Hisaki, pp. 112-114.
36. *KBKK*, item 594.
37. *KBKK*, item 87.
38. *KBKK*, item 15.
39. *KBKK*, item 526. The translation quoted is by Watson, *Japanese Literature in Chinese*, pp. 104-106. Published by permission of Columbia University Press.
40. *Godanshō*, pp. 31-32.
41. Primary sources on Kiyoyuki are in *DNS*, I.5, Engi 18/12/7. Tokoro has written biographical studies of him in two formats: a scholarly version that appeared as two journal articles "Kiyoyuki no zenhansei," and "Miyoshi no Kiyoyuki no kōhansei," *Geirin* 18.3 (June 1967); and a popular version, *Miyoshi no Kiyoyuki*, vol. 157 of *Jimbutsu sōsho* (1965). Kiyoyuki's writings are discussed by Kawaguchi in *Kambungakushi*, pp. 245-270. His most famous piece, "Statement of Opinion on Twelve Matters" (*Iken fūji junijō*) is partially translated in David John Lu, ed., *Sources of Japanese History* (New York, 1974), I, 60-65. For his examination, see *KBKK*, items 560-561; *KB*, Engi 17; and Tokoro "Kiyoyuki no zenhansei," pp. 177-179. Kiyoyuki's name sometimes is read incorrectly as "Kiyotsura."
42. Primary sources on Haseo are in *DNS*, I.4, Engi 12/2/10. A surviving fragment of his collected works, *Kikashū*, has become available in modern printed editions only recently. The best is *"Kikashū" kaidai shakubun*, ed. Kunaichō Shoryōbu, a pamphlet that accompanies the beautiful reproduction of the original manuscript published by Yoshikawa Kōbunkan in 1978. Other of his writings appear in various collections, including *GR*, vol. 3, p. 700; and *Honchō monzui* II, 54-62. The latter is a valuable autobiographical essay. Haseo has not received the attention he deserves from modern scholars. Studies include Satō Seijitsu, "Ki no Haseo," *Shigaku zasshi* 12.4:61-71 (October 1901); Tokoro Isao, "Sugawara no Michizane to Ki no Haseo no kankei," in *Koji ruien geppō* 25:6-8 (April 1969) and Sakamoto Tarō, "Sugawara no Michizane to Ki no Haseo," in *Shintō taikei geppō* 2, *Kitano* (April 1978), pp. 1-4. His writings are discussed in Kawaguchi, *Kambungakushi*, pp. 223-245. The identity of Haseo's original teacher, or teachers, is not certain. His autobiographical essay in *Honchō monzui* states only that he joined Michizane's faction after having begun his studies under a different man. Various names have been proposed, among them Tadaomi, Fumio, and Yoshika (Tokoro, "Kiyoyuki no zenhansei," pp. 191-192). The best guess is Ōkura no Yoshiyuki (832-922), a scholar with close ties to the Fujiwara, for when a group of former students commemorated Yoshiyuki's seventieth year by composing a series of poems, Haseo provided the introduction (*Zatsugen hōwa*, in *GR* vol. 6, pp. 415-416). Unfortunately, this theory too has flaws (Gotō Akio, pp. 164-183). Kiyoyuki's comment about Haseo is in *Gōdanshō*, pp. 215-216.
    Michizane examined two other candidates in addition to Kiyoyuki and Haseo. Little is known of one, but the other, Ono no Yoshiki, achieved some reputation as a poet. Michizane later lamented his death, noting, "As a friend he was neither close nor distant, and he was not my student." *KBKK*, item 502; for Yoshiki, see *DNS*, I.3, Engi 2, pp. 110-114.
43. Momo, pp. 125-132, 157-169, 312-318; Hisaki, pp. 98-101, 193-205; Kawaguchi, *Kambungakushi*, pp. 126-130; Akiyama, "Michizane no shijin keisei," pp. 183-202; Iyanaga, "Michizane no zenhansei," pp. 166-172.

44. *KBKK*, items 145, 151, 198, 330.
45. *KBKK*, item 98.
46. Watson, *Japanese Literature in Chinese*, p. 76.
47. Akiyama, "Michizane ron no danshō," p. 44. A more clinical analysis of Michizane's presumed nervous disorders is offered by Ōmaru Isamu, a psychiatrist who has taken an interest in Michizane ("Sugawara no Michizane ni miru shinkeishitsu," in *Kyūshū shinkei seishin igaku* 20.2:120-124 [August 1974]).
48. *KBKK*, item 118.
49. For Korenori, see *Rikkokushi sakuin*, IV, 41. Michizane's replies to his poems are in *KBKK*, items 119-121. Also see Watson, *Japanese Literature in Chinese*, pp. 78-79.
50. *KBKK*, item 90.
51. *KBKK*, item 114.
52. *KBKK*, items 46, 243, 245, 258. For examples of Po Chü-i's poems written on walls, see Arthur Waley, *The Life and Times of Po Chü-i, 772-846 A.D.* (New York, 1949), pp. 100, 207. The last three of the poems Michizane wrote on walls were composed while he was serving in the provinces. Perhaps paper was not readily available?
53. *KBKK*, item 92. These poems appear in *KBKK* before the ones Michizane exchanged with the ambassadors from Parhae; however, they seem to be out of chronological order (*KBKK*, p. 87). For Masanori, see *Rikkokushi sakuin*, IV, 45; and *SB*, IV, 4.
54. *KBKK*, items 153-172. Those translated are 161 and 167.
55. Michizane once referred to Tadaomi as his father-in-law (*KBKK*, item 93) and *Kitano Tenjin goden* states his wife's name and age (p. 4). Kawaguchi and Kimpara estimate that Michizane was married around 866, when he would have been 23 and Nobukiko 18 (Kawaguchi, *Kambungakushi*, p. 183; Kimpara, p. 234). For material on Takami, see *DNS*, I.4, Engi 13, pp. 563-564. The careers of Michizane's sons and grandson are discussed in Makabe Toshinobu, "Michizane no shison no dōsei ni tsuite," *Kokugakuin zasshi* 74.10:40-50 (October 1973).
56. *KBKK*, item 117. The translation is Watson's from *Japanese Literature in Chinese*, pp. 90-91; published by permission of Columbia University Press. One couplet is omitted because its meaning is unclear. For additional references to Amaro, see *KBKK*, item 122 (also translated by Watson, *Japanese Literature in Chinese*, p. 92) and item 140.
57. *KBKK*, items 260, 302, 308, 437, 475, 477, 483, etc.; *Kitano Tenjin goden*, p. 5.

CHAPTER 4: GOVERNOR OF SANUKI

1. *SJ*, Ninna 2/1/2, 20; *Honchō monzui*, II, 194-195; Iyanaga, "Ninna ninen," pp. 555-556. The customary new year's celebrations are described in Yamanaka, pp. 94-166.
2. *SJ*, Ninna 2/1/7, 8, 11, 14, 16, 2/1, 5/18; Iyanaga, "Michizane no zenhansei," pp. 173-175; Yoshimura, pp. 202-203.
3. *KBKK*, item 183; *SJ*, Ninna 2/1/21.
4. *Haku Rakuten shishū*, vol. 11 of *Zoku kokuyaku kambun taisei, bungakubu* (1957) contains both the Chinese original and a Japanese translation of Po Chü-i's poem (II, 402). Michizane described the incident in *KBKK*, item 184.
5. *SNK*, Jōwa 9/8/29; Kitayama, *Heian kyō*, pp. 155-157. The conventional view of aristocratic disdain for provincial offices is found in, for example, Ivan Morris, *The World of the Shining Prince* (New York, 1964), pp. 79-86.
6. Yoshimura, pp. 58-61.

7. *KBKK*, item 187.
8. *Kitano Tenjin goden*, p. 3; *Kanke goden*, p. 85; *KB*, Kampyō 5; Abe, *Heian zenki seijishi*, pp. 201-202.
9. *Nichūreki*, vol. 23 of *Kaitei shiseki shūran* (1901), p. 235; *Fujiwara no Yasunori den*, in *Kodai seiji shakai shisō*, ed. Yamagishi Tokuhei, Takeuchi Rizō, Ienaga Saburō, and Ōsone Shōsuke, vol. 8 of *Nihon shisō taikei* (1979), pp. 70, 284 (*Kambun* texts from *Nihon shisō taikei* are cited with two page references because they appear twice, first in an annotated Japanese translation and second in the Chinese-language original); *KBKK*, items 269, 279. Extensive data on Sanuki appear in *Engi shiki*. They can be found easily by means of the index volume to the *Kōtei Engi shiki* edition edited by Kōten Kōkyūjo Zenkoku Shinshokukai (1929-1931). The more commonly used *KT* edition is not well indexed. For a detailed study of early Sanuki, see Fuke Sōei, *Kagawa ken tsūshi: kodai chūsei kinsei hen* (Takamatsu, Kagawa Prefecture, 1965), pp. 149-506.
10. *KBKK*, items 184, 186; *SJ*, Gangyō 8/12/5; Ninna 2/2/21; Iyanaga, "Michizane no zenhansei," pp. 173-175; Iyanaga, "Ninna ninen," pp. 552-563; Sakamoto Tarō, *Sugawara no Michizane*, pp. 65-68; Nishio Yōtarō, "Sanuki no kami jidai no Michizane," *Shien* 42:81-85 (December 1949); Segawa Hisae, "Sugawara no Michizane no Sanuki no kami jidai," in *Heianchō bungaku kenkyū: sakka to sakuhin*, ed. Waseda Daigaku Heianchō Bungaku Kenkyūkai (1971), pp. 636-640.
11. Hurst, *Insei*, pp. 68-73; Sakamoto Tarō, "Yoshifusa to Mototsune," pp. 169-178; Mezaki Tokue, "Fujiwara no Mototsune," a 1965 essay reprinted in his book *Ōchō no miyabi* (1978), see pp. 111-120; Tokoro Isao, "Kampyō no chi no saikentō," *Kōgakkan Daigaku kiyō* 5:109-112 (1967).
12. *Ryō no gige*, p. 30; *Ryō no shūge*, pp. 40-43.
13. *SJ*, Gangyō 8/5/9; Sakamoto Tarō, *Sugawara no Michizane*, pp. 59-60; Ishio Yoshihisa, *Nihon kodai no tennōsei to daijōkan seido* (1962), pp. 186-192; Abe, *Heian zenki seijishi*, pp. 196-198.
14. *SJ*, Gangyō 8/6/5; Sakamoto Tarō, "Yoshifusa to Mototsune," pp. 169-172; Mezaki, *Ōchō no miyabi*, pp. 120-123; Tokoro, "Kampyō no chi," p. 112.
15. Iyanaga, "Ninna ninen," pp. 549-552.
16. *Gōdanshō*, p. 22.
17. *KBKK*, item 187.
18. *KBKK*, item 186.
19. *KBKK*, item 188.
20. *Ryō no gige*, pp. 102-103; *Ryō no shūge*, pp. 317-332.
21. *KBKK*, item 219.
22. *KBKK*, item 221, translated by Watson in *Japanese Literature in Chinese*, pp. 96-98.
23. *Engi shiki*, pp. 648, 775, 780; *Ryō no gige*, p. 61; *Ryō no shūge*, p. 165; Yoshimura, pp. 48-58.
24. For officials appointed to Sanuki, see *Rikkokushi sakuin*, IV, 150-151; and *KB*, Kampyō 2.
25. *KBKK*, item 286. Also see items 277, 307, 317.
26. *SJ*, Ninna 2/12/28; *Ruijū sandai kyaku*, p. 316; Iyanaga, "Michizane no zenhansei," p. 189; Yoshimura, pp. 50-51.
27. *KBKK*, item 214, also translated by Watson in *Japanese Literature in Chinese*, p. 95.
28. *KBKK*, item 255.
29. *KBKK*, item 262.
30. *KBKK*, item 525.
31. *Kanke godenki*, p. 85; an illustration of the dance as it is performed today

appears in Nishikawa Osamu, ed. *Kagawa, Tokushima, Ehime, Kōchi*, vol. 15 of *Nihon no bunka chiri* (1970), p. 56.

32. *Fujiwara no Yasunori den*, pp. 71-72, 284; Sakamoto Tarō, *Sugawara no Michizane*, pp. 107-108; Tokoro, *Miyoshi no Kiyoyuki*, pp. 140-142.
33. *SJ*, Ninna 3/6/2. The descriptions of the inferior silk are found in *SJ*, Jōgan 6/8/9, and *Seiji yōryaku, KT* vol. 28, pp. 271-272. Also see Abe Takeshi, *Ritsuryō kokka kaitai katei no kenkyū* (1966), pp. 156-167.
34. Iyanaga, "Michizane no zenhansei," pp. 178-180, 188-189; Sakamoto Tarō, *Sugawara no Michizane*, pp. 76-77; Yoshimura, pp. 115-116; Sansom, p. 109.
35. *KBKK*, item 196.
36. *KBKK*, item 210.
37. *KBKK*, item 218.
38. *KBKK*, item 234; *Kanke godenki*, p. 85.
39. *KBKK*, item 235.
40. *KBKK*, item 236.
41. Nishio, pp. 103-106.
42. *SJ*, Gangyō 8/6/2, 2/28; Sakamoto Tarō, "Yoshifusa to Mototsune," pp. 169-174; Mezaki, *Ōchō no miyabi*, pp. 119-124; Iyanaga, "Ninna ninen," pp. 549-552; Tokoro, "Kampyō no chi," pp. 109-112; Hurst, *Insei*, pp. 73-74.
43. *SJ*, Ninna 3/8/22, 25, 26. Both the Minamoto who desired to become emperor and Yōzei's unhappiness concerning Uda are found in *Ōkagami*, Muramatsu Hiroshi, ed., vol. 21 of *NKBT*, pp. 46, 69; or in Helen McCullough's translation, *Ōkagami: The Great Mirror* (1980), pp. 75, 93-94.
44. The quotations are from a fragment of Uda's diary that is preserved in *Seiji yōryaku, KT* vol. 28, p. 238. This passage is cited, with some elaboration, in *Gukanshō*, ed., Okami Masao and Akamatsu Toshihide, vol. 86 of *NKBT*, pp. 153-154; or in Delmer M. Brown and Ichirō Ishida's translation, *The Future and the Past: A Translation and Study of the Gukanshō, an Interpretative History of Japan Written in 1219* (1979), p. 41. The roles of Mototsune's sister and Hiromi are mentioned in a letter Michizane wrote to Mototsune (discussed below, p. 180) that also appears in *Seiji yōryaku*, pp. 244-245.
45. Virtually all the extant primary data on the Akō Debate are found in *Seiji yōryaku*, pp. 232-246. Included are the fragment of Uda's diary already cited, the two edicts Hiromi drafted, the reply drafted by Haseo, various learned opinions on the nature of the term "*akō*," the opinion on how Hiromi should be punished, and finally, Michizane's letter to Mototsune. Unless otherwise indicated, data on the Akō Debate are all taken from this source. The previous use of the term "*akō*" occurred after Kōkō had first granted Mototsune the powers of chancellor. Mototsune naturally declined, and when he was again requested to serve, the term "*akō*" was used (*SJ*, Gangyō 8/6/5, 7/6, 8). Brief modern accounts of the incident can be found in virtually all the sources already cited on Michizane's life or the politics of the period. The best, however, is Tokoro's meticulously detailed and annotated "Kampyō no chi," pp. 112-115. Finally, Carl F. Taeusch has translated a colorful although not historically reliable account of the incident that appears in *Jikkinshō*, a thirteenth century collection of tales ("The Jikkinshō: An Annotated Translation of Chapter Four: 'A Caution against Talking Too Much of Other People's Affairs,' with Critical Introduction," Master's thesis, University of Michigan [1970], pp. 53-56). For comparisons of Mototsune and Yoshifusa, see Sakamoto Tarō, "Yoshifusa to Mototsune," pp. 174-178, and Mezaki, *Ōchō no miyabi*, pp. 111-119.
46. *Hokuzanshō*, vol. 4 of *Zōtei kojitsu sōsho* (1928), p. 600.
47. *Seiji yōryaku*, pp. 238-239.

48. *Fusō ryakki,* vol. 12 of *KT,* Kampyō 1/8/10.
49. *Nihon kiryaku,* Ninna 4/10/2.
50. *KBKK,* item 261.
51. *KBKK,* item 263.
52. *Hokuzanshō,* p. 601.
53. *Seiji yōryaku,* pp. 243-246. Although Michizane did not include this letter, his longest extant prose composition, in his anthologies, it has been added to *KBKK* as supplementary item 676. It is discussed in Iyanaga, "Michizane no zenhansei," pp. 184-186; and Sakamoto Tarō, *Sugawara no Michizane,* pp. 82-85.
54. The letter is not dated, but refers to events of the tenth month as having occurred "last month." For a detailed analysis of the timing of the letter, see Iyanaga, "Michizane no zenhansei," pp. 185-188. The importance of the Akō Debate to Michizane's subsequent career was first pointed out by Hagino Yasuyuki in "Akō mondai to Kankō sasen," *Rekishi chiri* 14.2:18-33 (August 1899). His presentation remains the most detailed discussion of the topic.
55. Hiromi died on Kampyō 2/5/16, and Mototsune on Kampyō 3/1/13 (*Nihon kiryaku*).
56. *KBKK,* item 243.
57. Nishio, pp. 87-93; and Segawa, pp. 641-647; Ōsone, pp. 1-10.
58. Brower and Miner, pp. 18-19, 223.
59. Konishi, "Kambungaku," pp. 899-902; Watson, *Japanese Literature in Chinese,* pp. 12-13; Kato, pp. 115-118.
60. *KBKK,* item 220; Segawa, pp. 647-648.
61. *KBKK,* item 222.
62. *KBKK,* item 256.
63. *KBKK,* items 247-249.
64. *KBKK,* item 228.
65. *KBKK,* items 200, 203, 204, 206, 208, 209. The poems from this set omitted here, *KBKK* items 201, 202, 205, and 207, all are translated in Watson, *Japanese Literature in Chinese,* pp. 93-94.
66. Kaneko, pp. 90-91.
67. Iyanaga, "Michizane no zenhansei," pp. 189-192; Takikawa Seijirō, "Okura no 'Hinkyū mondōka' to Kankō no 'Kansō jisshu'," *Nihon rekishi* 404:40-43 (January 1982).
68. Iyanaga, "Michizane no zenhansei," p. 192; Akiyama, "Bungaku shisō," pp. 39-40; Segawa, pp. 642-644; Nishio, pp. 93-99.
69. *KBKK,* items 29, 52, 53, 72, 93, 117, 125. Michizane's introduction (*KBKK,* item 551) is described in Yamaguchi Kōen, "Kankō no *Gen'yō daikai ronjo* to *Daikai shinanshō,*" *Bukkyō shigaku* 2.1:25-33 (January 1951). Yamaguchi notes that when he was reading the work for which Michizane wrote the introduction, *Gen'yō daikai ron,* he observed that the style of the introduction was distinctly more difficult than that of the work it introduced. Michizane's name did not appear in the text, and only later did he discover that the introduction was not by the same author as the main text. At the time Michizane wrote it, he was only twenty-two, but he was already writing in a more learned style than most of his contemporaries. For a biography of Ennin, see Edwin O. Reischauer, *Ennin's Travels in T'ang China* (New York, 1955) pp. 20-38.
70. *KBKK,* item 279. Other poems with Buddhist themes or references written in Sanuki include items 191, 196, 201, 250, 255, 257, 262, 289, 298, 310 and 311.
71. *KBKK,* item 194.
72. *KBKK,* item 301. His grey hair also appears in items 224, 254, and 297.

73. *KBKK,* item 260.
74. *KBKK,* item 308. Additional references to his family in the capital can be found in items 192, 261, 302 (a response to a poem he received from his eldest son) and 318.
75. *KBKK,* item 274. Michizane also laments that wine does not dispel his grief in items 196 and 298; however, he reports enjoying a few drinks in items 195, 214, 251, and 299.
76. *KBKK,* item 259. Michizane also mentions reading *Lao-tzu* and *The Spring and Autumn Annals* in item 223.
77. For exchanges with his family, see *KBKK,* item 302; with friends, item 198 (a response to a poem from Fumio), 225, 263 (to Tadaomi), 275, 285 (again to Tadaomi), 290 (to the governor of Bizen), 291 (replying to Tadaomi's answer to 285). Poems Tadaomi sent to Michizane appear in *Denshi kashū,* p. 353. References to Michizane's students are found in items 189, 190, 199, 241, 244, 245, and 305.
78. *KBKK,* item 264. Tokizane's visit was also the occasion for items 265 and 267.
79. *KBKK,* item 281.
80. *KBKK,* item 662.

CHAPTER 5: THE RISE TO HIGH OFFICE

1. *KBKK,* item 296.
2. *KBKK,* item 327; Iyanaga, "Michizane no zenhansei," pp. 188-189.
3. *KBKK,* item 325.
4. *KBKK,* items 323-325.
5. *KBKK,* items 599-600; *Kitano Tenjin goden,* p. 3; *Kanke godenki,* p. 85; *KB,* Kampyō 5. *KB* states that he was appointed in the third month. Although contradicted by all the other sources, that date does appear in the chronology in *KBKK,* p. 87. *Kanke godenki* claims that the second time he declined the office, his resignation was accepted, but this too seems highly unlikely. For the history and importance of the office, see Sansom, pp. 113-114.
6. *KB,* Kampyō 3. *KB* lists year by year appointments of high court nobles, and most of the information on appointments that appears in this chapter comes from that source. The most detailed study of court politics during these years is Tokoro, "Kampyō no chi," pp. 115-123. Tokoro provides a chart (with no page number) showing all appointments to important offices, pp. 882-901.
7. Masano Jun'ichi, "Minamoto no Yoshiari to Sugawara no Michizane," *Shishū* 14-15:22-27 (June 1981); Morita, *Seijishi,* pp. 195-201; and Tsunoda Bun'ei, "Sugawara no Michizane to Fujiwara shi: Atsugimi Shinnō no rittaishi o megutte," in *Michizane to Dazaifu,* I, 174. For primary sources on Yoshiari, see *DNS,* I.2, Kampyō 5/7/19.
8. Primary sources on Yasunori can be found in *DNS,* I.2, Kampyō 2/4/21. *Fujiwara no Yasunori den,* the early biography written by Kiyoyuki, is particularly important. Also see Abe, *Heian zenki seijishi,* pp. 145-156; and Tokoro, "Kampyō no chi," pp. 118-119.
9. *KB,* Engi 17; *KBKK,* item 351; *Chishō Daishi den, ZGR* vol. 8b, p. 716; Hagino, p. 186. The precise details of these two appointments are not as clear as Hagino indicates. Sukeyo did not depart for Mutsu until a year after his original appointment, when Michizane addressed a second farewell poem to him, and in the interval he seems to have retained his offices at court (*KBKK,* item 357; *Honchō monzui,* I, 884). Kiyoyuki's appointment presents ever greater complications,

363 · Notes to Pages 202–213

and possibly he did not go to Higo, although he was unquestionably removed from his honorable post as private secretary and two years later did go to serve as lieutenant governor of Bitchū. In *Chishō Daishi den,* another biography Kiyoyuki wrote, he clearly refers to this later appointment as an exile (p. 716). For a complete discussion of both these appointments, see Tokoro, "Kiyoyuki no zenhansei," pp. 185–187. Uda may not have been able to remove these men from the court as quickly as he would have liked, but both were eventually sent away.

10. Ikeda Genta, "Heian shoki," pp. 20–22; Akiyama Ken, "Waka Renessansu," in *Kyūtei saron to saijo,* ed. Yamanaka and Akiyama, pp. 148–154; Ryō Susumu, *Heian jidai* (1962), pp. 73–74.

11. The lectures are mentioned in *Kitano Tenjin goden,* p. 3; Michizane's daughters appear in *SB,* 4:61; and *Nihon Kiryaku,* Kampyō 8/11/26.

12. Tokoro, "Kampyō no chi," pp. 117–119.

13. *KBKK,* item 601.

14. Tokoro, "Kampyō no chi," pp. 119–120.

15. Tsuchida, pp. 575–578; Tokoro, "Kampyō no chi," p. 120. Tokoro provides a chart showing how many regulations were issued under the name of each high noble during Uda's reign (p. 139). Those issued by Michizane are included in Fujino, "Michizane nempyō," pp. 371–374. Fujino lists one more than does Tokoro.

16. *KBKK,* item 603.

17. The Rikkokushi contain only one mention of an imperial prison inspection (*SJ,* Gangyō 3/3/23), whereas over 50 amnesties are mentioned. The Chinese precedents for amnesties and prison inspections are discussed in Brian E. McKnight, *The Quality of Mercy: Amnesties and Traditional Chinese Justice* (Honolulu, 1981).

18. Morita, *Seijishi,* pp. 192–199.

19. *KBKK,* item 602; Abe, *Heian zenki seijishi,* pp. 210–214; Sakamoto Tarō, *Sugawara no Michizane,* pp. 95–97.

20. *Kampyō no goikai* (also pronounced *"Kampyō goyuikai"*), in *Kodai seiji shakai shisō,* pp. 107, 294 (This is the testament that Uda left to his successor. Its complete text does not survive, but the edition cited includes the best extant version, plus fragments gathered from other sources); *Nihon kiryaku,* Engi 10/2/25; *SB,* 3:379; Tsunoda, "Michizane to Fujiwara shi," pp. 161–162.

21. The interpretation presented largely follows Sakamoto Tarō, *Sugawara no Michizane,* pp. 98–100; and Tokoro, "Kampyō no chi," pp. 121–122. For a more elaborate theory on the selection of the crown prince, see Tsunoda, "Michizane to Fujiwara shi," pp. 147–179.

22. *KBKK,* introductory note to items 391–400.

23. *KBKK,* introductory note to items 401–417.

24. *KBKK,* item 410. Also see items 381, 385, 426.

25. In explaining Uda's abdication, Tokoro presents the religion theory ("Kampyō no chi," pp. 122–123); Kitayama, the aesthetic pleasures theory (*Heian kyō,* p. 348); and Sakamoto Tarō, the political frustration theory (*Sugawara no Michizane,* pp. 100–101). For Uda's continued involvement in government after his abdication, see Ryō, pp. 66–71. Mezaki provides a critique of the above works and a detailed analysis of Uda's activities after his retirement in "Uda Jōkō no in to kokusei," in *Engi Tenryaku jidai no kenkyū,* ed. Kodaigaku Kyōkai (1969), pp. 89–122.

26. Hurst, *Insei,* pp. 74–80.

27. *Kampyō no goikai,* pp. 107–108, 294; Tokoro, "Kampyō no chi," p. 123; Sakamoto Tarō, *Sugawara no Michizane,* pp. 98–100.

28. *Nihon kiryaku,* Kampyō 9/7/3, 13; *Fusō ryakki,* same dates plus p. 183 (a section not included in the chronological framework); *Tenso reishi shokushō roku,* in *GR,* vol. 2, p. 246.

29. *Kampyō goikai,* pp. 104-106, 293-294.

30. *Kampyō goikai,* pp. 109, 295. The moral of this story seems to be that Emperor Kammu was a forgiving ruler. Another version of it appears in a collection of tales compiled c. 1250-1350, with interesting variations. The later version has Kammu requesting the gate be lowered one foot because it was in a place where the winds blew fiercely. Kammu returned to discover that the carpenters had lowered it only 5 inches (the Heian "foot" [*shaku*] had 10 "inches" [*sun*] because it would not appear sufficiently grand if lowered one foot. The story concludes by extolling the emperor's foresight because the Rashōmon was blown down 3 times. (*Yotsugi monogatari* [also known as *Uji Dainagon monogatari*], in *ZGR,* vol. 32b, pp. 164-166). Historical records show that it was blown down at least twice, first in 816 and again in 980, after which it was apparently not rebuilt. In 1023, when Fujiwara no Michinaga needed foundation stones for a temple he was having built, he took some from the site of the Rashōmon (Ikeda Kikan, *Heian jidai no bungaku to seikatsu* [1968], pp. 86-89; Murai Yasuhiko, "Heian kyō no keisei," in *Kyōto no rekishi 1: Heian no shinkyō,* ed. Hayashiya Tatsusaburō [1970], pp. 253-259).

31. *Kampyō no goikai,* pp. 107, 294.

32. The story of Tokihira's affair with his uncle's wife appears in various collections of anecdotes. The version appearing in *Konjaku monogatari* has been translated by Marian Ury in *Tales of Times Now Past* (Berkeley, 1979), pp. 134-138. The events in the tale are not dated and many commentators have suggested that Uda was referring to the incident; however, judging from the ranks and ages of the principals given in at least the *Konjaku* version of the story, it apparently occurred c. 907-908.

33. *Kampyō no goikai,* pp. 107-108, 294. Another version of the text states that Michizane was promoted as "punishment" (literally, "a whipping") for his merit (in *GR* vol. 21, p. 2). The text cited is probably more reliable.

34. The full text of this edict does not survive. The passage quoted is found in *Nihon kiryaku,* Kampyō 9/7/3. A slightly different version of it is quoted in *KBKK,* item 606. The implications of this edict are discussed in Yamamoto Shinkichi, "Heian chūki no nairan ni tsuite," in *Zoku Nihon kodaishi ronshū,* ed. Sakamoto Tarō Hakase Koki Kinenkai (1972), III, 225-240.

35. *KB,* Shōtai 1-3; Morita, *Seijishi,* pp. 43-48; Yamamoto, pp. 221-232.

36. Early Japan's historiographic traditions are discussed in Sakamoto Tarō, *Nihon no shūshi to shigaku* (1958), pp. 1-38; and G.W. Robinson, "Early Japanese Chronicles: The Six National Histories," in *Historical Writing on the Peoples of Asia: Historians of China and Japan,* ed. W.G. Beasley and E.G. Pulleyblank (New York, 1961), pp. 213-228.

37. *MJ,* "Jo" (Introduction), which also appears in *KBKK* as item 554.

38. *SJ,* "Jo" (Introduction); *Nihon kiryaku,* Kampyō 4/5/1, Engi 1/8/2; Sakamoto Tarō, *Rikkokushi,* pp. 298-303.

39. *SJ,* Jōgan 3/3/14; Gangyō 4/8/30; Sakamoto Tarō, *Rikkokushi,* pp. 303-308; Saeki Arikiyo, "Sugawara no Michizane to Jikaku Daishi den," *Nihon rekishi* 434:75-82 (July 1984).

40. *KBKK,* items 360, 365, the former of which has been translated by Watson, *Japanese Literature in Chinese,* pp. 102-103; *Kitano Tenjin goden,* p. 5; *Kanke godenki,* p. 85; *Honchō shojaku mokuroku,* pp. 76-82.

41. Sakamoto Tarō, *Rikkokushi*, pp. 339-349, and "*Ruijū kokushi* ni tsuite," originally published in 1937 and reprinted in his *Nihon kodaishi no kisoteki kenkyū* (1964), pp. 317-329 (which includes a partial reconstruction of the table of contents, including lost chapters); and Sasayama Haruo, "*Ruijū kokushi* oboegaki," in *Shintei zōho kokushi taikei geppō* 17:3-6 (March 1965). The extant portions of *Ruijū kokushi* appear as vols. 5-6 of *KT*.
42. Sakamoto Tarō, *Rikkokushi*, pp. 331-338.
43. The prose introduction to *Shūishū* no. 40, a poem that also appears in *Shinsen Man'yōshū*, states that the poem was taken from *Kanke Man'yōshū*. Supporting the theory that Michizane was in some way responsible for the anthology are a number of highly reputable specialists, among them Kawaguchi, *Kambungakushi*, pp. 282-291; Kyūsojin Hitaku, *Gensenbon Shinsen Man'yōshū to kenkyū*, vol. 9 of *Mikan kokubun shiryō* ser. 1 (1958); and Nakashima, pp. 337-355.
44. The most comprehensive analysis of why Michizane could not have been associated with *Shinsen Man'yōshū* is Kumagai Naoharu, "*Shinsen Man'yōshū* no seiritsu," *Kokubungaku kenkyū* 60:1-14 (October 1976) and 61:12-22 (March 1977). Supporting arguments are found in Kaneko, pp. 233-263; and Kigoshi Takashi, "*Shinsen Man'yōshū* no kanshi no sakusha ni tsuite," *Kokugo* 4.4:4-13 (September 1956).
45. *KBKK*, item 674, pp. 44-45.
46. *KBKK*, unnumbered item, pp. 471-472.
47. *KBKK*, item 469.
48. *KBKK*, pp. 64-70.
49. *Fusō ryakki*, Enchō 4/5/21.
50. *KBKK*, item 674.
51. *KBKK*, items 347 and 360, both translated in Watson, *Japanese Literature in Chinese*, pp. 101-103.

CHAPTER 6: DIPLOMAT

1. Two standard surveys of early Sino-Japanese relations are Kimiya Yasuhiko, *Nikka bunka kōryūshi* (1955); and Mori Katsumi, *Kentōshi* (1955). In English, see Reischauer, *Ennin's Travels: Japan in the Chinese Dynastic Histories*, trans. Ryūsaku Tsunoda (1951); and Penelope A. Herbert, "Japanese Embassies and Students in T'ang China," University of Western Australia Centre for East Asian Studies Occasional Paper no. 4 (Nedlands, Australia, n.d.).
2. Parhae sometimes is romanized following Chinese pronunciation as "Pohai" or "P'ohai." In this text, Korean readings are used, both for the name of the kingdom and the names of people from it. The best source of information on Parhae is Chin Yü-fu, *Po-hai kuo-chih ch'ang pien*, originally published c. 1934 and reprinted as vol. 7 of *Chung-hua wen-shih ts'ung-shu* (Taipei, 1968). Chin has gathered all primary data from Chinese, Japanese, and Korean sources, and arranged them somewhat in the manner of a Chinese dynastic history. Useful Japanese studies include Toriyama Kiichi, *Bokkai shikō* (1915), and *Bokkai shijō no shomondai* (published posthumously in 1968 with some sections incomplete); Numata Raisuke, *Nichi-Man no kodai kokkō* (1933); and Niizuma Toshihisa, *Bokkai kokushi oyobi Nihon to no kokkōshi no kenkyū* (1969). Toriyama's *Bokkai shikō* appeared in a Chinese translation that for some reason was attributed to the eminent scholar Tsuda Sōkichi, who in fact published nothing on Parhae. In English, the only detailed study is an article translated from Russian: Aleksei Pavlovich Okladnikov, "The Mo-ho Tribes and the P'o-hai State," in

The Soviet Far East in Antiquity: An Archaeological and Historical Study of the Maritime Region of the U.S.S.R., ed. Henry N. Michael (Toronto, 1965).
3. Toriyama, Bokkai shikō, pp. 91–138, 227–286; Niizuma, pp. 48–131; Okladnikov, pp. 181–195.
4. Bunka shūreishū, pp. 227–228. Four other poems by ambassadors from Parhae appear in the same collection, pp. 210–212, 227–228; and two more are in the Keikokushū, pp. 319–320, 330–331. One final example, with a long prose introduction, was preserved in Ennin's diary (for a translation, see Ennin's Diary, pp. 261–263).
5. A detailed account of each mission from Parhae to Japan can be found in Niizuma, pp. 171–311, with passing mention of the less frequent Japanese missions to Parhae.
6. Niizuma not only described the formalities between Parhae and Japan, but seems to accept the fiction that Parhae was a vassal of Japan (Bokkai kokushi, pp. 317–333). In his much earlier study, Toriyama presented the more plausible view that Parhae adopted a humble attitude in order not to interfere with its friendly—and profitable—relations with Japan (Bokkai shikō, pp. 219–225). For a survey of East Asian diplomatic traditions, see John K. Fairbank, "A Preliminary Framework," the introductory essay to The Chinese World Order, which he also edited (Cambridge, Mass., 1968), pp. 1–14.
7. Ruijū kokushi, II, 358; Ruijū sandai kyaku, pp. 571–572; Toriyama, Bokkai shikō, pp. 191–192; Ishii Masatoshi, "Shoki Nichi-Botsu kōshō ni okeru ichi mondai," in Shigaku ronshū taigai kankei to seiji bunka, ed. Mori Katsumi Hakase Koki Kinenkai (1974) I, 81–112.
8. Niizuma, Bokkai kokushi includes the texts of all surviving poems written for poetic exchanges between Parhae and Japan (pp. 350–380). These exchanges also are discussed in Kawaguchi, Kambungakushi, pp. 138–145. For the calendar, see Shigeru Nakayama, A History of Japanese Astronomy (Cambridge, Mass., 1969), p. 71. The dancing girls are mentioned in various Chinese sources, including both the old and the new T'ang histories. The relevant passages from these and other works are quoted in Chin Yü-fu, pp. 14, 17, 25, 49. Kawaguchi speculates that these dancers may have been presented to the embassy from Parhae that came to Japan in 771 (KBKK, p. 665). For An Lu-shan, see SN, Tempyō hōji 2/12/10.
9. SJ, Gangyō 6/11/27; 7/1/1; Niizuma, pp. 291–295.
10. SJ, Gangyō 7/1/26.
11. SJ, Gangyō 7/2/24, 3/8.
12. SJ, Gangyō 7/2/21, 4/2, 21.
13. KBKK, item 104; SJ, Gangyō 7/4/21.
14. SJ, Gangyō 7/4/28, 29, 5/1, 2, 3. The Foreign Envoys' Quarters are discussed in Kawakatsu Masatarō, "Heiankyō no Kōrokan ni tsuite," in Kammuchō no sho-mondai, Kodaigaku Kyōkai ed. (Osaka, 1962), pp. 229–232. The tone of Parhae's messages is described, albeit rather uncritically, in Niizuma, pp. 317–324.
15. SJ Gangyō 7/5/5. The customary festivities are described in Yamanaka, pp. 196–207.
16. The poems Michizane wrote on the occasion of the Parhae ambassador's visit are KBKK, items 104–112; the one translated is item 106.
17. The seven poems Tadaomi wrote on the occasion, including the one translated, appear in Denshi kashū, pp. 350–351.
18. SJ, Gangyō 7/5/7, 8; Niizuma, pp. 334–340.
19. SJ, Gangyō 7/5/10.
20. Honchō monzui, I, 341–352; translated in Wetzler, pp. 67–71.
21. KBKK, item 555.

22. *KBKK*, item 111.
23. *KBKK*, item 123.
24. *SJ*, Gangyō 7/5/12, 14; *KBKK*, item 569. In 877, Michizane had also drafted an edict granting an ambassador from Parhae an unspecified office (*KBKK*, item 570). The rewards bestowed to the dancers in 842 were not specified.
25. *SJ*, Gangyō 7/10/29.
26. *KBKK*, item 633. Many Japanese scholars have discussed the abandonment of relations with China and in so doing have commented on this and the other documents translated below. The most convenient exegesis of the principal texts is in Ryō, pp. 44-49. Masumura Hiroshi's, "*Kanke bunsō no shiryō*," *Kagoshima Keidai ronshū* 16.3:305-342 (November 1975), the first in the author's series of four articles on the end of the missions, is a more detailed analysis of the same texts. Suzuki Yasutami's "Kampyō no kentōshi o meguru kisoteki kōsatsu," *Kokugakuin Daigaku kiyō* 13:61-100 (March 1975) also meticulously examines the texts. Suzuki has published a somewhat less detailed but more accessible version of the same material as "Sugawara no Michizane to Kampyō no kentōshi," in *Michizane to Dazaifu*, I, 27-51. Masumura responded to Suzuki in his "Kentōshi teihai no shosetsu: Suzuki-shi no ronsetsu," *Chiiki kenkyū* 6.1:53-73 (June 1976). Masumura and Suzuki both make valuable contributions to understanding the relevant documents and events, but neither's conclusions are completely convincing. The studies noted here also provide useful background on Chūkan.
27. *Nihon kiryaku* and *Fusō ryakki*, Kampyō 6/8/21.
28. *Kokinshū*, no. 993. For the official in charge of preparations and the scribe, see *KB*, Kampyō 7; Suzuki, "Kampyō no kentōshi," pp. 68-69; and Ryō, p. 54.
29. *KBKK*, item 601. The works cited in note 26 above contain valuable material on this document too.
30. *Nihon kiryaku*, Kampyō 6/9/30.
31. *Kanke godenki*, p. 86.
32. Suzuki, "Kampyō no kentōshi," pp. 72-79. For a very detailed critique of the various theories on why the missions were abandoned, see the second and third of Masumura's series of articles, "Kentōshi teihai no shosetsu: sōki no shosetsu," *Kadai shigaku* 23:2-20 (1975); and "Kentōshi teihai no shosetsu: kōki no shosetsu," *Kagoshima Keidai ronshū* 17.1:2-48 (July 1976). A more concise summary is in Suzuki, "Kampyō no kentōshi," pp. 61-64.
33. Masumura traces the conspiracy theory back to a 1903 article ("Sōki no shosetsu," pp. 7-12). A principal recent advocate of the conspiracy theory is the popular writer Nakamura Shin'ichirō, in various essays on Michizane, for example, "Sugawara no Michizane," in *Rekishi no Kyōto 3: gakusha to sōryo* (1970), pp. 69-71.
34. The idea that Japan no longer needed to learn from China was popular among prewar historians, and according to Suzuki, it still has supporters ("Kampyō no kentōshi," pp. 61-62, 96). The continuing respect for Chinese culture is stressed by Mori, pp. 187-198; and Sansom, pp. 129-130.
35. Mori, pp. 198-214.
36. This theory was originally presented, in slightly different versions, in Ryō, pp. 55-58; and Sakamoto Tarō, "Sugawara no Michizane to kentōshi," originally published in 1962 and reprinted in his *Kankō to sake*, pp. 34-37.
37. This theory is offered by Suzuki, "Kampyō no kentōshi," pp. 87-88.
38. *Engi shiki*, I, 80, 668-669; II, 1141-1142, etc.; *KBKK*, item 670.
39. Mori, pp. 69-71; Kimiya, pp. 117-121; Niizuma, pp. 312-340; Fairbank, pp. 1-14.
40. The earlier arrival date appears in both *Nihon kiryaku* and *Fusō ryakki*, Kampyō 6/5 (no day). *Fusō ryakki* consistently refers to these visitors from Parhae as "Chinese." The later arrival date appears in *Nihon kiryaku*, Kampyō 6/12/29.

For their reception in the capital, see *Nihon kiryaku*, Kampyō 7/5/4, 7, 11, 14, 15, 16.

41. *Kitano Tenjin godenki*, p. 4; *Nihon kiryaku*, Kampyō 7/5/15.
42. *KBKK*, item 419. The other poems written with the same rhyme are items 420–424.
43. *KBKK*, item 425.
44. *Fusōshū*, p. 195.
45. For an excellent treatment of Tokugawa Japan's diplomatic position, see Ronald P. Toby, *State and Diplomacy in Early Modern Japan: Asia in the Development of the Tokugawa Bakufu* (Princeton, 1984).

CHAPTER 7: FROM MINISTER TO EXILE

1. *Seikyūki*, I, 47, 58; Tokoro, "Kampyō no chi," pp. 123–124; Mezaki, "Uda Jō-kō," pp. 108–110.
2. *Seikyūki*, I, 50–51.
3. *KBKK*, items 578–581, 606–607; *Kitano Tenjin godenki*, p. 4.
4. *KBKK*, item 473. Also see item 472.
5. *KBKK*, item 482. The translation quoted is that of Watson, *Japanese Literature in Chinese*, p. 112. Published by permission of Columbia University Press.
6. Michizane's account, unfortunately, does not survive intact. A highly condensed version can be found in *Fusō ryakki*, Shōtai 1/10/20–11/1, 21 (included in *KBKK* as item 680). Another version, not only condensed but also translated in Japanese, is in *Gosenshū seigi*, in *ZGR* vol. 16b, pp. 623–624. Haseo recorded events of the first two days of the trip, and a complete but poorly preserved text appears in *Kikashū*, pp. 24–30 (also included in *KBKK* as item 679). All these sources, along with the *waka* written on the excursion and a few other data are found in *DNS*, I.2, Shōtai 1/10/20. The following narrative is based on these sources except where noted.
7. *Kokinshū*, no. 420; also translated in Watson, *Japanese Literature in Chinese*, p. 126.
8. *Kokinshū*, no. 421.
9. In addition to those quoted in this section, the poems appearing in imperial anthologies are: *Gosenshū*, nos. 1237, 2358 (by Michizane), and 1368; *Shinchokusenshū*, nos. 502, 1283, 1284; and *Shinshūishū*, no. 1385 (attributed to Michizane). The additional two poems appear in *Kenchū mikkan*, a commentary on *Kokinshū* by Fujiwara no Teika, and *Sosei Hōshi shū*, a collection of Sosei's works. These poems are included in *DNS*. Three poets, Minamoto no Noboru, Tachibana no Kin'yori, and Ariwara no Tomomoto, wrote poems that are preserved but not included in the narrative here.
10. *Fukuro sōshi*, in vol. 2 of *Nihon kagaku taikei*, ed. Sasaki Nobutsuna (1956), pp. 7–8.
11. *Gosenshū*, no. 1238.
12. *Gosenshū*, no. 1357. This poem is also in *Ōkagami*, vol. 21 of *NKBT*, p. 258; or in Helen McCullough's translation, *Ōkagami*, p. 220; and also is translated in Watson, *Japanese Literature in Chinese*, p. 127.
13. *Shinshūishū*, no. 1760. This is a rather late anthology, compiled in 1364, and so the authenticity of the poem is open to question. Its appearance in so late a collection, however, shows how lasting was the appeal of Uda's journey to Japanese poets.
14. As printed in *KBKK* (item 680), the last two characters in the first line mean

"small loom" (*shōki*). The translation follows *Fusō ryakki* as it appears in *KT*, which gives the characters as "heartloom," (*shinki*). The characters for "small" and "heart" are very similar in their script forms. Semantically, "heart" seems more likely to be correct, since the compound "*shinki*" is used in Chinese to mean simply "heart," and thus allows the possibility of understanding the poem either with or without the Japanese conceit of the autumn leaves forming a brocade.

15. *Shinkokinshū*, no. 869.

16. *KBKK*, items 421–422, 547. Again, Haseo wrote a detailed account of this excursion, including the text of the poems by Michizane and Tokihira, along with one by Uda and one of his own (*Kikashū*, pp. 23–24, also included in *KBKK* as item 677). Unfortunately, it is very poorly preserved.

17. *KBKK*, item 368. Also see items 352, 357, and 358.

18. *KBKK*, item 444.

19. *KBKK*, item 608.

20. *KBKK*, items 606, 607; Sakamoto Tarō, *Sugawara no Michizane*, pp. 103–105. For "edicts" by retired emperors, see Hurst, *Insei*, pp. 77–78.

21. *Nihon kiryaku*, Shōtai 2/2/14; *KB*, Shōtai 2; Tokoro Isao, "Sugawara no Michizane no hairu," in *Michizane to Dazaifu*, I, 85. Tokoro has written several articles focusing on different aspects of Michizane's exile. They are carefully written and meticulously documented, as are all his scholarly writings. Much has been written on the circumstances of Michizane's exile, but this is the best account.

22. *SB*, 4:61; *Nihon kiryaku*, Kampyō 8/11/26, Shōtai 1/11/21; *Kampyō goikai*, pp. 106–107, 294; *Kitano Tenjin godenki*, p. 6; Tokoro, "Michizane no hairu," pp. 86–88.

23. *Nihon kiryaku*, Engi 7/6/7; *Kyūreki*, in *Dai Nihon kokiroku* (1958), Tenryaku 4/6/15; Tokoro, "Michizane no hairu," pp. 93–95.

24. *KBKK*, item 477 (translated in Watson, *Japanese Literature in Chinese*, pp. 108–110); *Kitano Tenjin godenki*, pp. 5–6; *SB*, 4:59; *Seiji yōryaku*, p. 3; *Honchō monzui*, I, 1022; *KB*, Engi 2; Tokoro, "Michizane no hairu," p. 88.

25. Tokoro, "Kampyō no chi," p. 124. The figure on the number of regulations signed by Tokihira appears in an unpaginated chart at the end of the article. Tokoro indicates that during the period in question, Michizane issued only 6 regulations. Fujino, however, lists 9, of which 3 come from rather obscure sources ("Michizane nempyō," pp. 373–374). A search through less-used document collections might reveal that Tokihira too had signed more regulations than Tokoro indicates, and so the gap between Tokihira and Michizane could be even greater than the figures in the text indicate. The order that Kiyoyuki lecture on *Shih chi* appears in *Ruijū fushenshō*, p. 244.

26. *KBKK*, items 629–631, and p. 585; Tokoro, "Michizane no hairu," pp. 85–86; Tsunoda, "Michizane to Fujiwara shi," p. 174.

27. *KBKK*, item 629.

28. For Michizane's attempts to resign offices, see *KBKK*, items 609, 675; for Uda's attempts to promote him, *Fusō ryakki*, Shōtai 3/1/3, Eikan 2/6/29; and Hurst, *Insei*, p. 76. In a recent essay, "The Kōbu Policy: Court-Bakufu Relations in Kamakura Japan" (in *Court and Bakufu in Japan*, ed. Jeffrey P. Mass [New Haven, 1982], p. 7), Hurst relates Michizane's refusal to accept the title of chancellor to the concept of "disparity of status," which was proposed by Cornelius J. Kiley ("Estate and Property in the Late Heian Period," in John W. Hall and Jeffrey P. Mass, ed., *Medieval Japan: Essays in Institutional History* [New Haven, 1974], pp. 109–112). In fact, as minister of the right, Michizane already held an

office inappropriate to a person of his status, and as will be noted, this was one of the causes of his downfall.

29. This letter appears in both *Honchō monzui,* I, 1018-1021; and *Seiji yōryaku,* pp. 3-4.

30. Kivoyuki's statement to the court appears in *Nihon kiryaku,* Shōtai 3/10/21; and *Honchō bunshū, KT* vol. 30, p. 150. His more detailed statement, *Kakumei kammon,* is a separate item appearing in *Kodai seiji shakai shisō,* pp. 50-58, 278-281. Tokoro Isao has made a detailed study of Kiyoyuki's "revolutionary" ideas in "Miyoshi no Kiyoyuki to shin'yū kakumei ron," *Shintōshi kenkyū* 17.1:27-50 (January 1969).

31. *KB,* Shōtai 4.

32. *Seiji yōryaku,* pp. 2-3; *Nihon kiryaku,* Engi 1/1/25.

33. This anecdote appears in *Fusō ryakki,* Shōtai 4/1/25, which seems to imply that not Sugane but Haseo blocked Uda's entrance. *Gōdanshō,* however, states that Sugane was responsible (p. 166). Considering the close friendship between Michizane and Haseo, *Gōdanshō* is probably more accurate. Hurst suggests that the passage in *Fusō ryakki* means Haseo attended to rather than blocked Uda (*Insei,* pp. 76-77). Also see Tokoro, "Michizane to Haseo," pp. 6-8. According to *KB,* Sugane was sentenced to exile on the twenty-sixth day and pardoned on the twenty-seventh (Engi 8). Another source states that he was both sentenced and pardoned on the twenty-fifth, and also gives his blocking of Uda's entrance into the palace as the reason (*Kokin wakashū mokuroku,* in *GR,* vol. 13, p. 98).

34. *Seiji yōryaku,* p. 3.

35. *Nihon kiryaku,* Engi 1/1/30, 2/1; *KBKK,* item 483 (translated by Watson, *Japanese Literature in Chinese,* p. 113). The date of Tokiyo's tonsure is recorded in different sources as having occurred on widely different dates. Tokoro prefers the date appearing in *Nihon kiryaku:* Engi 5 (i.e. 905)/3/16, ("Michizane no hairu," p. 96). Fujino, however, follows *Ninnaji shoshi nempu* and *Tōji no chōja bunin* in placing the event on the second day of the second month, 901. The date given by Fujino is more plausible because even some sources giving later dates state that Tokiyo became a monk as a result of Michizane's being exiled. Presumably, those who drove Michizane from the court also forced Tokiyo to become a monk so as to remove him from the imperial succession. If that was the case, their action should have coincided with Michizane's exile, as the date given by Fujino does, rather than occurring in 905, two years after his death. Most of the relevant sources can be found in *DNS,* I.5, Enchō 5/9/10, the date of Tokiyo's death.

36. *Honchō monzui,* I, 1022-1024.

37. *Kakumei kammon,* pp. 281-284; *Nihon kiryaku* and *Fusō ryakki,* Engi 1/7/15.

38. *KBKK,* item 479.

39. *Nihon kiryaku,* Enchō 1/4/20; *Seiji yōryaku,* p. 4; Tokoro, "Michizane no hairu," pp. 63-73.

40. For Daigo's burning of the records, see *Seiji yōryaku,* p. 4; and *Gukanshō,* pp. 154-155 (Brown and Ishida, trans., p. 42). The most detailed argument for Michizane's innocence is found in Tokoro Isao, "Sugawara no Michizane no enzai kanken," *Geirin* 20.5:233-250 (October 1969).

41. The messenger's report was recorded in Daigo's diary, an excerpt of which is preserved in *Fusō ryakki,* Shōtai 4/7/10. For information on Kiyotsura, see *DNS,* I.6, Enchō 8/6/26 (pp. 260-262). In medieval times, Kiyoyuki's name was usually read as "Kiyotsura." Perhaps that was because he and Fujiwara no Kiyotsura had come to be confused with each other. Unlike Kiyoyuki, Kiyotsura does not seem to have been actively involved in the plot against Michizane; however, when he

was killed by lightning, he was seen as a victim of Michizane's angry ghost and thus connected with the plot, at least in people's imaginations.

42. Morita, *Seijishi*, pp. 201-204, 221; Mezaki, *Ōchō no miyabi*, pp. 141-145. Even Sakamoto Tarō, who argues for Michizane's innocence, acknowledges that this statement can be interpreted aṣ a confession of guilt (*Sugawara no Michizane*, p. 113).

43. Tokoro, "Enzai kanken," pp. 239-247. For data on Yoshi, see *DNS* I.2, pp. 842-843.

44. *Ōkagami*, p. 79 (McCullough translation, p. 102); *Kyūreki*, Tenryaku 4/6/15; *Nihon kiryaku*, Engi 3/11/20, 4/2/10.

45. Kitayama, *Heian kyō*, pp. 355-359; Morita, *Seijishi*, pp. 204-208; Sansom, pp. 144-145.

46. Tokoro, "Kiyoyuki no kōhansei," pp. 120-122. The names of Sugane, Hikaru, and Sadakuni are linked together as plotters in *Tenjinki*, which is dated 1194 and thus the oldest extant version *Kitano Tenjin engi*, the familiar account of Michizane's life and deification (in *Kitano*, p. 107). Hikaru's and Sadakuni's appointments appear in *KB*, Shōtai 4.

47. *Nihon kiryaku*, Shōtai 3/10 (no day); Tokoro, "Michizane no hairu," pp. 94-95.

48. Hurst, "The Kōbu Policy," p. 7.

49. *KBKK*, item 526.

50. Mezaki, "Uda Jōkō," pp. 110-112.

51. Nakamura, pp. 74-76.

52. Michizane's exile is described in Sakamoto Tarō, *Sugawara no Michizane*, pp. 115-126; Kawai Ginnosuke, "Kankō Tsukushi kakōki (jō)," *Shiseki to bijutsu* 30.3:104-112 (March 1960). (This is only the first half of what was supposed to be a two-part article; the conclusion apparently was never published); and Tokushige Asakichi, *Nihon bunkashi no kenkyū* (1938), which contains an essay on Michizane's exile, pp. 56-73.

53. *Shūishū*, no. 1006. This poem also appears in *Ōkagami*, some texts of which give the last line as *"Haru na wasureso"* (p. 72; McCullough trans., p. 96). The meaning of the poem does not change. This poem is also translated in Watson, *Japanese Literature in Chinese*, p. 129. For a detailed discussion of it, see Nakashima, pp. 355-375.

54. *Gosenshū*, no. 57. This poem is also translated in Watson, *Japanese Literature in Chinese*, p. 128.

55. *Kitano* contains reliable texts of the major versions of *Kitano Tenjin engi*. In the oldest, *Tenjinki*, the poems appear on p. 108; in the picture-scroll version, entitled *Kitano seibyō engi*, see p. 264. For studies of these texts, see items in Chapter 8, notes 10 and 14. The legend of the flying plum is discussed in Naganuma, pt. 2, pp. 115-120; Sakurai Mitsuru, "Sugawara no Michizane," *Rekishi kōron* 3.10:147-148 (October 1977); and Horiguchi Yasuo, "'Oimatsu' kō," in *Kanze* 44.1:6-8 (January 1977).

56. *Gempei seisuiki* (c. 1250-1300) contains both the alternate story and Shitagō's poem (in vol. 16 of *Kōchū Nihon bungaku taikei* [1921], pp. 283-284). The other treatments of the cherry blossom poem are in *Kitano Tenjin goengi;* an undated text in *Kitano*, p. 137; and *Rakuyō Kitano Tenjin engi*, an early Edo copy in ibid., p. 173.

57. *Shinkokinshū*, no. 1694.

58. This poem appears in many places, most notably *Sugawara denju tenarai kagami*, in *Bunraku jōrurishū*, ed. Yuda Yoshio, vol. 99 of *NKBT*, p. 137. The oracle is in *Kitano*, pp. 42-44 and is discussed in Chapter 8 (see note 10).

59. The noh play has been translated by Ueda Makoto as the title work in his *The Old Pine and Other Noh Plays,* (Lincoln, Nebraska, 1962), pp. 1-11. For the legend behind it, see Horiguchi, pp. 8-12. In traditional orthography, only the word "grown old" was written *"oinu"*; "grown" and "followed" were "ohinu," but even in the Heian period, the actual pronunciations probably were similar.

60. Kitamura Kigin (1624-1705), a pioneer classicist, stated that the cherry poem was written before Michizane's departure for Sanuki, although he does not give a reason (*Hachidaishū zenchū,* Yamagishi Tokuhei, ed., [1961], includes notes by Kigin; for his comment on this poem, see p. 207). In a recent commentary, Kubota Jun suggests that poems in *Shinkokinshū* attributed by Michizane might be forged; although he too fails to provide strong evidence (*Shin'kokin wakashū zenhyōshaku* [1977], VIII, 12-13).

61. For a detailed comparison of Michizane's poem with those of Po Chü-i and Yuen Chen, see in particular Kawaguchi Hisao, "Sugawara no Michizane no bungaku to Gen Shin, Haku Rakuten no bungaku: Dazaifu ni okeru 'Joi ippyakuin' shi o megutte," in *Michizane to Dazaifu,* pp. 103-146; and also Kimpara's essay, "Sugawara no Michizane no kanshi—*Kanke kōshū* shosaishi o chūshin ni," which appears both in ibid., pp. 215-229, and in his book *Heianchō kanshibun,* pp. 258-283.

62. *KBKK,* item 484.

63. *KBKK,* item 514.

64. *Kitano Tenjin godenki,* p. 5; *KBKK,* p. 524 (an undated note appearing after the final poem in *Kanke kōshū.* It is followed by three further poems that Michizane is said to have written posthumously).

65. *Kitano Tenjin godenki,* p. 5; *Kanke godenki,* p. 87; *Nihon kiryaku,* Engi 3/2/25. Ōmaru Isamu, the psychiatrist who diagnosed Michizane's emotional problems, also speculated on his cause of death (*Sugawara no Michizane* [1980], pp. 119-120, 125-126). Michizane noted his ill health in *KBKK,* items 484, 500 (translated by Watson in *Japanese Literature in Chinese,* pp. 118-119), 504, and 513.

66. The stories of Michizane's transfiguration and death appear in *Tenjinki,* pp. 113-114. For the history of the shrine, see Oda Fujio, "Chikuzen Anrakuji shi: kodai makki made," *Kyūshū shigaku* 12:10-11 (June 1959).

CHAPTER 8: MICHIZANE AS TENJIN

1. Prayers at Kitano are mentioned in *SNK,* Jōwa 3/2/1 and Seikyūki, II, 37-38. Imperial visits and other early references to Kitano are indexed in *Rikkokushi Sakuin,* III, 353; and IV, 357. Tenjin worship before Michizane is discussed in Hayashiya Tatsusaburō's 1959 essay "Tenjin shinkō no henreki," reprinted in his *Koten bunka no sōzō* (1964), pp. 203-206; confusion of the different Tenjin is reported in Jean Herbert, *Shintō: At the Fountainhead of Japan* (London, 1967), pp. 28-29, 369.

2. For the first *Goryōe,* see *SJ,* Jōgan 5/5/20. Tenjin as an angry spirit is discussed in Shibata Minoru, "Goryō shinkō to Tenjin," in *Michizane to Dazaifu,* II, 335-351; Hayashiya, pp. 207-211; Morita, *Ōchō seiji,* pp. 169-181; Sakurai Yoshirō, *Kamigami no hembō: shaji engi no sekai kara* (1976), pp. 64-69; and Hori, pp. 111-117.

3. Dazaifu Temmangū is publishing *Dazaifu, Dazaifu Temmangū shiryō* (Fukuoka, 1964-), a chronologically arranged set of documents pertaining to the city and the shrine, edited by Takeuchi Rizō and modeled on *DNS.* The founding of the Anrakuji, first noted in a document dated 976, is in III, Engi 5/8/19; the new building, III, Engi 19 (p. 399); the first Shinto rite, VI, Kōwa 3/8/21. For studies

373 · Notes to Pages 311-326

of the institution, see Oda, pp. 4-22; Nishitakatsuji, pp. 69-113, 168-179; and Sakamoto Ken'ichi, "Shintōshijō no Sugawara no Michizane," in *Michizane to Dazaifu*, I, 320-324.

4. *Kitano Tenjin godenki*, p. 5; and *Honchō monzui*, which includes an examination essay on "the speech of birds and beasts" by the younger son, I, 392-404. For a detailed study of Michizane's descendants, see Makabe, "Michizane no shison," pp. 40-50. Sugawara efforts to deify their ancestor are discussed in Hayashiya, pp. 211-213; and Sakamoto Ken'ichi, pp. 324-326.

5. For early versions of Tokihira's and the crown prince's deaths, see *Nihon kiryaku*, Engi 9/4/4 and Enchō 1/3/21; for more colorful ones, *Tenjinki*, pp. 115-116; and *Daihōshi Jōzō den*, in *Zokuzoku gunsho ruijū*, vol. 3 (1907), pp. 465, 469. The evolution of these stories is analyzed in Kasai Masaaki, *Tenjin engi no rekishi* (1973), pp. 75-83; Kiyoyuki and his sons' roles are discussed in Tokoro, *Miyoshi no Kiyoyuki*, pp. 215-218.

6. For the prince's death and Michizane's pardon, see *Nihon kiryaku*, Enchō 1/3/21, 4/20; and *Seiji yōryaku*, p. 4; for the palace lightning, both *Nihon kiryaku* and *Fusō ryakki*, Enchō 8/6/26. Also see Kasai, pp. 84-86.

7. *Shōmonki*, vol. 2 of *Nihon koten bunko*, ed. Hayashi Rokurō (1975), pp. 104-105. This incident is discussed in Sakaguchi Tsutomu, "*Shōmonki* ni okeru Masakado no sokui ni tsuite," in *Kodai chūsei no shakai to minzoku bunka*, ed. Wakamori Tarō Sensei Kanreki Kinen Rombunshū Henshū Iinkai (1976), pp. 357-385; Wakamori, "Sugawara no Michizane," pp. 113-115; and Morita, *Ōchō seiji*, pp. 190-191.

8. Dōken's account survives in two versions, *Nichizō muki* (*Kitano*, pp. 61-73), which is detailed but poorly preserved; and *Dōken shōnin meidoki* (appearing in *Fusō ryakki*, Tengyō 4/3, and also included in *Kitano*, pp. 77-80), which is shorter but well preserved. Dōken's experiences are discussed in Kasai, pp. 86-93; Shibata, pp. 345-349; and Sakurai Yoshirō, pp. 69-73.

9. The story of Ayako first appears in *Kitano Temman Daijizai Tenjingū Yamashiro no kuni Kadono no kōri Uwabayashi no gō ni hajimete tatsuru engi* in *Kitano*, pp. 8-9 and 30-35. Sources on the Shidara deities appear in *DNS* I.8, Tengyō 8/7/28-8/3. The incident is discussed in Morita, *Ōchō seiji*, pp. 182-190; and Sakurai Yoshirō, pp. 79-85.

10. The second oracle appears as *Tengyō kunen [946] sangatsu futsuka sarunotoki Temman Tenjin no gotakusenki*, in *Kitano*, pp. 42-44; although in other published versions of the same document (for example, *GR* I, 494) the date in the title is one year later, *tenryaku gannen* (947), and that seems to be the correct date, for it appears in other sources. The Shinto priest's visit to Kitano is recorded in *Saichin kimon*, in *Kitano*, p. 10. *Kanke godenki* combines both stories of the shrine's founding, pp. 87-88. Nishida Nagao analyzes these texts in his essay "Kitano Temmangū no sōken," first published in 1961 and reprinted in his *Jinja no rekishiteki kenkyū* (1966), pp. 175-224. Also see Kasai, pp. 93-102; and Sakurai Yoshirō, pp. 73-79.

11. For Heichū, see *Dazaifu, Dazaifu Temmangu shiryō* IV, Tenryaku 1/8/11. The present head priest, Nishitakatsuji Nobusada, discusses his family's history in *Dazaifu Temmangū*, pp. 150-167. Morosuke's prayer and the document placing the shrine under Sugawara control appear in *Kitano*, pp. 11, 29-30.

12. The 986 prayer is in *Honchō monzui*, II, 802-803. For Kitano Shrine's official recognition and Michizane's final promotions, see *DNS* II.1, Eien 1/8/5; Shōryaku 2/6/24, 4/6/26, inter 10/20; and II.5, Kankō 1/inter 9/13, 10/1, 10/11.

13. *Tenjinki*, p. 127; Endō, p. 110-112; Naganuma, 4.2:139-144.

14. Various texts of *Kitano Tenjin engi* appear in *Kitano,* and the illustrated version is beautifully reproduced in both Minamoto Toyomune, ed., *Kitano Tenjin engi,* vol. 9 of *Shinshū Nihon emakimono zenshū* (1977); and Komatsu Shigemi, ed., *Kitano Tenjin engi,* vol. 21 of *Nihon emaki taisei* (1978). Studies include Kasai, *Tenjin engi;* Sakurai Yoshirō, pp. 86-102; Ōno Isao, "*Kitano Tenjin engi* no seiritsu ni tsuite," *Shigaku zasshi* 67.9:1-23 (September 1958); and, Miyeko Murase, "The Tenjin Engi Scrolls—A Study of Their Genealogical Relationship," PhD dissertation, Columbia University, 1962. The use of picture scrolls in proselytizing is discussed by Barbara Ruch in "Medieval Jongleurs and the Making of a National Literature," in *Japan in the Muromachi Age,* ed. John Hall and Toyoda Takeshi (Berkeley, 1977), pp. 288-290. She also presented a paper that focused more specifically on religious picture scrolls, including *Kitano Tenjin engi,* at the Association for Asian Studies Conference, Chicago, March 1973.

15. Texts describing Tenjin's conversion to Zen include *Ryōseiki, Tenjin den'eki,* and *Kanjin nissō jueki,* which appear in *Kitano* on pp. 393-396, and 429-434. Also see Endō, pp. 137-164; Takeuchi Hideo, pp. 42-46; Naganuma, *Shirin,* 4.4:144-152; and Murata Masashi, "Totō Tenjin shisō no genryū," in *Michizane to Dazaifu,* I, 375-401.

16. Michizane and *renga* are discussed in Endō, pp. 181-195; and Takeuchi Hideo, pp. 54-82, 248-259. Eileen Katō has translated Sōgi's account of his visit to Dazaifu as "Pilgrimage to Dazaifu: Sōgi's *Tsukushi no Michi no Ki,*" *Monumenta Nipponica* 34.3:333-367 (Autumn 1979). For *kyōka,* see James T. Kenney, "A Brief History of the Kyōka and the Edo Kyōka Movement," in Theodore Bowie, *Art of the Surimono* (Bloomington, Indiana, 1979), pp. 28-29.

17. Kaibara Ekken's views appear in his *Dazaifu Temmangū kojitsu,* in *Ekken zenshū,* ed. Ekkenkai, (1973), V, 852-854. Rai San'yō's are in his *Nihon seiki,* in *Rai San'yō zensho: zenshū chū,* ed. Kisaki Aikichi and Rai Seiichi (Hiroshima, 1932), pp. 143-144. Confucian opinions of Tenjin are surveyed in Endō, pp. 166, 171-172, 223-234; and Takeuchi Hideo, pp. 212-213, 232-240.

18. Endō, pp. 234-237.

19. Ibid., pp. 238-303. Versions of the *Tenjin sutra* are found in ibid., pp. 270-271 and Takeuchi Hideo, pp. 48-49. For the prewar higher schools, see Donald Roden, *Schooldays in Imperial Japan: A Study in the Culture of a Student Elite* (Berkeley, 1980), pp. 61, 101-102; and for postwar Tenjin worship, see Endō, pp. 358-398.

20. See Horiguchi, pp. 6-12 for Michizane in noh drama; Endō, pp. 318-326, and Takeuchi Hideo, pp. 240-242, for puppet and kabuki representations; and *Sugawara and the Secrets of Calligraphy* for *Sugawara denju tenarai kagami.*

Bibliography

Because many primary sources require special bibliographic treatment, they are listed separately from secondary sources. All primary sources are arranged by title and are provided with brief annotations to indicate authorship and date (or the lack of certainty about the work's provenance) and to explain the nature of the work. English translations of the texts, when they have also been cited, are also noted, although their full entries appear among the secondary sources, where important modern collections of documents are also found. All Japanese works, both primary and secondary sources, are published in Tokyo, except as noted.

Many primary sources appear in four important collectanea, each of which has been reprinted many times, sometimes by different publishers, sometimes with different numbering of the volumes, and sometimes in different editions. The editions used in this study are:

Nihon koten bungaku taikei 日本古典文学大系 . Iwanami Shoten, 1957–1969.

Shinkō gunsho ruijū 新校群書類従 . Comp. Hanawa Hokinoichi 塙保己一 . Naigai Shoseki, 1928–1937.

Shintei zōho kokushi taikei 新訂増補国史大系 . Comp. Kuroita Katsumi 黒板勝美 . Yoshikawa Kōbunkan, 1929–1964.

Zoku gunsho ruijū 続群書類従 . Comp. Hanawa Hokinoichi. Zoku Gunsho Ruijū Kanseikai, 1931–1933.

PRIMARY SOURCES

Bunka shūreishū 文華秀麗集 . The second imperial anthology of *kanshi*, sponsored by Emperor Saga; completed in 818 by a committee headed by Fujiwara no Fuyutsugu 藤原冬嗣 . In *Kaifūsō, Bunka shūreishū, Honchō monzui* 懷風藻．文華秀麗集．本朝文粹 , ed. Kojima Noriyuki 小島憲之 , vol. 69 of *Nihon koten bungaku taikei.*

Chōya gunsai 朝野群載 . A diverse collection of *kambun* writings initially compiled by Miyoshi no Tameyasu 三善為康 (1049–1139) in 1116, with later additions. Vol. 29 of *Shintei zōho kokushi taikei.*

Chishō Daishi den 智證大師傳 . A biography of the monk Enchin 圓珍 (814–891, posthumously known as Chishō Daishi 智證大師), written by Miyoshi no Kiyoyuki c. 902. In *Zoku gunsho ruijū*, vol. 8b.

Daihōshi Jōzō den 大法師淨藏傳 . A biography of the monk Jōzō written anonymously in 1229 on the basis of two earlier biographies that are now lost. In vol. 3 of *Zokuzoku gunsho ruijū*. Kokusho Kankōkai, 1907.

Dazaifu Temmangū kojitsu 大宰府天滿宮故實 : Kaibara Ekken's account of Michizane's life, Tenjin worship, and the Dazaifu Shrine, completed in 1684. In vol. 5 of *Ekken zenshū* 益軒全集 , ed. Ekkenkai. Kokusho Kankōkai, 1973.

Denshi kashū 田氏家集 . A collection of Shimada no Tadaomi's *kanshi*, probably compiled after the Heian period. In vol. 6 of *Shinkō gunsho ruijū.*

Dōken shōnin meidoki 道賢上人冥途記 . An account of Dōken's experiences that is preserved in *Fusō ryakki* under the date Tengyō 4/3. In *Kitano*, ed. Makabe Toshinobu, vol. 11 of *Shintō taikei: jinja hen.* Shintō Taikei Hensankai, 1978.

Engi shiki 延喜式 . A collection of government regulations begun under the sponsorship of Fujiwara no Tokihira in 905 and completed in 927. In *Kōtei Engi shiki* 校訂延喜式 , ed. Kōten Kōkyūjo Zenkoku Shinshokukai. Ōoka Shoten, 1929–1931.

Fujiwara no Yasunori den 藤原保則傳 . A biography of Fujiwara no Yasunori, written by Miyoshi no Kiyoyuki in 907. In *Kodai seiji shakai shisō* 古代政治社会思想 , ed. Yamagishi Tokuhei 山岸德平 , Takeuchi Rizō 竹内理三 , Ienaga Saburō 家永三郎 , and Ōsone Shōsuke 大曽根章介 , vol. 8 of *Nihon shisō taikei* 日本思想大系 . Iwanami Shoten, 1979.

Fukuro sōshi 袋草紙 . A study of *waka* poetics written c. 1156 by Fujiwara no Kiyosuke 藤原清輔 (1104–1177). In vol. 2 of *Nihon kagaku taikei* 日本歌學大系 , ed. Sasaki Nobutsuna 佐佐木信綱 . Kazama Shobō, 1956.

Fusō ryakki 扶桑略記 . A generally reliable chronicle covering the years from Emperor Jimmu　神武　to 1094, compiled by the monk Kōen　皇圓　(d. 1196). Vol. 12 of *Shintei zōho kokushi taikei.*

Fusōshū　扶桑集　. A *kanshi* collection compiled c. 995-998 by Ki no Tadana　紀齊名　(959?-999). Only 2 of 16 chapters survive. In vol. 6 of *Shinkō gunsho ruijū.*

Gempei seisuiki　源平盛衰記　. An account of the Gempei wars, thought to have been written c. 1250-1300, perhaps by Hamuro Tokinaga　葉室時長　(dates unknown); includes many anecdotes not found in the more familiar *Heike Monogatari*　平家物語　. Vols. 15-16 of *Kōchū Nihon bungaku taikei*　校註日本文學大系　. Kokumin Tosho, 1921.

Gōdanshō　江談抄　. A collection of anecdotes told by Ōe no Masafusa 大江匡房　(1041-1111) and recorded c. 1104-1107 by Fujiwara no Sanekane　藤原實兼　(1085-1112). In *Kohonkei Gōdanshō chūkai*　古本系江談抄注解　, ed. Gōdanshō Kenkyūkai. Musashi Shoin, 1978.

Gosenshū　後撰集　. The second of the imperial *waka* anthologies, sponsored by Emperor Murakami　村上　(r. 946-967). Compilation began in 951 by a committee of Ōnakatomi Yoshinobu　大中臣能宣　(922-991) et al. In *Kokka taikan,* ed. Matsushita Daizaburō and Watanabe Fumio. Kadokawa Shoten, 1963.

Gosenshū seigi　後撰集正義　. A commentary to the *Gosenshū,* written c. 1304, authorship unknown. In *Zoku gunsho ruijū,* vol. 16b.

Gukanshō　愚管抄　. The first interpretative history of Japan, written c. 1219 by the monk Jien　慈圓　(1155-1225). Okami Masao 岡見正雄　and Akamatsu Toshihide　赤松俊秀　ed., vol. 86 of *Nihon koten bungaku taikei.* (Translated as *The Future and the Past* by Delmer M. Brown and Ichirō Ishida).

Hokuzanshō　北山抄　. A detailed record of court customs written c. 1012-1020 by Fujiwara no Kintō　藤原公仕　(966-1041). Vol. 4 of *Zōtei kojitsu sōsho*　増訂故實叢書　, ed. Zōtei Kojitsu Sōsho Henshūbu. Yoshikawa Kōbunkan, 1928.

Honchō monzui　本朝文粋　. A diverse collection of *kambun* writings compiled c. 1037-1045 and attributed to Fujiwara no Akihira 藤原明衡　(989-1066). In *Honchō monzui chūshaku* 本朝文粋註釋　, ed. Kakimura Shigematsu　柿村重松　. 2 vols. Fuzambō, 1968.

Honchō reisō　本朝麗藻　. A collection of *kanshi* compiled c. 1007 by Takashina no Moriyoshi　高階積善　(dates unknown). Only the second of 2 chapters survives. In vol. 6 of *Shinkō gunsho ruijū.*

Honchō shojaku mokuroku　本朝書籍目録　(also read *Honchō shoseki mokuroku*). The earliest extant bibliography of Japanese writings, compiled c. 1285-1290 and sometimes attributed to Fujiwara no Sanefuyu　藤原實冬　(1242-1303). In *Honchō shojaku mokuroku kōshō*　本朝書籍目録考證　, ed. Wada Hidematsu 和田英松　. Meiji Shoin, 1940.

Kakumei kammon　革命勘文　. Miyoshi no Kiyoyuki's analysis of

why the year 901 was inauspicious, written in that year. In *Kodai seiji shakai shisō*, ed. Yamagishi Tokuhei, Takeuchi Rizō, Ienaga Saburō, and Ōsone Shōsuke, vol. 8 of *Nihon shisō taikei*. Iwanami Shoten, 1979.

Kampyō no goikai 寛平御遺誡 . Emperor Uda's testament written at the time of his abdication in 897, giving instructions to his successor, Emperor Daigo. The extant text is incomplete, but the edition cited includes both the fullest version plus fragments that survive in other works. In *Kodai seiji shakai shisō*, ed. Yamagishi Tokuhei, Takeuchi Rizō, Ienaga Saburō, and Ōsone Shōsuke, vol. 8 of *Nihon shisō taikei*. Iwanami Shoten, 1979.

Kanchūki 勘仲記 . The diary of Fujiwara no Kanenaka 藤原 兼仲 (1244–1308); originally covering the years 1268–1300, but with sections covering a total of 13 years now lost. Vols. 34–36 of *Zōho shiryō taisei* 増補史料大成 . Kyoto, Rinsen Shobō, 1982.

Kanjin nissō jueki 菅神入宋授衣記 . A late Muromachi period version of the legend of Tenjin's journey to China to study Zen. In *Kitano*, ed. Makabe Toshinobu, vol. 11 of *Shintō taikei: jinja hen*. Shintō Taikei Hensankai, 1978.

Kanke bunsō 菅家文草 . Michizane's collection of his prose and poetry in Chinese that he presented to Emperor Daigo in 900. In *Kanke bunsō, Kanke kōshū*, ed. Kawaguchi Hisao. Vol. 72 of *Nihon koten bungaku taikei* (cited as *KBKK*).

Kanke den 菅家傳 . A detailed genealogy of the Sugawara family with entries as late as 1837, not to be confused with *Kitano Tenjin goden*, which is often cited as *Kanke den*. In *Kitanoshi*, ed. Kitano Jinja, vol. 2. Kokugakuin Daigaku Shuppambu, 1910.

Kanke godenki 菅家御傳記. The second-oldest account of Michizane's life, compiled in 1106 by Sugawara no Nobutsune 菅原陳經 (dates unknown). Generally reliable, with indications of the sources it used. In *Kitano*, ed. Makabe Toshinobu, vol. 11 of *Shintō taikei: jinja hen*. Shintō Taikei Hensankai, 1978.

Kanke kōshū 菅家俊集 (also known as *Kanke kōsō* 菅家 俊草). Michizane's collection of his *kanshi* written in Dazaifu. In *Kanke bunsō, Kanke kōshū*, ed. Kawaguchi Hisao. Vol. 72 of *Nihon koten bungaku taikei* (cited as *KBKK*).

Keikokushū 經國集 . Last imperial anthology of *kambun* literature; sponsored by Emperor Junna, completed in 827 by a committee headed by Yoshimine no Yasuyo 良岑安世 (785–830). Only 6 of 20 chapters survive. In vol. 24 of *Kōchū Nihon bungaku taikei*. Kokumin Tosho, 1936.

Keirin ihōshō 桂林遺芳抄 . A guide to Muromachi-period examination procedures written in 1515 by Sugawara Kazunaga 菅原 和長 (1460–1529). In vol. 21 of *Shinkō gunsho ruijū*.

Kikashū 紀家集 . A collection of Ki no Haseo's *kambun* writings. Only 1 of 20 chapters survives and it is poorly preserved. In "*Kikashū*" *kaidai shakubun* 紀家集解題釈文 ed. Kunaichō Shoryōbu. Yoshikawa Kōbunkan, 1978.

Kitano seibyō engi　北野聖廟縁起　. The oldest and most famous illustrated version of Michizane's life and deification, c. 1219. In *Kitano*, ed. Makabe Toshinobu, vol. 11 of *Shintō taikei: jinja hen.* Shintō Taikei Hensankai, 1978.

Kitano Temman Daijizai Tenjingū sōken Yamashiro no kuni Kadono no kōri Uwabayashi no gō ni hajimete tatsuru engi　北野天満大自在天神宮創建山城國葛野郡上林郷縁起　. Tajihi no Ayako's version of the founding of Kitano Shrine as written by one of her relatives in 960. In *Kitano*, ed. Makabe Toshinobu, vol. 11 of *Shintō taikei: jinja hen.* Shintō Taikei Hensankai, 1978.

Kitano Tenjin goden　北野天神御傳　(also known as *Kanke den*). The oldest biography of Michizane, written c. 931–947, probably by one of his grandsons. For detailed discussion of this important text, see two articles by Makabe Toshinobu, "Egara Tenjinja bon *Kanke den* no shutsugen," and "*Kanke den* no hensha kō—Monjō Hakase Sugawara no Arimi no katsuyaku," both cited under Secondary Sources. In *Kitano*, ed. Makabe Toshinobu, vol. 11 of *Shintō taikei: jinja hen.* Shintō Taikei Hensankai, 1978.

Kitano Tenjin goengi　北野天神御縁起　. A version of *Kitano Tenjin engi* of uncertain date that, unlike most texts, is in *kambun*. In *Kitano*, ed. Makabe Toshinobu, vol. 11 of *Shintō taikei: jinja hen.* Shintō Taikei Hensankai, 1978.

Kokinshū　古今集　. The first imperial *waka* anthology, sponsored by Emperor Daigo; completed in 905 by Ki no Tsurayuki et al. In *Kokka taikan*, ed. Matsushita Daizaburō and Watanabe Fumio. Kadokawa Shoten, 1963.

Kokin wakashū mokuroku　古今和歌集目録　. A commentary on the *Kokinshū* attributed to Fujiwara no Nakazane 藤原仲實 (1057–1118). In vol. 13 of *Shinkō gunsho ruijū*.

Kugyō bunin　公卿補任　. An annual record of high court nobles from the reign of Emperor Jimmu through 1868, begun in the ninth century. Vols. 53–57 of *Shintei zōho kokushi taikei* (cited as *KB*).

Kyūreki 九曆 . The diary of Fujiwara no Morosuke 藤原師輔 (908–960) covering the years 947–960 in the extant version. In *Dai Nihon kokiroku* 大日本古記録 , ed. Tōkyō Daigaku Shiryō Hensanjo. Iwanami Shoten, 1958.

Midō kampaku ki　御堂關白記　. The diary of Fujiwara no Michinaga. Fourteen out of 30 chapters survive covering the years 998–1021. In *Dai Nihon kokiroku*, ed. Tōkyō Daigaku Shiryō Hensanjo. Iwanami Shoten, 1952.

Montoku jitsuroku　文德實錄　. The fifth of the Rikkokushi, completed in 879 by a committee under Fujiwara no Mototsune. Covers the years 850–858. In vol. 3 of *Shintei zōho kokushi taikei* (cited as *MJ*).

Nichizō muki　日藏夢記　. The most detailed account of Dōken's experiences that survives only in a somewhat mutilated text. In *Kitano*, ed. Makabe Toshinobu, vol. 11 of *Shintō taikei: jinja hen.* Shintō Taikei Hensankai, 1978.

Nichūreki 二中歴 . An encyclopedic compendium on court customs, completed c. 1444–1448. Vol. 23 of *Kaitei shiseki shūran* 改定 史籍集覧 . Kondō Kappanjo, 1901.

Nihon kiryaku 日本紀略 . A chronicle modeled on the Rikkokushi covering the years from the age of the gods through 1036. Author and date unknown. Vol. 10 of *Shintei zōho kokushi taikei*.

Nihon kōki 日本後紀 . The third of the Rikkokushi, completed in 840 by a committee under Fujiwara no Otsugu 藤原緒嗣 (773–843). Covers the years 792–833. Only 10 of 40 chapters survive. In vol. 3 of *Shintei zōho kokushi taikei* (cited as *NK*).

Nihon seiki 日本政記 . A history of Japan that the scholar Rai San'yō was working on at the time of his death in 1832. In *Rai San'yō zensho: zenshū chū* 頼山陽全書 全集中 , ed. Kisaki Aikichi 木崎愛吉 and Rai Seiichi 頼成一 . Rai San'yō Sensei Iseki Kenshōkai. Hiroshima, 1932.

Nihon shoki 日本書紀 (or *Nihongi* 日本紀). The first of the Rikkokushi, completed in 720 by a committee under Prince Toneri 舎人 (d. 735); covers the years from the age of the gods through 696. Vol. 1 of *Shintei zōho kokushi taikei* (cited as *NS*).

Nittō shingu shōgyō mokuroku 入唐新求聖教目録 . The monk Ennin's bibliography of works he brought back from China, compiled in 847. In vol. 60 of *Taishō shinshū daizōkyō* 大正新修 大藏經 , ed. Takakusu Junjirō 高楠順次郎 . Taisho Issaikyō Kankōkai, 1928.

Ōkagami 大鏡 . An early Japanese-language court history, written c. 1085–1125. Muramatsu Hiroshi 村松博司 ed., vol.21 of *Nihon koten bungaku taikei*. (Translated as *Ōkagami: The Great Mirror* by Helen McCullough).

Rakuyō Kitano Tenjin engi 洛陽北野天神縁起 . A version of *Kitano Tenjin engi* copied in the early Edo period. In *Kitano*, ed. Makabe Toshinobu, vol. 11 of *Shintō taikei: jinja hen*. Shintō Taikei Hensankai, 1978.

Ruijū fusenshō 類聚符宣抄 . A collection of official documents dating from the years 737 to 1093; compiler and date of compilation unknown. Eight of 10 chapters survive. Vol. 27 of *Shintei zōho kokushi taikei*.

Ruijū kokushi 類聚國史 . Entries from the Rikkokushi arranged topically; compiled by Sugawara no Michizane c. 892. Only 61 of 200 chapters survive. Vols. 5–6 of *Shintei zōho kokushi taikei*.

Ruijū kudaishō 類聚句題抄 . A late Heian collection of *kudaishi* 句題詩 , i.e., *kanshi* that take a familiar line of poetry as their theme. In vol. 12a of *Zoku gunsho ruijū*.

Ruijū sandai kyaku 類聚三代格 . A collection of government regulations from the Nara and early Heian periods, compiled in the late Heian period. Fifteen of 30 chapters survive. Vol. 25 of *Shintei zōho kokushi taikei*.

Ryō no gige 令義解 . An official commentary to the *Yōrō*

ryō, completed in 836 by a committee of Kiyowara no Natsuno 清原夏野 (782–837) et al. Vol. 22 of *Shintei zōho kokushi taikei.*

Ryō no shūge 令集解 . An unofficial compendium of commentaries on the *Yōrō ryō,* compiled by Koremune no Naomoto 惟宗 直本 (859?–930?), c. 859–884. Thirty-six of 50 chapters survive. Vols. 23–24 of *Shintei zōho kokushi taikei.*

Ryōseiki 兩聖記 . The earliest version of the story of Tenjin journey to China to study Zen, written by Fujiwara Nagachika 藤原 長親 c. 1394. In *Kitano,* ed. Makabe Toshinobu, vol. 11 of *Shintō taikei: jinja hen.* Shintō Taikei Hensankai, 1978.

Ryōunshū 凌雲集 . The first imperial *kanshi* anthology, sponsored by Emperor Saga and completed c. 814 by a committee of Ono no Minemori 小野岑守 (778–830) et al. In vol. 3 of Kojima Noriyuki, *Kokufū ankoku jidai no bungaku.* Hanawa Shobō, 1978.

Saichin kimon 最鎮記文 . An account of the founding of Kitano Shrine by the monk Saichin, written c. 959. In *Kitano,* ed. Makabe Toshinobu, vol. 11 of *Shintō taikei: jinja hen.* Shintō Taikei Hensankai, 1978.

Sandai jitsuroku 三代實錄 . The last of the Rikkokushi, its initial compilation committee included Michizane, but it was completed in 901 by a committee under Fujiwara no Tokihira; covers the years 858–887. Vol. 4 of *Shintei zōho kokushi taikei* (cited as *SJ*).

Seiji yōryaku 政事要略 . A collection of materials relating to governmental procedures, compiled c. 1008 and attributed to Koremune no Masasuke 惟宗允亮 (late tenth–early eleventh century). Only 26 of 140 chapters survive. Vol. 28 of *Shintei zōho kokushi taikei.*

Seikyūki 西宮記 (also read *Saikyūki* or *Saigūki*). Considered the diary of Minamoto no Takaakira 源高明 (913–982), but, in fact, a topically arranged description of court customs. Vols. 37 and 40 of *Zōtei kojitsu sōsho,* ed. Zōtei Kojitsu Sōsho Henshūbu. Yoshikawa Kōbunkan, 1930.

Shinchokusenshū 新勅撰集 . The ninth imperial *waka* anthology, sponsored by Retired Emperor Gohorikawa 後堀河 (r. 1221–1232) and completed c. 1234 with Fujiwara Teika 藤原定家 (1162–1241) as editor. In *Kokka taikan,* ed. Matsushita Daizaburō and Watanabe Fumio. Kadokawa Shoten, 1963.

Shinkokinshū 新古今集 . The eighth imperial *waka* anthology, sponsored by Retired Emperor Gotoba 後鳥羽 (r. 1183–1198) and initially completed in 1206, but with later revisions. Edited by a committee including Fujiwara Teika et al. In *Kokka taikan,* ed. Matsushita Daizaburō and Watanabe Fumio. Kadokawa Shoten, 1963.

Shinshūishū 新拾遺集 . The nineteenth imperial *waka* anthology, sponsored by Emperor Gokōgon 後光嚴 of the "northern dynasty:' (r. 1353–1731) at the request of Shogun Ashikaga Yoshiakira 足利義 詮. Completed in 1364 with Fujiwara no Tameaki 藤原爲明 as principal editor. In *Kokka taikan,* ed. Matsushita Daizaburō and Watanabe Fumio. Kadokawa Shoten, 1963.

Shoku Nihongi 續日本紀 . The second of the Rikkokushi, completed in 797 by two committees, one under Sugano no Mamichi 菅野眞道 (738-811) and the other under Fujiwara no Tsugutada 藤原繼繩 (727-806); covers the years 697-791. Vol. 2 of *Shintei zōho kokushi taikei* (cited as *SN*).

Shoku Nihon kōki 續日本後紀 . The fourth of the Rikkokushi, completed in 869 by a committee under Fujiwara no Yoshifusa; covers the years 833-850. In vol. 3 of *Shintei zōho kokushi taikei* (cited as *SNK*).

Shōmonki 將門記 . An account of Taira no Masakado's rebellion, thought to have been written in 940 by monks in the Kantō area. Ed. Hayashi Rokurō 林陸朗 , vol. 2 of *Nihon koten bunko* 日本古典文庫 . Gendai Shichōsha, 1975.

Shūgaishō 拾芥抄 . An encyclopedic description of court customs, originally compiled during the thirteenth century, with later additions. Vol. 32 of *Zōtei kojitsu sōsho,* ed. Zōtei Kojitsu Sōsho Henshūbu. Yoshikawa Kōbunkan, 1928.

Shūishū 拾遺集 . The third imperial *waka* anthology, thought to have been compiled c. 1000 principally by Retired Emperor Kazan 花山 (968-1008, r. 984-986) and Fujiwara no Kintō. In *Kokka taikan,* ed. Matsushita Daizaburō and Watanabe Fumio. Kadokawa Shoten, 1963.

Sompi bummyaku 尊卑分脈 . A comprehensive genealogy of court families, based on early Muromachi texts with later additions and revisions. Vols. 58-60 of *Shintei zōho kokushi taikei* (cited as *SB*).

Sugawara denju tenarai kagami 菅原傳授手習鑑 . A play for the puppet theater, first performed in 1746 and written by Takeda Izumo 竹田出雲 (1691-1756), Namiki Senryū 並木千柳 (1695?-1751?), Miyoshi Shōraku 三好松洛 (1696?-1771?), and Takeda Koizumo 竹田小出雲 (d. 1753). In *Bunraku jōrurishū* 文樂淨瑠璃集 , ed. Yuda Yoshio 祐田善雄 , vol. 99 of *Nihon koten bungaku taikei.* (Famous scenes from this play have been translated often; Stanleigh Jones has translated the whole play as *Sugawara and the Secrets of Calligraphy*).

Sugawara shi keizu 菅原氏系圖 . The name of 5 genealogies of the Sugawara family that appear in *Zoku gunsho ruijū.* The ones referred to in chapter 1 note 61 date respectively from the mid-fifteenth century, the mid-sixteenth century, and the early seventeenth century. In vol. 7b of *Zoku gunsho ruijū.*

Taiki 台記 . The diary of Fujiwara no Yorinaga 藤原賴長 (1120-1156), covering the years 1136-1155, with numerous gaps in the extant text. Vols. 23-25 of *Zōho shiryō taisei.* Kyoto, Rinsen Shoten, 1982.

Tengyō kunen sangatsu futsuka sarunotoki Temman Tenjin no gotakusenki 天慶九年三月二日酉時天滿天神御詫宣記 . Miwa no Yoshitane's account of the founding of Kitano Shrine. In *Kitano,* ed. Makabe Toshinobu, vol. 11 of *Shintō taikei: jinja hen.* Shintō Taikei Hensankai, 1978.

Tenjin den'eki 天神傳衣記 . An undated account of Tenjin's journey to China to study Zen. In *Kitano*, ed. Makabe Toshinobu, vol. 11 of *Shintō taikei: jinja hen*. Shintō Taikei Hensankai, 1978.

Tenjin kegenki 天神化現記 . The earliest account of the boy Michizane's mysterious appearance at his father's mansion, dating from c. 1070. In *Kitano,* ed. Makabe Toshinobu, vol. 11 of *Shintō taikei: jinja hen*. Shintō Taikei Hensankai, 1978.

Tenjinki 天神記 . The oldest extant version of *Kitano Tenjin engi,* dated 1194. In *Kitano,* ed. Makabe Toshinobu, vol. 11 of *Shintō taikei: jinja hen*. Shintō Taikei Hensankai, 1978.

Tenso reishi shokushō roku 天祚禮祀職掌録 . A description of enthronement ceremonies for emperors from Uda through Gohana-zono 後花園 (r. 1428-1464). Originally compiled c. 1336, with later additions. In vol. 2 of *Shinkō gunsho ruijū*.

Toshi bunshū 都氏文集 . A collection of Miyako no Yoshika's *kambun* writings; only 3 of 6 chapters survive. In vol. 6 of *Shinkō gunsho ruijū*.

Wakan rōeishū 和漢朗詠集 . A collection of couplets from *kanshi,* by both Japanese and Chinese poets, and *waka* arranged by theme for chanting. Compiled by Fujiwara no Kintō, c. 1011. In *Wakan rōeishū, Ryōjin hishō* 和漢朗詠集・梁塵秘抄 , ed. Kawaguchi Hisao and Shida Engi 志田延義 , vol. 73, *Nihon koten bungaku taikei.*

Wen-hsuan 文選 . A major anthology of Six Dynasties literature that was compiled by Hsiao T'ung 蕭統 (501-531) c. 526 and was widely read in early Japan. Ed. Obi Kōichi 小尾郊一 , vols. 26-32 of *Zenshaku kambun taikei* 全釈漢文大系 . Shūeisha, 1974-1976.

Yotsugi monogatari 世継物語 (also known as *Uji dainagon monogatari* 宇治大納言物語). A late thirteenth century collection of anecdotes. In vol. 32b of *Zoku gunsho ruijū*.

Zatsugen hōwa 雜言奉和 . A collection of 44 *kanshi* compiled c. 947-957. In vol. 6 of *Shinkō gunsho ruijū*.

SECONDARY SOURCES

Abe Takeshi 阿部猛 . *Ritsuryō kokka kaitai katei no kenkyū* 律令国家解体過程の研究 (A study of the process of the collapse of the *ritsuryō* state). Shinseisha, 1966.

——. *Heian zenki seijishi no kenkyū* 平安前期政治史の研究 (A study of early Heian political history). Seishinsha, 1974.

——. *Sugawara no Michizane: kyūseiki no seiji to shakai* 菅原道真九世紀の政治と社会 (Sugawara no Michizane: ninth-century politics and society). Kyōikusha, 1979.

Aida Hanji 會田範治 . *Chūkai Yōrō ryō* 註解養老令 (The annotated Yōrō Civil Code). Yūshindō, 1964.

Akiyama Ken 秋山虔 . "Kodai kanjin no bungaku shisō" 古代

官人の文学思想 (Literary thought of ancient bureaucrats), *Kokugo to kokubungaku* 32.4:30–40 (April 1955).

———. "Sugawara no Michizane ron no dansho" 菅原道真論の断章 (Thoughts on Sugawara no Michizane), *Kokugo to kokubungaku* 34.10:37–45 (October 1957).

———. "Waka Runessansu" 和歌ルネッサンス (The *waka* renaissance), in *Nihon bungaku no rekishi 3: kyūtei saron to saijo,* 日本文学の歴史 3: 宮廷サロンと才女 . Ed. Yamanaka Yutaka 山中裕 and Akiyama Ken. Kadokawa Shoten, 1967.

———. "Sugawara no Michizane no shijin keisei" 菅原道真の詩人形成 (Sugawara no Michizane's development as a poet), in *Sugawara no Michizane to Dazaifu Temmangū.* Ed. Dazaifu Temmangū Bunka Kenkyūjo, vol. 1. Yoshikawa Kōbunkan, 1975.

Aoki Kazuo 青木和夫 . "Ritsuryō kokka no kenryoku kōzō" 律令国家の権力構造 (The power structure of the *ritsuryō* state), in *Iwanami kōza Nihon rekishi 3: kodai 3* 岩波講座日本歴史 3: 古代 3 . Iwanami Shoten, 1976.

Aoki Masaru 青木正兒 . "Shō no rekishi to jigi no hensen" 嘯の歴史と字義の變遷 (A history of whistling [*hsiao*] and changes in the meaning of the character), in *Aoki Masaru zenshū* 青木正兒全集 , vol. 8. Shunjūsha, 1971.

Borgen, Robert. "The Origins of the Sugawara: A History of the Haji Family," *Monumenta Nipponica* 30.4:405–422 (Winter 1975).

———. "The Japanese Mission to China of 801–806," *Monumenta Nipponica* 37.1:1–28 (Spring 1982).

Brower, Robert H., and Earl Miner. *Japanese Court Poetry.* Stanford, Stanford University Press, 1961.

Chin Yü-fu 金毓黻 . *Po-hai kuo-chih ch'ang-pien* 渤海國志長編 (A complete history of the kingdom of Parhae). Published c. 1934 and reprinted in *Chung-hua wen-shih ts'ung-shu* 中華文史叢書 , vol. 7. Taipei, 1968.

Collcutt, Martin. *Five Mountains: The Rinzai Zen Monastic Institution in Medieval Japan.* Cambridge, Harvard University, Council on East Asian Studies, 1981.

The Complete Works of Chuang Tzu, tr. Burton Watson. New York, Columbia University Press, 1968.

Confucian Analects, tr. James Legge, in *The Chinese Classics,* vol. 1. Oxford, Clarendon Press, 1892.

Crump, James. "'Borrowed' T'ang Titles and Offices in the Yōrō Codes," in *Occasional Papers: Center for Japanese Studies.* Ann Arbor, University of Michigan Press, 1952.

Dai Nihon Shiryō 大日本史料 (Japanese historical materials) Comp. Tōkyō Daigaku Shiryō Hensanjo. Tōkyō Daigaku Shuppankai, 1901– (cited as *DNS*).

Dai Nihon shoga meika taikan　大日本書画名家大鑑
(Famous Japanese calligraphers and painters). Ed. Araki Tadashi
荒木矩　. Dai Nihon Shoga Meika Taikan Kankōkai,
1934.

Davis, A. R. "The Double Ninth Festival in Chinese Poetry: A Study in
Variations upon a Theme," in *Wen-lin: Studies in the Chinese Humani-*
ties. Ed. Chow Tse-tung. Madison, University of Wisconsin Press, 1968.

Dazaifu, Dazaifu Temmangū shiryō　大宰府・大宰府天満宮
史料　(Dazaifu and Dazaifu Temman Shrine historical materials).
Ed. Takeuchi Rizō. Dazaifu, Dazaifu Temmangū, 1964– .

des Rotours, Robert. *Le Traité des Examens.* Paris, Libraire Ernest Leroux,
1932.

———. *Traité des Fonctionnaires et Traité de l'Armée.* Leiden, E. J. Brill,
1947.

Doe, Paula. *A Warbler's Song in the Dusk: The Life and Work of Ōtomo*
no Yakamochi (718–785). Berkeley, University of California Press,
1982.

Dumoulin, Heinrich. *A History of Zen Buddhism,* tr. Paul Peachey. New
York, Pantheon Books, 1963.

Edwards, E. D. "Principles of Whistling—*Hsiao-Chih*—Anonymous," *Bulle-*
tin of the School of Oriental and African Studies 20:217–229 (1957).

Eiga Monogatari: A Tale of Flowering Fortunes, tr. William H. and Helen
C. McCullough. Stanford, Stanford University Press, 1980.

Endō Taisuke　遠藤泰助. *Temman Tenjin shinkō no kyōikushiteki*
kenkyū　天満天神信仰の教育史的研究　(Ten-
jin worship: a study in educational history). Kōdansha, 1966.

Ennin's Diary: The Records of a Pilgrimage to China in Search of the Law,
tr. Edwin O. Reischauer. New York, Ronald Press, 1955.

Fairbank, John K. "A Preliminary Framework," in *The Chinese World*
Order. Ed. John K. Fairbank. Cambridge, Harvard University Press,
1968.

Fenollosa, Ernest. *The Chinese Character as a Medium for Poetry.* Ed. Ezra
Pound. 1936. Reprint San Francisco, City Lights Books, n.d.

Fujino Hideko　藤野秀子　. "Sugawara no Michizane nempyō"
菅原道真年表　(Chronology of Sugawara no Michizane), in *Sugawara*
no Michizane to Dazaifu Temmangū. Ed. Dazaifu Temmangū Bunka
Kenkyūjo, vol. 2. Yoshikawa Kōbunkan, 1975.

———. "Sugawara no Michizane, Temmangū, Tenjin shinkō kankei bunken
mokuroku"　菅原道真・天満宮・天神信仰関係文献
目録　(Bibliography of materials relating to Sugawara no
Michizane, Temman shrines, and Tenjin worship), in *Sugawara no Mi-*
chizane to Dazaifu Temmangū. Ed. Dazaifu Temmangū Bunka Kenkyūjo, vol. 2. Yoshikawa Kōbunkan, 1975.

Fuke Sōei　福家惣衛　. *Kagawa ken tsūshi: kodai chūsei kinsei hen*
香川県通史：古代中世近世編　(A survey history

of Kagawa prefecture: ancient, medieval, and early modern). Takamatsu, Kagawa Prefecture, Ueda Shoten, 1965.

The Future and the Past: A Translation and Study of the Gukanshō, an Interpretive History of Japan Written in 1219, tr. and ed. Delmer M. Brown and Ichirō Ishida. Berkeley, University of California Press, 1979.

Gengo geijutsu no hana hiraku 言語芸術の花 ひらく (The blossoming of the flower of the linguistic arts), vol. 3 of *Nihongo no rekishi* 日本語の歴史 (History of the Japanese language). Ed. Doi Tadao 土井忠生. Heibonsha, 1964.

Gotō Akio 後藤昭雄. *Heianchō kambungaku ronkō* 平安朝漢文学論考 (Essays on Heian literature in Chinese). Ōfūsha, 1981.

Hachidaishū zenchū 八代集全註 (Anthologies from eight reigns, fully annotated). Ed. Yamagishi Tokuhei 山岸徳平, 3 vols. Yūseidō (1960).

Hagino Yasuyuki 萩野懐之. "Akō mondai to Kankō sasen" 阿衡問題と菅公左遷 (The Akō problem and Michizane's exile), *Rekishi chiri* 14.2:18–33 (August 1899).

Haku Rakuten shishū 白樂天詩集 (A collection of Po Chü-i's poetry), vol. 11 of *Zoku kokuyaku kambun taisei, bungakubu* 續國譯漢文大成. 文學部. Tōyō Bunka Kyōkai, 1957.

Hall, John W. *Japan from Prehistory to Modern Times.* New York, Delacourt Press, 1970.

Haruna Yoshishige 春名好重. *Jōdai nōsho den* 上代能書伝 (Biographies of ancient calligraphers). Mokujisha, 1972.

Hayakawa Shōhachi 早川庄八. *Nihon no rekishi 4: ritsuryō kokka* 日本の歴史4: 律令国家 (History of Japan vol. 4: the *ritsuryō* state). Shōgakkan, 1974.

Hayashi Rokurō 林陸郎. *Jōdai seiji shakai no kenkyū* 上代政治社会の研究 (A study of ancient politics and society). Yoshikawa Kōbunkan, 1969.

Hayashiya Tatsusaburō 林屋辰三郎. *Koten bunka no sōzō* 古典文化の創造 (The creation of classical culture). Tōkyō Daigaku Shuppankai, 1964.

Herbert, Jean. *Shintō: At the Fountainhead of Japan.* London, Allan and Unwin, 1967.

Herbert, Penelope A. "Japanese Embassies and Students in T'ang China," University of Western Australia Centre for East Asian Studies Occasional Paper no. 4. Nedlands, Australia, n.d.

Hisaki Yukio 久木幸男. *Daigakuryō to kodai jukyō* 大学寮と古代儒教 (The university and ancient Confucianism). Saimaru Shuppankai, 1968.

Holzman, Donald. "Literary Criticism in China in the Third Century A.D.," *Asiatische Studien/Etudes Asiatiques* 28.2:113–149 (1974).

————. *Politics and Poetry: The Life and Works of Juan Chi (A.D. 210–263)*. Cambridge, Cambridge University Press, 1976.

Hori, Ichiro. *Folk Religion in Japan*. Chicago, University of Chicago Press, 1968.

Horiguchi Yasuo 堀口康生 . "'Oimatsu' kō" 「老松」考 (A study of "Oimatsu"), *Kanze* 44.1:6–12 (January 1977).

Hurst, G. Cameron, III. *Insei: Abdicated Sovereigns in the Politics of Late Heian Japan, 1086–1185*. New York, Columbia University Press, 1976.

————. "The Kōbu Policy: Court-Bakufu Relations in Kamakura Japan," in *Court and Bakufu in Japan*. Ed. Jeffrey P. Mass. New Haven, Yale University Press, 1982.

Ikeda Genta 池田源太 . "Heian shoki ni okeru monjō no keikoku-teki seikaku" 平安初期における文章の經国的性格 (The concept of literature as a support of the state in the early Heian period), in *Kammuchō no shomondai* 桓武朝の諸問題 . Ed. Kodaigaku Kyōkai. Osaka, Kodaigaku Kyōkai, 1962.

————. *Nara Heian jidai no bunka to shūkyō* 奈良平安時代の文化と宗教 (Culture and religion of the Nara and Heian periods). Kyoto, Nagata Bunshōdō, 1977.

Ikeda Kikan 池田亀鑑 . *Heian jidai no bungaku to seikatsu* 平安時代の文學と生活 (Literature and life of the Heian period). Shibundō, 1966.

Inoue Kaoru 井上薫 . *Nihon kodai no seiji to shūkyō* 日本古代の政治と宗教 (Ancient Japanese politics and religion). Yoshikawa Kōbunkan, 1961.

————. *Kodaishi no gunzō* 古代史の群像 (Portraits from ancient history). Sōgensha, 1980.

Inoue Tetsujirō 井上哲次郎 . *Sugawara no Michizane* 菅原の道真 (Sugawara no Michizane). Hokkai Shuppansha, 1936.

Ishii Masatoshi 石井正敏 . "Shoki Nichi-Botsu kōshō ni okeru ichi mondai" 初期日渤交渉における一問題 (One issue in early relations between Japan and Parhae), in *Shigaku ronshū taigai kankei to seiji bunka* 史学論集対外関係と政治文化 , vol. 1. Ed. Mori Katsumi Hakase Koki Kinenkai. Yoshikawa Kōbunkan, 1974.

Ishio Yoshihisa 石尾芳久 . *Nihon kodai no tennōsei to daijōkan seido* 日本古代の天皇制と太政官制度 (The ancient Japanese emperor and Council of State system). Yūhikaku, 1962.

Iwahashi Koyata 岩橋小彌太 . *Jōdai kanri seido no kenkyū* 上代官吏制度の研究 (A study of the ancient bureaucratic system). Yoshikawa Kōbunkan, 1964.

Iyanaga Teizō 弥永貞三 . "Ninna ninen no naien" 仁和二年の内宴 (The palace banquet in the second year of the Ninna era), in *Nihon kodaishi ronshū* 日本古代史論集 . Ed. Sakamoto Tarō Hakase Kanreki Kinenkai, vol. 2. Yoshikawa Kōbunkan, 1962.

——. "Sugawara no Michizane no zenhansei" 菅原道真の 前半生 (Sugawara no Michizane's early years), in *Nihon jimbutsushi taikei* 日本人物史大系 . Ed. Kawasaki Tsuneyuki 川崎 庸之 . Asakura Shoten, 1963.

——. "'Shunjitsu kakei' no shi: Ōtemmon no hen to Michizane o tori-maku hitobito," 「春日暇景」の詩：応天門の変と 道真をとりまく人々 (The poem "Resting on a Spring Day": The Ōtemmon Incident and people involved with Michizane), *Shintei zōho kokushi taikei geppō* 25:1–5 (July 1965).

——. "Kodai no sekiten ni tsuite" 古代の釈奠について (Concerning the ancient Confucian memorial rites), in *Zoku Nihon kodaishi ronshū* 続日本古代史論集 . Ed. Saka-moto Tarō Hakase Koki Kinenkai, vol. 3. Yoshikawa Kōbunkan, 1972.

Japan in the Chinese Dynastic Histories, tr. Ryūsaku Tsunoda. Ed. L. Car-rington Goodrich. Perkins Asiatic Monographs no. 2. South Pasadena, California, P. D. and Iona Perkins, 1951.

Johnson, David G. *The Medieval Chinese Oligarchy*. Boulder, Colorado, Westview Press, 1977.

Kakimura Shigematsu 柿村重松 . *Jōdai Nihon kambungakushi* 上代日本漢文学史 (History of ancient Japanese lit-erature in Chinese). Nihon Shoin, 1947.

Kanda Hideo 神田秀夫 . "Kambungaku" 漢文学 (Literature in Chinese), in *Shimpan Nihon bungakushi 1: Jōdai* 新版日本 文学史 1：上古 . Ed. Hisamatsu Sen'ichi 久松潜一 . Shibundō, 1971.

Kaneko Hikojirō 金子彦二郎 . *Heian jidai bungaku to Hakushi monjū: Michizane no bungaku kenkyūhen dainisatsu* 平安時代 文學と白氏文集：道眞の文學研究篇第二 冊 (Heian literature and *Po-shih wen-chi*: research on Michizane's literature, vol. 2). Geirinsha, 1978.

Kanke bunsō, Kanke kōshū, ed. Kawaguchi Hisao, vol. 72 of *Nihon koten bungaku taikei*. Iwanami Shoten, 1966.

Kankō Shōtokuroku 菅公頌德録 (A Memorial volume to Lord Sugawara). Ed. and pub. Kitano Jinja. Kyoto, 1944.

Kanshi, kambun, hyōron 漢詩・漢文・評論 (Poetry in Chinese, prose in Chinese, criticism), vol. 11 of *Kenkyū shiryō Nihon koten bungaku* 研究資料日本古典文学 . Ed. Ōsone Shō-suke, Kubota Jun 久保田淳 , Hinotani Teruhiko 檜谷昭彦 , Horiuchi Hideaki 堀内秀晃 , Miki Sumito 三木紀人 , and Yamaguchi Akiho 山口明穂 . Meiji Shoin, 1984.

Kasai Masaaki 笠井昌昭 . *Tenjin engi no rekishi* 天神縁起 の歴史 (A history of *Tenjin engi*). Yūzankaku, 1973.

Kato, Shuichi. *A History of Japanese Literature: The First Hundred Years,* tr. David Chibbett. New York, Kodansha International, 1979.

Kawaguchi Hisao 川口久雄 . *Heianchō Nihon kambungakushi no kenkyū* 平安朝日本漢文学史の研究 (A study of the history of Heian Japanese literature in Chinese). Meiji Shoin, 1964.

──── . *Seiiki no tora: Heianchō hikaku bungaku ronshū* 西域の虎：平安朝比較文学論集 (The tiger of the western regions: studies in comparative literature of the Heian period). Yoshikawa Kōbunkan, 1974.

──── . "Sugawara no Michizane no bungaku to Gen Shin, Haku Rakuten no bungaku: Dazaifu ni okeru 'Joi ippyakuin' shi o megutte" 菅原道真の文学と元稹・白楽天の文学：太宰府における叙意.一百韻詩をめぐって (The literature of Sugawara no Michizane and the literature of Yuan Chen and Po Chü-i: concerning the Dazaifu one-hundred couplet poem), in *Sugawara no Michizane to Dazaifu Temmangū.* Ed. Dazaifu Temmangū Bunka Kenkyūjo, vol. 1. Yoshikawa Kōbunkan, 1975.

──── and Wakabayashi Tsutomu 若林力 . *Kanke bunsō Kanke kōshū shiku sōsakuin* 菅家文草菅家後集詩句総索引 (Concordance of poems in *Kanke bunsō* and *Kanke kōshū*). Meiji Shoin, 1978.

Kawai Ginnosuke 川井銀之助 . "Kankō Tsukushi kakōki (jō)" 菅公筑紫下行記（上） (Michizane's journey to Kyushu [part 1]), *Shiseki to bijutsu* 30.3:104-112 (March 1960) (Part 2 was never published).

Kawakatsu Masatarō 川勝政太郎 . "Heiankyō no Kōrokan ni tsuite" 平安京の鴻臚館について (Concerning the Foreign Envoys' Quarters in the Heian capital), in *Kammuchō no shomondai.* Ed. Kodaigaku Kyōkai. Osaka, Kodaigaku Kyōkai, 1962.

Kawase Kazuma 川瀬一馬 . *Kojisho no kenkyū* 古辞書の研究 (A study of ancient dictionaries). Kōdansha, 1955.

Keene, Donald. *Landscapes and Portraits: Appreciations of Japanese Culture.* Palo Alto, Kodansha International, 1971.

Kenney, James T. "A Brief History of the Kyōka and the Edo Kyōka Movement," in Theodore Bowie, *Art of the Surimono.* Bloomington, Indiana, Indiana University Art Museum, 1979.

Kigoshi Takashi 木越隆 . "*Shinsen Man'yōshū* jōkan no kanshi no sakusha ni tsuite" 新撰萬葉集上巻の漢詩の作者について (Concerning the authorship of the *kanshi* in *Shinsen Man'yōshū*, chapter 1), *Kokugo* 4.4:4-13 (September 1956).

──── . "Michizane no shi to *Hakushi monjū*" 道真の詩と白氏文集 (Michizane's poems and *Po-shih wen-chi*), in *Nihon kambungakushi ronkō* 日本漢文学史論考 . Ed. Yamagishi Tokuhei. Iwanami Shoten, 1974.

Kiley, Cornelius J. "Estate and Property in the Late Heian Period," in *Medieval Japan: Essays in Institutional History.* Ed. John W. Hall and Jeffrey P. Mass. New Haven, Yale University Press, 1974.

Kimiya Yasuhiko 木宮泰彦 . *Nikka bunka kōryūshi* 日華文化
交流史 (A history of Sino-Japanese cultural exchange). Fuzambō, 1955.

Kimpara Tadashi 金原理 . *Heianchō kanshibun no kenkyū*
平安朝漢詩文の研究 (Research on Heian prose
and poetry in Chinese). Fukuoka, Kyūshū Daigaku Shuppankai, 1981.

———. "Sugawara no Michizane no kanshi—*Kanke kōshū* shosaishi o chūshin ni" 菅原道真の漢詩「菅家後集」所載詩を
中心に (Sugawara no Michizane's *kanshi*—focusing
on those in *Kanke kōshū*), in *Sugawara no Michizane to Dazaifu Temmangū*. Ed. Dazaifu Temmangū Bunka Kenkyūjo, vol. 1. Yoshikawa
Kōbunkan, 1975.

Kitano 北野 (Kitano), ed. Makabe Toshinobu 真壁俊信 . *Shintō
Taikei: jinja hen* 神道大系神社編 , vol. 11. Shintō Taikei
Hensankai, 1978.

Kitano Tenjin engi 北野天神縁起 (*Kitano Tenjin engi*),
ed. Minamoto Toyomune 源豊宗 , vol. 9 of *Shinshū Nihon emakimono zenshū* 新修日本絵巻物全集 . Kadokawa
Shoten, 1977.

Kitano Tenjin engi 北野天神縁起 (*Kitano Tenjin engi*),
ed. Komatsu Shigemi 小松茂美 , vol. 21 of *Nihon emaki taisei*
日本絵巻大成 . Chūō Kōronsha, 1978.

Kitanoshi 北野誌 (Documents on the Kitano Shrine). Ed. Kitano
Jinja. 3 vols. Kokugakuin Daigaku Shuppanbu, 1909–1910.

Kitayama Shigeo 北山茂夫 . *Nihon no rekishi 4: Heian kyō*
日本の歴史 4：平安京 (The history of Japan, vol. 4: the
Heian capital). Chūō Kōronsha, 1965.

———. "Sekkan seiji" 摂関政治 (Regental government), in *Iwanami kōza Nihon rekishi 4: kodai 4*. Iwanami Shoten, 1967.

Kobayashi Yoshinori 小林芳規 . *Heian Kamakura jidai ni
okeru kanseki kundoku no kokugoshiteki kenkyū* 平安鎌倉時代
に於ける漢籍訓読の国語史的研究
(Philological research in Japanese readings of Chinese texts
in the Heian and Kamakura periods). Tōkyō Daigaku Shuppankai, 1967.

Kojima Noriyuki 小島憲之 . *Jōdai Nihon bungaku to Chūgoku bungaku* 上代日本文學と中國文學 (Ancient
Japanese literature and Chinese literature), 3 vols. Hanawa Shobō,
1962–1965.

———. *Kokufū ankoku jidai no bungaku* 國風暗黒時代の
文學 (Literature in the dark age of the native style), 3 vols. to date.
Hanawa Shobō, 1968–

Kojima Yoshio. 小島吉雄 *Shinkokin wakashū no kenkyū, zokuhen* 新古今和歌集の研究：續編
(A study of the *Shinkokinshū*, continued). Shin Nihon Tosho, 1946.

Kokka taikan 國歌大觀 (Compendium of Japanese poetry).
Ed. Matsushita Daizaburō 松下大三郎 and Watanabe
Fumio 渡邊文雄 . Kadokawa Shoten, 1963.

Kokyō ibun 古京遺文 (Literary remains of the old capital). Ed. Yamada Takao 山田孝雄 and Katori Hozuma 香取秀真 . Bunseidō, 1965.

Kōkyū no subete 後宮のすべて (All about court ladies). Special issue of *Kokubungaku* 25.13 (October 1980).

Konishi Jin'ichi 小西甚一 . "Kambungaku" 漢文学 (Literature in Chinese), in *Heianchō bungakushi* 平安朝文学史 . Ed. Hisamatsu Sen'ichi and Nishishita Kyōichi 西下経一 . Meiji Shoin, 1965.

———. "The Genesis of the *Kokinshū* Style," tr. Helen C. McCullough. *Harvard Journal of Asiatic Studies* 38.1:61–170 (June 1978).

Kubota Jun 久保田淳 . *Shinkokin wakashū zenhyōshaku* 新古今和歌集全評釈 (*Shinkokinshū* completely annotated), 9 vols. Kōdansha, 1976–1978.

Kumagai Naoharu 熊谷直春 . "*Shinsen Man'yōshū* no seiritsu" 新撰万葉集の成立 (The creation of *Shinsen Man'yōshū*), *Kokubungaku kenkyū* 60:1–14 (October 1976) and 61:12–22 (March 1977).

Kyūsojin Hitaku 久曽神昇 . *Gensenbon Shinsen Man'yōshū to kenkyū* 原撰本新撰萬葉集と研究 (The original text of *Shinsen Man'yōshū* and a study of it), vol. 9 of *Mikan kokubun shiryō* 未刊國文資料 , ser. 1. Mikan Kokubun Shiryō Kankōkai, 1958.

Liu, James J. Y. *Chinese Theories of Literature.* Chicago, University of Chicago Press, 1975.

Lu, David John, ed. *Sources of Japanese History.* 2 vols. New York, McGraw-Hill Book Co., 1974.

Makabe Toshinobu 真壁俊信 . "*Tenjin engi* ni okeru Michizane kegen dan no seiritsu" 天神縁起における道真化現段の成立 (The creation of the story of Michizane's appearance in human form in the *Tenjin engi*), *Kokugakuin zasshi* 69.6:44–55 (July 1968).

———. "Egara Tenjinja bon *Kanke den* no shutsugen" 荏柄天神社本「菅家伝」の出現 (The origin of the Egara Tenjin Shrine text of *Kanke den*), *Nihon rekishi* 292:13–20 (September 1972).

———. "Kankō ni okeru shijitsu to denshō" 菅公に於ける史実と伝承 (Michizane: history and legend), *Shintōshi kenkyū* 21.2:16–32 (March 1973).

———. "Michizane no shison no dōsei ni tsuite" 道真の子孫の動静について (Concerning the activities of Michizane's descendants), *Kokugakuin zasshi* 74.10:40–50 (October 1973).

———. "*Kanke den* no hensha kō—Monjō Hakase Sugawara no Arimi no katsuyaku" 「菅家伝」の編者考：文章博士菅原在躬の活躍 (Thoughts on the compiler of *Kanke den*:

the activities of Professor of Literature Sugawara no Arimi), *Nihon rekishi* 310:82–89 (March 1974).

Maki Hidemasa 牧 其 正 . "Shiin kō" 資 陰 考 (A study of hereditary privilege), *Ōsaka Shidai hōgaku zasshi* 2.1:99–125 (January 1955).

Masano Jun'ichi 正 野 順 一 . "Minamoto no Yoshiari to Sugawara no Michizane" 源 能 有 と 菅 原 道 真 (Minamoto no Yoshiari and Sugawara no Michizane), *Shishū* 14–15:22–27 (June 1981).

Mashimo Goichi 真 下 五 一 . *Sugawara no Michizane seitanchi no kenkyū* 菅 原 道 真 生 誕 地 の 研 究 (A study of Sugawara no Michizane's birthplace). Kazama Shobō, 1972.

Masumura Hiroshi 増 村 宏 . "Kanke bunsō no shiryō" 菅 家 文 草 の 史 料 (Historical sources in *Kanke bunsō*), *Kagoshima Keidai ronshū* 16.3:305–342 (November 1975).

———. "Kentōshi teihai no shosetsu: sōki no shosetsu" 遣 唐 使 停 廃 の 諸 説 : 早 期 の 諸 説 (Early theories on the abandonment of envoys to the T'ang), *Kadai shigaku* 23:1–20 (1975).

———. "Kentōshi teihai no shosetsu: kōki no shosetsu" 遣 唐 使 停 廃 の 諸 説 : 後 期 の 諸 説 (Late theories on the abandonment of envoys to the T'ang), *Kagoshima Keidai ronshū* 17.1:1–48 (July 1976).

———. "Kentōshi teihai no shosetsu: Suzuki-shi no ronsetsu" 遣 唐 使 停 廃 の 諸 説 : 鈴 木 氏 の 論 説 (Mr. Suzuki's theory on the abandonment of envoys to the T'ang), *Chiiki kenkyū* 6.1:53–73 (June 1976).

Matsuura Sadatoshi 松 浦 貞 俊 . "Chokusen sanshū kenkyū oboegaki" 勅 撰 三 集 研 究 覚 書 (Research notes on the three imperial anthologies), *Kokugo to kokubungaku* 34.10:21–29 (October 1957).

Matsuura Tomohisa 松 浦 友 久 . "Pu-fun ch'iung-yao hsieh; Lai-chan lü-k'e chin" 不 分 瓊 瑤 屑 : 來 霑 旅 客 巾 (Alas, the jewel dust; Comes and soaks the traveler's handkerchief), *Kambungaku kenkyū* 11:12–21 (January 1963).

McCullough, William H. "Japanese Marriage Institutions in the Heian Period," *Harvard Journal of Asiatic Studies* 27:103–167 (1967).

McKnight, Brian E. *The Quality of Mercy: Amnesties and Traditional Chinese Justice.* Honolulu, The University Press of Hawaii, 1981.

Mezaki Tokue 目 崎 徳 衛 . "Uda Jōkō no in to kokusei" 宇 多 上 皇 の 院 と 国 政 (Retired Emperor Uda and national government), in *Engi Tenryaku jidai no kenkyū* 延 喜 天 暦 時 代 の 研 究 . Ed. Kodaigaku Kyōkai. Yoshikawa Kōbunkan, 1969.

———. *Ōchō no miyabi* 王 朝 の み や び (The elegance of the imperial court). Yoshikawa Kōbunkan, 1978.

Miller, Richard J. *Japan's First Bureaucracy: A Study of Eighth Century Government.* Cornell University East Asia Papers no. 19. Ithaca, N.Y., China-Japan Program, Cornell University, 1979.

Minakata, Kumakusa. "The Art of Whistling." 1925. Reprinted in *Minakata Kumakusa zenshū* 南方熊楠全集 , vol. 10. Heibonsha, 1973.

Miyakawa, Hisayuki. "An Outline of the Naitō Hypothesis and Its Effects on Japanese Studies of China," *Far Eastern Quarterly* 14.4:533–552 (August 1955).

Miyazaki Ichisada 宮崎市定 . *Kakyo* 科挙 (Civil service examinations). Osaka, Akitaya, 1946.

———. *China's Examination Hell: The Civil Service Examinations of Imperial China,* tr. Conrad Schirokauer. New Haven, Yale University Press, 1981.

Momo Hiroyuki 桃裕行 . *Jōdai gakusei no kenkyū* 上代學制の研究 (A study of the ancient school system). Meguro Shoten, 1947.

Mori Katsumi 森克己 . *Kentōshi* 遣唐使 (Envoys to the T'ang). Shibundō, 1955.

Morita Tei 森田悌 . *Heian jidai seijishi kenkyū* 平安時代政治史研究 (A study of Heian political history). Yoshikawa Kōbunkan, 1978.

———. *Ōchō seiji* 王朝政治 (Court government). Kyōikusha, 1979.

Morris, Ivan. *The World of the Shining Prince.* New York, Alfred A. Knopf, 1964.

———. *The Nobility of Failure: Tragic Heroes in the History of Japan.* New York, Holt, Rinehart and Winston, 1975.

Murai Yasuhiko 村井康彦 . *Heian kizoku no sekai* 平安貴族の世界 (The world of Heian aristocrats). Tokuma Shoten, 1968.

———. "Heian kyō no keisei" 平安京の形成 (The formation of the Heian capital), in *Kyōto no rekishi 1: Heian no shinkyō* 京都の歴史 1: 平安の新京 . Ed. Hayashiya Tatsusaburō. Gakugei Shorin, 1970.

Murao Jirō 村尾次郎 . *Ritsuryōsei no kichō* 律令制の基調 (The foundation of the *ritsuryō* system). Hanawa Shobō, 1960.

Murase, Miyeko. "The Tenjin Engi Scrolls—A Study in their Genealogical Relationship." PhD dissertation, Columbia University, 1962.

Murata Masashi 村田正志 . "Totō Tenjin shisō no genryū" 渡唐天神思想の源流 (The origins of the idea of Tenjin's journey to China), in *Sugawara no Michizane to Dazaifu Temmangū.* Ed. Dazaifu Temmangū Bunka Kenkyūjo, vol. 1. Yoshikawa Kōbunkan, 1975.

Mushakōji Minoru 武者小路穣 . "Shinsen'en no bun'yū" 神泉苑の文遊 (Literary gatherings at the Shinsen'en), in *Nihon bungaku no rekishi 3: kyūtei saron to saijo.* Ed. Yamanaka Yutaka and Akiyama Ken. Kadokawa Shoten, 1967.

———. "Tōka no arashi" 唐化の嵐 (The storm of sinification), in *Nihon bungaku no rekishi 3: kyūtei saron to saijo.* Ed. Yamanaka Yutaka and Akiyama Ken. Kadokawa Shoten, 1967.

Naganuma Kenkai 長沼賢海 . "Temman Tenjin shinkō no hen-sen" 天満天神の信仰の變遷 (The evolution of Tenjin worship), *Shirin* 4.2:130–144; 4.3:114–120; 4.4:144–154 (April–October 1919).

Nakamura Shin'ichirō 中村真一郎 . "Sugawara no Michizane" 菅原道真 (Sugawara no Michizane), in *Rekishi no Kyōto 3: gakusha to sōryo* 歴史の京都 3 : 学者と僧侶 . Tankōsha, 1970.

Nakashima Nobutarō 中島信太郎 . *Sugawara no Michizane: sono hito to bungaku* 菅原道真：その人と文学 (Sugawara no Michizane: the man and his literature). Taiyō Shuppan, 1981.

Nakayama, Shigeru. *A History of Japanese Astronomy.* Cambridge, Harvard University Press, 1969.

Nihon bungaku zenshi 2: chūko 日本文学全史 2 : 中古 (Complete history of Japanese literature vol. 2: mid-ancient [Heian]). Ed. Akiyama Ken. Gakutōsha, 1978.

Nihon kodai jimmei jiten 日本古代人名辞典 (Biographical dictionary of ancient Japan). Ed. Takeuchi Rizō, Yamada Hideo 山田英雄 , and Hirano Kunio 平野邦雄 , 7 vols. Yoshikawa Kōbunkan, 1958–1977.

Niida Noboru 仁井田陞 . *Tō rei shūi* 唐令拾遺 (Collected fragments of the T'ang Civil Codes). Tōkyō Daigaku Shuppankai, 1964.

Niizuma Toshihisa 新妻利久 . *Bokkai kokushi oyobi Nihon to no kokkōshi no kenkyū* 渤海国史及び日本との国交史 の研究 (A study of the history of Parhae and its relations with Japan). Tōkyō Denki Daigaku Shuppankyoku, 1969.

Nishida Nagao 西田長男 . *Jinja no rekishiteki kenkyū* 神社 の歴史的研究 (Historical studies of Shinto shrines). Hanawa Shobō, 1966.

Nishikawa Osamu 西川治 , ed. *Kagawa, Tokushima, Ehime, Kōchi* 香川・徳島・愛媛・高知 (Kagawa, Tokushima, Ehime, and Kōchi prefectures), vol. 15 of *Nihon no bunka chiri* 日本の 文化地理 . Kōdansha, 1970.

Nishio Yōtarō 西尾陽太郎 . "Sanuki no kami jidai no Michizane" 讃岐守時代の道真 (Michizane's term as governor of Sanuki), *Shien* 42:79–109 (December 1949).

Nishitakatsuji Nobusada 西高辻信貞 . *Dazaifu Temmangū* 太宰府天満宮 (The Dazaifu Temman Shrine). Gakuseisha, 1970.

Nomura Tadao 野村忠夫 . *Ritsuryō kanjinsei no kenkyū* 律令 官人制の研究 (A study of the *ritsuryō* bureaucratic system). Yoshikawa Kōbunkan, 1970.

———. *Kanjinsei ron* 官人制論 (A study of the bureaucratic system). Yūzankaku, 1975.

———. *Kodai kanryō no sekai* 古代官僚の世界 (The world of the ancient bureaucrats). Hanawa Shobō, 1976.

Numata Raisuke 沼田頼輔 . *Nichi-Man no kodai kokkō* 日滿 の古代國交 (Ancient relations between Japan and Man-churia). Meiji Shoten, 1933.

Oda Fujio 小田富士雄 . "Chikuzen Anrakuji shi: kodai makki made" 筑前安樂寺史：古代末期まで (A his-tory of Anrakuji in Chikuzen province: through the late ancient period), *Kyūshū shigaku* 12:4–22 (June 1959).

Ogata Hiroyasu 尾形裕康 . *Nihon kyōiku tsūshi* 日本 教育通史 (Survey history of Japanese education). Waseda Daigaku Shuppambu, 1960.

Okada Masayuki 岡田正之 . *Nihon kambungakushi* 日本 漢文学史 (History of Japanese literature in Chinese). Yoshikawa Kō-bunkan, 1954.

Ōkagami, the Great Mirror: Fujiwara no Michinaga and His Times, tr. Helen Craig McCullough. Princeton, Princeton University Press, 1980.

Okladnikov, Aleksei Pavlovich. "The Mo-ho Tribes and the P'o-hai State," in *The Soviet Far East in Antiquity: An Archaeological and Historical Study of the Maritime Region of the U.S.S.R.* Arctic Institute of North America—Anthropology of the North: Translations from Russian Sources, no. 6. Ed. Henry N. Michael. Toronto, University of Toronto Press, 1965.

The Old Pine Tree and Other Noh Plays, tr. Makoto Ueda. Lincoln, Uni-versity of Nebraska Press, 1962.

Ōmaru Isamu 王丸勇 . "Sugawara no Michizane ni miru shinkeishi-tsu" 菅原道真にみる神経質 (Nervousness seen in Sugawara no Michizane), *Kyūshū shinkei seishin igaku* 20.1:120–124 (August 1974).

———. *Sugawara no Michizane* 菅原道真 (Sugawara no Michizane). Kongō Shuppan, 1980.

Ōno Isao 大野功 . "*Kitano Tenjin engi* no seiritsu ni tsuite" 「北野 天神縁起」の成立について (An account of the compilation of the *Kitano Tenjin engi*), *Shigaku zasshi* 67.9:1–23 (September 1958).

Ōsone Shōsuke 大曽根章介 . "Sugawara no Michizane: shijin to kōju" 菅原道真：詩人と鴻儒 (Sugawara no Michi-zane: poet and Confucian), *Nihon bungaku* 22.9:1–10 (September 1973).

Ozawa Masao 小沢正夫 . "Kambungaku" 漢文学 (Literature in Chinese), in *Shimpan Nihon bungakushi 2: chūko* 新版日本 文学史 2：中古 . Ed. Hisamatsu Sen'ichi. Shibundō, 1971.

"Pilgrimage to Dazaifu: Sōgi's *Tsukushi no Michi no Ki*," tr. Eileen Katō. *Monumenta Nipponica* 34.3:333–367 (Autumn 1979).

The Platform Sutra of the Sixth Patriarch, tr. Philip B. Yampolsky. New York, Columbia University Press, 1967.

Pollack, David. "The Informing Image: 'China' in *Genji Monogatari*," *Mon-umenta Nipponica* 38.4:359–375 (Winter 1983).

Ponsonby Fane, Richard A. B. "Kitano Temmangū: Patron Saint of Learning." 1937. Reprinted in *Visiting Famous Shrines in Japan*, Dr. Richard Ponsonby Fane Series, vol. 6. Kyoto, The Ponsonby Memorial Society, 1964.

Pulleyblank, Edwin G. *The Background of the Rebellion of An Lu-shan*. London, Oxford University Press, 1955.

Reischauer, Edwin O. *Ennin's Travels in T'ang China*. New York, Ronald Press, 1955.

Reischauer, Jean and Robert Karl. *Early Japanese History*. 1937. Reprint Gloucester, Massachusetts, Peter Smith, 1967.

Rikkokushi sakuin 六國史索引 (Index to the Rikkokushi). Ed. Rikkokushi Sakuin Henshūbu, 4 vols. Yoshikawa Kōbunkan, 1963–1969.

Ritsuryō 律令 (*Ritsuryō*). Ed. Inoue Mitsusada 井上光貞, Seki Akira 関晃, Tsuchida Naoshige 土田直鎮, and Aoki Kazuo. Vol. 3 of *Nihon shisō taikei*. Iwanami Shoten, 1976.

Robinson, G. W. "Early Japanese Chronicles: The Six National Histories," in *Historical Writing on the Peoples of Asia: Historians of China and Japan*. Ed. W. G. Beasley and E. G. Pulleyblank. New York, Oxford University Press, 1961.

Roden, Donald. *Schooldays in Imperial Japan: A Study in the Culture of a Student Elite*. Berkeley, University of California Press, 1980.

Ruch, Barbara. "Medieval Jongleurs and the Making of a National Literature," in *Japan in the Muromachi Period*. Ed. John Hall and Toyoda Takeshi. Berkeley, University of California Press, 1977.

Ryō Susumu 龍肅. *Heian jidai* 平安時代 (The Heian period). Shunjūsha, 1962.

Saeki Arikiyo 佐伯有清. *Shinsen shōjiroku no kenkyū: kenkyūhen* 新撰姓氏録の研究：研究篇 (Studies of the *Shinsen shōjiroku*). Yoshikawa Kōbunkan, 1963.

———. *Tomo no Yoshio* 伴善男 (Tomo no Yoshio), vol. 156 of *Jimbutsu sōsho* 人物叢書. Yoshikawa Kōbunkan, 1970.

———. "Sugawara no Michizane to *Jikaku Daishi den*" 菅原道真と慈覚大師伝 (Sugawara no Michizane and the *Biography of Jikaku Daishi* [Ennin]), *Nihon rekishi* 434:75–82 (July 1984).

Sakaguchi Tsutomu 坂口勉. "*Shōmonki* ni okeru Masakado no sokui ni tsuite" 「将門記」における将門の即位について (Masakado's accession in *Shōmonki*), in *Kodai chūsei no shakai to minzoku bunka* 古代中世の社会と民俗文化. Ed. Wakamori Tarō Sensei Kanreki Kinen Rombunshū Henshū Iinkai. Kōbundō, 1976.

Sakamoto Ken'ichi 阪本健一. "Shintōshijō no Sugawara no Michizane" 神道史上の菅原道真 (Sugawara no Michizane from the perspective of Shinto history), in *Sugawara no Michizane* to Dazaifu Temmangū. Ed. Dazaifu Temmangū Bunka Kenkyūjo, vol. 1. Yoshikawa Kōbunkan, 1975.

Sakamoto Shōzō 坂本賞三 . Nihon no rekishi 6: sekkan jidai 日本の歴史 6: 摂関時代 (The history of Japan vol. 6: the age of regents and chancellors). Shōgakkan, 1974.

Sakamoto Tarō 坂本太郎 . Nihon no shūshi to shigaku 日本の修史と史学 (Japanese historiography). Shibundō, 1958.

———. Sugawara no Michizane 菅原道真 (Sugawara no Michizane), vol. 100 of Jimbutsu sōsho. Yoshikawa Kōbunkan, 1962.

———. "Fujiwara no Yoshifusa to Mototsune" 藤原良房と基経 (Fujiwara no Yoshifusa and Mototsune), in Rekishi to jimbutsu, 歴史と人物 . Ed. Nihon Rekishi Gakkai. Yoshikawa Kōbunkan, 1964.

———. Kankō to sake 菅公と酒 (Michizane and wine). Tōkyō Daigaku Shuppankai, 1964.

———. Nihon kodaishi no kisoteki kenkyū 日本古代史の基礎的研究 (Basic research on ancient Japanese history). Tōkyō Daigaku Shuppankai, 1964.

———. Rikkokushi 六國史 (The six national histories). Yoshikawa Kōbunkan, 1970.

———. "Sugawara no Michizane no shōgai" 菅原道真の生涯 (The life of Sugawara no Michizane), in Sugawara no Michizane to Dazaifu Temmangū. Ed. Dazaifu Temmangū Bunka Kenkyūjo, vol. 1. Yoshikawa Kōbunkan, 1975.

———. "Sugawara no Michizane to Ki no Haseo" 菅原道真と紀長谷雄 (Sugawara no Michizane and Ki no Haseo), Shintō taikei geppō 2: Kitano (April 1978), pp. 1-4.

Sakurai Mitsuru 桜井満 . "Sugawara no Michizane" 菅原道真 (Sugawara no Michizane), Rekishi kōron 3.10:147-153 (October 1977).

Sakurai Yoshirō 桜井好郎 . Kamigami no hembō: shaji engi no sekai kara 神々の変貌：社寺縁起の世界から (The transfiguration of the gods: from the world of accounts of shrine and temple origins). Tōkyō Daigaku Shuppankai, 1976.

Sansom, George B. A History of Japan to 1334. Stanford, Stanford University Press, 1958.

Sasaki Nobutsuna 佐佐木信綱 . "Kankō no waka ni tsuite" 菅公の和歌について (Concerning Michizane's waka), in Kankō shōtokuroku. Ed. and pub. Kitano Jinja, Kyoto, 1944.

———. "Kajin toshite no Sugawara no Michizane" 歌人としての菅原道眞 (Sugawara no Michizane as a waka poet), Kaizō 15.4:232-239 (April 1933).

Sasayama Haruo 笹山晴生 . "Ruijū kokushi oboegaki" 類聚国史おぼえがき (Notes on Ruijū kokushi), in Shintei zōho kokushi taikei geppō 17:3-6 (March 1965).

———. "Heian shoki no seiji kaikaku" 平安初期の政治改革

(Political reforms of the early Heian period), in *Iwanami kōza Nihon rekishi 3: kodai 3*. Iwanami Shoten, 1976.

Satō Seijitsu 佐藤誠實 . "Ki no Haseo" 紀長谷雄 (Ki no Haseo), *Shigaku zasshi* 12.4:61–71 (October 1901).

Sawada Mizuho 澤田瑞穗 . "Shō no genryū" 嘯の源流 (The origin of whistling [*hsiao*]), *Tōhō shūkyo* 44:1–13 (October 1974).

Segawa Hisae 瀨川ヒサヱ . "Sugawara no Michizane no Sanuki no kami jidai" 菅原道真の讃岐守時代 (Sugawara no Michizane's term as governor of Sanuki), in *Heianchō bungaku kenkyū: sakka to sakuhin* 平安朝文学研究：作家と作品 . Ed. Waseda Daigaku Heianchō Bungaku Kenkyūkai. Yūseidō, 1971.

Seki Akira 関晃 . "Ritsuryō kizoku ron" 律令貴族論 (Essay on the *ritsuryō* aristocracy), in *Iwanami kōza Nihon rekishi 3: kodai 3*. Iwanami Shoten, 1976.

Shibata Minoru 柴田實 . "Goryō shinkō to Tenjin" 御靈信仰と天神 (Belief in angry spirits and Tenjin), in *Sugawara no Michizane to Dazaifu Temmangū*. Ed. Dazaifu Temmangū Bunka Kenkyujō, vol. 1. Yoshikawa Kōbunkan, 1975.

Shimmura Izuru 新村出 . "Kankō no 'Umi narazu' no outa ni tsukite" 菅公の「海ならず」の御歌について (Concerning Michizane's poem "Not the Sea"), in *Kankō Shōtokuroku*. Ed. and pub. Kitano Jinja, Kyoto, 1944.

Spaulding, Robert M., Jr. *Imperial Japan's Higher Civil Service Examination*. Princeton, Princeton University Press, 1967.

Sugawara and the Secrets of Calligraphy. Ed. and tr. Stanleigh H. Jones, Jr. New York, Columbia University Press, 1985.

Sugawara no Michizane to Dazaifu Temmangū 菅原道真と太宰府天満宮 (Sugawara no Michizane and the Dazaifu Temman Shrine). Ed. Dazaifu Temmangū Bunka Kenkyūjo, 2 vols. Yoshikawa Kōbunkan, 1975.

Suzuki Yasutami 鈴木靖民 . "Kampyō no kentoshi o meguru kisoteki kōsatsu" 寛平の遣唐使をめぐる基礎的考察 (A fundamental investigation of the Kampyō era envoys to the T'ang), *Kokugakuin Daigaku kiyō* 13:61–100 (March 1975).

———. "Sugawara no Michizane to Kampyō no kentōshi" 菅原道真と寛平の遣唐使 (Sugawara no Michizane and the Kampyō era envoys to the T'ang), in *Sugawara no Michizane to Dazaifu Temmangū*. Ed. Dazaifu Temmangū Bunka Kenkyūjo, vol. 1. Yoshikawa Kōbunkan, 1975.

Taeusch, Carl F. "*The Jikkinshō:* An Annotated Translation of Chapter Four: 'A Caution against Talking Too Much of Other People's Affairs,' with Critical Introduction." Master's thesis, University of Michigan, 1970.

Taga Akigorō 多賀秋五郎 . *Tōdai kyōikushi no kenkyū*

唐代教育史の研究　　　(A study of the history of T'ang education). Fumaidō, 1953.

Takahashi Takashi 高橋崇 . *Ritsuryō kanjin kyūyosei no kenkyū* 律令官人給与制の研究 (A study of the salary system of *ritsuryō* bureaucrats). Yoshikawa Kōbunkan, 1970.

Takatori Masao 高取正男 . *Sugawara no Michizane: onryō no kami kara gakumon geinō no kami e* 菅原道真：怨霊の神から 学問芸能の神へ (Sugawara no Michizane: from god of vengeful ghosts to god of learning), vol. 4 of *Nihon o tsukutta hitobito* 日本を創った人びと . Heibonsha, 1978.

Takeuchi Hideo 竹内秀雄 . *Temmangū* 天満宮 (Temman shrines). Yoshikawa Kōbunkan, 1968.

Takeuchi Rizō 竹内理三 . *Ritsuryōsei to kizoku seiken* 律令 制と貴族政権 (The *ritsuryō* system and the political power of aristocrats), 2 vols. Ochanomizu Shobō, 1958.

Takikawa Seijirō 滝川政次郎 . *Ritsuryō no kenkyū* 律令 の研究 (A study of the *ritsuryō* codes). Tōkō Shoin, 1966.

―――. "Okura no 'Hinkyū mondōka' to Kankō no 'Kansō jisshu' " 憶良の「貧窮問答歌」と菅公の「寒早十首」 (Okura's "Dialogue of Poverty Song" and Michizane's "Ten Poems on Early Cold"), *Nihon rekishi* 404:40–43 (January 1982).

Tales of Times Now Past, tr. Marian Ury. Berkeley, University of California Press, 1979.

Toby, Ronald P. *State and Diplomacy in Early Modern Japan: Asia in the Development of the Tokugawa Bakufu.* Princeton, Princeton University Press, 1984.

Tokoro Isao 所功 . *Miyoshi no Kiyoyuki* 三善清行 (Miyoshi no Kiyoyuki), vol. 157 of *Jimbutsu sōsho.* Yoshikawa Kōbunkan, 1965.

―――. "Miyoshi no Kiyoyuki no zenhansei" 三善清行の前 半生 (Miyoshi no Kiyoyuki's early years), *Geirin* 17.5+6:172–195 (December 1966).

―――. "Miyoshi no Kiyoyuki no kōhansei" 三善清行の後 半生 (Miyoshi no Kiyoyuki's later years), *Geirin* 18.3:118–143 (June 1967).

―――. "Kampyō no chi no saikentō" 寛平の治の再検討 (Government of the Kampyō era [889–898] reexamined), *Kōgakkan Daigaku kiyō* 5.107–139 (1967).

―――. "Miyoshi no Kiyoyuki to shin'yū kakumei ron" 三善清行の 辛酉革命論 (Miyoshi no Kiyoyuki's *shin'yū* revolution theory), in *Shintōshi kenkyū* 17.1:27–50 (January 1969).

―――. "Sugawara no Michizane to Ki no Haseo no kankei" 菅原 道真と紀長谷雄の関係 (The relationship between Sugawara no Michizane and Ki no Haseo), *Koji ruien geppō* 25:6–8 (April 1969).

―――. "Sugawara no Michizane no enzai kanken" 菅原道真の

冤罪管見　　　　(Views on Sugawara no Michizane's being falsely accused), *Geirin* 20.5:233-250 (October 1969).

——. "Kokuga 'kanchō' no gainen to jittai" 国街「官長」の概念と実態　(The concept and practice of provincial "chief officer"), *Nihon rekishi* 264:85-106 (May 1970).

——. "Kankō ryōke no kyōiku katsudo"菅江両家の敎育活動 (Educational activities of the Sugawara and Ōe families), in *Nihon kyōiku bunkashi* 日本敎育文化史　　　. Ed. Yūki Rikurō 結城陸郎 . Meigen Shobō, 1975.

——. "Sugawara no Michizane no hairu" 菅原道真の配流(Sugawara no Michizane's exile), in *Sugawara no Michizane to Dazaifu Temmangū*. Ed. Dazaifu Temmangū Bunka Kenkyūjo, vol. 1. Yoshikawa Kōbunkan, 1975.

Tokushige Asakichi 德重淺吉　　. *Nihon bunkashi no kenkyū* 日本文化史の研究 (Studies in Japanese cultural history). Meguro Shoten, 1938.

Toriyama Kiichi 鳥山喜一　. *Bokkai shikō* 渤海史考　(A history of Parhae). Meguro Shoten, 1915.

——. *Bokkai shijō no shomondai* 渤海史上の諸問題 (Issues in the history of Parhae). Kazuma Shobō, 1968.

Tsuchida Naoshige 土田直鎮　　. "Shōkei ni tsuite" 上卿について　(Concerning *shōkei* [the superior official on duty]), in *Nihon kodaishi ronshū*. Ed. Sakamoto Tarō Hakase Kanreki Kinenkai, vol. 2. Yoshikawa Kōbunkan, 1962.

Tsunoda Bun'ei 角田文衞　. *Murasaki Shikibu to sono jidai* 紫式部とその時代　(Murasaki Shikibu and her age). Kadokawa Shoten, 1966.

——. *Ōchō no eizō: Heian jidaishi no kenkyū* 王朝の映像：平安時代史の研究　(Images of the imperial court: studies in Heian history). Tōkyōdō, 1970.

——. *Nihon no kōkyū* 日本の後宮　　(Japan's court ladies). Gakutōsha, 1973.

——. "Sugawara no Michizane to Fujiwara shi: Atsugimi Shinnō no rittaishi o megutte" 菅原道真と藤原氏：敦仁親王の立太子をめぐって　(Sugawara no Michizane and the Fujiwara family: concerning the selection of Atsugimi as crown prince), in *Sugawara no Michizane to Dazaifu Temmangū*. Ed. Dazaifu Temmangū Bunka Kenkyūjo, vol. 1. Yoshikawa Kōbunkan, 1975.

Tsurugashi tsūshi 敦賀市通史　(A survey history of Tsuruga city). Ed. and pub. Tsurugashi Kyōiku Iinka, 1956.

Twitchett, Denis. "The Composition of the T'ang Ruling Class: New Evidence from Tunhuang," in *Perspectives on the T'ang*. Ed. Denis Twitchett and Arthur F. Wright. New Haven, Yale University Press, 1973.

Wada Hidematsu 和田英松 . "Sugawara no Michizane no hisseki ni tsuite" 菅原道眞の筆蹟に就いて　　(Concerning Sugawara no Michizane's calligraphy), *Kokka* 32.1:3-5 (July 1921); 32.2:39-45 (August 1921).

———. *Kokusho itsubun* 國書逸文 (Fragments of lost Japanese books). Privately printed by Mori Katsumi, 1940.

———. *Kanshoku yōkai* 官職要解 (Dictionary of official titles). 1943. Reprint Meiji Shoin, 1979.

Wakamori Tarō 和歌森太郎 . *Sake ga kataru Nihonshi* 酒 が 語る日本史 (Japanese history as told by wine). Kawade Shobō Shinsha, 1971.

———. "Sugawara no Michizane" 菅原道真 (Sugawara no Michizane), in *Jimbutsu Nihon no rekishi 3: Ōchō no bunka* 人物日本の 歴史 3：王朝の文革 . Shōgakkan, 1976.

Waley, Arthur. *The Life and Times of Po Chü-i, 772–846 A.D.*. New York, Macmillan, 1949.

Watanabe Kan 渡辺寛 . "Tenjin shinkō kenkyūshi josetsu" 天神 信仰研究史序説 (Introduction to the historiography of Tenjin worship), in *Sugawara no Michizane to Dazaifu Temmangū*. Ed. Dazaifu Temmangū Bunka Kenkyūjo, vol. 2. Yoshikawa Kōbunkan, 1975.

Watson, Burton. *Early Chinese Literature*. New York, Columbia University Press, 1962.

———. "Michizane and the Plums," *Japan Quarterly* 11.2:217-220 (April–June 1964).

———. *Japanese Literature in Chinese, Volume One: Poetry and Prose in Chinese by Japanese Writers of the Early Period*. New York, Columbia University Press, 1975.

Wetzler, Peter Michael. "Yoshishige no Yasutane: Lineage, Learning, Office, and Amida's Pure Land." PhD dissertation, University of California, Berkeley (1977).

White, Douglass Alan. "Ch'eng-kung Sui's 'Poetic Essay on Whistling: The *Hsiao-fu.*'" Honors thesis, Harvard College, Cambridge, 1964.

Wixted, John Timothy. "The *Kokinshū* Prefaces: Another Perspective," *Harvard Journal of Asiatic Studies* 43.1:215-238 (June 1983).

Yamagishi Tokuhei 山岸徳平 . *Nihon kambungaku kenkyū* 日本漢文学研究 (A study of Japanese literature in Chinese), in vol. 1 of *Yamagishi Tokuhei chosakushū* 山口徳平著作 集 . Yūseidō, 1972.

Yamaguchi Kōen 山口光圓 . "Kankō no Gen'yō daikai ronjo to Daikai shinanshō" 菅公の顯揚大戒論序と大戒 指南抄 (Michizane's *Gen'yō daikai ronjo* and *Daikai shinanshō*), *Bukkyō shigaku* 2.1:25-33 (January 1951).

Yamamoto Shinkichi 山本信吉 . "Heian chūki no nairan ni tsuite" 平安中期の内覧について (Concerning the right of private examination during the mid-Heian period), in *Zoku Nihon kodaishi ronshū*. Ed. Sakamoto Tarō Hakase Koki Kinenkai, vol. 3. Yoshikawa Kōbunkan, 1972.

Yamanaka Yutaka 山中裕 . *Heianchō no nenjū gyōji* 平安朝
の年中行事　　　(Annual events of the Heian court). Hanawa Shobō, 1972.
Yokoo Yutaka 横尾豊　　. *Heian jidai no kōkyū seikatsu* 平安
時代の後官生活　　　(The life of court ladies in the Heian
period). Kashiwa Shobō, 1976.
Yoshimura Shigeki 吉村茂樹　. *Kokushi seido* 国司制度
(The provincial governor system). Hanawa Shobō, 1962.

Glossary

Abe no Okiyuki 安部興行
Akame 赤目
Akashi 明石
Akishino 秋篠
akō 阿衡
Amaterasu 天照
Amenohohi 天穗日
An Lu-shan 安祿山
Anrakuji 安樂寺
Ariwara 在原
—— no Narihira 業平
—— no Tomomoto 友干
Asano no Katori 朝野
　鹿取
Ashikaga 足利
ason 朝臣
Ate 安殿
Atsugimi 敦仁
Awa 阿波
Ayae Jizai Tenjin 文江自在
　天神

bekkō 別貢
Bidatsu 敏達
Bitchū 備中
bō 卯
Bungo 豐後

Bunka shūreishū 文華秀麗
　集
Bun'ya no Tokizane 文屋時實
Butsumyō kyō 佛名經

Chang Heng 張衡
Ch'ang-an 長安
Ch'ang-sha 長沙
Chao 召
Chao Ping 趙炳
Cheng 鄭
Cheng I-en 鄭益恩
Cheng-chü 鄭渠
Ch'i 齊
Chia I 賈誼
chiao 交
Chiao-yuan 焦原
Chigi 地祇
Chikamatsu Monzaemon
　近松門左衛門
Chikubu 竹生
Chin 晉
Ch'in 秦
chin-shih 進士
Chiyō shakuen 治要策苑
chō 町
Chou 周

403

Chu Pao 朱褒
Chu Po 朱博
Ch'ü Yuan 辰辰
Chuang-tzu 莊子
chūben 中辨
chueh 角
chūgū no daibu 中宮大夫
Chūgūshiki 中宮職
Ch'ui 倕
Chūkan 中瓘
chūnagon 中納言
Ch'un-ch'iu 春秋
chün-tzu 君子

Daichi doron 大智度論
Daigakuryō 大學寮
daigeki 大外記
Daigo 醍醐
Daihannya kyō 大般若經
daijin 大臣
daijō daijin 太政大臣
daijōe 大嘗會
Daijōkan 太政官
dainagon 大納言
dainaiki 大内記
danjō daihitsu 彈正大弼
Danjōdai 彈正臺
Dazai no gon no sochi 大宰權師
Dazaifu 大宰府
Dengyō Daishi 傳教大師
Dōken 道賢
Dōkyō 道鏡

Emonfu 衛門府
Engi 延喜 (era name)
engi 緣起 (accounts of shrine origins)
Engi shiki 延喜式
Ennin 圓仁
Enryakuji 延曆寺
Erh-ya 爾雅
Etchū 越中

Fan Li 范蠡
Feng Yen 馮衍
fu 賦

Fu Yueh 傳說
Fujiwara 藤原
—— no Akitada 顯忠
—— no Fuyuo 冬緒
—— no Harukage 春景
—— no Haruko (Onshi) 溫子
—— no Kadanomaro 葛野麻呂
—— no Kiyosuke 清輔
—— no Kiyotsura 清貫
—— no Kusuko 藥子
—— no Michinaga 道長
—— no Morosuke 師輔
—— no Mototsune 基經
—— no Nakahira 仲平
—— no Sadakuni 定國
—— no Sugane 菅根
—— no Sukeyo 佐世
—— no Tadafusa 忠房
—— no Tadahira 忠平
—— no Tokihira 時平
—— no Tsunesuke 恆佐
—— no Yasuko (Onshi) 穩子
—— no Yasunori 保則
—— no Yoshifusa 良房
—— no Yoshio 是雄
—— no Yoshitsumu 良積
—— no Yukimichi 如道
Fukura 福良
fukushi 副使

Gaku ryō 學令
Gangyō 元慶
ge 外
geki 外記
gemba no suke 玄蕃助
Gembaryō 玄蕃寮
Gimbō kanritsu 銀牓翰律
gimonjōshō 擬文章生
giri 義理
Gōdanshō 江談抄
gon 權
Goryōe 御靈會
gunji 郡司
gyōbu kyō 刑部卿
Gyōbushō 刑部省
gyotai 魚袋

Hachiman 八幡
Hagui 羽咋
Haji 土師
—— no Furuhito 古人
hakase 博士
Han 漢 (dynasty and river)
hangan 判官
haniwa 埴輪
Han-shu 漢書
Harima 播磨
Haruzumi no Yoshitada
　春澄善繩
Hayashi Razan 林羅山
Hayashi Gahō 林鵞峯
Heichū 平忠
Heizei 平城
Hibasuhime 日葉酢媛
Hie 比叡
Hiei 比叡
Higo 肥後
Hirata Atsutane 平田篤胤
hisangi 非參議
Hokkaidō 北海道
Hokke 北家
Hokke Sammaidō 法花
　三昧堂
Hokkeji 法華寺
Honchō ichinin isshu
　本朝一人一首
Honchō monzui 本朝文粹
honkan 本官
Hou-Han-shu 後漢書
Hsiang 湘
hsiao 嘯
hsieh 屑
hsing 行
hsueh 雪
Huang Hsien 黃憲
Huang Pa 黃霸
Hui-ch'ang 會昌
Hyakunin isshu 百人一首
hyōbu no shō 兵部少輔
Hyōbushō 兵部省

Ichijō 一條
Inaba 因幡
Inari 稻荷

Inoue Tetsujirō 井上哲次郎
Ise 伊勢
Ishikawa no Michimasu
　石川道益
Izumo 出雲
Izumo no Kuninomiyatsuko 出雲國造

Jibushō 治部省
jijū 侍從
Jingikan 神祇官
Jingoji 神護寺
Jōgan 貞觀
Jōwa 承和
Jōwa no hen 承和の變
Jōzō 淨藏
Juan Chi 阮籍
Junna 淳和

kabane 姓
kabuki 歌舞使
Kaga 加賀
kageyushi no chōkan 勘解由使
　長官
kageyushi no jikan 勘解由使
　次官
Kaibara Ekken 貝原益軒
Kaifūsō 懷風藻
Kaihōji 開法寺
Kaishō bunruijū 會昌
　分類集
K'ai-yuan ching 開元經
kakumei 革命
kambun 漢文
kami (deity) 神
kami (governor) 守
kami (president) 頭
Kammu 桓武
Kamo 賀茂
kampaku 關白
Kampyō 寬平
kan 卷
Kan Zōdaishōkoku 菅贈
　大相國
Kangakuin 勸學院
kanjin 官人
Kanke bunsō 菅家文草
Kanke kōshū 菅家後集

Kanke Man'yōshū 菅家萬葉集

Kanke Rōka 菅家廊下

Kannon 觀音

kanshi 漢詩

Karai 火雷

Katano 片野

Katsura Rikyū 桂離宮

Kawachi 河内

Kawashima 川嶋

Kaya 河陽

kebiishi no bettō 檢非遣使別當

Kebiishichō 檢非遣使廳

Kehi 氣比

Keichū 契沖

Keikokushū 經國集

keishi 家司

Kenchū mikkan 顯注密勘

kentō taishi 遣唐大使

kentōshi 遣唐使

kenzeishi 檢稅使

ki 貴

Ki 紀

—— no Haseo 長谷雄

—— no Natsui 夏井

—— no Tsurayuki 貫之

Kibi no Makibi 吉備眞備

kiden 紀傳

Kimbu 金峰

Kinoshita Jun'an 木下順庵

Kisshōin 吉祥院

Kisshōten 吉祥天

Kitano 北野

Kitano Tenjin engi 北野天神緣起

Kiyama 城山

kō ("lecture") 講

kō ("to go") 行

kō ("to associate") 交

Kōbaiden 紅梅殿

Kōbō Daishi 弘法大師

Kogaku 古學

Koguryŏ 高句麗

Kojiki 古事記

Kōka ryō 考課令

Kokinshū 古今集

Kōkō 光孝

koku 石

Kokugaku 國學

Konoefu 近衞府

Kōrokan 鴻臚館

Kose no Fumio 巨勢文雄

Kose no Kanaoka 巨勢金岡

Kōya 高野

Kōzuke 上野

K'uei 蹇

kugyō 公卿

Kūkai 空海

Kunaishō 宮内省

Kung Sui 襲遂

Kuo-tzu chien 國子監

Kura 倉

kurai 位

kurōdo no bettō 藏人別當

kurōdo no tō 藏人頭

Kurōdodokoro 藏ノ所

Kusuko no hen 藥子の變

kyō 卿

kyōka 狂歌

Lao-tzu 老子

Li Chu 離朱

Li Fang 李昉

Li Huan 李環

Liang 梁

Li-chi 禮記

Li-pu 禮部

Liu K'uan 劉寬

Liu Liang 劉梁

Liu Yueh-shih 劉越石

Lo Pin-wang 駱賓王

Lun-yü 論語

Lun wen 論文

Ma Ku 麻姑

Maeno Ryōtaku 前野良澤

Makimuku 纏向

Man'yōshū 萬葉集

Matsuyama 松山

Meng-men 孟門

Mimbushō 民部省

Mimune no Masahira 三統理平
Minabuchi no Toshina 南淵年名
Minamoto 源
―― no Hikaru 光
―― no Noboru 昇
―― no Shitagō 順
―― no Yoshi 善
―― no Yoshiari 能有
Mino 美濃
Miwa no Yoshitane 神良種
Miyaji no Tomoe 宮道友兄
Miyako no Yoshika 都良香
Miyanotaki 官瀧
Miyoshi no Kiyoyuki 三善清行
moku no kami 木工頭
Mokuryō 木工寮
monjō 文章
Monjōin 文章院
monjōshō 文章生
Montoku 文德
Montoku jitsuroku 文德實錄
muraji 連
Murakami 村上
Mutsu 陸奥
myōbō 明法
myōgyō 明經

Nagaoka 長岡
naiki 内記
nairan 内覧
naishi no kami 尚侍
naishi no suke 典侍
Naishi no tsukasa 内侍司
Nakai 中井
Nakako (Hanshi) 班子
Nakatsukasashō 中務省
Naniwa 難波
Nanke 南家
Nembutsu sammai kyō
  念佛三昧經
nengō 年號
Nihon Daijō Itokuten
  日本太政威德天
Nihon sandai jitsuroku
  日本三代實錄
Nihon shoki 日本書記
Nimmyō 仁明

ninjō 人情
Ninna 仁和
Ninnaji shoshi nempu
  仁和寺諸師年譜
Nobukiko 宣來子
Nomi no Sukune 野見宿禰
Noto 能登

Ōe 大江
―― no Koreo 維緒
―― no Masafusa 匡房
Ogyū Sorai 荻生徂徠
Oimatsu 老松
oinu 老いぬ (grown old)
oinu 生ひぬ (grown)
oinu 追ひぬ (followed)
Ōjin 應神
Ōkuma Shigenobu 大隈重信
Ōkura no Yoshiyuki 大藏善行
Ōkurashō 大藏省
Ōmi 近江
Ōmi ryō 近江令
Ōnakatomi no Kunio
  大中臣國雄
on'i 蔭位
Ono no Komachi 小野小町
Ono no Yoshiki 小野美材
Ōtemmon 應天門
Ōtomo 大伴
―― no Tabito 旅人
Owari 尾張

Pae Chŏng 裴頲
Pae Ku 裴璆
Paekche 百濟
Pai-ch'ü 白渠
Pai-i fang 百一方
Pan 班
Pan Ku 班固
P'an Yueh 潘岳
Pao-p'u tzu 抱朴子
Parhae 渤海
Pien 汴
Pien ho-t'ung lun
  辨和同論
Po Chü-i 白居易
Po-hu t'ung 白虎通

pu-fen 不分

Rai San'yō 賴山陽
Raikō 雷公
Rashōmon 羅城門
renga 連歌
Rengadō 連歌堂
Rengaya 連歌屋
Rikkokushi 六國史
ritsuryō 律令
rokuji 錄事
Ruijū kokushi
　　類聚國史
ryaku 略
ryō 寮
Ryō no gige 令義解
Ryōin'in 良因院
ryōri 良吏
Ryōunshū 凌雲集
Ryūmon 龍門
Ryūmonji 龍門寺

Sabenkankyoku 左辨官局
sachūben 左中辨
sadaiben 左大辨
sadaijin 左大臣
Sadami 定省
saemon no kami 左衛門督
Saga 嵯峨 (emperor and recluse)
Saichin 最鎮
Saichō 最澄
sakon'e no taishō
　　左近衛大將
sakyō no daibu 左京大夫
Sami 佐味
san 贊
Sandai jitsuroku 三代實錄
sangaku 散樂
sangi 參議
San'intei 山陰亭
San-shih 三史
Sanuki 讚岐
sashōben 左少辨
Sawara 早良
seiri 政理
Seiryō 清涼

Seiwa 清和
Sekiten 釋奠
sesshō 攝政
Settsu 攝津
shaku 尺
shakutai 借貸
Shang 商
Shang-yuan 上源
Shidara 志多良
Shih Hsiang 師襄
Shih-chi 史記
Shih-ching 詩經
shikibunden 職分田
Shikibushō 式部省
Shikiin ryō 職員令
Shikike 式家
Shimada no Tadaomi 島田忠臣
Shimada no Yoshiomi 島田良臣
Shimotsuke 下野
shin 辛
Shinano 信濃
Shingon 眞言
shinki 心機
Shinkokinshū 新古今集
Shinsen Man'yōshū
　　新撰萬葉集
Shinsen'en 神泉苑
shinshi 進士
Shintei shushiki 新定酒式
shintō 臣等 ("we")
shitōkan 四等官
shō 省 (ministry)
shō 少輔 (junior assistant minister)
shōben 少辨
shōen 莊園
shōgeki 少外記
shōjō 少掾
shōki 小機
Shōnagonkyoku 少納言局
shōnaiki 少内記
Shoryōryō 諸陵寮
Shoryōshi 諸陵司
Shōtai 昌泰
Shōtoku 聖德
Shu-ching 書經
Shūen 宗淵
Shūin risshi 集韻律詩

Shūishū 拾遺集
Shun 舜
shūsai 秀才
Silla 新羅
Sōgi 宗祇
soi 初位
Sompi bummyaku 尊卑分脈
Sosei 素性
Sosei Hōshi shū
素性法師集
Su Wu 蘇武
Sugano no Korenori 菅野惟肖
Sugawara denju tenarai kagami
菅原傳授手習鑑
Sugawara In 菅原院
Sugawara 菅原
—— no Amaro 阿滿
—— no Atsumochi 淳茂
—— no Fumitoki 文時
—— no Kiyokimi 清公
—— no Koreyoshi 是善
—— no Michizane 道眞
—— no Takami 高視
—— no Yoshinushi 善主
Sui 隋
suiko 出擧
Suinin 垂仁
suke 介 (lieutenant governor)
suke 助 (vice-president)
sukune 宿禰
Su-men 蘇門
Sumiyoshi 住吉
sun 寸
Suzaku 朱雀
Suzakuin 朱雀院

Tachibana 橘
—— no Hayanari 逸勢
—— no Hiromi 廣相
—— no Kin'yori 公頼
Taihō 大寶
T'ai-p'ing kuang-chi 太平廣記
Taira 平
—— no Arinao 有直
—— no Masakado 將門
—— no Masanori 正範
—— no Suenaga 季長

taishi 大便
Tajihi no Ayako
多治比奇子
Takayama Chogyū 高山樗牛
Takechi 高市
Tamaki 珠城
Tamba 丹波
Tameko (Ishi) 為子
Tamuke 手向
Tan 丹
Tarō 太郎
Tatsuta 龍田
tayū 大輔
Temman Daijizai Tenjin
天滿大自在天神
Temmangū 天滿宮
Tempai 天拜
Tendai 天台
Tenjin 天神
Tenjin kyō 天神經
Tenjinkō 天神講
Tenjin-sama 天神樣
tennō 天皇
ten'yaku no kami 典藥頭
Ten'yakuryō 典藥寮
Tien-lun 典論
Ti-ching p'ien 帝京篇
tōgū no daibu 東宮大夫
tōgū no gakushi 東宮學士
tōgū no suke 東宮亮
Tōgū setsuin 東宮切韻
Tōgūbō 東宮坊
Tōji no chōja bunin
東寺長者補任
Tokiyasu 時康
Tokiyo 齊世
toku 讀
tokugōshō 得業生
Tomari 泊
Tomo no Tomoko (Yūshi)
伴友子
Tomo no Yoshio 伴善男
toneri 舍人
tonomo no kami 主殿頭
Tonomoryō 主殿寮
torii 鳥居
Tosa 土佐

Totō Tenjin 渡唐天神
Tōtōmi 遠江
Ts'ao P'i 曹丕
Tso-chuan 左傳
tsūki 通貴
Tsuruga 敦賀

Ubenkankyoku 右辨官局
Uchi no Kura no Tsukasa 内藏寮
uchūben 右中辨
Uda 宇多
udaiben 右大辨
udaijin 右大臣
uemon no kami 右衛門督
uji 氏
ukon'e no taishō 右近衛大將
ukyō no daibu 右京大夫
Unrin'in 雲林院
ushōben 右少辨
Utari 鵜足

wa 和
waka 和歌
Wakan rōeishū
   和漢朗詠集
Wake 和氣
Wakon kansai 和魂漢才
Wakon yōsai 和魂洋才
Wang Chao-chün 王昭君
Wang Chi 王季
Wang Chi-hsin 王積薪
Wang Hyo-lyŏm 王孝廉
Wang No 王訥
Wang Ts'an 王粲
Wang Tu 王度
Waseda 早稻田

Wei 魏
Wei K'o 魏顆
Wei Wu-tzu 魏武子
Wen 文 (king and emperor)
Wen 溫 (province)
Wen-hsuan 文選
wen-hua 文化
Wu 吳
Wu Ting 武丁
Wu-ching 碁經

yamabushi 山伏
Yamanoe no Okura 山上憶良
Yamashiro 山城
Yamato 大和
Yamatohiko 倭彦
Yang Hsiung 揚雄
Yangtze 揚子
Yen 燕
Yen Hui 顏回
Yin 印
Yodo 淀
yōnin 遙任
Yōrō ryō 養老令
Yoshimine no Yasuyo 良岑安世
Yoshiyori 良因
Yōzei 陽成
yū 酉
yü 羽
Yuan Chen 元稹
Yueh 越
yueh-fu 樂府

Zaō Bosatsu 藏王菩薩
Zeami 世阿彌
zōnin 雜任

Index to the Poems

MICHIZANE'S *KANSHI*

OTHER POETRY IN CHINESE

WAKA

Index

Abe no Okiyuki, Michizane's admiration for, 161, 179
Absentee appointment (*yōnin*), 36, 52, 99, 142; Michizane's 125, 147; in Sanuki, 160
Academic cliques, 129, 131; of the Sugawara, 130, 178; rivalry among, 133-134, 135-137, 153-154, 256; and the Akō Incident, 173, 178
Administration, political, 9-17; chart of, 10; provincial, 36, 126, 147-148, 158, 160, 168-169, 189; Saga's reforms of, 39; Chinese models for, 79; professors' relation to, 85; Uda's reforms of, 208
Administrative officials (*shitōkan*), 12
Akashi, Michizane's poem written at, 181
Akishino family, 24
akō, 287; vs. *kampaku*, 175-176; meaning in China, 176, 177, 179-180; scholars' views on, 176; Michizane's view of, 179-180
Akō Incident, 175-181, 184, 192, 271; Michizane's role in, 173,

177-178, 179, 202; and academic cliques, 173, 178; Hiromi's letter to Michizane about, 179; Michizane's letter to Mototsune about, 179-181
Analects (*Lun-yü*), 39, 97-98
Amaterasu: as a "Tenjin," 309
Ambassador (*taishi*), Fujiwara no Kadonomaro as, 32; Michizane as, 123, 228, 242, 243 (illustration, 244-245), 249-250; Wang Hyo-lyŏm as, 229
Amenohohi, 24
Amida: Michizane's faith in, 190
An Lu-shan, Rebellion of, 231
Anrakuji, 310, 311; and Michizane's descendants, 321, 324
Aristocrats. See Status, aristocratic
Ariwara no Narihira, 62, 146
Assistant director of the Bureau of Buddhism and Aliens (*gemba no suke*): Michizane as, 116
Assistant handmaid (*naishi no suke*): Michizane's daughter as, 202
Assistant master of the crown prince's quarters), 10; Michizane as, 210
Ate, Prince. See Heizei, Emperor

Hibasuhime, Empress, 24
Hideyoshi, 253
Hie, 320
Hirata Atsutane (1776-1843): and
Tenjin worship, 330
Hiromi. *See* Tachibana no Hiromi
hisangi. See Honorary consultant
Historical writings, 18, 61, 62;
Michizane's compilation of, 2,
198, 217, 218, 220-221; as means
of imperial legitimacy, 18, 217,
226; relation to literature, 82-
83; Six national, 216, 219;
Nihon sandai jitsuroku, 216-219;
Ruijū kokushi, 218-220; topical
arrangement of, 220; China mis-
sions recorded in, 227
History of the Former Han Dynasty
(Han-shu), 82, 125, 194
History of the Later Han Dynasty
(Hou-Han-shu), 48, 56, 82, 124,
125; Koreyoshi's lectures on, 96-97
Hokke (Northern House), 7, 38, 210,
285
Hokke Sammaidō (Lotus Meditation
Hall), 321
Hokkeji, 261
Honchō monzui (Choice of literature
of this realm), 183
honkan (specialists), 12
Honorary consultant (*hisangi*):
Kiyokimi as, 49, 52, 203; Toki-
hira as, 203
Hou-Han-shu. See History of the
Later Han Dynasty
hsiao (whistling), 60; Kiyokimi's
poem on, 44-45; Chinese essay
on, 46
Huang Hsien, 96, 97
Hyakunin isshu (One hundred poems
by one hundred poets), 262
Hyōbushō. *See* Ministry of War

Ichijō, Emperor (980-1011; r. 986-
1011), 324
Imperial Police Office (Kebiishichō),
10, 39

Inari (god of harvest), 2
Initial rank (*soi*), 13. *See also* Rank
Inoue Tetsujirō (1855-1944), 4
Ishikawa no Michimasu (d. 805),
32, 33
Izumo no Kuninomiyatsuko, 25

Jibushō. *See* Ministry of Civil Affairs
Jingikan. *See* Department of Shrines
Jingoji, 54
Jōzō, 315; and Tokihira's death, 311,
314
Junior assistant minister of ceremon-
ial: Michizane as, 124-125; 232;
Sukeyo as, 153
Junior assistant minister of popular
affairs: Michizane as, 117-119,
122, 123
Junior assistant minister of war
(*hyōbu no shō*): Tadaomi as, 92;
Michizane as, 117
Junior secretary of province (*shōjō*):
Kiyokimi as, 31
Junna, Emperor (786-840; r. 823-
833), 39, 42, 112

Kadonomaro. *See* Fujiwara no
Kadonomaro
Kaga: Michizane as supernumerary governor of, 125-126; Koreyoshi as supernumerary governor
of, 126; and mission from Parhae,
231-232
kageyushi no chōkan. See Chief investigator of the records of outgoing officials
Kaibara Ekken (1630-1714): and
Tenjin worship, 329, 334
Kaifūsō (Fond recollections of
poetry), 6, 41
Kaihōji, 169
Kaishō bunrui jū (Classified literary
works of the Hui-ch'ang era), 61
K'ai-yuan ching (Classic of the K'ai-
yuan era), 275-276
kakumei ("revolution"): Kiyoyuki's
prediction of, 277

Sugawara no Kiyokimi *(continued)*
career as official of, 48–49, 160–
161; death of, 50; dormitory
founded by, 127
Sugawara no Koreyoshi (812–880),
50–67, 103, 106, 117, 134; as a
student, 51; offices held by, 51–
52, 130; as court scholar, 51–53;
spiritual inclinations of, 57–60,
66, 218; as Michizane's teacher,
96, 100; students of, 130; and
factionalism, 137
Sugawara no Michizane (845–903):
legends about, 3, 89, 102, 103,
106, 123, 258–259, 290–294,
304, 308–309, 311, 314–315,
320–321, 327, 334; as god of
literature, 3, 309, 324, 325,
330; as symbol of his age, 5–8;
and the plum tree, (illus. ii),
64, 89–90, 123, 290–291 (illus.
292–293), 294, 301–302, 327;
and Buddhism, 66, 163–165,
169; and civil service exams,
70–71, 85; professorial vs.
bureaucratic roles, 85–86, 113,
119, 141, 149–150, 156, 216,
273, 275, 288; formal poetry
of, 91, 95, 143–144, 182–183,
198, 224–225; as an archer, 103,
106, (illus. 108–109); and civil
service exams, 103, 106, 107,
110–112, 113, 114, 129, 190,
256; rank of, 114, 115, 116,
117, 118, 129, 213, 214–215,
278, 287, 324; drafting of edicts
by, 120, 121, 315; petitions
written by, 120, 242–243; first
poetic narrative by, 122; and
Confucianism, 123, 141, 144,
160; influence of at court, 126,
137; students of, 130, 134,
272, 279; as an examiner, 131,
136, 288; and criticism, 137–
139; poems on walls by, 141,
181; informal poetry of, 142–
144, 145, 182–183, 225, 256,

289–290; and Taoism, 144, 171–
173, 199; children of, 144–146,
193; wives of, 145–146; and
Uda's patronage, 152, 197, 202,
270, 272, 275; historical works
by, 198; ill health of, 199; career
vs. Tokihira's, 203–207 (chart
204–205), 213, 216, 217; review
of prisoners by, 207–208; opinion on tax rice by, 208–209; as
Uda's confidant, 210, 212–213,
257; and *waka*, 224, 262, 268,
290, 291; exile of, 278, 282,
296–301 (illus. 302–303); posthumous pardon of, 282, 314,
315; reasons for downfall of,
287–289; death of, 304; as
thunder god, 308, 309, 311,
314, 315 (illus. 316–317), 318,
320; and return of family to
capital, 311; posthumous promotions granted to, 324. *See
also* Tenjin
Sugawara no Takami (876–913),
144, 272
Sugawara no Yoshinushi (803–852),
7, 50, 69, 112, 249; as lieutenant governor, 152
*Sugawara Secrets of Calligraphy,
The* (*Sugawara denju tenarai
kagami*), 3, 4, 304; modeled
after Chikamatsu's play,
331
suiko (government interest-bearing
loans), 220
Suinin, Emperor, 24
Sukeyo. See Fujiwara no Sukeyo
sukune, 13
Sumiyoshi: poems written at, 267–
268; shrine at, 268
Supernumerary (*gon*) governor:
Kiyokimi as, 36; Tadaomi as, 92;
Michizane as, 125, 278, 289;
Koreyoshi as, 126; Tokihira as,
204
Supernumerary provincial secretary:
Michizane as, 116

About the Author

Robert Borgen is professor of Japanese and history at the University of California, Davis, where he currently chairs the Department of Chinese and Japanese. This book—and related shorter articles—evolved from his University of Michigan doctoral dissertation on Sugawara no Michizane. Professor Borgen's subsequent research and publications have concerned the eleventh-century Japanese monk Jōjin, who made a pilgrimage to China and left a detailed account of his travels there.